Democratic politics is a collective enterprise, not simply because individual votes are counted to determine winners, but more fundamentally because the individual exercise of citizenship is an interdependent undertaking. Citizens argue with one another, they inform one another, and they generally arrive at political decisions through processes of social interaction and deliberation.

This book is dedicated to investigating the political implications of interdependent citizens within the context of the 1984 presidential campaign as it was experienced in the metropolitan area of South Bend, Indiana. Hence, this is a community study in the fullest sense of the term. National politics is experienced locally through a series of filters unique to a particular setting. And this study is concerned with understanding that setting and its consequences for the exercise of democratic citizenship.

Several different themes structure the undertaking: the dynamic implications of social communication among citizens, the importance of communication networks for citizen decision making, the exercise of citizen purpose in locating sources of information, the constraints on individual choice that arise as a function of contexts and environments, and the institutional and organizational effects that operate on the flow of information within particular settings.

CITIZENS, POLITICS,
AND SOCIAL COMMUNICATION

Cambridge Studies in Political Psychology and Public Opinion

General Editors

James H. Kuklinski and Robert S. Wyer, Jr.
University of Illinois, Urbana-Champaign

Editorial Board

Stanley Feldman, State University of New York, Stony Brook
Roger D. Masters, Dartmouth College
William J. McGuire, Yale University
Norbert Schwarz, Zentrum für Umfragen, Methoden und Analysen, ZUMA, Mannheim, FRG
David O. Sears, University of California, Los Angeles
Paul M. Sniderman, Stanford University and Survey Research Center, University of California, Berkeley
James A. Stimson, University of Iowa

   This series has been established in recognition of interest in political psychology in recent years. The series will focus on work that pertains to the fundamental question: What kinds of mental processes do citizens employ when they think about democratic politics and respond, consciously or unconsciously, to their political environments? We will also include research that explores the macro-level consequences of such processes.

   We expect that many of the works will draw on developments in cognitive and social psychology and relevant areas of philosophy. Appropriate subjects would include the use of heuristics, the roles of core values and moral principles in political reasoning, the effects of expertise and sophistication, the role of affect and emotion, and the nature of cognition and information processing. The emphasis will be on systematic and rigorous empirical analysis and a wide range of methodologies will be appropriate: traditional surveys, experimental surveys, laboratory experiments, focus groups, in-depth interviews, as well as others. We intend that these empirically oriented studies will also consider normative implications for democratic politics generally.

   Politics, not psychology, will be the focus, and it is expected that most works will deal with mass public and democratic politics, although work on non-democratic publics will not be excluded.

Other books in the series:

CITIZENS, POLITICS, AND SOCIAL COMMUNICATION

Information and influence in an election campaign

ROBERT HUCKFELDT
State University of New York
at Stony Brook

JOHN SPRAGUE
Washington University
in St. Louis

CAMBRIDGE
UNIVERSITY PRESS

Published by the Press Syndicate of the University of Cambridge
The Pitt Building, Trumpington Street, Cambridge CB2 1RP
40 West 20th Street, New York, NY 10011-4211, USA
10 Stamford Road, Oakleigh, Melbourne 3166, Australia

First published 1995

Printed in the United States of America

Library of Congress Cataloging-in-Publication Data
Huckfeldt, R. Robert.
Citizens, politics, and social communication: information and
influence in an election campaign / Robert Huckfeldt, John Sprague.
p.   cm.
ISBN 0-521-45298-8
1. Elections – Indiana – South Bend Metropolitan Area.   2. Political
parties – Indiana – South Bend Metropolitan Area.   3. Communication in
politics – Indiana – South Bend Metropolitan Area.   4. South Bend
Metropolitan Area (Ind.) – Politics and government.   5. Presidents –
United States – Election – 1984.   I. Sprague, John D.   II. Title.
JS1459.S43A84   1994
324.9598'038 – dc20   94-8335

A catalog record for this book is available from the British Library.

ISBN 0-521-45298-8 hardback

Contents

Acknowledgments

This book represents a rare event among students of electoral politics: the opportunity to design an election study from first principles – our own first principles. The danger of such an undertaking is that we are unable to absolve the collectors of the data from any blunders. Full responsibility for the mistakes, oversights, and missed opportunities belongs to the two of us. And there were certainly errors, both of oversight and insight. If we could do it over again, we would change some things – such as increasing the level of competition and volatility in the 1984 presidential election – but the basic contours would remain the same. The delight of carrying out this study was that we *did* exercise control, from beginning to end, of the design and its implementation. This allowed us to construct an analysis and design anchored in a set of theoretical and substantive ideas regarding the role of social communication in politics. And our primary acknowledgment thus goes to the National Science Foundation for originally supporting this undertaking through grants SES-8318899 to the University of Notre Dame, SES-8415572 and SES-8706940 to Indiana University, and SES-8319188 and SES-8706935 to Washington University.

Other important sources of support came from the University of Notre Dame, Indiana University, and Washington University. We are particularly grateful to the College of Arts and Sciences and the Office of Research and Graduate Development at Indiana for making funds available to carry out additional interviews with discussants. Finally, Catherine Cirksena, Jon Masland, Mike Greenwell, and the rest of the staff of the Center for Survey Research at Indiana undertook heroic efforts to make this project a success.

A wonderfully diverse army of colleagues provided us with indispensable advice and criticism along the way: Bob Boynton, Laurily Epstein, Lee Epstein, Hartmut Esser, Heinz Eulau, Chris Gilbert, Bernie Grofman, Margie Hershey, Max Kaase, Kit Kenney, Hans-Dieter Klingemann, Mike Krassa, Jim Kuklinski, Dave Leege, Jeff Levine, Mike McBurnett, Michael McGinnis, Jeff Mondak, Elinor Ostrom, Franz Pappi, John Roos, Bob Salisbury, Steve Schneck, Mark Schneider, Karl Schuessler, Paul Sniderman, Harvey Starr, Don Stabrowski, Bob Stein, Lew Westefield, John Williams, Rick Wilson, Jerry Wright, and a series of anonymous reviewers.

We would especially like to thank our collaborators on other projects, not only for their advice and insight, but also for tolerating our digressions and lapses of attention from joint endeavors: Carol Kohfeld, Ted Carmines, Paul Beck, and Russ Dalton. Two of the chapters in this book were based on earlier collaborative efforts with Eric Plutzer and the late Tina Brickell. Finally, more than a few graduate students at the University of Notre Dame, Indiana University, and Washington University have participated in seminars where they were either direct or indirect participants in working out the ideas that serve as the basis for this project.

Several chapters in this book are based on previously published essays. For granting us permission to rely on these materials, we are grateful to the publishers of the *American Political Science Review, American Journal of Political Science, Journal of Politics,* and *Political Science: The State of the Discipline II.*

Finally, this book is dedicated to the citizens of St. Joseph County, Indiana.

September 1993

I

Democratic politics and social communication

1

The multiple levels of democratic politics

> All politics is local politics.
> – Hon. Thomas P. (Tip) O'Neill

Politics in a democracy revolves around the decisions of individual citizens, but individual citizens make their choices at particular times and places, located in multiple environments operating at a variety of levels. In this way the reality of a national election is played out in countless specific locations across the nation, and the behavior of individual voters is often best understood within these subnational locales. In keeping with such a perspective we have undertaken a study of voters and democratic elections at a particular time in a particular place: the 1984 presidential election as it occurred in the South Bend, Indiana, metropolitan area.

Voters in South Bend experienced the national spectacle of an election campaign during 1984, and, like all elections, the 1984 election was not a matter of individual choice for South Bend voters. It took place whether they desired it or not. Many South Bend residents would have preferred to spend their idle mental moments musing about the Cubs' pennant hopes, organizing next spring's garden, or planning sailing trips on Lake Michigan. Regardless of their own preferences, however, an election was taking place, and elections alter the lives of citizens who value democracy. Indeed, even citizens who do not take democratic responsibilities seriously are unable to avoid the altered environment of an election campaign: Dan Rather, the *South Bend Tribune,* bumper stickers, yard signs, party workers, candidate mailings, and informal discussions all served as inescapable reminders for South Bend residents. In short, and as John Stuart Mill has informed us, democratic politics includes a substantial element of coercion: Citizens unavoidably pay heed to the events and debates and issues that impinge upon their lives from all sides.[1]

---

1 The classic statement of democratic coercion by majority opinion was set forth by John Stuart Mill (1956: 7): "Like other tyrannies, the tyranny of the majority was at first, and is still vulgarly, held in dread, chiefly as operating through the acts of the public authorities. But reflecting persons perceived that when society is itself the tyrant – society collectively over the separate individuals who compose it – its means of tyrannizing are not restricted to

How are we to understand the nature of coercion in democratic politics? First, it need not be pernicious – it has the capacity to produce socially desirable as well as undesirable consequences. In contrast to Mill, who saw social coercion as the enemy of individual liberty, we see it as liberty's natural result. Social coercion is only meaningful when individuals are in a position to choose, and in this context coercion becomes the by-product that one individual's choice has for the choices of others. Second, coercion is ubiquitous because none of us exercises complete control over our own experience, and thus coercion arises as a primary, involuntary element of social and political life. Indeed, the key to understanding the power of individual freedom in democratic politics is to recognize the influence that individuals have over one another. Finally, although coercion is an inevitable element of social and political life, its outcome is both problematic and contingent. Some individuals resist, others overcome, and still others fail to pay attention.

This means that, in addition to being coercive, elections are also social. Casting a vote in the isolation of a voting booth is an act of individual choice, but it is also the end product of a systematic social and political process that is set into motion by the political stimulus of the campaign. The residents of South Bend did not experience the events of 1984 as social isolates, and the political decisions they made were not arrived at in an autonomous manner. Election campaigns are socially shared experiences, and the politics of democratic decision making is truly collective in nature. It is collective not simply because votes are aggregated to determine the winner. Rather the collective nature of democratic politics and the pursuit of individual interests through politics are rooted in the nature of social life: Voting is social as well as political and thus mass political behavior rests on fundamental social interdependencies among citizens.

Finally, election campaigns are dynamic. They occur through time, and this temporal dimension has important consequences for democratic politics. For most South Bend citizens, politics occupied a tertiary status during 1983. As 1984 proceeded, however, politics came to occupy an increasingly important position in most people's sets of interests and concerns. The coercive nature of the campaign meant that politics was forced to the personal attention of individual citizens, and the social nature of the campaign meant that these individual concerns became a part of social exchange. Thus the dynamic structure of political campaigns moves citizens

the acts which it may do by the hands of its political functionaries. Society can and does execute its own mandates; and if it issues wrong mandates instead of right, or any mandates at all in things with which it ought not to meddle, it practices a social tyranny more formidable than many kinds of political oppression, since, though not usually upheld by such extreme penalties, it leaves fewer means of escape, penetrating much more deeply into the details of life, and enslaving the soul itself." Our own view toward the role of social coercion in democratic politics is more benign, but we recognize it as coercion nonetheless.

from political quiescence to political activation, and this transformation is accomplished through environmentally specific channels of social and political communication.

The socially coercive, interactive, and dynamic aspects of electoral politics are national in scope – they are experienced by citizens in Bangor, Chicago, El Monte, and every other community across the country. But the character of that experience may be radically dissimilar depending upon where it occurs. We recognize this lack of uniformity as characteristic of the political process. When Tip O'Neill says that all politics is local, he recognizes the boundedness of democratic politics. When television newscasters MacNeil and Lehrer interview the editors of newspapers across the country, they recognize the disjunctures in information flow that can only be observed from a local perspective. When someone asks how a message or event will play in Peoria, they recognize that the collective response of Peoria's citizens must be understood from a collective, environmentally specific vantage point. In politics, localities matter.

What are the features of political life that must be understood from such an environmentally specific perspective? The list is long, but factors related to the social and political organization of the electorate loom especially large. By political organization we include electoral laws, levels of partisan competition and control, and the locally specific strategies of party organizations – factors that affect the political communication that occurs between political parties and citizens. By social organization we include all the factors that affect the transmission of political information through social communication – churches, secondary organizations, work groups, families, networks of political discussion.

A key idea is that the locally specific roots of national electoral politics lie in the environmentally contingent (localized) supply of political information. These environmental contingencies are both social and political, and they give rise to correspondingly distinctive interpretations of political affairs. As a result, democratic politics can be seen as occurring at multiple levels of meaning, where individual citizens make their choices subject to locally imposed informational constraints. We turn first to the social communication of political information, and to the potential of such communication for influence.

SOCIAL INFLUENCE AND SOCIAL CONTEXTS

The nature and content of social influence and social communication in election campaigns are fundamentally structured by the social context – by the social composition of the environments where individuals reside, work, go to church, and so on. This proposition is supported by an increasing number of empirically documented relationships, only some of which are related to voting and elections. The modern intellectual roots of contextual analysis can be located in the work of Emile Durkheim, Herbert Tingsten, V. O. Key, and the early election studies of several Columbia University sociologists – most notably, but not exclusively, Berelson, Lazarsfeld, and McPhee (1954), followed in the same tradition by Ennis (1962), Segal and Meyer (1974), and others. Over the past 100 years, these efforts have articulated several themes that continue to provide a focus for contextual theories: behavioral interdependence, multiple levels of observation, and the necessity of cross-level inference.

In his classic study of suicidal impulses, Durkheim (1951) examined perhaps the most individualistic of all acts – taking one's life – and argued that such behavior could best be understood as socially contingent. That is, the same person with the same characteristics and predispositions was more or less likely to engage in the act, depending upon social surroundings – in this case, he argued, the extent to which Catholics and Protestants were surrounded by those of similar or divergent faith and confession. Contextual analysis in particular, and structural analysis in general, have moved far beyond the initial work of Durkheim, but he made the crucial observation that it is meaningful to understand social (and hence political) reality as occurring simultaneously and interdependently at multiple levels, and these multiple levels lie at the heart of contextual analysis even today (Harder and Pappi 1969; Boyd and Iversen 1979; Iversen 1991). The earliest efforts at cross-level inference involved measurement at a single level but inference across levels (see Tingsten 1963). This usually meant that social scientists observed in the aggregate but theorized about individuals whose behavior varied as a function of the environment – an enterprise that was called into question by a subsequent obsession with ecological fallacies (Robinson 1950; Goodman 1953, 1959; Hannan 1971; Hannan and Burstein 1974; Alwin 1976; Achen 1986; Shively 1987; Hanushek, Jackson, and Kain 1974).

The work of V. O. Key consistently displays such a sensitivity to multiple levels of analysis and meaning, but nowhere is this more true than in *Southern Politics* (1949). One of the most compelling analyses of structural influence in political life comes in Key's demonstration that white racial hostility in the South varied as a function of black population concentrations. He demonstrated, for example, that southern whites were more likely to participate in politics if they lived in counties with higher concentrations of black citizens – a pattern that perhaps continues to the present (Alt forthcoming). Indeed, Key explains much of the internal variations in southern politics according to the presence or absence of black populations – the racial context.

By contemporary standards, Key's (1949) methodology was fairly primitive and limited by the availability of data, although surely of extraordinary originality. But his insights have stood the test of time and replication, both inside and outside the South, in studies conducted by Matthews and

Prothro (1963), Wright (1976, 1977), Giles and Evans (1985), Bobo (1983, 1988), and Huckfeldt and Kohfeld (1989). These studies and others show that white racial hostility is a common feature of American political life, and that it frequently varies as a direct function of blacks' presence in the population. Furthermore, when Key investigated the problem of racial hostility in the post–World War II South, he saw it through the lens of politics and purpose. In particular, he saw it in terms of a white population that was taking political steps to realize its own interests. According to Key (1949: 5) the central problem in the black belt was "the maintenance of control by a white minority." Thus, in Key's analysis, political self-interest is the concept used to explain racial hostility – even racial hostility that is contextually contingent. By avoiding an explanation rooted in the social psychology of prejudice, Key shows us that contextual analyses of politics are not necessarily wed to social psychology either. Rather, a contextual analysis might be thoroughly political in its focus upon interests and the mobilization of interests. This is theoretically significant for contextual analyses because it offers a conjunction of motivated behavior, driven by a social condition, with political consequences. In his analysis Key weds rationality and social context as jointly required to give an adequate theoretical account of the politics under analysis.

A final building block for the foundation of contextual analysis was laid when, first, Lazarsfeld introduced the sample survey as a tool of serious social science and, second, the Columbia sociologists used it to demonstrate the importance of social influence in election campaigns. Whereas Key and others used aggregate data to make inferences regarding the behavior of individuals, the Columbia sociologists used individual-level data to make inferences regarding social processes and the dependence of individual behavior upon larger social aggregates. The most sophisticated empirical analysis of the early Columbia tradition occurs in the work of Berelson et al. (1954) – a 1948 community-based election study located in Elmira, New York. Although the authors do not explicitly state the problem as one involving multiple levels of analysis and observation, and nearly all their observation is at the level of individuals, it is clear that they place the distinction between the individual and the aggregate at the forefront of their theoretical efforts. In their own words (1954: 122): "Whatever the psychological mechanisms, the social and political consequence is much the same: the development of homogeneous political preferences within small groups and along lines of close social ties connecting them. During a campaign political preferences are 'contagious' over the range of personal contacts." While Key recognized the importance of behavioral interdependence in making inferences from aggregates to individuals, the Columbia sociologists recognized its importance in making inferences from individuals to aggregates. In both instances, the foundation was being laid for a contextual, multilevel understanding of politics.

Too much has probably been made of the disjuncture between the Columbia and Michigan schools of electoral research. Certainly the authors of *The American Voter* (Campbell et al. 1960) gave clear recognition to the importance of both individuals and groups within democratic politics. It is still the case, however, that the Columbia school established a tradition of electoral research that has operated concurrently and yet apart from the dominant Michigan tradition. What sets this Columbia tradition apart? The Columbia sociologists largely ignored the issue of national representativeness in their effort to locate the structures and environments of the individual citizen. The Michigan social psychologists largely ignored the importance of contexts, structures, and environments in their effort to arrive at a representative picture of the American electorate.

What then is the legacy of these earlier efforts? First, individuals are viewed as interdependent and individual choice is seen as partially contingent upon the choices of other individuals. Second, the socially contingent nature of political choice leads to a conception of political behavior that is characterized by multiple levels: Individuals are to be understood within the larger social aggregates of which they are part, and aggregate behavior is to be understood as more than the simple accumulation of individually determined preferences. Third, there is a methodological imperative – measurement that informs political relationships is to be taken at multiple levels if cross-level inferences are to be rooted in observation. But even if observation occurs at a single level, attention is directed to the cross-level consequences of interdependence. Fourth, the relationships point toward a time-ordered process of social influence: An individual is embedded within a particular context, the context structures social interaction patterns, political information is conveyed through social interaction, and the individual forms a political response based upon this information. Such a dynamic must be incorporated, at least implicitly, within any contextual explanation for electoral politics. Fifth and finally, the nature and content of social influence varies systematically across both individuals and environments in ways that require careful attention to the mechanisms responsible for producing social influence in politics.

How does such a legacy compare with the intellectual perspective typically invoked to study American electoral politics? Studies of electoral politics often seek to abstract an individual from time, place, and surroundings. The epistemological foundation of such an effort is the mythically representative citizen chosen probabilistically to represent everyperson. But such a myth ignores the reality that every citizen is located within a setting, and the characterization of the citizen apart from the setting lacks meaning. In other words, a probability model of independent balls in an urn replaces the flesh and blood of real electorates. The real electorate is composed of interrelated, interacting, interdependent citizens. The artificially constructed electorate is an aggregate of independent, isolated, atomized individuals. The problem is not probability theory – the problem lies instead in the particular probability model chosen to arrive at a representation of the electorate. Studies of electoral politics require an explicit recognition of interdependence, but such studies typically rely instead on the myth of the independent citizen. This practice divorces political behavior from the settings and contexts that provide local, and hence individual, meaning to national politics.

CONTEXTS, STRUCTURES, AND ENVIRONMENTS

What is a contextual effect? How does a context differ from a structure or an environment? Various labels have been applied to individually exogenous factors that serve to influence individual behavior, and the broadest definition of a contextual effect is tied to any such individually extrinsic factor. According to such a definition, a contextual effect operates when individual behavior depends upon some individually external factor after all individual-level determinants have been taken into account. That is, a contextual effect exists when individually intrinsic explanations cannot account for systematic variations in behavior across environments (Hauser 1974).

Such a definition is certainly appropriate for many purposes, but it is broad, including within its coverage a wide range of disparate environmental factors: institutional variations, media coverage, and social network effects. A more focused definition, building upon the work of Przeworski and Teune (1970) and Eulau (1986), suggests a distinction that establishes contextual effects as a subset of environmental effects (Huckfeldt 1986: 13). Przeworski and Teune (1970: 56) define contextual factors as aggregates of individual properties and argue that the importance of these factors arises through social interaction. Eulau defines an environmental effect as any behavioral influence that arises from factors external to the individual. In contrast, contextual effects as construed here are due to social interaction within particular environments, and social contexts are created as a result of these interactions. (For a somewhat different approach, see Books and Prysby 1991.)

The primary advantage of narrower definitions of context is that they serve to build on the intellectual foundation laid by Durkheim, Tingsten, Key, and the Columbia sociologists – a foundation that was renewed by Blau (1956, 1957, 1960a, 1960b), Davis (1966), and Davis, Spaeth, and Huson (1961). Blau was fundamentally concerned with the individual consequences arising due to location in populations with different social compositions. He identified such effects as structural effects, but their similarity to the contextual effects of Eulau and Przeworski and Teune is clear (Blau 1957: 64).

In their extension of Blau's work, Davis and his colleagues (Davis et al. 1961) argue that calling such effects structural effects confuses these factors with the broader range of phenomena generally included within the boundaries of social structure. For example, the fact that more highly educated people tend to earn more money can be seen as an effect of social structure, but that is not what either Blau or Davis has in mind, and thus Davis and his colleagues adopt the term "compositional effects."

Where does this leave us? An environmental effect is any effect on individual behavior that arises due to extraindividual factors. In contrast, a contextual effect is any effect on individual behavior that arises due to social interaction within an environment. We adopt that view here. Both effects are more generally seen as being structural consequences of individual standing and location within particular social and political orders, and thus they can be seen as subsets of social and political structure.

We do not limit our analyses to contextual effects thus defined, but rather incorporate more general considerations of other environmental influences as well. Moreover, our definition of contextual effects leaves several related issues unaddressed. In particular, what constitutes social interaction? And how does social interaction relate to issues of individual preference and control?

SOCIAL INTERACTION AS A MECHANISM OF POLITICAL INFLUENCE

The electorate is composed of interdependent citizens tied together by complex patterns of social interaction. But when we argue that individual political choice is subject to systematic patterns of social interaction, and that contextual effects on political behavior operate through the mechanism of social interaction, we are not saying very much. Social interaction can be characterized along a variety of dimensions: intimacy, frequency, level of political content, the extent to which the interaction is purposeful or recreational, the extent to which it is voluntary or coerced, the substantive content of the interaction. At one extreme, social interaction occurs when lovers hold hands while they stroll in the park. At another, it also occurs when one neighbor sees a political yard sign on another neighbor's lawn. The relative political impact of these various interactions is an open question. But it would be a gross error to believe that social interaction is politically relevant only when it occurs among intimates who interact on a voluntary basis. In this impersonal sense, then, we can say that the county-level, racial-hostility effects documented by Key were due to a process of social interaction. In yet a different way, the autoworker who involuntarily shares a workplace location with a co-worker whom he finds obnoxious may still learn a great deal about politics, one way or another, through an ongoing and continual process of social interaction.

For many purposes it is especially useful to contrast voluntary and involuntary social interaction, and to use that distinction to consider the role played by individuals in controlling their own agendas of social interaction. It is probably best to illustrate these matters with an example – the classic study of associational patterns among autoworkers conducted by Finifter (1974). Finifter investigated friendship patterns at the factory and produced an important result. In these overwhelmingly Democratic workplaces, Republicans were more politically sensitive than Democrats in their choice of workplace friendships. In such a setting it is useful to think of the factory as an environment with an attendant context created by the distribution of political preferences among its work force. In this sense, then, the context is imposed upon the people who work at the factory. Once they decide to take the job – or to attend a church or live in a neighborhood or bowl in a league – they have little control over the people they encounter as part of their activities within the boundaries of the environment. Thus, contexts are external to individuals, even if the composition of the context depends upon the mix of people contained within it.

This is not to say that citizens are necessarily the helpless victims of a social reality that lies beyond their control. Finifter's Republican autoworkers were surrounded by Democrats, and their response was selectively to create friendship groups with other Republicans – friendship groups that served as politically protective environments. In other words, people have more control over some forms of social interaction than others. These autoworkers had little control over the people who shared their work area, but they had much more control over their lunchtime associates. Thus a friendship group reflects the efforts made by individuals to impose their own preferences upon their social contexts, and the composition of a friendship group is subject to the multiple, interdependent, cascading choices of people who share the same social space – the people who compose the context.

At the same time, associational choice is limited and incomplete, even in controlling voluntary forms of social interaction. Associational choice is not determinant in the construction of social interaction patterns because the choice of an associate operates within the constraints imposed by a context. To present an extreme example, a Mondale voter was unable to discuss politics with another Mondale voter if she was located in a context where everyone else supported Reagan. Alternatively, if there is only one Republican working at the automobile factory, he will either eat lunch with other Democrats or he will eat alone. And thus the efficacy of individual control over the choice of politically like-minded discussants is subject to the distribution of politically like-minded discussants within the context. Choosing a place of residence is self-selection, of course, but it also is constraining and leads to non-self-selected information exposure (Brown 1981). Similarly, employment may be freely chosen, but once work is begun many subsequent choices are circumscribed by the particular workplace setting – the dilemma of Finifter's Republican autoworkers.

Individual control over interaction patterns is also incomplete because such control responds to multiple preferences, with different weights, many of which are unformed or at best poorly formed (Zaller 1992). All of us want friends who are smart, pleasant, great bridge players, and politically enlightened. But only activists and political scientists are likely to put an overwhelmingly important weight on political enlightenment. Indeed, many citizens have uninformed and perhaps unformed political preferences which only become articulate *after* associates are chosen and persuasion and education and social learning occur. To say that associational choice is probabilistic is *not* to say that it is unimportant or inconsequential. An important issue that must be addressed in this book is the relationship between involuntary social interaction, voluntary social interaction, and individual choice.

In summary, different forms of social interaction vary in the extent to which they are controlled by individual choice. But even voluntary social interaction is the product of individual choice operating probabilistically within the boundaries of externally imposed contexts. Moreover, the context presents a menu of choices that is inherently stochastic as well: If you move into a Democratic neighborhood, the odds are that you may live next door to a Democrat and his yard signs and bumper stickers, but maybe not. The important point is not that choice and control are lacking, or that individual preference is socially determined (Key and Munger 1959), but rather that choice operates probabilistically within an externally imposed, systematically biased, and necessarily stochastic environment. How can such a conception of social interaction and its political import be incorporated within a microtheory of political choice?

MICROTHEORIES OF CONTEXTUAL INFLUENCE

The individual provides the ultimate unit of analysis in a contextual theory of politics, and the analyses of this book rest on a premise of methodological individualism. We understand individual choice as being located at the intersection between individual purpose, individual cognition, and individual preference on the one hand, and environmentally imposed opportunities and constraints on the other hand. Citizens are always understood within a particular setting – a setting that attaches probabilistically to the menu of choices that is available to the individual. Indeed, this joining of biased environments to rational individual political decision making was modeled in a persuasive fashion by McPhee and his co-workers three decades ago in his dynamic model of the voting process, a model specifically designed to incorporate the idea of influence of a stochastically biased information environment (probabilistically) sampled by the rational individual citizen (McPhee and Smith 1962; McPhee and Ferguson 1962; McPhee with Smith and Ferguson 1963; also see Calvert 1985).

At the same time, a contextual theory of politics resists methodological reductionism, and with it the idea that any explanation of democratic politics must be judged by its ability to get inside the heads of the individual voter. In other words, a contextual analysis of politics is not coincident with the effort to reduce politics to its lowest common denominator. Such an effort is inconsistent with our premise that the interdependence of individuals is the key to a compelling explanatory reconstruction of political behavior. And thus politics can be understood from the vantage point of the individual psyche, but only as individual psyches interact to produce political outcomes. Correspondingly, once a contextual analysis of politics is subsumed under the effort to understand individual motivation, it ceases to engage in a multilevel analysis, and hence ceases to be contextual.

The importance of microtheories to contextual analysis is not that they explain individual behavior, but rather that they more fully articulate the nature of interdependence among citizens and hence add to our understanding of politics as a corporate outcome – the level at which politics has meaning and substance (Eulau 1986). The task – the specification of behavioral interdependence – lies at the heart of contextual analysis. The questions become: Under what conditions does one citizen affect another? And what are the circumstances that give rise to interdependent behavior? Stated somewhat differently, what are the individual and corporate mechanisms that translate the context into a force operating upon individual behavior?

There is no silver bullet that serves as the answer to all these questions – there is no official microtheory of contextual influence. This is particularly the case because there is a range of divergent forms of contextual influence and appeals to an explanatory contextual hypothesis. Key (1949) and Matthews and Prothro (1963) demonstrated that southern whites were more likely to engage in racial oppression if county populations were more heavily black in their racial composition. Butler and Stokes (1974) demonstrated that British workers were more likely to vote Conservative if they lived among middle-class populations – a result that is disputed by Kelley and McAllister (1985). Langton and Rapoport (1975) demonstrated that Santiago workers were more likely to be class-conscious if they lived among other workers. Carmines and Stimson (1989) demonstrated that a reorganization of civil-rights voting cleavages in the Congress led to a reorganization of these cleavages in the population at large. All of these can be seen as contextual effects, but there the similarity ends. Some of these contextual effects involve assimilation between individuals and groups, while others involve conflict as the product of group intersection (Huckfeldt 1986). Some of these contextual effects involve fundamental social and political loyalties, whereas others involve more ephemeral judgments and attachments.

Our substantive concern in this book is more limited in scope. We are interested in social influence during an election campaign – the manner in which citizens' political choices become interdependent. Three building blocks become crucial for this task: (1) the purposes of individual citizens, (2) a microsociological conception of individual choice, and (3) social learning.

CITIZEN PURPOSE

There is nothing about social influence that is inherently at odds with rationality in politics. Contextual theories do not argue that citizens are irrational, but only that they are interdependent. As Key (1949) shows us, one aspect to the evil logic of the Old South was that the racial context stimulated a racial-hostility effect among whites through their own perceived self-interest. Moreover, various forms of interdependence can be instrumental for many citizens in many circumstances.

Anthony Downs (1957) argued that citizens are faced with an important dilemma when they seek to become informed about politics. They need information to realize where their interests lie, but information is costly. Indeed, even modest information costs can swamp the benefit that is likely to be obtained through politics, once individual acts are discounted by the likelihood that they will have political consequence. Given such a problem, rational citizens seek to reduce their information costs – they seek to obtain political information on the cheap – and one effective way to realize that goal is by obtaining information from other individuals. Information obtained in this fashion may, of course, be biased and partial to others similarly situated, but it is nonetheless useful (Calvert 1985).

Socially obtained information results in several efficiencies. First, the information comes tailor-made. If a citizen wants to know about the current status of nuclear arms–reductions talks, he may or may not find relevant information in the newspaper or on the television news, but he can formulate an explicit informational request to an associate who might know. Second, citizens might exercise control over the source. Most citizens have little control over the bias of the evening newspaper or the network news. But they are likely to exercise more control over the bias of their personal information sources. That is, citizens can request information from people who, based on their joint history in some common context, are known to have general viewpoints similar to their own.

A variation on the Downsian view is offered by various cognitive models of decision. Inspired by the early work of Simon (1957), this general viewpoint recognizes the inherent limitations upon the capacities of citizens to make informed choices in complex areas, and focuses on the shortcuts citizens employ to make reasonable and informed decisions (Ottati and Wyer 1990; Lodge and Hamill 1986; Lodge, McGraw, and Stroh 1989). One shortcut is to obtain information from trusted sources (Carmines and Kuklinski 1990), and one of the trusted sources might be another citizen (Mondak 1990). Thus a cognitive model of decision making might potentially complement a contextual theory of politics, and indeed might offer a microtheory to explain contextual effects.

A point of potential divergence between these various viewpoints and a contextual theory of politics lies in the underlying conception of choice and control over political information. Downs views informational choice as being determinant: He implicitly assumes that people have the freedom to choose their own sources of information with certainty, and thus social influence becomes a direct reflection of the citizen's own prior beliefs. Correspondingly, many cognitive models stress the extent to which individuals engage in selective information seeking and interpretation (Ottati and Wyer 1990: 189–91; Iyengar 1990), thereby screening and reinterpreting incoming information within the general context of their own preexistent orientation (or schema). And thus it is not clear that influence occurs at all, at least to the extent that the target of influence exercises direct or indirect control over the message that is received. Such conceptions of information processing have the potential to deny interdependence – to deny that (1) an individual's behavior is fundamentally predicated upon the behavior of other individuals and that (2) explanations of an individual's behavior must look beyond the individual in question.

MICROSOCIOLOGICAL MODELS

Most advocates of a microtheory for contextual effects look toward psychology or economics as sources of inspiration in constructing a mechanism to explain structural influences upon individual behavior. As Raymond Boudon (1986) informs us, however, the individualistic tradition in sociology also supplies a microtheoretical alternative, with roots that trace to the work of Weber (1966). This tradition is sociological in its emphasis upon the extraindividual factors that impinge on individual behavior, but its unit of analysis is the individual, and it incorporates some form of methodological individualism as a microtheory of human behavior.

Microsociological reasoning can be illustrated with respect to personal influence in politics. What makes for political influence in personal relationships? The implicit (social psychological) assumption carried over from many political socialization studies is that intimacy is responsible for personal influence on political orientations, even though socialization research offers little support for such an assertion (Jennings and Niemi 1968; Tedin 1974). Even without empirical support, a reliance upon intimacy continues to drive a great deal of reasoning regarding social influence and contextual effects (Eulau and Rothenburg 1986). Following the lead of Burt (1987), we refer to arguments relying upon intimacy as social cohesion models. In contrast, a microsociological explanation would point toward the social locations of both the target and the source of influence. For example, a structural equivalence explanation pursues the notion that one citizen should have more influence over another to the extent that they share the same locations in social structure (Burt 1987). Such reasoning provides an entirely different vantage point from which to assess contextual effects in politics.

Consider neighborhood effects from the social cohesion perspective: Why should citizens be influenced by the politics of the neighborhood when we know that, in the modern world, neighbors are seldom friends but merely residents of the same social space? Certainly neighborhood effects are difficult to explain from a social cohesion perspective. But reconsider neighborhood effects from the vantage point of structural equivalence: Neighborhoods may be important because residents share common structural locations. If this is the case, it is not cohesion, discussion, and persuasion that are at issue, but rather information. When I see the yard signs and bumper stickers in my neighborhood, I am being informed regarding the political preferences that are appropriate for someone who is like me.

What is the individual-level motive force for conformity? Burt (1987) argues a form of status anxiety in his reanalysis of the Coleman, Katz, and Menzel (1966) study of diffusion patterns in the medical community's adoption of a medical innovation. Boudon (1986) draws on Weber (e.g., 1966: 31–4) to urge the adoption of a rational actor motivation and a conception of contextually bounded rationality. Our own position is that different motives are better equipped to explain different behaviors. In the case of yard signs and bumper stickers, it seems reasonable to assume that their informational value is best explained on the basis of shared interests. When we drive down the streets of our neighborhoods and see Democratic yard signs, or when we see co-workers wearing Democratic campaign buttons, or when we see Democratic bumper stickers in the workplace parking lot, we are being informed regarding the political perferences of people with whom we share interests. The influence of such information is independent of intimacy – indeed it may not even be verbally transmitted – but it is entirely reasonable that citizens pay heed.

Viewed more generally, how does the microsociological model of political information processing differ from that of the economist or the cognitive psychologist? First and foremost, a microsociological argument views choice and control over information as being incomplete and probabilistic (Huckfeldt 1983b). It is not that people do not intend to collect information about politics that corresponds with their own political biases and predispositions, but rather that they are frequently unable. This means, in turn, that: (1) socially obtained political information (indeed all political information) is not simply a reflection of prior preference, (2) people obtain discrepant information that has influence potential, and hence (3) individual citizens are interdependent.

Why might the choice and control of political information operate probabilistically? First, the control over information is probabilistic because the search for information is expensive. Remember what we are addressing. The location of an informal source of information means finding someone with whom to discuss matters of interest, or at least someone from whom to gather information. If choice operates deterministically, citizens do not share their concerns with others until they have located the correct bias. If the correct bias is hard to find, the search must continue. Who is willing to pay the social cost of such an extended search? People who demand political conformity in surrounding social relationships are the most likely candidates, either due to their own lack of tolerance for discrepant views or their own commitment to a particular bias (Finifter 1974). This means, of course, that the extent to which choice is probabilistic depends upon the strength of an underlying preference. Some people are more discriminating than others, but no one exercises complete and total control over incoming information because, if for no other reason, a person must determine the bias of potential information sources in the first place in order to discriminate.

Second, informational choice is probabilistic with respect to any particular preference because it responds to multiple preference dimensions. We often discuss politics with the same people with whom we discuss baseball and fly casting. This is not to say that social relationships are not specialized, but only that specialization adds to the cost of information search and thus one more way to economize is to make a single source serve multiple functions. Some specialization is inevitable – most of us have good friends with whom we would never discuss politics. But specialization comes at a price. In general, life is easier when one contact serves as a source of information for fly casting *and* politics. Thus, when we choose a contact, we are often implicitly optimizing in several directions and compromising among them all, further attenuating individual control and increasing the probabilistic component of choice with respect to any single underlying preference.

Third, informational choice is incomplete because so much of it is obtained inadvertently. When we see a respected co-worker wearing a campaign pin, we have collected an important piece of information. We know that someone with good judgment, and with a particular set of interests, has decided to support a particular candidate. We did not ask him for his opinion – we did not even exercise choice in collecting the information – but the import of such information should not be ignored.

Fourth, control over informally supplied information from social sources is also incomplete because the basis of informational choice is absent – the underlying preference upon which choice rests is incomplete. In other words, we should not forget that it is possible to ask honest, naive questions with little preconception regarding how such information might be reconciled with some preexisting political bias. None of this is meant to deny the existence or importance of a bias either on the part of the sender or receiver of the information. Rather, it is only meant to suggest that such biases are incomplete and capable of being informed. And since they are incomplete, they cannot serve as ironclad criteria in the discrimination among all information sources.

Finally, informational choice is probabilistic because some information is better than no information. Citizens are able to take account of the source's own bias when they evaluate information, or at least they believe that they can. And thus it makes eminently good sense to collect information even if it comes from a wrongheaded source. This does not mean that such information does not have an impact, or that social influence is nullified, but only that people may indeed purposefully expose themselves to information that comes from a source that runs counter to their own bias.

If citizen control over information operates deterministically, then the composition of the incoming stream of information becomes inconsequential for the composition of the information that is ultimately obtained. To the extent that citizens enforce their political predispositions upon informational choice, then the menu of informational alternatives no longer matters. Citizens simply wait it out – they refuse to choose an information source until they find one that they like, even if this means *never* locating an information source. Such a model of information control produces its own by-products, of course. To the extent that citizens exercise such control, they are more likely to extend their search for information, to be unable to locate reliable information sources, and thus to be politically isolated (Huckfeldt 1983b). Alternatively, to the extent that informational choice is probabilistic, the incoming stream of information becomes a crucial consideration. What affects the content and composition of this incoming stream? The answer lies in media exposure and in the multiple bases of social experience to which citizens are exposed.

BEHAVIORAL CONTAGION AND SOCIAL LEARNING

Thus far we have established two elements of our microtheory. First, citizens value political information but they prefer to obtain it inexpensively. Second, the supply of political information is inevitably and systematically biased at its source, and these biases lie beyond the control of individual citizens. The third and final component addresses the following question: How does information affect preference? We address this question by reconsidering the nature of social learning and behavioral contagion.

Behavioral contagion as a micromechanism of contextual influence is articulated best in terms of a social learning process (Sprague 1982; McPhee 1963). According to this view, citizens are rewarded or punished for political viewpoints that agree or conflict with the viewpoints of other people whom they encounter. The process is repetitive in time and subject to the reinforcement schedule that is probabilistically characteristic of a particular context. That is, white voters in Mississippi experienced distinctive reinforcement schedules in the 1984 presidential election when roughly 85 percent of them voted for Ronald Reagan. Black voters in Mississippi encountered dramatically different reinforcement schedules in 1984 when roughly 90 percent of them voted for Walter Mondale.

For some people, learning theory conjures up images of Skinnerian rats being manipulated in a maze, but such a connotation need not be attached to learning theory as it is applied to politics. Citizens certainly make efforts to control their own reinforcement schedules – there were probably some white Mondale voters in Mississippi who were able to surround themselves with associates who also voted for Mondale. And thus, the schedule of reinforcement can be seen to vary across both individuals and contexts.

Moreover, a learning theory maintains its focus upon individuals as their own preferences and predispositions collide with those of other individuals. Reconsider McPhee's (1963) vote simulator: (1) An individual receives a piece of information from the larger (biased) political environment. (2) He then forms a response based upon his own predisposition. (3) He shares that response with others. (4) The others then reward or punish that response with agreement or disagreement. (5) If disagreement occurs, he samples his (biased) information context broadly conceived, reconsiders his opinion, and shares it once again. (6) And so it goes.

This model has several important advantages. First, it allows both individual predisposition and context to be incorporated within a microtheory of contextual influence. Context enters as the information environment and also as the specialized population from which the individual samples associates with whom to share opinions and responses. Individual predispositions enter as the citizen processes information, formulates an initial response to external political stimuli, and responds to disagreement. The motor that drives the model is disagreement. Only through disagreement does change occur, and, thus, to the extent that people are part of politically homogeneous populations, we see less change, and, when change *does* occur, it typically increases the homogeneity of the microcontext.

Another advantage of a learning theory model is that it leads directly to a series of expectations regarding the circumstances under which contextual influence should be most pronounced (Sprague 1982). First, the efficiency of learning increases as the delay in reinforcement decreases and the frequency of reinforcement increases. On this basis we might expect that routine, ongoing, social contacts should be especially influential (McCloskey and Dahlgren 1959; Straits 1990) because their striking power, or immediacy in both time and space, is greatest. Second, continuous reinforcement over a short period of time produces dramatic effects that decay rapidly at the end of reinforcement. Hence, individually idiosyncratic political opinions that are exposed to social influence during an election campaign should be especially subject to change, but these opinions are likely to become individually idiosyncratic once again at the end of the campaign period (see Berelson et al. 1954). Third, individual motivation plays a crucial role in learning efficiency – motivated citizens make efficient learners. And thus it is not at all clear that only disinterested, uninformed citizens should be subject to social influence (Huckfeldt and Sprague 1990). As Converse (1962) and Orbell (1970) remind us, however, incoming information must compete with stored infomation, and thus the long-term and short-term consequences of motivation are complex and interdependent.

In summary, we are offering a threefold argument regarding the translation of the social context into a force on individual behavior. First, citizens are purposeful in their search for information with a politically congenial bias. Second, their control over information is incomplete, and thus the bias of the information they receive is the complex product of their own preferences intersecting with the content of the incoming stream of information to which they are exposed. Third, when citizens encounter political information that disagrees with their own viewpoints, they may rationally reassess their positions, and herein lies the potential for influence. In these ways, the multiple levels of democratic politics are tied together, and the environmentally contingent stream of incoming political information becomes part of each citizen's social experience.

THE MULTIPLE BASES OF SOCIAL EXPERIENCE

The political influence of environmentally contingent information is best understood relative to the various bases of social experience. At one and the same time, citizens live in households, among immediate neighbors, located in the middle of larger neighborhoods, surrounded by a city, a county, a state, and a region. Coupled with these relatively inescapable geographically based environments is a whole series of less geographically dependent environments: workplaces, churches, taverns, bowling leagues, little leagues, health clubs, and so on. And each of these environments, whether it be geographically or nongeographically based, serves to establish constraints and opportunities acting upon social interaction.

None of these environments is necessarily more important than any other in influencing citizen behavior. In particular, it is a mistake to believe that more intimately defined environments are more important than environments which are larger and more impersonal. Indeed, the work of Erikson, Wright, and McIver (1993) demonstrates quite persuasively that American states are the most appropriate environmental units for many purposes of political analysis. The important point is that opportunities for social interaction are circumscribed by availability, availability is influenced by a range of environments defined at various levels, and thus social experience arises in a particular place and time.

Just as individual choice is not determinate in the selection of information sources, neither is the environment. Citizens do not simply roll over and accept whatever comes along in terms of social interaction opportunities. All of us avoid association with some individuals while we pursue it with others. And thus individual social experience is best seen as the end result of a complex interplay between individual choice and environmental supply. Just as the environment is composed of multiple and intersecting dimensions of experience (work, neighborhood, church, tavern), so also is individual associational preference multidimensional, responding to a range of different goals and objectives. To the extent that social experience carries political content, these life domains become important to the diffusion of political information and to the resulting preferences and choices of citizens.

In short, individual discretion plays an important role in defining social space and thereby determining social exposure. Learning theory points toward the importance of exposure, and a range of empirical findings shows that, for example, organizational involvement can serve both to shield individuals from and expose individuals to contextual influence (R. Putnam 1966; Segal and Meyer 1974; Cox 1974). In point of fact, social contexts are created at least in part by an individual's construction of a social space. And thus the social context reflects a series of socially structured decisions regarding where to live, work, worship, drink beer, bowl, and so on. The social context experienced by any individual is the point of intersection between all these environments. As an empirical matter, we will be fortunate if we can obtain contextual measures on one or two environments at a time (Wald, Owen, and Hill 1988, 1990), but the inconveniences of measurement should not obscure the underlying theoretical issues.

POLITICAL ORGANIZATION AND SOCIAL COMMUNICATION

Thus far we have argued that social communication is central to political life, and that the informal transmission of political information produces an interdependent electorate. In other words, the electorate is socially organized in ways that make it misleading for purposes of systematic political analysis to extract an individual citizen from a particular social location. But what does this social organization have to do with political organization? Are we simply engaged in a new form of social determinism that seeks to express politics and political behavior as the product of social forces – as a residue and appendage of social life?

Quite the opposite, our argument is that the role and power of politics and political organization are frequently undervalued by failing to take account of the social organization of the electorate. By comprehending the electorate as an aggregation of independent citizens, the potential of political organization remains unrealized for two reasons. First, it is important to recognize that the information transmitted by partisan organizations is quite frequently conveyed through informal, social means. Yard signs, bumper stickers, lapel buttons, telephone and neighborhood canvasses all represent the systematic effort of one person to influence another person usually at the behest of a political organization. Indeed, to the extent that partisan organizations are successful at the task of political mobilization, it most likely depends on the vehicle of social communication.

Second, in many of these efforts, partisan organization quite skillfully exploits social organization. Partisan organizations heighten the credibility of their messages through the choice of credible messengers, and often the most credible messengers are the friends and neighbors and co-workers whose viewpoints we take seriously. Moreover, partisan organizations heighten and extend the impact of the information they convey by carefully targeting their messages to particular locations within the social structure – locations that are likely to further the diffusion of their messages.

In summary, if we view electorates as being composed of individually isolated citizens, then the task of political parties becomes impossible. An individually isolated electorate suggests that party organizations must recruit voters in single-file fashion. Each vote must be secured, and every citizen convinced, individually. Such an undertaking is unimaginable, and against such a backdrop it is understandable that so many analyses of party organization have reached skeptical conclusions regarding their likely success. In contrast, if citizens are interdependent, if they are tied together through structured patterns of social interaction, then the opportunity for partisan organization is transformed, and the potential for partisan mobilization is transformed as well. In particular, the task of partisan mobilization becomes highly strategic: How can political messages be transmitted in ways that are likely to be diffused through an interdependent electorate in an optimal manner?

RESEARCH QUESTIONS

The present effort is designed to study social influence during an election campaign within a contextually structured process of social influence. Several questions guide this research: What are the most important micromechanisms of social influence during an election campaign? How is the social context translated into a source of political influence? What are the dynamic consequences of social influence for the changing attitudes, opinions, and preferences of the electorate during a political campaign? What roles do political parties play in exercising social influence? And more. Questions such as these cannot be addressed with the standard technologies of voting studies, and thus our attention turns to the design implications of the theoretical perspective we have adopted.

2

A research strategy for studying
electoral politics

The substantive and theoretical aims of this project give rise to a particular set of observational challenges, and the project's design is thus motivated by several theoretical imperatives. We are arguing that citizens are interdependent – that they obtain important political information through processes of social communication – and hence democracy and democratic politics occur at multiple levels of meaning and observation. An exclusive focus on isolated citizens runs the risk of ignoring the thoroughgoing imbeddedness that characterizes the individual acquisition of political information. An exclusive focus on social or political aggregates runs the risk of ignoring the nonadditive consequences of social and political interaction among citizens who constitute particular electorates. As a consequence, the theoretical focus of this book is on the citizen who resides within a particular social and political setting, who obtains political information from a limited menu of alternative choices, and who thus controls the flow of information only incompletely and imperfectly.

Such a theoretical perspective has observational consequences that are far from trivial. It is not enough, for example, to add a few more questions to an interview protocol soliciting citizens' perceptions of their environments. Indeed, one of the goals of this book is to understand more fully the manner in which these very perceptions are the product of a complex interplay among individual preference, attempts at individual control, and the external constraints imposed by a particular setting. We have enjoyed the rare opportunity to construct a research design from first principles, guided by the particular aims of our research program. This chapter devleops that design within an analysis of the theoretical imperatives on which it is based.

We begin at the beginning, by providing a general description of our study site – the South Bend metropolitan area. Our focus then shifts to an analysis of the underlying observational problems of cross-level analysis and inference. Finally, we translate the general discussion of cross-level inference and contextual analysis into a set of specific design requirements, as well as explaining the procedures used in the South Bend study.

SOUTH BEND AS A STUDY SITE

Why South Bend? The answer to this question is, first and foremost, because we know something about it! Many of the questions addressed in this book are demanding in terms of the knowledge required to carry out the necessary analyses. We need to know where the neighborhood boundaries lie, how the primary elections are administered, how the party organizations plot strategy, and much more. This book represents an effort at hands-on political science – it is predicated on the belief that democratic politics cannot be understood adequately from afar. Such an effort requires more than survey data – it requires an understanding of the political and social organization surrounding the voter.

Moreover, the South Bend metropolitan area is well suited for studying the contextual basis of individual behavior and the multiple levels of meaning in democratic politics. Several factors contribute to its value as a research site. First, South Bend is small enough to make it a manageable object of study, but sufficiently large and diverse to be truly urban, manifesting many of the policy problems and qualities of interest to political scientists. The population of the city is approximately 100,000 and the metropolitan area includes somewhat more than a quarter million residents. In addition, South Bend is a self-contained metropolitan area, with four television stations, numerous radio stations, and a daily newspaper.

While South Bend is small in relationship to many other urban areas, it serves as a microcosm of the urban industrial areas of the Northeast and Midwest. Located in the heart of the Great Lakes industrial corridor, South Bend has experienced many of the same problems that have plagued other urban areas in the region: physical deterioration, out-migration of capital and human resources, a corresponding decline in the tax base, racial tension, violent crime, and a controversial public school desegregation process. In addition, the combination of a dwindling tax base and state-controlled tax levy has resulted in a tight squeeze on basic services within the city.

The city's central business district has been deserted by the area's major retailers, and redevelopment in the downtown area focuses on civic, cultural, and service functions. The metropolitan area has suffered from the long-term decline of its once strong manufacturing sector, symbolized by the 1963 closure of South Bend's Studebaker operations. Demographic trends have affected the health of South Bend as well. While the population of Indiana is expected to increase slightly during the rest of the century, St. Joseph County's population is expected to decline. In short, the South Bend area faces many of the problems that are typical of the region.

Along with problems also come advantages. South Bend lies very close to the southeast corner of Lake Michigan, and thus its residents enjoy easy access to the waters and beaches of the lake, as well as to a farmer's market that offers the fruits and vegetables of the farming areas that thrive in the lake's relatively temperate climate. Lying southeast of the lake also means that South Bend lies in the Great Lakes snowbelt, and South Bend residents are not unaccustomed to voting in the snow, even in November. The South Bend area enjoys other benefits as well: a culturally heterogeneous population that includes Hispanics and blacks as well as a range of European ethnic groups, inexpensive housing and a relatively low cost of living, a symphony orchestra, a revitalizing downtown and a strong neighborhood life, with neighborhood bars, ethnic restaurants, and a wide variety of religious parishes. Shortly after our study's field work was completed, the city became the home of the South Bend White Sox – a Chicago White Sox organization farm team that plays in South Bend's newly constructed Stan Covaleski Stadium. In summary, South Bend may not be as spectacular as Chicago or as chic as San Francisco, but most of its residents feel that it is a good place to live, and it supplies a way of life that is not uncommon among many Americans.

Perhaps the most important feature making South Bend an excellent research site is its internal diversity. Neighborhoods range in socioeconomic status from the very poor to the very wealthy, and in cultural attributes from the declining inner-city neighborhoods, to the modest but well-manicured working-class neighborhoods, to the affluent suburban subdivisions in outlying areas. South Bend has also been characterized by the presence of ethnic groups and ethnic neighborhoods. A number of neighborhoods in South Bend and its sister city, Mishawaka, were originally settled by Eastern Europeans and Belgians. Over the past several decades, blacks have settled in some of these neighborhoods, but European ethnic groups still predominate in a number of metropolitan area neighborhoods. Poles, the largest such group, traditionally dominated West Side politics in the city of South Bend, whereas Hungarians settled in the South Side area known as Rum Village, and Belgians settled in Mishawaka. (All three areas are included within the neighborhoods chosen for our study.) At one time these ethnic villages maintained their own vibrant social institutions: taverns, political clubs, parish organizations, foreign-language newspapers. The vitality of these groups has declined in recent years, but they are still important to the life of the community (Stabrowski 1984).

In summary, this election study is a community study in the fullest sense of that term. The project is an attempt to understand the choices of voters within the settings and community where those choices were made. It is not, however, a study of South Bend. We make no claims to provide a representative picture of the South Bend population, or of South Bend voters. Indeed our sampling plan contains major purposive elements: Part of the design is intentionally *non*random, guided instead by the theoretical focus of the research. Before addressing the specifics of the research design, we turn to the more general challenge of cross-level inference and its implications for this project.

CROSS-LEVEL INFERENCE AND CONTEXTUAL ANALYSIS

At one level, it may seem painfully apparent and trivially obvious that individual experience is contingent on the environment, and that individual behavior is predicated on such an environmentally contingent experience. As a matter of observation and analysis, however, connecting the behavior of citizens to social and political environments has proved to be an elusive undertaking. Part of the difficulty lies in an often myopic focus on the theoretically abstract and isolated individual. Another part of the problem arises as a reaction to early, crude, and misleading efforts to make individual level inferences on the basis of aggregate information. And still another difficulty is due to the historical development of methods and technologies for studying electoral politics. The fundamental problem of making the analytical connection between individuals and environments is, however, more profound than these fairly obvious problems might suggest. In particular, the problem of making such a connection is rooted in both real and imagined problems of cross-level inference. In the discussion that follows we examine multilevel analyses of politics with respect to these issues.

As a starting point and illustration, reconsider the pathbreaking work of Tingsten (1963) in his analysis of socialist voting in Stockholm during the 1920s and 1930s. Figure 2.1 is a graphical presentation of Tingsten's data on working-class support for the socialists in Stockholm precincts, and it shows that the socialist vote increases in working-class precincts. But the significance of these data extends far beyond this simple observation. First, notice that the data of Figure 2.1 are best described by an s-curve (a logistic distribution fits these data with extraordinary accuracy). If the probabilities of socialist support among workers and nonworkers were constant, that is, if each person had a fixed individual-level probability of supporting the socialists given his or her class-membership status, then the data should be clustered around a straight line. (We have imposed the line of perfect proportionality, or uniform returns to scale, $Y = X$, as an aid in studying the plots.) The important point here is that individual propensity to vote socialist cannot be constant across precincts and also yield the pattern exhibited in Figure 2.1. Furthermore, the nonconstancy is systematic, that is, in precincts with high working-class densities the socialists get a disproportionate share of the vote and the converse holds in precincts with low working-class densities.

Figure 2.1 only provides data at a single aggregate level, and even though these Stockholm precincts are very small aggregate units, we are thus forced to theorize regarding the individual-level effects that might generate such a pattern. In contrast, Tingsten also offers evidence regarding turnout among Stockholm workers that does not require such an inferential leap because it provides what is, in essence, observation at two levels. As luck

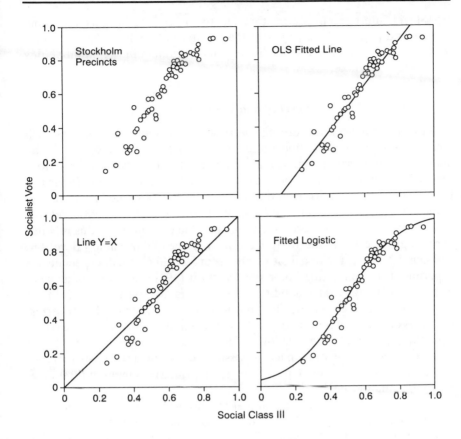

Figure 2.1. Tingsten's data.

would have it, Swedish census officials calculated the individual level rate of voting participation among those classified as working class and reported it by precinct; Tingsten had the good theoretical sense to consider that rate as a (linear) function of working-class densities within the precinct. In considering these class-specific turnout rates, we are not required to infer the behavior of workers on the basis of the population at large. We observe this rate directly and see that it varies as a function of working-class densities. There is no ecological inference problem or compositional measurement problem in these data. And thus Tingsten's work signifies a breakthrough. His combination of aggregate observation with individual-level inference explicitly recognized the nonadditive consequences that derive from behavioral interdependence, and his analysis of turnout is the earliest cross-level analysis with individual-level measurement that we have been able to identify in the literature.

More than fifty years ago, Tingsten was able to navigate the waters of cross-level inference in a way that led to productive insights regarding politics and political behavior. But the tradition of analysis that he represented would be eclipsed by technology and argument in the methodology of the social sciences.

Level of analysis fallacies

Two events that occurred during the postwar era redirected the research focus of contemporary political science. The first was the adoption of the national random-sample survey as a means of data collection in serious scholarly research on mass political behavior, especially voting behavior. Prior to this time, empirical studies of electoral politics relied most heavily upon aggregate data obtained from the public record – election returns and census data. There were, of course, notable exceptions to this reliance upon aggregate data: the early Columbia studies (Lazarsfeld, Berelson, and Gaudet 1948); the imaginative efforts of Harold Gosnell, especially his experiment in stimulating voter participation (1927); and others as well. But with the increased availability of survey data, and particularly with the establishment and growth of the American National Election Study series, the focus of electoral politics began to shift from the electorate to the voter, from the aggregate to the individual. Thus, at the beginning of the 1950s, a methodological innovation made it possible for political scientists to adopt the framework of individual psychology as a primary element in their arsenal of explanatory devices.

At the same time that mass political psychology became a methodological alternative, the practice of political sociology was rendered suspect among many scholars. The catalytic event for the eclipse of political sociology among political scientists was the publication of W. S. Robinson's (1950) critique of aggregate data analysis and cross-level inference in his exposé of the ecological fallacy. Robinson's argument continues to provide a conundrum for many political scientists. Indeed, forty years after its publication, a small eminent group of methodologists are still struggling to come to grips with its implications (Erbring and Young 1979; Achen 1986; Shively 1987; Hanushek et al. 1974).

We do not intend to recapitulate the entire argument surrounding Robinson's original article and its later critiques and extensions. But the general problem lies at the core of contextual analysis, and to the extent that the ecological fallacy poses a problem, contextual analysis provides the solution. Since the publication of Robinson's argument, generations of social scientists have eschewed aggregate analysis in fear of committing an ecological fallacy, and this meant that the tradition of aggregate analysis went out of style among many social scientists. Caution is an admirable trait, especially among social scientists, but the motivating fear warrants reexamination because the ecological fallacy is not logically different from a corresponding individualistic fallacy. Indeed, both are the result of unspecified contextual effects.

For purposes of demonstration, suppose that the empirical issue concerns the relationship between individual income and support for a particular Republican mayoral candidate in a city election. That is, we are interested in the manner in which citizen support for the candidate varied as a function of citizen income level. A number of research strategies are open to us. We might simply regress the candidate's proportional vote within neighborhoods (or precincts or tracts) on the mean income level within the neighborhood. Alternatively, taking Robinson's admonition seriously, we might contract a polling firm to conduct a random-sample survey of citizens within the city, and in that survey we might ask respondents their income levels and how strongly they support or oppose the candidate. Remember that in both instances we are interested in the behavior of individual citizens. Is the aggregate strategy as bad as the ecological fallacy makes it seem? Is the survey of individual citizens the solution to our problem?

Consider first the aggregate strategy. What stands in the way of inferring individual behavior on the basis of aggregate data? For purposes of illustration, we select three bogus neighborhoods with three respondents in each neighborhood and construct scenarios on that basis. In order to facilitate comparison, we assume (1) that the survey question provides an unbiased estimate of the individual probability that each respondent voted for the candidate and (2) a correspondence of metrics between aggregate measures for the neighborhoods and respondent means within the neighborhoods.

Figure 2.2 is a scatterplot of candidate support on income: Each observation is an individual respondent and each neighborhood sample is enclosed by an elipse. In each panel of Figure 2.2, a line is drawn to represent the regression of the neighborhood mean for candidate support on the neighborhood income mean, and thus we can easily compare the aggregate relationship for the neighborhood means to the individual relationships within neighborhoods. Only in the first panel would we correctly infer a positive individual-level relationship within neighborhoods on the basis of the positive aggregate relationship. In the second panel we would infer a positive relationship when, in fact, the relationship within the neighborhoods was flat, and in the third panel we would infer a positive relationship when the individual relationship within neighborhoods was negative.

There is, of course, nothing new to any of this (see Przeworski and Teune 1970). These are simply variations on the scenarios that drove many political scientists to reject aggregate analysis and embrace individual-level data as a cure. But are they a cure? Do individual-level data solve these problems?

Returning to the three panels of Figure 2.2, what would happen if we estimated a single individual-level model on the basis of pooled individual-level data for the three neighborhoods? Figure 2.2 is redrawn as Figure 2.3,

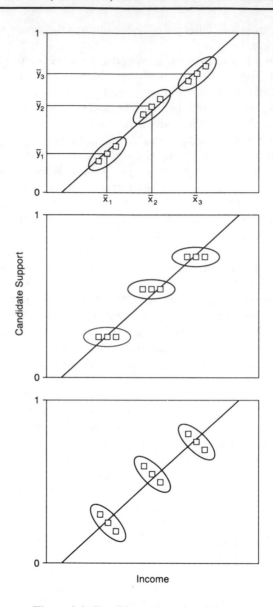

Figure 2.2. Possible aggregation fallacies.

absent the neighborhood means, but with lines drawn to represent the *individual-level* regression of y on x for the pooled sample. What is the result? As before, for each panel, we would obtain a positive slope even though such an individual-level relationship only held within the neighborhoods of the first panel.

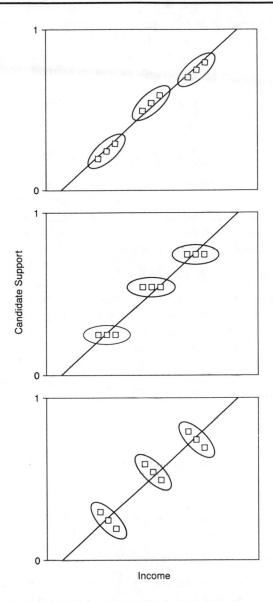

Figure 2.3. Possible individualistic fallacies.

None of this is anything more than conjecture and line drawing, and we could continue to generate a long list of observational perversities with respect to relationships within, between, and across the three neighborhoods. But this exercise serves to illustrate an important point: The potential for an ecological fallacy is not logically different from the attendant potential of an individual-level fallacy. Suppose that the third panel of Figure 2.3 is accurate. Is it meaningful to argue that higher income is related to a higher level of support when, in fact, the relationship is reversed within neighborhoods? In this particular instance, the pooled individual-level model corresponds to the aggregate model, but one model would produce an ecological fallacy, the other would produce an individual-level fallacy, and both would be wrong.

The Boyd–Iversen model

A direct strategy for dealing with both the ecological fallacy and the individual-level fallacy has been proposed by Boyd and Iversen (1979). They provide a canonical and straightforward formulation for examining a range of possibilities (also see Iversen 1991). Following Boyd and Iversen, consider first a simple individual-level model:

$$y_{ij} = a_j + b_j x_{ij} \tag{1}$$

where y_{ij} and x_{ij} are the candidate support scores and the income levels for the ith individual in the jth context. Even if the requisite individual-level data are available, there may be some profound dangers in ignoring the contextual dependence of a_j and b_j on their local environments by simply regressing y on x using the pooled individual-level data. (For example, the intercept varies as a function of $x_{.j}$ in both the second and third panels of Figures 2.2 and 2.3.)

The simplest Boyd–Iversen generalization is to express both the slope and the intercept of the individual-level model as a linear function of the group means.

$$a_j = a' + a''x_{.j} \tag{2}$$

$$b_j = b' + b''x_{.j} \tag{3}$$

Substituting equations 2 and 3 into equation 1 produces the single equation form.

$$Y_{ij} = a' + a''x_{.j} + b'x_{ij} + b''x_{.j}x_{ij} \tag{4}$$

The resulting multilevel model can be estimated in several different ways (Boyd and Iversen 1979; Alwin 1976; also Iversen 1991), but, most important for present purposes, notice what the model demands in terms of evidence. Not only are observations on individuals required, but also observations on the aggregates of which they are a part.

The important point of this exercise is that contextual theories of politics grant no particular epistemological status to the ecological fallacy. Rather, the ecological fallacy and the individual-level fallacy are both examples of specification error (Hanushek et al. 1974). As a logical matter, it is no more dangerous to infer individual behavior from aggregate-level data than it is to infer individual behavior from individual-level data. Indeed, if a'' and b'' are both zero, then either aggregate- or individual-level data will provide equally revealing inferences regarding the behavior of individuals. It is only when contextual effects are present ($a'' <> 0$ and(or) $b'' <>0$) that either the ecological fallacy or the individual-level fallacy poses a problem. Stated somewhat differently, ecological fallacies and individual-level fallacies are both the result of unspecified contextual effects.

The Boyd–Iversen model provides no guidance regarding appropriate levels of aggregation, the mechanisms that link together the multiple levels of meaning in democratic politics, or the substantive and theoretical basis for understanding individuals in context. The model does, however, provide several important measurement insights. It helps to illuminate the danger of observing politics at a single level. Moreover, it provides several statistical and measurement strategies that we incorporate in the South Bend study.

DESIGN REQUIREMENTS

Against the general background of these cross-level inference problems, a number of specific factors dictate the specifics of the South Bend study research design: the contextual focus of the research, a concern with the translation of social contexts into political influence, a theoretical concern with dynamics, and our desire to examine political choice at multiple levels of meaning. In order to carry out such a research project, it was necessary to construct a data set with the following minimal characteristics.

1. The data set must have multiple measures on individuals collected through time. We interviewed 1,500 South Bend area residents at three points in time during the 1984 election campaign. The first interview took place after the Indiana primary but before the national party conventions. The second interview occurred during the heart of the campaign – after Labor Day and before the election. The final interview with the main respondents occurred after the election.

Table 2.1 summarizes the sampling design and shows the attrition rate from the first two waves of interviewing. The end product of this effort is three cross-sectional surveys, a three-wave panel of 926 respondents, and a two-wave panel of 1,254 respondents. All interviewing was done over the phone through the use of computer-assisted telephone interviewing by the Center for Survey Research at Indiana University. Total interview time per respondent for the combined three waves averages slightly in excess of ninety minutes.

2. The data set must include extensive information on the social structures within which our respondents reside. The sampling frame is constructed around neighborhoods, but our concern with social influence and social

Table 2.1. *Summary survey statistics for main respondent interviews*

	First wave 6/11-7/17	Second wave 9/11-11/3			Third wave 11/12-12/11			
	"A"	"A"	"B"	Total	"A"	"B"	"C"	Total
Complete interviews	1,491	1,091	415	1,506	926	328	257	1,511
Retention rate	—	73%	—	—	85%	79%	—	—
Average interview length (minutes)	25	35	43	37	32	31	39	33

Note: "A" respondents were first interviewed in the first wave, "B" respondents in the second wave, and "C" respondents in the third wave.

contexts does not stop at the neighborhood level. The second wave of the survey includes extensive batteries of questions regarding the various domains within which respondents' lives are organized: work, organizational involvements, recreational pursuits, church membership, and family, as well as neighborhood. For example, each of the respondents to the survey was asked whether he or she attended church services, as well as the particular congregation attended.

3. *The data set must include measures regarding the political activity and orientations of the respondents' informal associates, particularly the people with whom they discuss politics.* In short, the data set must include social network information that is relevant to politics and political discussion. Furthermore, these measures should not wholly depend on the perceptions of the main respondents. Previous research suggests that respondents do an accurate job in perceiving their friends' social characteristics, but an inaccurate job in perceiving their friends' political orientations (Laumann 1973). Thus information on the main respondents' associates is gathered both from the main respondents and the associates themselves.

The third and final interview with the main respondents concluded with a battery of questions regarding the "three people you talked with most about the events of the past election year." The wording of the question focused intentionally upon discussion, and avoided any mention of friendship. The relationship between the main respondent and her discussant was, in turn, established within the battery of questions. Moreover, the respondents were asked a range of questions regarding their perceptions of the discussants.

A second source of social-network information comes from the discussants themselves. Subsequent to the three-wave survey of the main respondents, interviews were conducted with more than 900 discussants. This snowball component to the survey produced interviews that averaged approximately twenty minutes in length. In addition to standard postelection questions regarding voting preferences, political activity, and political opinions, the schedule included a battery of social-network questions that allow an investigation of reciprocity within the main respondents' discussion networks.

4. *The data set must include information that allows us unambiguously to connect citizens with political organization.* The key to such a connection is to use the same information used by partisan organizations – the public-record voter registration lists and participation histories included on the St. Joseph County voter tape. Such information is widely used by local party organizations nationwide, and South Bend is no exception in this regard. In keeping with Indiana election procedures, the voter tape includes a record for each registered voter in the county, and it contains information regarding whether the individual voted in past elections and which party ballot the individual chose in past primary elections. Thus, by merging this information together with the survey, we are able to determine whether respondents are registered to vote, how frequently respondents voted in elections, and a measure of behavioral partisanship for each respondent defined according to primary ballot choice. In addition to the standard reverse record checks regarding past voter participation, this information helps us see voters through the same lens as political parties, categorized according to the past public records of their behavior.

5. *The data set must include sufficient respondents within neighborhoods to provide context-specific estimates regarding the aggregate characteristics of neighborhood populations.* Moreover, at various points in the analyses we will obtain context specific slope estimates from the regression of an individual dependent behavior on an individual characteristic (Boyd and Iversen 1979). Thus the sample is concentrated within sixteen South Bend area neighborhoods, producing subsamples of approximately ninety-four respondents within each neighborhood at each wave of the survey. This design feature is particularly important: It means that every item on the survey can be aggregated to the level of neighborhood and treated as a compositional estimate of the neighborhood population.

Why did we choose neighborhoods as primary sampling units rather than bowling leagues or churches or workplaces? We grant no particular epistemological status to geography in general or neighborhoods in particular as determinants of social or political life. Indeed, we look forward to studies in the future that *do* adopt secondary organizations and workplaces as primary sampling units, much as Wald and his colleagues (1988, 1990) have adopted churches.

At the same time, geography is important, and urban geography is especially important (Keller 1968; Suttles 1972; Huckfeldt 1986). The *way* in which urban geography is important is an open question, however, that is sometimes a matter of dispute. We do not view the neighborhood as a necessarily cohesive or intimate form of social organization, nor do we look toward the neighborhood as a hotbed of widespread, interlocking, intense social ties. Rather, we see neighborhoods and neighboring in much less intense, more circumscribed, but still crucially important roles.

Neighborhoods are important because they determine proximity and exposure – they serve to structure important elements of involuntary social interaction (Huckfeldt 1983b). Where we live determines the churches that are nearby, where we do our shopping, the bumper stickers and yard signs that surround us. Moreover, neighborhoods serve as staging grounds for a variety of voluntary social activities. Everything else being equal, it is easier to pursue a friendship or join a group that is locationally convenient. For example, by focusing upon particular neighborhoods, we also focus upon particular churches. Approximately 40 percent of our third-wave respondents report attending about twenty churches. And thus by concentrating our sample within particular neighborhoods we also concentrate it within particular congregations, a design advantage that will be made clear in a later chapter. Two issues regarding urban geography and neighborhoods must be addressed in the course of our research. First, in what ways are neighborhoods important to politics and the political behavior of individual citizens? Second, how does the role of the neighborhood coincide, diverge, and compare with respect to other forms and levels of political and social organization?

An important resource for this research project has been the wealth of information available on South Bend area neighborhoods. Social scientists at the University of Notre Dame have been deeply involved in identifying South Bend neighborhood boundaries, and St. Joseph County was a full participant in the Census Bureau's 1980 neighborhood data reporting program. Thus not only can we identify the natural social boundaries of South Bend area neighborhoods with some confidence, but we can also make use of 1980 census data aggregated according to these boundaries. This means, in turn, that we are able to employ measures of the neighborhood context that derive both from the surveys and from standard census measures. Reliability analyses suggest a high degree of correspondence between census and survey measures of neighborhood contexts, with common variance between education and income measures from the two sources in excess of 80 percent. All of the neighborhood measures used in the analysis of this book are taken from aggregated survey measures.

Neighborhoods are chosen purposively to maximize variation along lines of social status and ethnic background. Some of these neighborhoods contain significant black minorities, but all are predominantly white in racial composition. Thus the resulting sample is not intended to provide a representative sample of the population at large. The respondents are chosen randomly within neighborhoods, however, and this means that the within-neighborhood sample can be used to provide estimates of population parameters for the neighborhood populations.

South Bend study data collection procedures

Data collection for the South Bend study occurred in a series of stages. The earlier stages involved the selection of neighborhoods to be included in the study. Later stages involved the interviewing of main respondents, the construction of a sample frame for political discussants, the interviewing of discussants, and the merger of public-record voter registration data. We document the stages in some detail because the data collection enterprise is central to the theoretical undertaking we have defined, the data collection procedures are different in important ways from standard survey technology, and we hope that others will build on our successes and learn from our failures.

Stage 1: Choosing neighborhoods. The research design originally called for three interviews with 1,500 respondents equally divided across fifteen neighborhoods, or 100 respondents per neighborhood. The first stage of the project consisted of choosing the South Bend area neighborhoods where surveying would occur, a task made easier because St. Joseph County participated in the U.S. Bureau of the Census neighborhood data program. Thus, detailed 1980 census statistics were reported by neighborhood for nearly the entire metropolitan area. Neighborhood boundaries were defined by three different agencies within St. Joseph County: South Bend and Mishawaka neighborhoods were identified by their respective city planning departments, and neighborhoods lying outside these two cities were identified by the St. Joseph County Area Planning Commission.

After eliminating neighborhoods that were too small to be of use in the study – neighborhoods with fewer than 2,000 residents – two main criteria were used in selecting neighborhoods: the status level of the neighborhoods, and neighborhood ethnic composition. Neighborhoods were chosen, first and foremost, to maximize social-status variation. As a second consideration, neighborhoods were chosen to maximize variation in white ethnic composition. A fundamental design decision was made to focus the study upon the white population. Social influence in politics operates among both whites and blacks, but one project cannot study both populations successfully due to the social fissure separating racial groups in American society, and in South Bend as well.

Two sources of information proved indispensable in choosing neighborhoods for the study: neighborhood census data and maps obtained from the Area Planning Commission, and the expertise of Professor John Roos of the University of Notre Dame. Roos accompanied the principal investigators on windshield tours of potential study neighborhoods, as well as sharing his insights regarding the metropolitan area and its neighborhoods. Through his work with the South Bend urban observatory, Roos participated in a neighborhood identification program that served as a precursor for St. Joseph County's participation in the neighborhood census program. This experience together with his other involvements in South Bend community and political affairs made him a storehouse of valuable information and advice for this project.

At the end of this stage of the project, sixteen neighborhoods were defined and chosen to be included in the study. Thus, 1,500 interviews produced an average of 94 respondents in each neighborhood at each wave of the survey. Ten neighborhoods were located in the city of South Bend, four in Mishawaka, and two in suburban St. Joseph County. In several instances the study neighborhoods were defined as combinations of adjacent neighborhoods defined by local planning authorities.

Stage 2: Neighborhood household enumerations. In order to obtain random samples of people living within the study neighborhoods, it was necessary to develop, as nearly as possible, complete enumerations of neighborhood households, names, and phone numbers. This was accomplished using a commercially marketed street directory – a listing of household names, addresses, and phone numbers organized by street for the South Bend metropolitan area.

This stage required that all the streets for a neighborhood be located within the directory, and that all households for those streets be added to a neighborhood's enumeration. As part of this process, slight alterations were also made in neighborhood boundaries in an effort to arrive at the highest possible level of neighborhood integrity. The South Bend area has a low level of unlisted telephone numbers, and the city directory appeared to provide more coverage than the phone book. During the course of the project, names were frequently located in the city directory that were not available in the phone book. The complete set of neighborhood enumerations were transported to the Center for Survey Research at Indiana University for the drawing of telephone interviewing samples within each neighborhood.

Stage 3: The first wave of the survey. The first wave of the survey provided baseline measures on 1,500 respondents prior to the general election campaign. In keeping with this goal, interviewing took place during the last three weeks of June and the first two weeks of July 1984. All interviewing was completed prior to the time that either of the presidential candidates was chosen by the party conventions. A total of 1,491 respondents were interviewed, and the average interview took twenty-five minutes to complete. (These respondents will be referred to as the "A" respondents.)

The survey design randomly chose households within a neighborhood, and then randomly chose either the man or woman of the house to interview. For example, if John Smith was listed as the name for a particular household, then the interviewer asked to speak with either Mr. John Smith or Mrs. John Smith. If the interviewer asked for Mrs. John Smith and no one by that name existed, then the interviewer asked for Mr. John Smith.

The response rate for the first-wave interview was 64 percent: Telephone contact was made with 2,316 households and interviews were completed in 64 percent of the instances in which contact was established. That is not an extremely high response rate by random-digit-dialing (RDD) standards. RDD surveys aim for a 70 to 75 percent response rate. Several factors account for the lower rate.

First, the interview required a significant amount of the respondent's time, and the respondents were given an estimate of interview length before it began. Second, and more important, the design of the study required that quotas of interviews be completed across a range of neighborhoods, and the quotas were more difficult to achieve in lower-status neighborhoods. Thus, RDD surveys undoubtedly produce an upper-status bias that the present study helps to reduce, but in doing so the response rate suffers.

Finally, each wave of the survey was undertaken within a focused time frame with a firm completion deadline. In the first wave this deadline was the nomination of the presidential candidate at the Democratic convention. This narrowly focused interviewing period precluded the luxury of extensive call-blacks to complete interviews. In keeping with this last point, only 22 percent of the contacted households produced "refusals" – instances in which the potential respondent told the interviewer on two separate occasions that she or he did not wish to participate. That refusal rate is well within the acceptable range for RDD surveys.

The response rates for new respondents drops further in the final two waves, and this drop-off is readily explained in terms of these final two factors. Indeed, the effect of these two conditions is exacerbated in the second and third waves.

Among the topics covered on the first wave were general participation history, primary-election participation, general policy opinions, opinions regarding important national problems, psychic involvement in politics and the election campaign, and intended vote. Additionally the instrument included a complete battery of demographic questions for the respondent and the respondent's spouse, as well as standard measures of political loyalties and preferences: political party identification, liberal–conservative identification, and so forth.

Stage 4: The second wave of the survey. This second preelection wave was designed to locate respondents sociologically. The instrument included five batteries of questions regarding respondents' neighborhoods, workplaces, organizational involvements, recreational pursuits, and families. Questions regarding the political salience of each domain were asked, as well as a battery of questions regarding political discussion and the respondent's reliance upon informal, socially derived information regarding politics.

In addition to questions regarding the respondent's social environments, the instrument also included questions regarding candidate preference and perception, policy opinions and expectations regarding the economy and foreign affairs, as well as a series of questions concerning various policy concerns. Thus, while the second wave of the survey had a concentrated emphasis on social influence in politics, it also included standard pre-election survey items that allow comprehensive consideration of factors affecting the vote.

The second-wave interviews were conducted in a period beginning one week after Labor Day and ending the weekend before the election. This instrument was administered as part of the study, averaging thirty-seven minutes per interview. Out of the 1,491 first-wave respondents, 1,091 or 73 percent were reinterviewed as part of the second wave. These "A" respondents were supplemented with 415 interviews of new, previously uninterviewed ("B") respondents, bringing the second-wave total to 1,506 respondents. As before, the respondents were distributed evenly across the sixteen neighborhoods.

The response rate among the new "B" respondents was 44 percent. This lower response rate is due to an intensification of previously discussed factors. First, the attrition rate between waves for "A" respondents was higher in the lower-status neighborhoods, and this meant that "B" respondents were disproportionately located in lower-status neighborhoods where the response rate tends to be lower. Second, the time frame for interviewing new respondents became even tighter in the second wave. The interviewing of "B" respondents was delayed as long as possible in an effort to recover a maximum number of "A" respondents. Thus, a larger number of potential respondents needed to be introduced in order to generate the requisite number of interviews in the short time frame. As a result, the actual refusal rate dropped even lower in the second wave to only 13 percent.

Stage 5: The third wave of the survey. The third wave of the survey contained sections on media use, political party contacting and participation in the campaign, voting behavior in the election, and opinions regarding campaign issues. The standard postelection questions were supplemented by a series of questions regarding local politics and local political figures and questions regarding group attitudes, and finally by a series of questions regarding the respondents' social networks. The third-wave instrument required an average of thirty-three minutes to administer.

The social-network questions formed the most innovative battery of questions in the third wave. The identification of the network was imbedded in an explicitly political frame of reference: Respondents were asked to provide the names of three people with whom they talked with most about the events of the election campaign. Sixteen questions were asked regarding each person mentioned by the respondent, including the person's last name and the street he or she lived on. This last information makes possible the snowball component to the survey – interviews with network members other than the main respondent.

Out of the 1,511 respondents to the third wave of the survey, 1,254 had been interviewed previously (926 "A" respondents and 328 "B" respondents). The response rate for the 257 new "C" respondents was 42 percent. This continued low response rate was due to the same factors operating previously in the second wave. Indeed, the refusal rate among "C" respondents dropped to only 5 percent.

Our biggest regret regarding the design of the study was that we reinterviewed the "B" respondents at the third wave of the survey. If we had not done this, we would have been able to interview nearly 600 new respondents, thereby providing a large, previously uninterviewed cross-section after the election. Chapter 5 demonstrates how valuable this would have been.

Stage 6: Constructing lists of discussants. Approximately 750 main respondents provided usable last names and addresses for 1,800 network members. Roughly one-third of these were people living in the same household – almost always fellow family members. These numbers meant that the project was much more successful at securing identifying information for discussants than the principal investigators had anticipated. Indeed, the original research budget only provided funds for 500 interviews with network members, but twice that number of interviews would easily have been possible. Subsequent efforts generated supplemental funds to pay for more than 400 additional interviews, for a total of more than 900 discussant interviews.

Even with last names and streets of residence for the discussants, tracking down 1,800 phone numbers is a time-consuming and daunting task. Personnel at the Center for Survey Research displayed remarkable persistence in compiling the enumeration of discussants from which the final wave of interviews was conducted. The highest priority was placed on interviewing a single discussant for each main respondent who was not a relative and did not live in the same household. A lower priority was placed upon interviewing a second discussant who was not a relative in the same household, a spouse, or another relative. These priorities maximized the number of interviews with discussants who were not relatives and did not live in the same household, but they also produced a data set that lends itself well to a comparison of the political information coming from spouses with information coming from discussants who are not relatives and live separately from the main respondent. These procedures do not, however, lend themselves well to the standard calculation of response rates, such as those shown for the earlier waves in Table 2.1.

Stage 7: Discussant interviews. Interviewing of discussants began on January 15, 1985. The survey instrument for these interviews was designed to be completed in an average time of fifteen minutes. It elicited basic campaign-related political involvement and behaviors, a limited amount of information on political opinions, basic demographic information, and a shortened battery of network questions. The network questions were included primarily to investigate reciprocity in network links for the main respondents. That is, to what extent did the discussant reciprocate the network link by naming the main respondent as a political discussant?

Stage 8: Merging the voter tape with the survey. As described earlier in this chapter, individual-level registration and voting-participation information was obtained in machine readable form from St. Joseph County. These data were, in turn, attached to the appropriate survey records for the main respondents. Thus, for each survey participant, these data provide an official record of whether the individual was registered to vote, an individual record of participation in elections, and a record of which party's ballot the individual selected in primary elections.

SUMMARY

In summary, this project has assembled a unique data set that allows us to address individual behavior as it is imbedded within a variety of overlapping, intersecting social domains. In the trade-off between representativeness and imbeddedness, we have intentionally chosen in favor of the latter. The resulting sample is randomly selected within a predetermined sampling frame, but the sampling frame is not constructed to be a randomly probabilistic representation of South Bend, or of St. Joesph County, or of northern Indiana. At the same time, the sample is certainly typical of the people and places that constitute the South Bend area and its population. More important for the purposes of this study is the fact that it is uniquely suited to studying the multiple levels of democratic politics.

In the sections and chapters that follow, we employ these data to examine a range of topics and issues related to social communication in democratic politics. In the next section (Chapters 3 through 5) we consider the dynamic consequences of social influence. In the third section (Chapters 6 through 10) we focus on the nature of social and political interdependence among citizens by exploring the relationships between the networks and contexts of political information. Finally, in the fourth section (Chapters 11 through 13) we consider the role of organizations and institutions in mediating and directing social influence in politics.

II

Electoral dynamics and social communication

3

The social dynamics of political preference

This chapter reviews the McPhee (1963) model of partisan dynamics in an election campaign. The model is used as a vantage point from which to address several questions. What is the relationship between social structure and the dynamics of political preference? What are the conditions under which social structure might generate either durability or change in the distribution of political opinion? How can we reconcile social influence and social structure with rational individuals and democratic citizenship?

What is the engine that drives the dynamics of public opinion and political preference during an election campaign? Should we focus on issues and issue development (Carmines and Stimson 1989)? On media coverage and agenda control (MacKuen and Combs 1981; Erbring, Goldenberg, and Miller 1980)? Or on the state of the economy and pocketbook voting (Tufte 1975; Kramer 1975; N. Beck 1989)? All these questions must be answered in the affirmative because each set of factors provides one answer to the question regarding why preferences change. Each explanation is persuasive, and others are as well, but all must be understood within the context of how people obtain and process information about politics.

How *do* people obtain political information? Do they depend primarily on politicians' speeches, newspaper editorials, Federal Reserve reports? Or is such information better seen as the raw stimuli of politics – stimuli that must be processed and integrated on the part of citizens? The purpose of this book is, first, to examine the manner in which the processing of political information occurs through channels of social communication and interaction and, second, to consider the implications of politically relevant social interaction for the functioning of democratic politics. Do citizens obtain information directly from the external political environment and then process that information as independent decision makers guided by their own decision rules, their own assessments of costs and benefits, their own calculations regarding the likely outcomes of public policy? Or do they make decisions on the basis of shared deliberations, shared information, and a shared social experience? If democratic politics *is* anchored in shared interdependent decision making on the part of individual citizens, what are the consequences for the dynamics of democratic politics?

In short, our purpose is to examine the political consequence of social interdependence among citizens in a democracy, and such a purpose further complicates an already difficult observational task. The dynamic of public opinion is always difficult to observe, even during the course of an election campaign. As political scientists we typically study partisan preference in the context of elections either of independent samples taken at multiple points in time, or by repeated observations of the same sample. When we reinterview the same respondents, the periods between observations are often several months, and we really know very little regarding issues of contamination due to reinterviewing and sample attrition. In this and other ways the study of partisan dynamics is seriously complicated by techniques of observation and measurement – complications that are not absent in our own analysis.

The problems become even more difficult in a study of social influence in politics because we are almost certainly unable to observe directly the process of social interaction with political content. Moreover, we may not sample related events with anything approaching the frequency necessary to assess directly the significance of social communication regarding politics for the ebb and flow of partisan preferences and attachments. Rather, our strategy in this study is to combine an analysis of time-ordered observations with a focus on the informational environments of our respondents in order to address the social dynamics of political preference.

The processes of social interaction that might drive partisan dynamics are related to a classic problem of social determinism addressed more than four decades ago by some of the earliest voting studies. That is, how can we reconcile a meaningful model of democratic citizenship – a model that assigns an important role to competent and rational individuals – with widespread evidence that citizens' preferences and opinions are conditioned on their social and political surroundings? Our purpose in this chapter is to reexamine the problem by first addressing the underlying puzzle of social determinism with respect to preference change. We then consider the observational consequences (and difficulties) inherent in such a view of partisan dynamics. And we develop the close connections between citizen purpose, the mechanism of social interaction, the problem of social determinism, and the dynamics of an election campaign.

CITIZEN PURPOSE, SOCIAL DETERMINISM, AND POLITICAL DYNAMICS

The characteristic finding in studies of mass political behavior that conjures up the problem of social determinism is the marked lack of independence in the political beliefs, opinions, and behavior of people who share a common social environment – especially people who belong to the same small primary groups. A classic illustration of these empirical patterns is found in the work of McClosky and Dahlgren (1959), a line of inquiry that is carried into the modern era by Jennings, Niemi, Beck, and others in their studies of the generational transmission of politics and partisanship (see Jennings and Niemi 1968, 1974, 1981; P. Beck and Jennings 1975; P. Beck 1976). Starkly posed, the problem of social determinism was recognized not only as an attack on the role of individual control and individual volition, but also as an attack on politics as a separate and integral life domain. If political preferences were determined according to social position and membership in social groups, the independence of both politics and citizenship was fundamentally called into question (Key and Munger 1959). That is, if politics is only the residue of social position, social attachment, and social characteristics, then the study of democratic politics becomes merely another sideshow in the study of social life.

The most extreme form of this nonindependence of beliefs in primary groups is perhaps the similarity in political behavior of husbands and wives. One common explanation for political homogeneity among marriage partners is a shared antecedent social location that is directly related to commonly shared (and temporally prior) attitudes, leading in turn to the choice of a marriage partner with compatible belief systems and political values. Another common explanation is that one marriage partner or the other – most typically the wife – unthinkingly and irrationally defers to the political belief system of the politically expert spouse. Alternatively it might be argued that husbands and wives share a common social and economic experience, quite rationally come to hold beliefs consistent with that experience, value one another's opinions because they are rooted in the same interests and experiences, and hence come to similar political positions.

This latter explanation, rather than accounting for the observed similarity either on the basis of an initial and determinate choice of likes by likes, or on the basis of a submerged individuality, is considerably more subtle. It is the fundamental guiding idea underlying the concept of structural equivalence (Burt 1987), but what is most important about the idea from a theoretical perspective is the role assigned to social structure. It is social and economic structure that supplies the experience to an individual, and this experience has a time dimension – it is dynamic. Thus even if initial preferences *are* fixed, experience may lead to changing manifestations of their implications. More realistically, experience may lead citizens to modify their preferences in the longer term, contingent in part upon information received from others who share the same experience. Even if marriage partners *do* choose each other on the basis of political beliefs, it is reasonable to suppose that these beliefs could be modified and mutually adjusted on the basis of shared interpretations of a common social experience.

Moreover, individual discretion is not submerged in such a process. Rather, the individual plays a crucial discriminating role in the give-and-take of social communication with political content.

Many frequent and recurring associations are more coercive than marriage. Work group associates in particular are often inflicted on the individual whether or not he or she chooses to participate. Members of work groups often cannot be avoided due to the nature of common tasks in such systems of organized cooperation. An occasional person may achieve approximately perfect misanthropy in a work environment, but it is surely difficult to remain a social isolate in most work settings. Social or economic structure provides a stream of experience and social interaction over time, which sometimes has political content. Hence, although some everyday associations are quite freely chosen, others are imposed on individuals as an unintended by-product of everyday life, and both may produce interactions with political content that are sustained through time. And thus the questions arise: Do these associations and the interactions they sustain have political consequence? Is there social influence? How does it operate?

THE McPHEE FORMULATION

The problem of social determinism typically arises as one of reconciling (1) free individual choice arrived at by freely reasoning individuals with (2) the regularly observed political agreement that so typically results among people who share common social locations. McPhee (1963) provided an argument, thirty years ago, that serves as a point of reconciliation between freely independent decision making and socially provided information. His argument runs along the following lines. When individuals engage in social interaction with political content they may reveal to one another their political preferences or attitudes or opinions. When such revelations take place, the partners to the interaction will learn that they are either in agreement or disagreement with respect to one or more subjects of discussion. The item of greatest interest to the organization of democratic politics is candidate preference during an election campaign, and we carry out the argument for that situation. In the event that discussion partners discover a mutual common choice, further information search is not stimulated, although this mutual discovery of common candidate preference may very well be reinforcing. In the event that *disagreement* is discovered, the consequences are more interesting and, indeed, provide a specific dynamic for change in candidate preference.

When disagreement is present between two people who interact socially, two options are available: Either the disagreement goes unrecognized or the participants must reassess their positions. We should not dismiss the first option too quickly. A great deal of slippage occurs through social communication. Some preferences go unreported, other preferences are incorrectly perceived, and many disagreements are artfully avoided by steering communication toward safer waters (MacKuen 1990). Moreover, a great deal of this slippage is likely to be biased systematically both by the political positions and opinions of the participants and by the setting of the interaction. Indeed, a central part of our analysis is aimed at a better understanding of the biases that distort socially communicated messages regarding politics.

If disagreement *is* recognized, the participants must inevitably engage in a reconsideration of the opinion or preference or choice. Either one's current opinion is retained in the face of contrary opinion from a partner in social interaction, or the position must be adjusted. It is unnecessary to make the claim that adjustment is automatic, or any claim that the opinion will be changed to conformity. Indeed, if I drive a rusty 1965 Volkswagen and see a Republican bumper sticker on my brother-in-law's new Cadillac Seville, his contrary preferences may reinforce my own intention to vote for the Democrat. It is only necessary that a reassessment of one's own opinion is undertaken. And note that this is a behavior fully consistent with a theoretical model of individual citizens as rational calculators. What should a reasonable citizen do when confronted with the fact that some person in his or her immediate social environment holds a divergent preference or opinion? The knowledge of disagreement is new information, and depending upon characteristics of the source, the receiver, and their relationship, this new information may be particularly salient. Under these conditions, a reassessment of whether his or her current candidate choice is the correct one would appear to be eminently reasonable and rational.

In this formulation, social structure operating through social interaction does not transfer units of influence, nor is the receiver of the new information compelled to change his or her opinion, nor does social influence occur as some form of mysterious social telepathy. Rather, in the normal course of daily living, a citizen discovers a discrepancy between her beliefs and the beliefs of others, and *this discovery is directly consequent on engaging in social interaction*. The citizen is presented with the compelling possibility that he or she has made a wrong calculation with respect to politics – a possibility rendered salient by the source of the new knowledge and the context in which it is learned. Contingent upon a variety of other factors, some sort of reassessment of one's own position clearly appears in order.

The process thus described does not require that citizens be rational actors, but it is entirely consistent with rational action. Other psychological mechanisms would suffice, but they would not be coincident with rational theories of political behavior. (For example, a dissonance-reduction mechanism could be used to predict reassessment and change.) The value of McPhee's formulation is that it *does* fit so well with theories of rationality in human behavior, while simultaneously providing a role for social structure, and also specifying a dynamic process.

What form might reassessment take? In the original McPhee computer model, a one-time stylized sampling of political information from the campaign was implemented (also see Shaffer 1972). More generally it is clear that citizens are bombarded continually by events from the external political environment – events they often must evaluate and to which they often must respond. But depending on the importance of the event and the attentiveness of the citizen, these idiosyncratic responses do not remain private matters – they are shared through various forms of social interaction. In short, citizens form their own responses to political stimuli, and they share these responses with others. If their responses and interpretations receive social support, the process is terminated. *But if their responses are met by disagreement,* they are likely to continue their search for information (cf. Calvert 1985). The argument is now at a critical juncture, for the nature of the information search is, in McPhee's formulation, the source of the observed positive correlation in beliefs among people who share a common social setting.

The central insight is that citizens live in socially structured ways, and thus the search for political information is conducted in a context biased by social structure. If an individual consults his or her social environment for additional information, the content of the information probabilistically reflects the environment. For example, when you discover that an acquaintance holds divergent positions on political matters, you may indeed question your own beliefs and undertake a search for still more information. But this search will be undertaken in the same environment, and thus the same bias is invoked when you discuss these matters with another individual, or encounter other information typical of that environment.

Anthony Downs (1957) offered his own formulation of this problem when he observed that citizens might reduce information costs by obtaining information from other individuals. One reason that such a practice generates savings is that an individual might realize economies by relying on other individuals with similar biases. This only works, of course, if individuals exercise substantial discretion regarding their informal sources of political information – if individual control over the environmental supply of political information is relatively complete. In many instances, of course, such control is far from complete, and individuals must do the best they can with the sources of information that are available. But this is just another way of putting the proposition that the environment of socially supplied information, like the environment of media-supplied information, provides a distinctive bias. The rational actor is thus trapped by her place in social and economic structure, and particularly by the distinctive mix of information that attaches to that structural locale. The trap is probabilistic rather than deterministic, and no law of behavior or convention requires the individual to conform to the biases in her surroundings. But if other political actors are rational as we suppose, the bias in the environment must reflect that collective rationality, and the individual who does alter his or her belief after information search may have simply come to a more complete understanding of the rational self-interests of fellow citizens who are located in ways economically and socially similar to herself.

Note that availability rather than intimacy is the triggering mechanism for this process. Similarly situated individuals may rationally come to homogeneity of beliefs through dynamic processes that are socially stimulated by nonintimates. It need not be your friends who require that you learn political beliefs and attitudes appropriate to your social and economic conditions. Work group associates or fellow church members or just people in the neighborhood may be quite sufficient. All that is required is that you pay attention to what these other actors say, that their opinions have some operational effect for you, and hence that you engage in the search for new relevant political information in the (informationally biased) environment in which you live and work.

Thus McPhee's logic reconciles (1) rational decision making by independent individuals with (2) observed political belief correlations in social groups, by appealing to (3) rational reconsideration of political belief triggered by disagreements, which are (4) discovered by the individual through processes of social interaction. Rational citizens rationally decide. Social and economic structures accidentally, but nevertheless systematically, mold homogeneity by repeatedly triggering individual reassessments of political beliefs.

PROBLEMS OF OBSERVATION

Some people may change their vote choices in the course of some election campaigns. Others may at least marginally alter their partisan loyalties. Still others may be undecided in their vote choices, at least initially. In a world designed for the political scientist, there would be some economically and scientifically feasible technique to monitor the social interactions of individuals in order to assemble a record that might be used to determine the dynamic effects of observed disagreement in political discussion. No such measurement strategy is known to us, and more indirect inference strategies are thus necessary.

At the outset it is important to recognize that stability rather than change is wholly consistent with, and indeed implied by, a central role for social interaction in determining political beliefs. Although other explanations may be offered, if reassessment of political positions after disagreement in political discussion is a significant mechanism for the dynamics of political beliefs, then the durability of preference distributions may be precisely what is expected on theoretical grounds.

To the extent that social groups are biased in the distribution of political preference, then agreement will overwhelm disagreement through the dynamics of reconsideration, and an increase in the bias will yield an increase in the extent of agreement within social relationships. To restate this fundamentally important point for emphasis: *A biased distribution of opinion dynamically gives rise to higher levels of agreement within social groups.* Furthermore, the relationship between biased distributions of opinion and political agreement does not depend on political discretion and individual control in the choice of discussion partners.

To see that this is the case, consider a population in which all individuals have either Democratic or Republican preferences, and assume temporarily that this population is perfectly unbiased – half are Democrats and half are Republicans. If we assume that interaction is random, and if we assume a sufficiently large population to avoid the problem of sampling without replacement, then the probability that any given interaction will involve two Democrats is $.5^2$ or .25. Similarly, the probability that any given interaction will involve two Republicans is also .25. Alternatively, there is a .25 probability that the first person in the encounter is a Democrat and the second a Republican, and a .25 probability that the first is a Republican and the second a Democrat. This means that, in the complete absence of bias, there is an equal likelihood of agreement (.5) and disagreement (.5).

What happens when bias is introduced into the social group? Subject to the constraints imposed in the previous example, Figure 3.1 plots the probability of agreement against the extent of bias, where bias is defined in terms of Democratic proportions – values greater than .5 signify a Democratic bias and values less than .5 signify a Republican bias. At the point of no bias, the probability of agreement is the same as the probability of disagreement (.5). As bias increases in either a Republican or Democratic direction, so does the probability of agreement. The point is quite clear: Increases in bias produce increased levels of agreement, at an ever increasing rate, until disagreement is totally eliminated when there is no one with whom to disagree.

We have assumed, quite conservatively, that interaction is random. What happens if interaction is strongly self-selected – Downsian Democrats seeking out other Democrats and Downsian Republicans seeking out other Republicans? Indeed, and by necessity, agreement levels will increase. In summary, agreement is exaggerated either by the presence of a political bias in the distribution of the population, or by politically inspired self-selection in patterns of social interaction.

But recall that agreement does not furnish the occasion for reassessment. It may reinforce existing beliefs, but it provides no compelling reason to seek new information. Hence, because we may thus expect disagreement to be lower in frequency than agreement, the frequencies of reassessment will be smaller than the frequencies of confirmatory reinforcement, and the subsequent overall influence on change in belief from social interaction thus smaller.

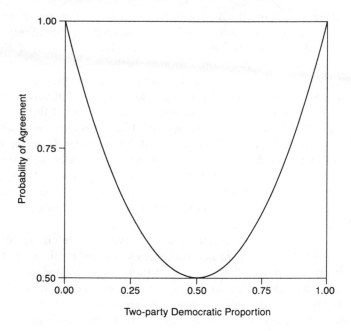

Figure 3.1. Agreement as a function of bias. *Note:* $y = (x)(x) + (1 - x)(1 - x) = 1 - 2x + 2x^2$

These arguments point toward important sources of asymmetry supporting the political status quo. Groups that are evenly divided in political
opinion, or approximately so, must be rare. Asymmetry in the distribution
of beliefs within groups is likely to be characteristic, particularly when we
take account of the tendency for individuals to seek out politically like-
minded associates. And such asymmetry is inherently conservative in the
social sense – it tends to reproduce the existing distribution of opinion. To
the extent that political beliefs are reassessed proportionally to disagreements, and to the extent that the information environments characteristic
of a group are biased proportionally to the opinion in that group, the
engine of social interaction should move citizens dynamically toward prevailing opinion within the group. But because politically unbiased groups
must be rare, the prevailing opinion toward which political discussion
mechanisms move the members of groups will, in general, reflect an asym-
metric opinion distribution. And asymmetrical opinion distributions in social groupings are biased in favor of the status quo – biased in favor of
continuity and stability in political beliefs, not change.

The scholar seeking evidence of political change, such as change in partisan dynamics, is doubly handicapped by this conspiracy of rationality and
social structure. If the group is homogeneous there will be (1) no disagree-

ment and hence (2) no motive for individuals to acquire new information through social interaction and thus (3) no observed change driven by social interaction. Moreover, the politically motivated self-selection of discussion partners and other associates only reinforces these outcomes.

These arguments combine to support a common conclusion. Social interaction very well may be one of the important engines that drive changes in partisanship and other political attitudes and beliefs, but if the mechanisms work as posited here, social interaction mechanisms are also important engines driving the temporal durability of opinion distributions. And the more homogeneous the overall social structure is locally, the more likely the observed effects of social interaction will be political stability rather than political change. This stability arises because common social experience in homogeneous microenvironments provides few occasions for the rational reassessment of beliefs.

Under what circumstances, then, *are* we likely to see change driven by social interaction? If individuals somehow develop opinions that are divorced from the opinion that prevails in their surroundings, and if mechanisms of social interaction are subsequently invoked, we ought to see rapid adjustment to prevailing opinion brought about by the very mechanisms we have discussed. But in view of these mechanisms, how might individual opinion become divorced from its surroundings in the first place? Two circumstances stand out as proximate causes. First, in McPhee's original formulation, the initial incentive for information search was provided by stimuli taken from the external political environment. In other words, the microenvironments we have described are not self-contained. They are constantly being bombarded by the real (external) world of political events. And the individual's initial response to these events is framed idiosyncratically – individual citizens form first responses to these events, which they in turn share with others. Thus the microenvironments must work overtime to bring these idiosyncratic opinions into line with prevailing opinion – a prevailing opinion that is, after all, itself a creation of these microenvironmental processes.

Second, it is not only opinion but also interest and attentiveness that vary across individual citizens. Under normal circumstances, citizens who care little about politics spend less time searching for information than the committed citizens who care a great deal. But once again, the external world of politics intervenes. Dramatic political events – events such as presidential election campaigns – stimulate those citizens who do not care as well as those who do. Indeed, the overall change in interest and attentiveness is likely to be highest among those who do not regularly spend time on information search – the citizens whose opinions are likely to be least firmly tied to prevailing sentiment. But these are the citizens who are likely to be most dependent on socially conveyed information when they are stimulated to search, and thus we might expect to see occasional but dramatic episodes of socially stimulated change occurring among them.

These arguments are only that, arguments. But there are two important points to be made. First, under alternative sets of circumstances, the arguments predict that social interaction mechanisms may be construed as the underpinning of either stability or change in political preference distributions. Second and just as important, the arguments predict a quantitative ratio of sorts: In times of political quiescence, change events (disagreement) should exhibit low frequencies relative to no-change events (agreement). But in politically tumultuous times – times during which people's lives are disrupted by the external world of politics – disagreement should increase in frequency relative to agreement, and thus we should expect that social interaction might become an important engine driving the dynamic of partisan preference.

The elements of formal and empirical attacks on modeling the dynamic consequences of this theory are straightforward but demanding. Not only probability distributions for individual preference are required, but also probability distributions on preferences surrounding the individual. Moreover, a specification of the probability of interaction is required, presumably conditioned on the properties of the groups, as well as the probability that the interaction is political, and – if political – the probabilities of agreement or disagreement. Indeed, successful attempts at modeling along these lines are fairly rare, and it was the very complexity of the many probability distributions involved that led McPhee and his collaborators to formulate these processes as a computer simulation rather than pursue the more rugged algebra implied by a more pristine, mathematical formulation. We believe that a formal model modeling exercise is fruitful, and we begin by presenting one in Chapter 4. But evidence is useful too, and we proceed to an empirical analysis of partisan dynamics in Chapter 5.

4

Durability, volatility, and social influence

The goal of this chapter is to assess the dynamic consequences of social structure and social influence for the distribution of political preferences during an election campaign. Two questions are addressed: First, under what circumstances does social structure and social influence lead to durability and volatility in mass political preferences? Second, do different explanations for social influence necessarily lead to different conclusions regarding its dynamic implications?

The durability and volatility of political preferences are key issues in the study of mass political behavior, and identifying their origins is a major preoccupation within political research. But the relationship between social influence, social structure, and the dynamics of partisan preference has been a source of some confusion. Social structural explanations for political preference have been accused of "static social determinism" (Stokes 1966: 19) at the same time that particular political processes depending on social structure – bandwagon effects, behavioral contagion – are typically associated with volatile, rapidly changing preference distributions. Indeed, we have already argued that social influence might lead either to stable preferences or to rapid change, and the purpose of this chapter is to specify the circumstances under which social structure and social influence might give rise to durability and volatility in political preference distributions.

This chapter's analysis is primarily an exercise in exploring logical consequences. Several mathematical models are developed to examine the theoretical implications involved in different models of social influence. A first, preliminary task is to articulate alternative positions regarding durability and volatility as functions of social influence. The second task is to consider several explanations for social influence on political preference and translate these explanations into mathematical, dynamic representations. Finally, we examine the consequences of these representations for the durability and volatility of political preferences. Before proceeding, we examine the statics and dynamics that underly changes in political preference during an election campaign.

SOCIAL STATICS AND POLITICAL DYNAMICS

Many citizens demonstrate durable preferences that persist through the course of an election campaign, but other citizens demonstrate volatile preferences that are subject to (sometimes) rapid change. The relative mix of durability and volatility depends, of course, on a great many factors – including political events that are specific to a particular election. As an example of volatility, the *New York Times*–CBS News polling organization conducted a 1980 postelection reinterview of individuals originally interviewed four days before the election. This panel survey showed that 21 percent of registered voters changed their vote intentions during the last four days of the campaign.[1]

The 1980 campaign was perhaps a special case of highly volatile preferences and an election that was not decided until the last days of the campaign, and in many ways the 1984 election presented an opposite case. Reagan was never in real danger of losing the 1984 election, and, except for the brief period following his poor showing in the first presidential debate, a Republican victory was never seriously in doubt. But even in 1984, a substantial proportion of the population reported indecision during the course of the election campaign.

Table 4.1 examines changes in vote intention during the election campaign among the South Bend panel respondents who, at the earlier interviews, said that they expected to vote. Before the summer party conventions officially chose presidential candidates, we asked respondents for whom they would vote if the election was between Reagan and Mondale. Once more, during the general election campaign and after the candidates were chosen, we again asked respondents for whom they would vote. Thus, the table produces a view of two overlapping panels. The respondents in Part A were interviewed at all three waves, and the respondents in Part B were interviewed, minimally, at the final two waves. Both parts of the table show that approximately 75 percent of the panel respondents had an earlier preference for one of the candidates that they maintained through the election. About 5 percent of the first-wave respondents switched candidates, reporting an earlier intention for one candidate but a reported vote for the other. But this figure slips to only 1.2 percent between the second and third waves.

Thus the panel data show little evidence of large-scale preference change during the election, although there is substantial evidence of resolved indecision, and a relatively minor amount of backsliding – incidents of people who express an intention to vote for a particular candidate but then report not voting. A panel design such as this one may very well be biased in favor of stable preferences, and we will consider this possibility in Chapter 5. But for present purposes it is sufficient to observe that (1) about one-fourth of

1 *New York Times*–CBS News Poll, reported in *New York Times* (November 9, 1980).

Table 4.1. *Vote intention change in the election among people who expected to vote at earlier interviews*

A. *Expected vote in hypothetical "trial heat" between Reagan and Mondale, before the conventions in the summer of 1984*

	Expected vote (summer)			
	Don't know	Reagan	Mondale	Total
Postelection reported vote				
Didn't vote	1.5%	2.3	4.0	7.8
Reagan	5.7	44.5	2.6	52.7
Mondale	3.8	2.6	33.1	39.5
Total	11.0	49.3	39.7	$N = 821$

B. *Expected vote in election, during the fall general election campaign*

	Expected vote (fall)			
	Don't know/ Uncertain	Reagan	Mondale	Total
Postelection reported vote				
Didn't vote	2.8%	1.8	1.5	6.1
Reagan	10.2	43.1	.6	54.0
Mondale	8.0	.6	31.3	39.9
Total	21.0	45.5	33.4	$N = 1,083$

those respondents who expressed an intention to vote made up their minds for whom to vote during the course of the 1984 general election campaign and (2) only a trivial percentage of voters admitted changing preferred candidates during the course of the election campaign. What were the dynamic circumstances underlying both the durability and volatility of these preferencs in the election campaign? Which things stayed constant and which things changed?

The statics of any election campaign are impressive. Few people realize significant changes in religious affiliation, marital and family status, social group membership, educational level, social status, or in basic social loyalties during the course of a campaign, and very few South Bend respondents report a significant change in partisan loyalty. Table 4.2 shows the joint distribution of party identification before and after the election,[2] and it indicates that only 1 percent of our respondents report an actual change in party affiliation, moving from strong or weak support for one party to strong or weak support for the other. Moreover, 89 percent of the panel

2 Respondents were asked their party identification on two different occasions: the first time they were interviewed and in the postelection interview. Thus, for most respondents Table 4.2 indicates change from summer to postelection, and for others it shows change from early fall to postelection.

Table 4.2. *Joint distribution of party identification, before and after election*

	At preelection interview							
	S.D.	W.D.	I.D.	Ind.	I.R.	W.R.	S.R.	Total
After election								
S.D.	17.22	3.54	1.35	.00	.17	.08	.08	22.45
W.D.	2.62	8.52	2.36	.59	.34	.34	.00	14.77
I.D.	.68	1.94	7.68	1.94	.59	.00	.00	12.83
Ind.	.42	.34	1.52	3.04	.76	.17	.00	6.24
I.R.	.25	.42	.76	3.21	7.59	1.94	.76	14.94
W.R.	.08	.25	.17	.17	2.11	6.08	1.27	10.13
S.R.	.00	.17	.00	.51	1.77	3.38	12.83	18.65
Total	21.27	15.19	13.84	9.45	13.33	11.98	14.94	$N = 1,185$

Note: S.D. = strong Democrat; W.D. = weak Democrat; I.D. = independent Democrat; Ind. = independent; I.R. = independent Republican; W.R. = weak Republican; S.R. = strong Republican.

falls either in cells along the main diagonal, or in cells adjacent to the main diagonal. That is, 89 percent of the sample either reported the same exact partisan loyalty, or a party loyalty only one step removed from the original report.

Finally, for most people, social environments prove to be enduring throughout a campaign. Most people live in the same neighborhoods, play poker with the same friends, and eat lunch with the same workplace associates. They attend the same churches and belong to the same organizations. In short, they are surrounded by the same mix of people before, during, and after the campaign.

What things change? First and foremost, politics changes. Images of candidates evolve and are manipulated by campaign organizations, political issues emerge, and the public significance of issues changes as well – the ups and downs of presidential debate performance; discussions of tax fairness and tax increases; arguments regarding abortion. Second, the political preferences of other people change. And just as important, citizens are forced to take heed of these preferences as discussions of the National League pennant race are increasingly replaced by discussions of the political campaign. In short, citizens are surrounded by the same people, but their interactions with these people increasingly carry political content – politics is forced onto the agendas of countless social encounters.

Thus, in the short-term horizon of a political campaign, some things stay constant and other things change. In broad strokes, things social stay constant and things political do not, where things social are defined to include basic social and political orientations that are socially transmitted during the early stages of political learning, and things political are defined to include the fluctuating political preferences of friends, associates, and the population in general. Can we focus on the social statics of an election campaign without becoming excessively deterministic? Can we focus on the political dynamics of an election campaign without becoming excessively idiosyncratic in our analysis of political change?

Electoral research has traditionally separated the determinants of political preference into (1) a long-term component consisting of things that stay relatively constant, and (2) a short-term component consisting of things that change. The underlying assumption of these categories is that long-term forces produce durability in American politics, whereas short-term forces produces volatility. Thus, Stokes (1986: 19) accused the 1940 Erie County study (Lazarsfeld et al., 1948) of "static social determinism" because its explanation for voting behavior focused too narrowly on things that stay constant – social position and group membership. Instead, Stokes focused on fluctuating candidate evaluations across presidential elections in his effort to explain electoral dynamics.

But such a conception of social structure and social influence ignores the crucial role they play in fostering *both* the volatility *and* durability of political preferences. That is, the social composition of most environments stays relatively constant, but an environment's political composition – the distribution of its political preferences – is sometimes subject to rapid change. Moreover, citizen attentiveness to surrounding political opinions and preference is volatile as well, and such volatility is a direct consequence of the stimulus of an election campaign. This chapter is intended to show that both the statics and dynamics of social influence have important dynamic consequences, not only for political durability, but also for political volatility. Explanations for political preferences that point toward social structure need not be guilty of static social determinism, and analyses of political change need not be wholly based on idiosyncratic political phenomena. Indeed, social structure and social influence have political consequences that are systematic and dynamic.

DURABILITY, VOLATILITY, AND SOCIAL INFLUENCE

One conception of social and group influence sees the social context as an additional layer of social order: The context creates political preferences that are more durable by tying together and unifying individuals within a social group. Another vision of contextual influence sees it as a force for volatility, magnifying perturbations to politics in epidemic-like fashion. An example of the former view – the social context as a source of political durability – is found in the work of Segal and Meyer (1974). In answer to mass-society theorists who view modern man as being atomistic, socially adrift, and associationally cut off, Segal and Meyer argue that individuals are anchored within particular environments: "Americans may not be inclined to radical ideologies or sudden shifts in party loyalties because intermittent persuasion cannot overcome the way a person's social setting structures his political beliefs" (1974: 231–2).

In contrast, Berelson et al. (1954: 122–32) show that social influence processes are responsible for short-run political volatility among some groups in the population. People were more likely to switch preferences during the course of the 1948 presidential election campaign if they occupied social positions that conflicted with their own predispositions: Switches in vote intention occurred more frequently among Protestants and white-collar workers who initially favored Truman, and among Catholics and blue-collar union members who initially favored Dewey. Thus, individuals surrounded by people with views different from their own were more likely to be politically volatile – they were more likely to change their political preferences. Indeed, Berelson and his associates argue that the group basis of electoral behavior is predictable over time because of the social environment's capacity to alter the behavior of politically deviant individuals. In a very real sense, individual volatility is the price that is paid for the durability of aggregate opinion distributions.

Other instances in which the social context is related to political volatility are also available. The concept of a political bandwagon is a contextual notion wedded to behavioral change: The bandwagon is to a political scientist, as the diffusion of innovation is to the sociologist, as rumor transmission is to the communication theorist. In each instance a particular context – defined along various dimensions – fosters a change in the behavior, opinion, or knowledge of individuals. At least in the case of the political bandwagon, such change is likely to be ephemeral and short-lived. Thus, an ambiguous statement of the relationship between contextual influence and the durability and volatility of political preferences is produced, and we entertain the notion that this ambiguity is at least partially rooted in different explanations regarding the mechanisms that translate the social context into a force for political change.

ALTERNATIVE EXPLANATIONS FOR CONTEXTUAL INFLUENCE

Contextual explanations for political behavior point toward the importance of population composition for the political choices made by individual members of the population. Individual preferences are not wholly determined by individual characteristics and predispositions. Rather, individual behavior is also influenced by the characteristics of a surrounding population: Working-class residents of Santiago, for example, were more likely to support Salvador Allende if they lived in working-class areas of the city (Langton and Rapoport 1975). Thus, a contextual explanation for political behavior emphasizes the interdependence of political choices made by individuals who share a common social space.

Such a compositional definition for the social context relies most directly on the work of Blau (1957) and Davis et al. (1961). The social context can be defined at a variety of different levels: family, workplace, neighborhood, county, and so on. Alternative contextual levels differ both in intimacy, and their capacity for altering the interaction patterns of population members. These differences between alternatively defined contexts present important issues that will be addressed in this study, but for present purposes it is only necessary to assume that social interaction patterns are, at least to some extent, circumscribed and constrained by the social context defined at some level, or at some combination of levels. Thus, in order to avoid sacrificing generality, the boundaries for the social context are intentionally left unspecified during this discussion.

Any contextual explanation ultimately gives credit to an underlying process of social interaction, but these explanations differ in the importance they assign to various kinds of social transmissions. Two fundamentally different microlevel mechanisms are frequently cited as the means whereby the context is translated into a source of political influence (Erbring and Young 1979; Sprague and Westefield 1979; Huckfeldt 1983a). One explanation points to the interactions that occur within and between social groups: An individual's political preferences are affected by the group memberships of other people in the context. A second explanation points to the interactions that occur within and between populations that demonstrate different political preferences: An individual's political preferences are affected by the preferences of other people in the context. These explanations are not necessarily contradictory: Indeed, they might work side by side in a complementary fashion. The explanations are different in their substantive implications, however, and these implications bear on issues of durability and volatility.

The first explanation, a social group model, gives attention to patterns of interaction that are structured by social densities: Different social contexts present different opportunities for interaction between and within social groups, and these interactions have important political consequences. For example, people who frequently come into contact with a particular group are sometimes more likely to identify with that group and adopt group norms. Even apart from group identification and group norms, these interactions might have politically important consequences. Consider the middle-class individual who lives in a working-class environment: He or she might maintain a sense of middle-class identity, but exposure to a working-class population might alter political attitudes regarding issues and candidates that affect the working class. Most important, the content of the interaction need not be explicitly political in order to have political implications: Our middle-class individual may have never discussed politics with any working-class neighbors, but political attitudes and preferences might still be affected. Thus, the social group model specifies a generalized milieu effect that does not depend on interpersonal communication with explicitly political content.

The second explanation, a behavioral contagion model, is more direct in the relationship that it asserts between political behavior and the social context. According to this explanation, one citizen obtains political information from other citizens, and thus it is typically the case that people are more likely to adopt a political preference if they are surrounded by other people who demonstrate the same preference. In short, the behavioral contagion model isolates interactions that occur with people who manifest the behavior in question, and people who do not, regardless of social groups. The social composition of a population is not nearly so important as its behavioral composition; the distribution of political preferences within the population is all that actually matters.

In summary, the crucial distinction between these two mechanisms relates to the contextual property that is given credit as being politically influential. The social group model points toward the influence of interactions that occur between and within social groups: The important contextual property is the social density of each group in the population. The behavioral contagion model gives credit to interactions that occur between people who manifest various combinations of political preferences: The important contextual property is the behavioral density of each preference in the population. A rigorous distinction between the two models is often problematic because social densities and behavioral densities are often closely related, and because the two models do not always produce sharply divergent consequences for static representations of politics. The two models do produce very different implications for the durability and volatility of individual preferences through time, however, and thus we turn to an examination of each model's dynamic implications.

DYNAMIC REPRESENTATIONS OF INDIVIDUAL PREFERENCE

We begin by constructing a simple mathematical representation of the social group model at the individual level. The discussion is made concrete by thinking in terms of the working class, the middle class, and support for the candidate of the working-class party. Define individual preference at time t as P_t: the extent of support given by an individual to the candidate of the working-class party. This measure is constructed on the $(0, 1)$ interval: A value of one indicates complete support, and a complete lack of support has value zero. Correspondingly, the extent of nonsupport is defined as $1 - P_t$.

A mathematical translation of the social group model is made using a gain–loss learning form where we assume that increases (gains) and decreases (losses) in the extent of candidate support occur proportionally to positive and negative reinforcement. Negative reinforcement acts to reduce the level of support at some rate. Positive reinforcement acts to reduce the level of nonsupport at some rate, thereby increasing the level of support.

$$\Delta P_t = R_1 (1 - P_t) - R_2 P_t \qquad (1)$$

where $\Delta P_t = P_{t+1} - P_t$; R_1 = the rate at which an individual's level of nonsupport is reduced due to positive reinforcement; and R_2 = the rate at which an individual's level of support is reduced due to negative reinforcement.

The theoretically crucial task lies in specifying the R_i as functions of the social context. We conceive these rates as products of (1) the likelihood of encountering the appropriate reinforcement, and (2) the relative influence of that reinforcement.

$$R_1 = gS \qquad (2)$$

$$R_2 = f(1 - S) \qquad (3)$$

where S = the contextually contingent probability that an individual will encounter positive reinforcement, defined as interaction with a member of the working class; $1 - S$ = the contextually contingent probability that an individual will encounter negative reinforcement, defined as interaction with a member of the middle class; g = the relative influence of positive reinforcement, or the rate at which an individual's level of nonsupport is reduced due to positive reinforcement in a context where all interaction is with working-class individuals; and f = the relative influence of negative reinforcement, or the rate at which an individual's level of support is reduced due to negative reinforcement in a context where all interaction is with middle-class individuals.

Equations 1 through 3 present a simple argument regarding the nature of political change through time. Even simple arguments are capable of producing important consequences, however, and much of this argument's power flows from logically imposed constraints on the rate operators. It must be the case that both R_1 and R_2 lie within the (0, 1) interval due to the structure of the model: Values less than zero produce either negative gains or positive losses in support, and values greater than one either produce increases in support that surpass an individual's previous level of nonsupport, or decreases in support that surpass an individual's previous level of support. All these possibilities present logical contradictions, and thus the following constraints apply:[3]

3 Thus it is also possible to set boundaries on g and f in terms of S and $1 - S$:

$$0 < g < 1/S$$
$$0 < f < 1/(1 - S)$$

These constraints maintain the logic of the gain–loss form: ($0 < R_1, R_2 < 1$), but they allow g and f to vary from zero to positive infinity. Such constraints are theoretically pleasing

$$0 < R_1, R_2 < 1 \tag{4}$$

Substituting equations 2 and 3 into equation 1 produces the complete model:

$$\Delta P_t = gS(1 - P_t) - f(1 - S)P_t \tag{5}$$

The model's reinforcement terms deserve careful attention. Imagine that $S = .8$, $g = .4$, and $f = .1$. Such a scenario suggests that (1) the probability of encountering positive reinforcement is four times greater than the probability of encountering negative reinforcement $S/[1 - S]$ and (2) the weight or influence of positive reinforcement (g) is four times greater than the weight or influence of negative reinforcement (f). Thus, the rate of decrease in nonsupport caused by positive reinforcement is sixteen times greater than the rate of decrease in support due to negative reinforcement.

Notice that the source of contextual influence – social composition – is static, or fixed in time. This (useful) simplification flows from our earlier argument. We are assuming that the individual probability of interaction with a member of a particular social group is contingent on the environment's social composition. Social densities change more slowly than individual behavior – at least in the metric of an election campaign – and that is the important point for these purposes. Readers should also note that we are not making random mixing assumptions for either of these individual-level models. That is, we are not assuming that the probability of working-class or middle-class interaction is simply the proportion of working-class or middle-class individuals in a particular context. Rather, we only assume that the probability of interaction is some unspecified function of underlying population densities.

The logic of the behavioral contagion model is similar to the logic of the social group model, with two important exceptions. First, the reinforcement rates are not affected by the likelihood of interaction within and between social groups, but rather by the likelihood of interaction within and between populations with particular political preferences. Second, the likelihood of various interactions is necessarily specific to a particular time, because aggregate behavior changes in step with individual behavior. We write the model as follows:

$$\Delta P_t = gM_t(1 - P_t) - f(1 - M_t)P_t \tag{6}$$

where M_t = the contextually contingent probability that an individual will encounter positive reinforcement at time t, defined as interaction with a supporter of the working-class party candidate; $1 - M_t$ = the contextually contingent probability that an individual will encounter negative reinforce-

because they suggest that group members might compensate for minority status by an infinitely extreme upweighting of positive reinforcement and downweighing of negative reinforcement.

ment at time t, defined as interaction with a nonsupporter of the working-class party candidate; g = the relative influence of positive reinforcement, or the rate at which an individual's level of nonsupport is reduced due to positive reinforcement in a context where all interactions are with individuals who support the candidate of the working-class party; and f = the relative influence of negative reinforcement, or the rate at which an individual's level of support is reduced due to negative reinforcement in a context where all interaction is with individuals who do not support the candidate of the working-class party.

The similarity of the two models extends to the logic underlying model parameters, and thus the constraints established in inequality 4 for the social group model are also applicable for the behavioral contagion model. Both models presented here are abstractions that are only aimed at capturing the contextual dynamic underlying political change. Thus, the models exclude a range of short-term factors that are clearly responsible for changes in candidate support, such as political events, media events, international crises, and candidates debates. These factors are assumed to operate as disturbances within a social influence process, and they are treated as displacements from a socially defined equilibrium.

ANALYTIC PROPERTIES

The social group model, as it is expressed in equation 5, is a linear first-order difference equation. And because the social context is treated as a parameter that is constant in time, the equation has constant (time invariant) coefficients. Linear first-order difference equations with constant coefficients have been studied in detail (Cadzow 1973; Goldberg 1958), and their analytic potential is fully developed. In order to exploit that potential we rearrange equation 5 algebraically as follows:

$$P_{t+1} = gS + (1 - gS + fS - f)P_t \qquad (7)$$

The reader will quickly see that equation 7 is isomorphic to the standard form.

$$\text{Standard form: } P_{t+1} = a_1 + a_2 P_t \qquad (8)$$

where:

$$a_1 = gS$$
$$a_2 = 1 - gS + fS - f$$

Two technical concepts directly related to difference equation models are especially important to our substantive treatment of contextual effects on durability and volatility: (1) the equilibrium and (2) the response time.

Both ideas are expressed as functions of the a_i, and thus each can be expressed as a function of the substantive model parameters.

The numerical equilibrium for a difference equation model is defined as a steady state that is independent of time: A model is at equilibrium if the sequence of values for P_t stays constant across time. Thus, in terms of model substance, behavior is at equilibrium if it does not change through successive time periods, and equilibrium is clearly related to the substantive notions of durability and volatility. Few individuals demonstrate political preferences that are truly at equilibrium, but in some theoretical sense it is surely reasonable to articulate the concept of a behavioral equilibrium subject to the disturbing shocks of short-term forces: political crises, candidates who shoot their own feet, scandals, and so on. The equilibrium for the standard form is given by: $a_1/(1 - a_2)$, and the equilibrium value for the social group model is expressed as:

$$P^* = gS/[gS + f(1 - S)] \tag{9}$$

The equilibrium for the social group model is the ratio of (1) the rate of change due to positive reinforcement, to (2) the sum of the rates of change due to positive reinforcement and negative reinforcement. We thus conceive a political equilibrium, closely related to durability and volatility, that is defined in terms of social influence.

The second concept, response time, refers to the time required for a return to equilibrium after some displacement away from equilibrium. In the vocabulary of dynamic systems, a stable model is one that returns to (or converges toward) equilibrium after some displacement away from equilibrium. Given the previously established parameter constraints, both models constructed here are stable in this technical sense: Each model tracks to an equilibrium, or steady state, over time.[4] Our concern is not whether the behavior returns to equilibrium, but rather how quickly the behavior returns to equilibrium. In keeping with this concern, durability is defined as an ordering concept: A more rapid return toward equilibrium indicates greater durability than a slower recovery. In other words, a political equilibrium is more durable through time if individuals return to it quickly after

---

4 Different modeling strategies treat instability (divergence) in different ways. A tradition within the study of international politics and arms control treats divergence as an empirically plausible outcome that corresponds to a runaway arms race (Richardson 1960). Another tradition, with historical roots that trace to behavioral psychology (Bush and Mosteller 1955), treats instability as a substantive impossibility because concern is typically focused on a naturally bounded outcome. For example, the probability of taking an action is necessarily bounded in a (0, 1) interval. Thus, if we are concerned with a dynamic representation of this probability, then specifying a model that allows for divergence beyond the interval is a logical contradiction. We follow this second tradition. Political support levels can be usefully seen as varying within the limits of complete support and complete nonsupport, both at the level of individuals and at the aggregate level as well. If behavior is conceived in this manner, then a properly specified model should not allow for the possibility of divergence.

some disturbance moves them away.[5] What does this mean in terms of the substance of our models?

Political behavior is more durable if an individual returns toward a behavioral equilibrium more quickly after some political event moves the individual away from equilibrium. Thus, political durability and political volatility are defined along different dimensions: Volatility is related to the magnitude of changes in a preference over time, but durability is related to the time required for a return to equilibrium.

Response time is a direct function of a_2, such that larger absolute values produce longer, slower responses, and it is therefore defined in the following way for the social group model.[6]

$$a_2 = \text{response time function} = 1 - [gS + f(1 - S)] \qquad (10)$$

Response time is crucial to our understanding of durability and volatility as functions of social influence, and we turn to its analysis.

SOCIAL GROUPS AND RECOVERIES TO EQUILIBRIUM

The response time specified by the social group model is a function of both positive and negative reinforcement effects, incorporating the probabilities that each type of reinforcement occurs and the relative influence for each type of reinforcement. Thus, the social context has a potentially direct effect on durability. Not only does individual sensitivity toward contextual stimuli affect individual durability, but durability is also subject to objective factors in the social context. Moreover, durability is increased by an increase in any effective reinforcement – positive or negative or both com-

---

5 An alternative conception of response time is system memory. According to Cortes, Przeworski, and Sprague (1974): "The memory of any system can be defined as the impact of some event that happened in the past on the current response of the system" (p. 231); and "any system that is stable forgets past events" (p. 237). Note that the system memory for a first-order model is not a single time period. Rather, it is the time required for a disturbance (or an input) to be forgotten, or for the system to approach equilibrium after a disturbance or input.

6 A value for a_2 less than zero produces a period-two oscillatory trajectory, but the parameter constraints of inequality 4 insure that a_2 must lie within the (0, 1) interval, thereby producing a monotonically convergent time path. The impossibility of period-two oscillation is, of course, the direct result of model construction. If we altered the model to include constant source effects (perhaps from the media: m) as well as contextual effects, the reinforcement terms might be redefined as:

$$R_1 = m + gS$$
$$R_2 = m + f(1 - S)$$

Thus, the combined constant source and contextual effects might produce period-two oscillation. Furthermore, equilibrium would be redefined in terms of both constant source effects and contextual effects. We adopt a different strategy: Our political equilibrium is defined wholly in terms of social influence, and social influence does not produce an oscillatory return toward a socially defined equilibrium. Constant source effects are treated as being variable: They are assumed to act as displacements within this socially defined process.

bined. Conflicting stimuli produce vacillation by creating an individual equilibrium that lies between those produced by purely negative or purely positive reinforcement effects, but it also creates a more rapid return to that equilibrium. These observations generate:

Result 1: The social group model asserts that response time shortens (durability increases) as the weighted sum of positive and negative reinforcement increases, where the weights operating on reinforcement are the relative influence given to each form of reinforcement. In other words, durability depends on both objective features of the social context – the likelihoods of negative and positive reinforcement – and subjective factors of attentiveness and sensitivity to contextual stimuli.

Figure 4.1 compares the response time for several specifications of the social group model. In each instance individual behavior is displaced to a level that is 50 percent of equilibrium, and the values shown on the vertical (y) axis denote the proportion of equilibrium attained at a particular time point – P_t/P^*. In this example we vary both (1) the probability of encountering negative–positive reinforcement, and (2) the relative influence of positive reinforcement. Thus, we consider the effect of individual sensitivity toward contextual stimuli, and the direct effect of the social context objectively defined. The figure clearly shows the differences in durability: After four time periods the upper time path has recovered to 90 percent of equilibrium while the lower time path has recovered only to 70 percent of equilibrium.

The examples of Figure 4.1 are extended to include numerous other scenarios in Table 4.3. The first panel shows that higher values of g produce greater durability, controlling for S and f; the second panel shows that higher values of f produce greater durability, controlling for S and g; and both panels show that higher values of S produce more or less durability depending on the ordinal relationship between g and f.

The third panel of Table 4.3 produces several special cases where individuals are equally sensitive to positive and negative reinforcement ($g = f$). This equality of stimuli effectiveness is an implicit assumption in many investigations of contextual effects, because few investigators extend their treatment of contextual influence beyond a single, simply defined contextual property. Reading across the values for S, the reader will notice that durability remains constant for a given specification of g and f. If an individual is equally sensitive to positive and negative reinforcement, both g and f can be replaced by q – a contextual sensitivity parameter – and the equation 5 model is rewritten as:

$$\Delta P_t = qS(1 - P_t) - q(1 - S)P_t = q(S - P_t) \tag{11}$$

Putting equation 11 into the standard form of equation 8 produces a value for a_2 that is simply equal to $1 - q$. Thus, changes in support occur

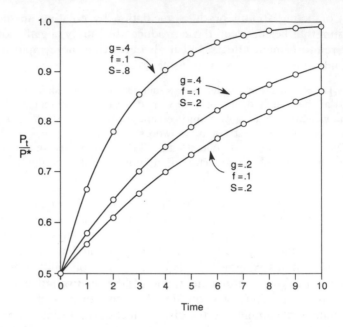

Figure 4.1. Social group effects upon individual political durability.

proportionally to the difference between the previous support level and the probability of positive reinforcement, and response time is wholly a function of individual sensitivity.

The form of equation 11 points to a variant of the social group model that emphasizes the importance of reference group norms as a vehicle for contextual influence. According to this argument, the political influence of context is subsumed by its influence on group loyalties: People surrounded by a particular social group identify with that group and adopt political preferences that are consistent with group norms. Thus, Langton and Rapoport (1975) argue that Santiago workers living in working-class environments were more likely to support Salvador Allende in the 1964 election because working-class contexts encouraged the adoption of a working-class identity with important political consequences.

A mathematical statement of this argument incorporates the idea of a political norm that is an unspecified function of a particular context. Define this norm as N: the acceptable level of political support for a candidate of the working-class party. This norm, which is measured in the same metric as P_t, translates the social context into political influence. In the short-term we should fully expect to see deviations between individual support levels and the group-level norm. In the long term a mechanism of social influence

Table 4.3. ***Number of time periods required to move from 50% to 90% of equilibrium for the individual-level social group model***

	g	f	S						
			.2	.3	.4	.5	.6	.7	.8
A.	.4	.1	10	8	7	6	5	5	4
	.3	.1	11	10	9	8	7	6	6
	.2	.1	13	12	11	10	10	9	9
B.	.1	.4	4	5	5	6	7	8	10
	.1	.3	6	6	7	8	9	10	11
	.1	.2	9	9	10	10	11	12	13
C.	.2	.2	8	8	8	8	8	8	8
	.4	.4	4	4	4	4	4	4	4

should bring individual behavior into correspondence with the norm. Specify this mechanism as:

$$\Delta P_t = r(N - P_t) \tag{12}$$

where N = the political norm as an unspecified function of context; and r = the rate of adjustment, in a single period of discrete time, between individual behavior and the group norm.

The model says, quite simply, that changes in the extent of party support from one time period to the next are the result of (1) discrepancies between individual behavior and the political norm, and (2) the rate at which those discrepancies are reduced. If r is positive, past behavior that lies below the norm produces an upward adjustment toward the norm, and past behavior that lies above the norm produces a downward adjustment toward the norm.

Notice that equation 11 is the simplest possible case of equation 12, where the norm is merely equal to the probability of positive reinforcement ($N = S$). And in correspondence with equation 11, the reference group mechanism implicitly assumes that response time is wholly a function of individual sensitivity to discrepancies between the political norm and past behavior. Regardless of the functional form tying the norm to the context, the objectively defined social context has no direct effect on political durability. These observations produce an expansion of the first result:

Result 2: According to the social group model, the durability of individual behavior is directly affected by the social context unless individuals are equally susceptible to the influence of positive and negative reinforcement – a highly unlikely situation. If contextual influence on politics is mediated through social loyalties and group norms, however, then durability is not directly affected by context, and is instead the direct function of individual sensitivity to the discrepancy between past behavior and the norm.

DOES DURABILITY PRODUCE VOLATILITY?

What is the relationship between political durability and political volatility? Recall that durability and volatility refer to different dynamic properties: Volatility is defined as the absolute magnitude of change, and durability is defined according to the speed of recovery toward equilibrium. A paradox is imbedded within these definitions: Higher levels of durability sometimes produce volatile, rapidly changing behavior in the short run. Part A of Table 4.4 shows an instance in which higher levels of durability produce higher levels of short-run volatility, but part B shows an instance in which higher levels of durability slightly reduce short-run volatility. The relationship between durability and volatility is complex because both durability and equilibrium generally depend on both individual sensitivity levels (g and f) and the objectively defined context.

Thus, a change in durability also produces a change in equilibrium, and volatility is directly dependent on the absolute magnitude of the difference between current behavior and equilibrium. A wider discrepancy creates a situation in which even low levels of durability produce higher levels of short-run volatility, and small discrepancies produce low levels of short-run volatility even for individuals with highly durable preferences.

Result 3: An increased level of contextual influence produces a higher level of political durability, but a higher level of volatility might be produced as a by-product of the faster recovery to equilibrium. Thus, contextual influence is sometimes related to higher levels of short-term volatility, and in these instances political durability produces political volatility.

This result raises several issues. First, the effects of the political environment have been treated as displacements from equilibrium, and these displacements have been uniformly and arbitrarily set at 50 percent of the equilibrium value.[7] Such a procedure ignores the role of social influence as a buffer between the individual and the political environment. In keeping with the research tradition that has grown up around the two-step flow of communication (E. Katz 1957), we might expect social influence to affect not only the return to equilibrium but the departure from equilibrium as well. And if contextually influenced individuals are less likely to depart from equilibrium in the first place, then they are also less likely to exhibit a rapid or volatile return.

---

7 As a matter of convenience we have been assuming events that produce displacements below equilibrium, but displacements can certainly occur above equilibrium as well. Such a displacement would be best expressed as a proportion of the distance between equilibrium and unity.

Table 4.4. *Short-run volatility as a function of durability for the individual-level social group model*

	g	f	S	Durability[a]	Volatility at period[b]				P*
					1	2	3	10	
A.	.4	.1	.2	10	.04	.03	.03	.01	.50
	.4	.1	.5	6	.10	.07	.06	.01	.80
	.4	.1	.8	4	.16	.10	.07	.00	.94
B.	.1	.4	.8	10	.04	.03	.03	.01	.50
	.1	.4	.5	6	.02	.02	.01	.00	.20
	.1	.4	.2	4	.01	.01	.00	.00	.06

Note: $P_0 = .5P^*$.

[a]Durability is measured as the number of time periods required to move from 50% to 90% of equilibrium. Thus, a lower number indicates a higher level of durability.

[b]Volatility is measured as the magnitude of change during the previous time period: $P_t - P_{t-1}$.

Who is least likely to depart from such an equilibrium? The attentive citizens who regularly monitor the political messages being transmitted through social networks of political communication would be most securely anchored. Is it possible to witness the socially stimulated dynamics among such citizens? In order to detect the dynamic among attentive citizens, it might be necessary to monitor not only their preferences but also their interactions on a nearly continual basis – an intrusive and prohibitively expensive undertaking. In general, and among all citizens, observing such a dynamic will be easier under some circumstances than under others. In particular, it should be easier among people whose ordinary level of attentiveness is low, but whose attention is at least temporarily stimulated by events in the political environment. Moreover, it should be easier – even among the attentive – when the political environment is bombarding individuals with conflicting cues and signals. Under such conditions, individuals are being displaced from the socially defined equilibrium at a high rate, and the socially defined equilibrium is concurrently and continually being redefined.

Thus, a statement of the relationship between the social context, political durability, and political volatility must be couched in conditional language. If one assumes proportionally equivalent displacements from equilibrium, a stronger contextual effect might produce a higher level of political volatility as a by-product of maintaining a higher level of political durability. Does this conditional language have any real world political relevance? It does if people form initial and idiosyncratic responses to stimuli from the political environment. Taking inspiration from McPhee (1963), we believe they do, particularly if the stimuli are strong and dramatic. Consider a citizen watching the 1984 candidate debates. She does not wait to form an opinion regarding candidate performance, but rather forms an initial response rooted in individual attitudes and beliefs.[8] At the same time, this response does not remain a matter of idiosyncratic concern, particularly if the opinion is important. As a result, discrepancies between initial responses and surrounding opinions soon become apparent, and the individual is nudged or pushed or jerked in the direction of surrounding opinion distributions. Again, contextually induced political durability does not always add to short-term volatility, but in many instances it can.

Second, by conceiving of political durability and volatility along different dimensions, we have produced an anomaly: Political durability might produce short-run volatility. This naturally raises the question of whether such a distinction between the two concepts is valid. The social group model specifies that greater sensitivity to contextual stimuli produces (1) a change in equilibrium and (2) a faster return to that equilibrium. Certainly this is a classic description of socially anchored politics. At the same time, however, such close ties to the socially determined equilibrium can produce rapid short-term adjustments after displacements. Thus, whether political behavior appears durable often depends on the frequency and magnitude of displacements from equilibrium. If the political environment is unstable, a socially anchored electorate might appear to be politically adrift and randomly fluctuating in its political preferences, when it is actually readjusting its behavior on the basis of socially communicated preferences.

BEHAVIORAL CONTAGION AND INDIVIDUAL RECOVERIES TO EQUILIBRIUM

What are the consequences of a behavioral contagion model for the durability and volatility of individual behavior? The logical similarity of this model to the social group model produces parallel terms for equilibrium and response time, such that:

$$P^* = gM_{t+k}/[gM_{t+k} + f(1 - M_{t+k})] \quad \text{(where } k = 0, 1, 2, \ldots) \quad (13)$$

$$a_2 = \text{response time function} = 1 - [gM_{t+k} + f(1 - M_{t+k})] \quad (14)$$

First consider equation 14, the response time for the behavioral contagion specification. Its form is identical to the social group model, except that a time-dependent behavioral density has replaced a time-invariant social density. When the proportion of workers at time $t + k$ equals the proportion of people who support the Democratic party at time $t + k$, the response time of the two specifications is the same at that time point. More important for our purposes, the response times of the two models rest on

---

8 According to the McPhee (1963) model: An individual (1) receives a stimulus from the environment, (2) forms a response, (3) shares the response socially, and (4) modifies the response on the basis of social influence.

the same logic: Increased levels of effective reinforcement produce faster returns toward equilibrium independent from the direction of the reinforcement. And increased levels of volatility might therefore be produced as a by-product of these faster recoveries.

The logic of the two models diverges more sharply when we compare the respective equilibrium terms: equations 9 and 13. The equilibrium for the social group model is specified as being constant across time, but the equilibrium for the behavioral contagion model is time-specific. That is, the equilibrium is constantly being redefined through time. Indeed, the concept of equilibrium loses meaning as a steady state through time because it must always be evaluated at a particular time point, *unless mass behavior has attained its own equilibrium.* This observation leads to:

Result 4: While the logic underlying the speed of return toward equilibrium is fundamentally the same for social group and behavioral contagion models, the models produce fundamentally different conceptions of equilibrium. Indeed, the behavioral contagion model produces an equilibrium that is constantly redefined by prevailing opinion and mass behavior, and the return to equilibrium is a never ending accommodation to a mixture of positive and negative reinforcement that may be highly volatile and rapidly altered.

AGGREGATE DURABILITY AND BEHAVIORAL CONTAGION

The behavioral contagion model implies that individual durability depends on aggregate durability. That is, the speed of an individual return toward equilibrium is constrained by the speed with which behavior in the mass attains its equilibrium. Thus we address the following question: What are the consequences of behavioral contagion for the durability of aggregate support levels? Our consideration has been at the level of individuals, but a contextually structured process of behavioral contagion also has aggregate consequences that do not necessarily coincide with individual-level implications. In order to undertake an investigation of these consequences, an aggregate version of the contagion model must be constructed.

The aggregate representation is specified to parallel its individual-level counterpart. As a first step we write a redefined gain–loss model:

$$\Delta M_t = C(L - M_t) - D(M_t - B) \tag{15}$$

where M_t = the proportion of the social context that supports the working-class party candidate at time t (see equation 6); C = the rate at which nonsupporters are recruited (converted) to become supporters; D = the rate at which supporters defect to become nonsupporters; L = upper limit of support for the working-class party candidate, so that $1 - L$ equals the proportion of the population that is not susceptible to the candidate's appeal; and B = lower limit of support for the working-class party's candidate, or the proportion of the population that both supports the candidate and is not vulnerable to defection.

The lower and upper limits on support levels, B and L respectively, represent the constraints operating on candidate appeal. Any candidate must be reconciled to a proportion of the population that could never be recruited. This subpopulation includes people who hold antipathies toward the candidate or the party, as well as politically inert individuals who lie beyond the reach of political campaigns and candidate appeals. Similarly, candidates can usually rely on some proportion of the population that will never defect, regardless of the competition and its appeal. Thus the dynamics of mass politics occur within these boundaries.

In order to arrive at an aggregate version of the contagion model, the defection and conversion rates are defined as follows:

$$C = cM_t \tag{16}$$

$$D = d(1 - M_t) \tag{17}$$

where c = the relative influence of interaction with supporters on the conversion rate of nonsupporters, or the rate of conversion among nonsupporters that is approached as M_t approaches one – as the population approaches complete support;[9] and d = the relative influence of interaction with nonsupporters on the defection rate of supporters, or the rate of defection among supporters that is approached as M_t approaches zero – as the population approaches complete nonsupport.

As in the individual level contagion model of equation 6, the social context is defined according to the distribution of political preferences. If one assumes positive values for d and c, a higher level of support for the working-class candidate increases the rate of conversion to, and decreases the rate of defection from, the ranks of those supporting the working-class party's candidate. We are, as a matter of convenience, assuming random interaction for the aggregate model. That is, we are assuming that the probability of interacting with a supporter of a party is equal to the proportion of the population that supports the party. (A major objective in later stages of this book is to investigate the relationship between population densities and social interaction probabilities.)

Algebraic manipulation produces the following response time function for the standard form of equation 8:

$$a_2 = \text{response time function} = 1 - cM_t + dM_t + cL - dB - d \tag{18}$$

$$I = 1 + c(L - M_t) + d(M_t - B - 1)$$

9 When M_t equals one the rate of conversion is a meaningless concept because everyone is already converted. Thus, language is used to suggest that c approaches some value as M_t approaches one.

As in the case of the individual level representation, behavioral contagion produces a complex specification of response time. Not only is a_2 time-dependent, but the aggregate contagion model is nonlinear because a_2 is a function of the system state – M_t. Indeed, this behavioral contagion specification is related to a large family of logistic models with a wide applicability ranging from field ecology (May 1974) to the diffusion of innovation (Coleman 1964: chap. 17). The substance of the model has dictated the form of the mathematical representation. Thus, an individual-level model of behavioral contagion translates into a first-order linear difference equation, but an aggregate model of behavioral contagion translates into the more familiar logistic form that reduces to a first-order nonlinear model.

The previously employed results for equilibrium and response time hold for linear equations with both constant and time-dependent coefficients, but they do not generally hold for nonlinear equations. Apart from these technical considerations, however, the logic underlying the substantive parameter constraints established in inequality 4 also holds for this representation, namely:

$$0 < D, C < 1 \qquad (19)$$

Thus an inspection of equation 15 shows that aggregate support levels will always be bounded within the $(0, 1)$ interval, and hence the model cannot produce a divergent time path.[10]

The effect of behavioral contagion on aggregate durability is examined in Table 4.5. The first row of the table shows row levels of contextual influence on both defection and conversion ($c = d = .1$). The resulting trajectory produces an extremely long and extended recovery, requiring thirty-two time periods to attain 90 percent of the equilibrium value. The second and third rows show modest increases in the effect of behavioral contagion on the recruitment rate, but these modest increases produce dramatic effects on durability, generating progressively faster recoveries toward equilibrium. The fourth and fifth rows of the table produce a surprise: Rather than increasing the level of durability, a stronger contagion effect on the defection rate generates a slight decline in durability. Finally, continued increases in the effect of contagion on the rate of defection once again lead to increases in durability. In summary, stronger contagion effects generally produce higher levels of aggregate durability, but the relationship between the contagion and the speed of recovery toward equilibrium is not consistent. Why is this the case?

Returning to equation 18, the response time function for the behavioral contagion model, we see that the speed of return to equilibrium is directly dependent on the previous support level – M_t. Recall that response time

---

10 In nonlinear difference equations global stability conditions frequently are lacking. However, Chaundy and Phillips (1936) produce general results for the quadratic, which are reworked by Sprague (1969). Also see Huckfeldt, Kohfeld, and Likens (1982).

Table 4.5. *Aggregate durability and volatility for the behavioral contagion model*

	c	d	Durability[a]	Volatility at period[b]				M*
				1	2	3	10	
1.	.1	.1	32	.01	.01	.01	.01	.40
2.	.2	.1	21	.02	.02	.02	.01	.56
3.	.4	.1	9	.04	.04	.04	.01	.64
4.	.4	.2	10	.04	.03	.03	.01	.56
5.	.4	.3	10	.04	.03	.03	.01	.47
6.	.4	.4	8	.04	.03	.03	.00	.40
7.	.4	.6	4	.06	.04	.02	.00	.32

Note: $M_0 = .5M^*$; $L = .7$; $B = .2$.

[a]Durability is measured as the number of time periods required to move from 50% to 90% of equilibrium. Thus, a lower number indicates a higher level of durability.

[b]Volatility is measured as the magnitude of change during the previous time period: $M_t - M_{t-1}$.

shortens – durability increases – as equation 18 approaches zero. Thus, if the contagion effect on the rate of conversion is greater than the contagion effect on the rate of defection $(c > d)$, larger values for M_t contribute toward a faster return. If the effect on conversion is smaller than the effect on defection $(c < d)$, larger values for M_t contribute toward a slower return.

Furthermore, the magnitude of the difference between the contagion effects on conversion and defection also affects the return toward equilibrium. Rearrange equation 18 as follows:

$$a_2 = 1 + cL - d(1 + B) + (d - c)M_t \qquad (20)$$

This form shows that the effect of M_t on the return to equilibrium is maximized when the difference between c and d is maximized. (Indeed, the resulting model is linear when c equals d.) These observations lead to:

Result 5: The aggregate behavioral contagion model specifies a complex contextual effect on political durability that depends on (1) the relative magnitudes of contagion effects on conversion and defection rates, (2) immediately preceding support levels, and (3) the difference between the contagion effects on the rates of defection and recruitment. Stronger contagion effects generally lead to higher levels of aggregate durability, but a stronger contagion effect can also reduce aggregate durability.

CONCLUSION

According to Berelson et al. (1954: chap. 7), group behavior is consistent between elections due to the social environment's ability to alter the behavior of politically deviant individuals. That is, social influence has the capacity to strengthen political boundaries between groups by bringing group members into line with the preferences that dominate within the group. Our results support this assertion, but they show that the dynamic consequences of social influence can be complex and unexpected, with important implications both for political durability and for political volatility.

What are the effects of contextual influence on political durability? The results generated by the social group model are clear and unambiguous: Higher levels of contextual influence create greater durability by producing a more rapid recovery toward equilibrium after displacement. The results generated by the behavioral contagion model are more complex. Individual-level durability is directly dependent on aggregate behavior, and increased levels of contextual influence generally, but not always, produce faster aggregate recoveries toward equilibrium. Thus, the speed of the individual return toward equilibrium is generally increased by a higher level of contextual influence at the aggregate level, but it can also be decreased. Finally, the behavioral contagion model implies that individual behavior is not only displaced from equilibrium by political events; it is also displaced by aggregate displacements from equilibrium. The behavior of one individual is affected by the behavior of other individuals and, like ripples in a pond, the displacements are self-perpetuating. At the same time that these displacements are self-perpetuating, however, they also diminish over time. Thus, the behavioral contagion process acts to produce recoveries toward equilibrium, but it also generates departures from equilibrium.

What are the effects of contextual influence on political volatility? In the process of producing a rapid recovery to equilibrium, higher levels of contextual influence sometimes result in higher levels of political volatility. The relationship between durability and volatility is complex, depending on the extent to which contextual influence depresses the initial departure from equilibrium, the magnitude of the discrepancy between equilibrium and the displaced behavior, and so on. The important point is as follows: Socially anchored politics is not static politics, and theories of political behavior motivated by social influence need not be guilty of "static social determinism." Indeed, without incorporating social influence within our explanations, an important element of the dynamic underlying political change is ignored.

Finally, short-run volatility should not be mistaken for social instability, or for the decomposition of politically cohesive groups. Rapid changes in behavior do not necessarily indicate the lack of a social fabric, or the existence of socially atomistic voters, or the breakdown of social groups and group politics (Kornhauser 1959). Rather short-run volatility at the individual level is sometimes produced by strong political ties to the social group, and social influence underlies the dynamics as well as the statics of political preference.

In the following chapter we set these words to music – we examine the empirical record from South Bend to see whether the development of vote intentions during the election campaign can be understood with respect to the distribution of surrounding intentions. In other words, to what extent can we understand individual votes as the end points of a social process?

5

Social dynamics in an election campaign

This chapter provides an empirical response to several questions regarding the dynamics of social influence in an election campaign: In particular, how does the structure of partisan preference change during the course of a campaign, both with respect to the voter's own social status and with respect to the social status of other citizens in the voter's surrounding environment? We are particularly concerned with individual and contextual effects on partisan identification and vote choice, and the interdependence between these two measurement levels is considered in order to assess differential individual sensitivity to the effects of the social context. A second series of analyses examines these relationships under variations in individual motivation and political attentiveness.

The social dynamic underlying electoral change can be observed either at the level of individuals or at the level of electorates. One alternative is to study the manner in which individual preferences change during the course of the campaign. And the other is to study the manner in which the pattern and distribution of aggregate preferences are altered. These are different issues that lead to different research strategies. The first requires that we observe individuals and their behavior through time, and that individual change be related to the social forces acting on individual preferences. The second requires that we inquire into the social boundaries that separate voters with different preferences and the extent to which these boundaries recede or emerge as a function of the campaign.

As we have seen in the previous chapter, the South Bend study is unlikely to support an examination of individual change during the campaign because very little individual movement can be detected. The citizen who intends to vote for one candidate but reports voting for another is a rare event in the South Bend study. Indeed, in the nation as a whole, the 1984 election campaign was notable for the lack of volatility in citizen preferences: Ronald Reagan began the campaign with a sizable lead in the opinion polls, and he maintained that lead through the election. The voting preferences of the South Bend respondents reflect these national trends, but this does not mean either that change is absent or that there is no social dynamic in operation. A considerable number of respondents were undecided before the election but reported a vote for one of the candidates after the election. Moreover, the repeated monitoring of individual preference may itself obscure the dynamic we are trying to observe, and such a possibility must be addressed in the analysis of this chapter. Finally, even limited levels of change at the individual level may have pronounced consequences for the aggregate distribution of political preference. For these reasons, the primary focus of this chapter is on the social dynamic underlying aggregate preference distributions during the campaign. And from this perspective, several questions are addressed: First, are political preferences in an election campaign structured by surrounding social contexts? Second, how does the social structure of political preference change during the course of the campaign? Finally, in what manner does the dynamic pattern of influence from the social context depend on individual social status and on individual attentiveness to politics?

THE SOCIAL DYNAMIC OF AGGREGATE PREFERENCE DISTRIBUTIONS

In their study of the 1948 election campaign, Berelson and his associates (1954: chap. 7) demonstrated that social influence was responsible for higher rates of volatility among individuals who held preferences that conflicted with the dominant political sentiment in their surrounding social environments. Protestants and white-collar workers who favored Truman at the beginning of the campaign were more likely to defect than Protestants and white-collar workers who preferred Dewey. Catholics and blue-collar union members who initially preferred Dewey were more likely to change their preference than fellow Catholics and blue-collar union members who favored Truman.

Individuals who hold political views unpopular in their social groups may remain undetected before the campaign. As the campaign accelerates, however, politics is introduced into countless social exchanges. Conversations with friends, yard signs in the neighborhood, and bumper stickers on co-workers' cars all have the effect of exposing dominant and dissenting political viewpoints. Thus, the members of a political minority come to recognize their minority status. This phenomenon produces an irony: Political volatility can be produced as a by-product of the bonds that tie individuals to groups. As Berelson et al. (1954: chap. 7) note, individual instability is the price that is paid to sustain the stability and cohesiveness of groups between elections.

Such a dynamic logic requires, of course, that individual preference be divorced from collective sentiment in the first place, and such a disjuncture is more likely to occur under some circumstances than others. A popular and charismatic incumbent president does not lead to volatile and rapidly changing preferences on the part of an undecided electorate. In this sense our task as students of campaign dynamics in the 1984 election is as enviable as that of Walter Mondale, and perhaps all three of us might have known better. But this is really just another way to make the observation that the social dynamic of electoral politics is antecedent to the political dynamic, and it is inherently conservative. If the political environment fails to bombard the public with messages that move and shake voters away from their moorings, then observing individual change that is stimulated by the social dynamic becomes a more difficult undertaking.

This does not mean that social structure is irrelevant, or that its attendant dynamic is completely absent, but only that socially stimulated volatility becomes more visible in politically disrupted environments – in environments where voters are unsure of their preferences or where they come into contact with opposing views. Moreover, even among the South Bend respondents in 1984, a sizable portion of the electorate had not yet decided on a candidate prior to the election, and we might expect that these citizens would look to their surroundings for political information. In short, even in relatively stable electoral environments, we expect partisan mobilization to be affected by the distribution of preferences within social contexts. Individual preferences should move in the direction of surrounding opinions, so that minorities become diminished as majorities become enlarged. The campaign sets into motion a social process that produces greater homogeneity within social groups, and greater diversity between social groups.

For purposes of these analyses, the group is defined as the neighborhood, and the social context is defined as the educational composition of the neighborhood population. Thus it is important to make clear the neighborhood's explanatory status (Eulau 1986). We are not arguing that neighborhoods are cohesive social communities, or that they are primary elements of social life. We only argue that they index relevant opportunities and constraints operating on the flow of political information. For example, Mondale voters living in Reagan neighborhoods might have fewer opportunities for discussion with Mondale supporters than Mondale voters who live in Mondale neighborhoods. Further, the consequence of these opportunities and constraints might extend beyond neighborhood boundaries. Localized social contacts create interaction opportunities beyond neighborhood boundaries, so that the social and political composition of the neighborhood population has consequences for discussion opportunities outside the neighborhood as well. In short, the educational composition of the neighborhood population is an index on structurally imposed social experience, just as individual education is an index on individually imposed social experience.

CHOOSING AN ANALYTIC MODEL

The analytic model employed in this chapter is intentionally simplified, with only three right-hand-side variables. Our central explanatory variable is the most commonly employed measure of individual social status – years of formal education. This is measured in the survey by self-report, and the mean for each neighborhood is computed from these self-reports. Finally, an interaction measure is included, formed as the multiplicative product of individual education and contextual mean education. It is possible, of course, to elaborate this model, but interpretation is complicated with little increase in understanding. We do not imagine the model provides a fully specified representation of the dynamics of vote choice or of partisan identification. Our goal is to produce a good analytic representation for answering the questions originally posed, with more complex analyses delayed until later chapters.

We use education as a measure of class and status because it is the best single proxy available in our survey, and perhaps in any survey, providing a powerful summary indicator of an individual's location in the social structure. There is a critical substantive issue at stake. One of the purposes of the analyses is to capture the political consequences of variation in those population characteristics which are typically structured by living patterns – especially patterns of residence. Education is one of those characteristics and probably the single most important one. The analyses seek to uncover the consequences of a socially differentiated world in which individuals are not randomly located within a national electorate, but rather systematically located within local social milieus that are both well defined and politically significant.

A common concern regarding contextual research is that a contextual fallacy is being committed: Explanatory power is attributed to a contextual factor that is actually the result of omitted individual level factors (Hauser 1974). We have subjected analyses of this chapter to additional individual controls, but the controls do not change any conclusions, and they certainly do not weaken the demonstrated effects of context. The controls are excluded from reported analyses because they serve to obscure the substantive interpretation, especially with respect to the effect of *individual* social status. Education is treated as a measure of class and status, and including multiple individual-level characteristics related to social status makes it difficult to compare contextual and individual social status effects in a direct manner. In short, adding additional individual-level controls more often has the misleading consequence of attenuating the apparent effect of *individual* social status rather than attenuating the effect of contextual social status.

The contextual fallacy is actually part of a larger concern regarding model specification. One reaction to our simple analytic model is that the model is seriously misspecified because it omits so many factors relevant to partisan preference. There are good reasons to expect that omitted relevant variables present minimal difficulties for the analyses reported here. As Maddala (1977: 153) emphasizes, omitted variables are only important to the extent that (1) the correlation between excluded and included factors is *both* substantial *and* in a uniform direction, and (2) *the ratio of error variance to the variance of included variables is large.* The nature of our research design ensures maximal variation on respondents' social environments, thereby minimizing the effect of excluded factors. Even if the first condition holds, which is not likely for many of the commonly measured variables in voting behavior, the likelihood that the second condition will hold is minimized by our research design.

The design of the research also creates some opportunities to check on the reasonableness of the model we employ in the analyses. Vote choice in a logistic representation can be compared with the dynamics of partisan identification utilizing linear regression procedures. Furthermore, samples were taken from three distinct time periods in the election process. Thus opportunities arise for cross-model validation due to the structure of the analyses and the original research design. The force of the cumulative results, with alternative model forms and alternative dependent variables, mutually reinforce the reasonableness of this modeling strategy. No table stands alone, and the joint effect is substantial.

THE DYNAMICS OF A NATURAL EXPERIMENT

For present purposes, the research design may be viewed as a quasi experiment that takes advantage of an externally applied experimental condition. An initial set of pretest measures was taken in the summer of 1984 before the national party conventions officially chose presidential candidates. The experimental condition – the election campaign – was then inflicted on the entire population, and a second set of measures was obtained during the campaign. Finally, a set of posttest measures was taken after the campaign, in November and December, giving us an opportunity to gauge the consequences of the naturally applied, but unavoidable, experimental condition of a democratic election campaign.

In the first wave of the survey, respondents were asked their preference in a hypothetical trial-heat election between Ronald Reagan and Walter Mondale. This survey question provides a pretest measure: All respondents who report that they would vote for Reagan are given value one and all other respondents are given value zero. A similar question was included in the second wave of the survey, conducted after Labor Day and before the election, and respondents in the final, postelection wave were asked how they actually voted. Thus, we have pretest and posttest measures of partisan mobilization, and for purposes of this chapter we consider Republican mobilization for the Reagan candidacy. The natural question arises: How did the campaign affect Republican mobilization?

This question is addressed in Table 5.1A, where a logit model is used to estimate the dynamic effects of social context on Reagan vote prefer-

Table 5.1A. *Logit estimation of Reagan vote preference before the conventions and after the election by education at the individual and contextual levels*

	Before conventions, June-July 1984	After election, November-December 1984
Intercept	-10.02	-15.40
	(2.52)	(3.47)
Individual education	.47	.84
	(1.60)	(2.59)
Neighborhood mean education	.64	1.06
	(2.09)	(3.14)
Interaction	-.027	-.055
	(1.22)	(2.24)
N	1,323	1,344

Note: The *t*-values for coefficients are shown in parentheses.

ences. The probability of supporting Reagan is estimated before the conventions, and the probability of reporting a vote for Reagan is estimated after the election. Three variables are included on the right-hand sides of the equation: individual education, mean neighborhood education, and the interaction between the two. Once again, we do not intend to suggest that education affects preference in any direct sense, but rather that (1) higher-social-status (better-educated) people are more likely to support Reagan, and thus (2) people surrounded by higher-status people are more likely to come into contact with Reagan supporters. The interdependence between individual and contextual education is included as a simple interaction term, allowing us to address the expectation that the contextual, dynamic structure of preferences varies across individuals.

While important contextual effects occur *both* before *and* after the election campaign, Table 5.1A shows that the coefficients' *t*-values become sharper from the preconvention to the postelection wave. Thus it would appear that these factors are more influential in structuring the vote at the end of the campaign. The model also predicts different patterns of individual and contextual effects across the campaign as a joint function of individual educational achievement and neighborhood educational distributions (Table 5.1B). At both points in time, higher-status individuals are less affected by context than lower-status individuals. But higher-status respondents become even less susceptible to neighborhood influence as the campaign progresses, while lower-status respondents become even more susceptible. The range on individual education at the first wave of the survey was from 3 years of schooling to 17 years (the value assigned to anyone with postgraduate education), with an average of approximately 13 years. The range on mean neighborhood education was from 11.6 years to 14.9 years.

Table 5.1B. *Predicted probabilities of Reagan vote preference before the conventions and after the election, estimated on the basis of Table 5.1A*

	Before conventions, June-July 1984:		After election, November-December 1984:	
	Mean neighborhood education		Mean neighborhood education	
	Low (11.6)	High (14.9)	Low (11.6)	High (14.9)
Individual education				
Low (3)	.11	.43	.08	.61
Average (13)	.36	.60	.38	.66
High (17)	.52	.66	.58	.68

Note: Numbers in parentheses refer to specified years of schooling.

A parallel analysis is carried out in Table 5.2, but vote choice is replaced by party identification as the criterion behavior, and the logit model is replaced by Boyd and Iversen's (1979) linear model with centered variables (see the appendix to this chapter). Party identification is measured on the standard seven-point scale where zero is strong Democrats and six is strong Republicans. Once again, the table shows that the same model takes on heightened explanatory power after the election. The variance accounted for by the model increases from .03 to .27, suggesting that the partisan preferences of the respondents are more fully structured at the culmination of the campaign.

Individual and contextual effects before and after the election are best calculated as partial derivatives of the respective equations – as the marginal effects of a unit change in the appropriate independent variable on the dependent variable. Thus the marginal effects of individual education are:

precampaign effect = .06 + .0027 (neighborhood education)

postcampaign effect = 1.09 − .074 (neighborhood education)

And the marginal effects of neighborhood education are:

precampaign effect = .34 + .0027 (individual education)

postcampaign effect = 1.49 − .074 (individual education)

These results are generally in keeping with the results of Table 5.1A. First, the political consequences of both individual and contextual social status increase on average during the course of the campaign. Second, the pro-Republican effect due to higher levels of contextual education is diminished at the culmination of the campaign by increased levels of individual education. Third, the pro-Republican effect due to higher levels of individual education is diminished at the culmination of the campaign by in-

Table 5.2. *Party identification as a function of individual and contextual education using OLS regression with centered variables, before the conventions and after the election*

	Before conventions, June-July 1984	After election, November-December 1984
Intercept	-2.91	-18.23
	(24.45)	(20.16)
Individual education	.06	1.09
	(3.32)	(3.33)
Neighborhood mean education	.34	1.49
	(6.07)	(22.21)
Interaction	.0027	-.074
	(.10)	(2.30)
R^2	.03	.27
N	1,315	1,371

Note: The *t*-values for coefficients are shown in parentheses.

creased levels of contextual education. And fourth, as a consequence, individual and contextual social status effects are more pronounced at the end of the campaign among lower-status people in lower-status contexts.

The first point is best illustrated by setting neighborhood education and individual education at their mean values – approximately 13 for both. A value of 13 signifies thirteen years of school, or a high school education plus one year of post–high school education. On average, the precampaign marginal effect of contextual education was .38 and its postcampaign marginal effect was approximately .53. Similarly, the precampaign marginal effect of individual education increased, on average, from .10 to .13.

In order to understand the political vulnerability of lower-status individuals to effects arising from the social context, compare the marginal effects of the neighborhood context among people with higher and lower levels of education. A ninth-grade education produces a precampaign marginal contextual effect of .32 and a postcampaign marginal contextual effect of .82. In contrast, a person with postgraduate training has a precampaign marginal effect of .23 and a postcampaign marginal effect of .29.

These magnitudes are fairly astonishing. Among the lower-status group, the effect of context increases nearly threefold across the election, while the effect barely increases at all among the second group. As a result, the marginal effect of context is *more than three times as great* among the lower-status group at the culmination of the campaign. Similar but less dramatic effects can be obtained for individual education. These results are consistent with the results of Franklin and Jackson (1983) on the movement in partisan identification during an election campaign, although we look to a different theory and different source to account for the observed dynamics.

Table 5.3. *Party identification as a function of individual and contextual education using OLS regression with centered variables, before the conventions and after the election, for three-wave panel respondents*

	Before conventions, June-July 1984	After election, November-December 1984
Intercept	-14.42	-18.16
	(20.46)	(22.96)
Individual education	.88	1.08
	(1.98)	(1.45)
Neighborhood mean education	1.22	1.53
	(14.75)	(17.40)
Interaction	-.060	-.076
	(1.51)	(1.79)
R^2	.21	.27
N	840	843

Note: The t-values for coefficients are shown in parentheses.

Table 5.3 is a replication of Table 5.2, but only for those respondents who were interviewed in all three waves. In contrast to the results of Table 5.2, these estimates are striking both for their high levels of consistency before and after the campaign, and for the consistently high level of contextual structure that they exhibit. In each instance, for every estimate, the results are approximately the same, even though the coefficients point toward higher levels of contextual structuring at the culmination of the campaign. The average marginal effect of individual education decreased from .10 to .09, and the average marginal effect of contextual education increased from .44 to .54. This relative stability poses an interesting puzzle: (1) Is consistency a measurement artifact? Do we produce consistency by asking the same question (party identification) more than once? (2) Is the consistency a self-selection artifact? Is there something special about the respondents who agree voluntarily to discuss politics with us at three separate occasions for a total of nearly ninety minutes?

The temporal consistency of Table 5.3 is unlikely to be wholly a product of reinterviewing because the respondents' preferences are contextually structured *both* before *and* after the election. Rather it would appear that the panel suffers primarily from selection bias: The panel respondents may be truly good citizens in the fullest sense of the term. They not only discuss politics willingly with interviewers on the phone; they are also likely to discuss it in many other social encounters as well. Their attitudes and preferences are more resistant to dynamic change during the campaign because *their viewpoints are less likely to become matters of idiosyncratic habit or opinion.* Rather their involvement in democratic politics is full and

Table 5.4. *Party identification at each wave in the survey as a function of individual and contextual education using OLS regression with centered variables, for first-time respondents*

	Survey wave		
	Before conventions	During campaign	After election
Constant	-2.91	-3.90	-13.93
	(24.45)	(3.46)	(1.10)
Education	.06	.62	.67
	(3.32)	(1.33)	(2.15)
Neighborhood mean education	.34	.35	1.07
	(6.07)	(2.16)	(6.61)
Interaction	.0027	-.038	-.035
	(.10)	(.42)	(.44)
R^2	.03	.01	.17
N	1,315	365	233

Note: The *t*-values for coefficients are shown in parentheses.

unrelenting, and it is deeply anchored in a point of social reference. Indeed, it is not that their preferences are unstructured by context, but rather that their preferences are structured early on, and that they stay structured throughout the campaign, continually reinforced and reaffirmed through social interaction with political content.

Finally, consider Table 5.4, which replicates the party identification analysis for first-time respondents at each wave of the survey. The second and third waves suffer from small *n*-sizes, but the results suggest that the strong contextual effect does not appear until the end of the campaign. Note particularly that these results lend some added assurance that the dynamic, contextual structure of preferences shown in Table 5.2 is not an artifact of measurement contamination due to reinterviewing. That is, because Table 5.4 is derived wholly from first-time interviews, it removes any potentially contaminating effects of reinterviewing and supports the pattern of effects shown in Table 5.2. This pattern of increasing structure through time is even more dramatic for noncentered regressions, which produce R^2 values of .06, .12, and .25 for first-time respondents in the first, second, and third waves respectively.

These results clearly call into question the utility of panel analyses for contextual studies of political dynamics. People who agree to participate in a panel have preferences that tend to be structured and stable, and repeated interviews only serve to make their preferences stabler. Other people appear to be much more volatile in terms of contextual structure, but we cannot obtain their participation in the panel. And thus, as a practical matter, the analysis of repeated cross-sections appears to be a preferable research strategy for assessing mass behavior dynamics.

ATTENTIVENESS AND CONTEXTUAL DYNAMICS

These results have demonstrated dynamic patterns of interdependence between the social context and individual status: The effect of individual status depends on context, and the effect of context depends on individual status. In the analysis that follows we consider another individual characteristic – attentiveness toward politics – and the manner in which this characteristic modifies our earlier results.

On the basis of social learning theory (Sprague 1982), we expect that learning occurs more efficiently when motivation is high, and thus the political consequences arising from the social context should depend not only on individual status but also on individual levels of interest and attentiveness. At each wave of the survey respondents were asked some variant of a political interest question that solicited their level of interest in the election campaign. The first-wave question was: "Would you say that you are very interested, somewhat interested, or not very interested in following the presidential campaign in 1984?" Responses are categorized so that respondents who report being "very interested" are treated as interested respondents and the remaining categories are treated as disinterested respondents. The third-wave question was: "And how much interest did you have in this year's election?" The possible answers were: a great deal, some, only a little, none at all. Respondents who answered "a great deal" are classified as being interested, and other response categories are classified as disinterested. An analysis of these questions for panel respondents shows the expected high level of correspondence. We treat the questions as indicators of attentiveness and expect that the dynamic structure of contextual influence should vary across interest or attentiveness levels. (Separate analyses show that levels of interest among first-wave respondents predict positively to subsequent participation in the survey; Interested first-wave respondents were more likely to be reinterviewed in the second and third waves.)

Results for interested respondents are displayed in Table 5.5. The table shows that party identification among interested respondents is structured by context both before and after the election, but the magnitude of the contextual effect is much more pronounced at the end of the election campaign. The explanatory power of the statistical model, as measured by the variance predicted, nearly doubles, and the magnitudes of the three slope coefficients for individual education, contextual education, and their interaction increase even more dramatically. People who pay attention to politics are affected by politics, and their political loyalties are more highly structured by their surroundings. (For a useful comparison see Converse 1962 and Orbell 1970.)

In contrast, Table 5.6 shows a far different dynamic pattern among disinterested respondents. In the summer before the election, disinterested re-

Table 5.5. *Party identification as a function of individual and contextual education using OLS regression with centered variables, before the conventions and after the election, for politically interested respondents*

	Before conventions, June-July 1984	After election, November-December 1984
Intercept	-10.97	-24.79
	(19.34)	(16.95)
Individual education	.40	1.42
	(1.37)	(1.97)
Neighborhood mean education	.98	1.98
	(11.68)	(18.02)
Interaction	-.026	-.098
	(.68)	(1.88)
R^2	.16	.29
N	712	815

Note: The t-values for coefficients are shown in parentheses.

Table 5.6. *Party identification as a function of individual and contextual education using OLS regression with centered variables, before the conventions and after the election, for politically disinterested respondents*

	Before conventions, June-July 1984	After election, November-December 1984
Intercept	8.77	-4.73
	(8.52)	(6.99)
Individual education	-.53	.17
	(3.04)	(1.48)
Neighborhood mean education	-.61	.44
	(6.33)	(3.51)
Interaction	.052	-.0055
	(1.09)	(.08)
R^2	.07	.02
N	602	553

Note: The t-values for coefficients are shown in parentheses.

spondents demonstrate a perverse contextual structure that is opposite the expected pattern of effects found among interested respondents, and among the sample as a whole. This structure is replaced after the election by the pattern displayed among interested respondents, although the magnitude of contextual influence is weaker. (A similar pattern of pre- and postelection structuring among disinterested respondents has been ob-

Table 5.7A. *Logit estimation of Reagan vote preference among politically interested respondents, before the conventions and after the election, by individual and contextual education*

	Before conventions, June-July 1984	After election, November-December 1984
Intercept	-13.66	-22.26
	(2.72)	(3.80)
Individual education	.68	1.33
	(1.86)	(3.15)
Neighborhood mean education	.99	1.61
	(2.57)	(3.62)
Interaction	-.049	-.093
	(1.75)	(2.94)
N	718	798

Note: The *t*-values for coefficients are shown in parentheses.

tained, for different elections, using national survey data in Huckfeldt and Sprague 1990.)

Before interpreting these results we return to the vote preferences of the respondents. Table 5.7A reestimates the logit model of Table 5.1A for interested respondents, and the results generally parallel those obtained for the whole sample in Table 5.1A, although the effects are supported by larger *t*-values and the dynamic is more pronounced for the politically attentive respondents. Finally, the *t*-values in Table 5.7A consistently increase in size from the early interview to the later interview, indicating an increase in explanatory power for the model at the end of the campaign.

The dynamic contextual structure predicted by the model is shown in Table 5.7B. As before, the contextual effect is consistently stronger among lower-status respondents, and its magnitude increases during the campaign among low-status respondents while it decreases among high-status respondents. In these instances, however, the interactive effect of individual and contextual social status is sufficiently strong to produce an inversion of the expected relationship between individual status and Reagan support in higher-status contexts. *Among politically interested respondents the campaign has the net effect of producing higher levels of polarization between status groups in low-status contexts while maintaining a reversal of political differences between status groups in high-status contexts.* Hence, even if high-status individuals encounter a low-status individual in high-status contexts, they are unlikely to see any political expression of class conflict. Who lives in such contexts? Probably, among others, college professors and those employed by the mass media who teach us that American politics is classless. Which indeed it is for them, because of their social location and immediate sociopolitical locale.

Table 5.7B. *Predicted probabilities of Reagan vote preference among politically interested respondents, before the conventions and after the election, estimated on the basis of Table 5.7A*

	Before conventions, June-July 1984: Mean neighborhood education		After election, November-December 1984: Mean neighborhood education	
	Low (11.6)	High (14.9)	Low (11.6)	High (14.9)
Individual education				
Low (3)	.14	.72	.06	.83
Average (13)	.33	.61	.42	.73
High (17)	.43	.56	.66	.69

Note: Numbers in parentheses refer to specified years of schooling.

The voting preferences of disinterested citizens are considered in Table 5.8. None of the coefficients take on crisp t-values, and thus it would appear that the voting preferences of disinterested respondents are unrelated to *either* individual *or* contextual social status.

These results show that the attentive citizenry is more likely to demonstrate preferences that are structured by its social milieu, and the extent to which its preferences are socially structured increases during the course of the election campaign. In contrast, the preelection preferences of disinterested respondents appear, at the very least, to be socially unstructured and individually idiosyncratic. The consequences of the campaign for the preferences of disinterested respondents are not entirely clear. Vote preference appears to be independent of the context both before and after the campaign, whereas party identification shows a moderate pattern of contextual structure at the culmination of the campaign.

What is the relative importance of individual and contextual social status to the political preferences of the attentive citizenry? Because the right-hand variables are orthogonal in the centered model, we can partition variation in party identification between individual, contextual, and interactive factors for the explained variation, the unexplained variation, and the total variation (Boyd and Iversen 1979: 70–5). This procedure is undertaken in Table 5.9, which analyzes variation in party identification after the election for interested respondents based on the model of Table 5.5.

Table 5.9 shows that 98 percent of the explained variation is due to context. Residual (unexplained) variation is fairly evenly divided between excluded individual and contextual factors, with only a minor amount due to excluded interactive factors. Nearly one-third of total variation is due to factors at the individual level, but more than two-thirds is due to factors at the contextual level. By focusing on row percentages rather than column percentages, the table shows that more than 40 percent of contextual varia-

Table 5.8. *Logit estimation of Reagan vote preference among politically disinterested respondents, before the conventions and after the election, by individual and contextual education*

	Before conventions, June-July 1984	After election, November-December 1984
Intercept	-4.52	-2.00
	(.68)	(.28)
Individual education	.13	-.11
	(.27)	(.20)
Neighborhood mean education	.10	.002
	(.20)	(.00)
Interaction	.007	.019
	(.18)	(.46)
N	604	543

Note: The *t*-values for coefficients are shown in parentheses.

Table 5.9. *Sources of variation in party identification after the election among attentive citizens, estimated on the basis of Table 5.5*

	Explained	Residual	Total
Individual	.01	.99	1.00
	.01	.43	.31
Contextual	.42	.58	1.00
	.98	.56	.68
Interaction	.21	.79	1.00
	.01	.02	.01
Total	.29	.71	
	1.00	1.00	

Note: The top number in each cell is the row proportion, and the bottom number is the column proportion. The total sum of squares for the table is 12,210 in units of centered party identification.

tion is explained by the model but only 20 percent of interactive variation and 1 percent of individual variation are explained.

Thus, Table 5.9 suggests several things. Our simple analytic model does a much superior job of accounting for contextual sources of variation than it does in accounting for individual sources of variation, but residual variation is still mostly due to contextual factors. This paradox is explained in the third column of the table: Most of the variation in party identification is due to contextual factors rather than individual-level factors.

We do not intend to deceive the reader. The results of Table 5.9 are affected by the model we have estimated, and by the nature of the sample we have constructed. Still, the table is compelling. Education is the most widely used measure of social status, and thus it is not unreasonable to focus on educational effects at various levels. The sample is purposefully drawn to maximize social status variation between contexts, but if social status could be explained in terms of individual characteristics and attributes, then we should not expect to see the disparity in the sources of total variation shown in the right-hand column.

When data are gathered on individuals who are divorced from time and place, the natural course of least resistance is to study individuals. In making a methodological commitment to the random-sample survey as the dominant device for understanding mass political behavior, social scientists have also made a theoretical commitment to focus on individual sources of variation. Table 5.9 suggests that such a commitment may be misplaced. In terms of social status effects in South Bend, the social context of political behavior is at least as important as a source of variation.

CONCLUSION

The most general conclusion to be reached from these analyses is that political preferences are more fully structured by the social context at the end of the election campaign than at the beginning. To repeat an earlier assertion: Democratic elections include a substantial element of social coercion. Electoral campaigns turn citizens' attention toward politics, and deviant preferences are brought into correspondence with their political surroundings. The election campaign serves as a political stimulus setting into motion a social influence process, and this in turn imposes social order on the political chaos of individually held, idiosyncratic opinions.

Second, the analysis shows important patterns of interdependence between the social context and two different individual characteristics: individual status and individual attentiveness to politics. In terms of individual status, lower-status individuals are more affected by context at the beginning of the campaign, and the election campaign serves to accentuate this fact. Moreover, it would appear that political attentiveness and interest are nearly preconditions for contextual influence. People who do not care about politics and elections are unlikely to be affected: Social learning requires motivation.

The combination of status and attentiveness produces important consequences. Indeed, at the end of the campaign the strong contextual effect among lower-status respondents, and the absence of such an effect among higher-status respondents, serve to reverse the normally expected relationship between individual status and vote choice among politically interested citizens in higher-status contexts. Thus, in higher-status contexts lower-status citizens become more Republican than higher-status citizens. In short, lower-status groups are more vulnerable to contextual influence, and the election campaign exploits this vulnerability, particularly among attentive citizens.

The results presented in this chapter support the importance of social influence in politics, and they urge a reassessment of the nature of individuals and groups in politics. Political preferences that are important do not remain idiosyncratic: Democratic politics is not something that takes place in the heads of individually isolated citizens. Important decisions – like presidential vote choice and attitudes toward political parties – become topics of social as well as individual concern, and even individual choices and preferences must be understood as being collective in nature.

The analyses of this chapter have remained at a relatively high level of aggregation, focusing on the extent to which political preferences are structured by relevant social boundaries during the course of an election campaign. In the chapters that follow we focus more narrowly on individual citizens and the ties that exist between individuals and groups. We are particularly concerned with the manner in which individual citizens obtain information through social contacts with other citizens, and the ways in which these contacts are influenced by both individual choice and environmental constraint.

APPENDIX: THE BOYD-IVERSON MODEL

The Boyd and Iversen (1979) model for contextual analysis is an important part of this chapter's analysis, and this appendix provides an explanation of its use. We begin by assuming that partisanship is related to individual-level social status. The model might be written as:

$$y_{ik} = d_{0k} + d_{1k}x_{ik} + f_{ik} \tag{1}$$

where y_{ik} is the seven-point party identification scale on the part of the ith individual in the kth context, and where x_{ik} is a measure of the same individual's social status. This model provides for the hypothesis that the behavioral laws tying group membership to group attitudes are specific to a given context: They vary across contexts, that is, across k values. Thus, the within-context parameters are determined by

$$d_{0k} = f(C_k) + u_k \tag{2}$$

$$d_{1k} = g(C_k) + v_k \tag{3}$$

where k indexes a particular context, C is a particular contextual property, and v and u are the residual effects of other contextual properties. The functions f and g are unspecified, and we follow Boyd and Inversen in assuming linearity as a first approximation. Thus write

$$d_{0k} = b_0 + b_2 x_{.k} + u_k \tag{4}$$

$$d_{1k} = b_1 + b_3 x_{.k} + v_k \tag{5}$$

where $x_{.k}$ is the mean population value for x_{ik} in the kth context – in this instance the mean social status level. In words, the behavioral laws specifying the relationship between an individual behavior and an individual characteristic are contingent on the context.

The model allows for three basic effects, as well as their various combinations. An individual level effect is present if b_1 is nonzero; a simple contextual effect is present if b_2 is nonzero; and an interaction effect is present if b_3 is nonzero. An individual effect is interpreted to mean that individual behavior is a function of an individual characteristic; a contextual effect means that individual behavior is a function of a contextual property; and an interaction effect means that the effect of context depends on individual characteristics and the effect of individual characteristics depends on context.

The two-equation model can be estimated directly by first estimating equation 1 *within each context*. If the resulting estimates of d_{0k} and d_{1k} are equal across the k contexts, then we can immediately assume that both b_2 and b_3 are zero. If the d coefficients are unequal across contexts, a second step consists of estimating the b_i in equations 4 and 5 by directly regressing both sets of d values on the group means. An alternative method for estimating individual, contextual, and interaction effects is the single-equation model. The two-equation model can be algebraically manipulated into this single-equation form by substituting equations 4 and 5 into equation 1, obtaining

$$y_{ik} = b_0 + b_1 x_{ik} + b_2 x_{.k} + b_3 x_{ik} x_{.k} + e_{ik} \tag{6}$$

where $e_{ik} = u_k + v_k x_{ik} + f_{ik}$. Thus the error term for the complete single-equation model, which can be applied to an aggregated data set as a whole, is a function of an individual-level variable as a product with one of the two-equation error terms. This error structure offers an opportunity to undertake at least a partial assessment of model specification.

A properly specified model should generate the same coefficient estimates, regardless of whether the two-equation or single-equation model is employed. All linear model slope coefficients in this analysis are obtained through the single-equation centered model, but in the course of the analysis they have been compared with those obtained from the algebraically equivalent, two-equation model obtained using weighted least squares with the context N size serving as the weight (Boyd and Iversen 1979: appendixes B and F). In every instance the coefficients are nearly equal. This is important, because it suggests that, as social science does not always go, the model is not seriously misspecified.

The Boyd and Iversen (1979) model has a number of advantages for

contextual analysis, but none is more important than their centering procedure. The problem of correlated independent variables frequently becomes
severe in contextual research: Individual and contextual measures are
likely to be positively correlated, and each is also positively correlated with
the interaction variable. Centering successfully resolves the problem of
correlated independent variables by transforming both the independent
and dependent variables in the equation. This centering procedure makes it
possible to preserve the original metric scale on the d coefficients, while
producing orthogonal independent variables. Consider again the previous
example. The dependent and independent variables would be translated
into their centered forms as follows:

$$y^*_{ik} = y_{ik} - d_{1k}x_{.k}$$

$$x^*_{ik} = x_{ik} - x_{.k}$$

$$x^*_{.k} = x_{.k} - x_{..}$$

where y^*_{ik}, x^*_{ik}, and $x^*_{.k}$ are the centered variables, and where $x_{..}$ is the
grand mean for the entire population. Notice especially the centered depen-
dent variable, y^*_{ik}. In order to achieve the centered form, an estimate of
the slope, d_{1k}, must be obtained within each context. Thus a sufficient
sample must be obtained within each context to regress y_{ik} on x_{ik} in their
uncentered forms.

All slope coefficients displayed in the tables have been translated back
into their uncentered forms. This only affects the intercept and the slope
coefficient for individual education, but it means that in interpretation all
the coefficients can be treated as operating directly on the uncentered
variables. Thus, such a translation recovers the original metric of the coefficients and allows them to be interpreted in a straightforward manner, as we
have done in the text.

III

Networks, political discussants, and social communication

6

Political discussion in an election campaign

This chapter begins an examination of political information networks during the course of a presidential election campaign. Our immediate goal is to address a series of descriptive issues regarding the nature of social interaction among citizens – particularly social interaction that carries political content. With whom do citizens discuss the election campaign? How does political discussion vary across different types of relationships? To what extent does political discussion take place within networks of socially and politically homogeneous individuals? A sample of South Bend area residents was interviewed three times during the election campaign, and they were asked to name the people with whom they discussed the election, as well as to supply information regarding these relationships. A sample of these discussants was interviewed subsequently, thereby expanding our ability to examine the political content of social interaction.

National surveys of political behavior are characterized by a methodological vice nearly inherent in their basic design. The power of randomly sampling individuals, which so effectively controls many sources of unknown error and allows generalization to the population of adult citizens, is not typically designed to take account of the social environments where respondents are found. The citizen is plucked from a distinctive social and political setting for reasons that are, at least in the abstract, compelling on both methodological and scientific grounds. But inevitably, if unintentionally, such a sampling design creates a profound bias in the analyses and questions that might be addressed. And thus it also produces a bias in the nature of systematic theory developed to understand mass political behavior. The typical result has been that the sociological basis of citizen activity, preference, and choice is short-changed in favor of individualistic psychological and economic motivations.

It would not be fair to say that the group basis of politics or political influence is totally ignored, not would it be fair to say that individual reports cannot be, or have not been, used to pursue sociological influences on political behavior. Indeed, in many instances they can be used quite effectively, and we will use such self-reports in the analyses of this chapter. But the fact remains that the individual respondent's environment is not measured independently of the individual's self-report, and, perhaps more important, a strong intellectual tendency is fostered to pursue a highly individualistic mode of analysis and theorizing about politics and political behavior. Indeed, the history of voting studies since the advent of the national random probability sample has been the abandonment of the sociologically rich, community-based studies arising from the Columbia school of sociologists (see Berelson, Lazarsfeld, and McPhee 1954) in favor of the social-psychologically rich, individualistic, national random samples arising from voting studies in the Michigan tradition (see Campbell et al. 1960).

There are, of course, compelling counterexamples using national survey data: the Converse (1969) analysis of time and partisan stability, Miller's (1956) analysis of the county political context and its influence on the vote, R. Putnam's (1966) examination of the mechanisms underlying community influence. The important point for present purposes is that these authors (and others) were the Pacific salmon swimming upstream – a frequently endangered species undertaking a difficult voyage. In this instance the difficulty of the task was heightened by the dominant technology employed to make the trip.

None of this is intended to diminish theoretical advances in the study of electoral politics generated by forty years of national election studies. Indeed, our own efforts are inextricably connected to (and dependent on) the national election study research tradition. At the same time, no observational perspective is theoretically neutral, and the national random survey carries along with it a distinctive observational perspective that fosters some theories and arguments while it disables others. Not surprisingly, the national random survey is particularly disabling for theories of electoral politics that invoke a combination of space, time, environment, context, information, and interdependence.

The present chapter is an introduction to one part of our effort at relocating individual citizens within the social and political matrices where they lead their daily lives. Rather than plucking individuals out of the distinctive settings that surround them, our intention is to understand their political preferences and choices as being fundamentally contingent on locationally specific patterns of social interaction. In particular, with whom do they discuss the election campaign? How does political discussion vary across different types of relationships? To what extent does political discussion take place within networks of socially and politically homogeneous individuals? These questions and others cannot be addressed solely on the basis of self-reports, and neither can they be addressed absent a research design that is intentionally constructed to reintroduce the environments of citizens into political analysis. Our attention thus shifts to specific features of the research strategy.

IDENTIFYING POLITICAL DISCUSSANTS

A primary goal of the South Bend study was to construct a research design around the social contexts within which real citizens live and act politically. This goal rests on the theoretical premise that the American electorate is nonexistent as a behavioral entity in everyday life when considered *simply as an aggregation of individual citizens who are isolated and independent from one another.* Advisors for national political candidates may view such an electorate as real, and perhaps for them it is, at least as a reality about which they reason and allocate resources. For the individual citizen, however, reality takes the form of an opinion held by an acquaintance at work, a neighbor, a husband, or perhaps a priest or minister. Social settings such as these, and the political discussion networks sustained within them, are typically ignored by the national random probability sample. Hence, the South Bend study was designed as a return to a community-based sample with an explicit focus on the immediate social settings within which citizens and their behavior are imbedded.

The analyses reported here are based primarily on the third-wave, post-election interview of main respondents in combination with a subsequent survey of more than 900 people identified by the main respondents as discussants. The names of these discussants were obtained in a straightforward fashion: We asked for the first names of people with whom third-wave respondents talked politics, *not friends or close friends.* The precise wording of the question was:

We are interested in the sort of political information and opinions people get from each other. Can you give me the *first* names of the three people you talked with most about the events of the past election year? These people might be from your family, from work, from the neighborhood, from church, from some other organization you belong to, or they might be from somewhere else. All I need are the first names.

If no names of political discussants were forthcoming we followed up with an additional probe:

Well then, can you give the first name(s) of person(s) with whom you were most likely to have informal conversations during the course of the past few months?

About 89 percent of our third-wave respondents furnished the first name of at least one political discussant and another 6 percent furnished the name of someone with whom they had regular conversations. It is especially important to recapitulate and emphasize that neither the first question nor the following probe asked the third-wave respondents to name friends. We do not assume that meaningful political interaction only occurs among friends, and this assumption pays important dividends at several points in the analyses of this and later chapters.

Subsequent to obtaining these first names of discussants, a battery of questions was employed to gather information about each political discussant according to the perceptions of the main respondent. After this battery of questions was completed, we made the crucial attempt to obtain sampling frame information for interviews with the political discussants. The question was:

We might like to ask these people a few short questions about their views regarding the last election. Would you mind giving me their last names and the street they live on?

On the basis of the responses to this last question a sampling frame of approximately 1,800 persons was constructed and follow-up interviews were completed with 929 persons so identified. In addition to these 929, another 55 discussants had already been interviewed in our third wave, but for obvious reasons we did not reinterview these individuals. (While the 55 are not included in the analyses of this chapter, they are included in several later analyses.)

The questions that motivate this chapter are concerned with dyadic relationships, and the resulting data set provides two different opportunities for examining dyads. The main respondents identified first names for more than 4,000 discussants, as well as answering a battery of questions regarding the characteristics of the relationships and persons thus identified. These data are identified in tables as the perception data, and they provide an important basis for the analyses of this and later chapters.

Additionally, we are able to construct a matrix of more than 900 dyads in which both the main respondent and the discussant have been interviewed, and these data are identified in tables as the network data. In the population of political discussion dyads generated by this procedure, a significant number of main respondents, and a much smaller number of discussants, appear more than once. Main respondents appear in the data set more than once if they gave us the names and addresses of multiple discussants, and we were successful in obtaining multiple discussant interviews. A discussant appears more than once if more than one main respondent names the person as a discussant, and if we were able to interview the individual. Only five of our interviewed discussants were named by more than one main respondent. And for the total set of dyadic relationships between people *unrelated* by blood or marriage, about 22 percent involve repeated use of a main respondent. The resulting data set – absent the 55 main respondents who named other main respondents as discussants – consists of 934 main respondent–discussant dyads.

In summary, these procedures yield two different matrices of discussion dyads: one that depends on the perceptions of main respondents and includes more than 4,000 dyads, and another with more than 900 dyads that uses information collected from both the main respondent and the discussant. It is possible to characterize both sets of dyads in a number of ways that respond to the questions motivating this chapter, and those possibilities are exploited here.

POLITICAL DISCUSSION AS AN INFORMATION CHOICE

Citizens obtain political information from a great many sources – politicians' speeches, media reports, mass mailings – but they also obtain it from one another through various forms and means of social interaction. Not all information obtained through social interaction comes via the means of political discussion. Some of it comes from lapel pins, yard signs, and bumper stickers. Other information comes through subtle but often powerful forms of nonverbal communication. Moreover, political discussion itself takes on many forms: lunchtime arguments among professional economists regarding the likely consequences of trade liberalization, a father-in-law's unsupported condemnation of a particular candidate as a crook, and so on. In short, political discussion is only one means of communicating information through social interaction, and such discussion is highly diverse in terms of its sophistication, focus, and potential for influencing the participants.

Two common features of information obtained through political discussion are especially important to our argument. First, citizens often use sophisticated strategies to process socially obtained information. Consider the case of Charles Barkley – an Olympic basketball star, a dominant power forward in the National Basketball Association, and a Bush voter in 1988. According to Mr. Barkley (*Sports Illustrated,* February 13, 1989, p. 9): "My family got all over me because they said Bush is only for the rich people. Then I reminded them, 'Hey, I'm rich.' "

Some might argue with Mr. Barkley's choice of candidates, but few would argue with the sophisticated strategy he employed for processing information: He judged the information relative to the source, and he judged the imputed interests of the source relative to his own self-perceived interests. In articulating his strategy of information processing, Mr. Barkley focuses our attention on an important point: Citizens are not the helpless dupes of a social setting that extinguishes individual control over the evaluation of information and the exercise of political choice. Mr. Barkley encountered disagreeable information, but he did not simply change his opinion. Rather, the information forced him to reevaluate his vote choice and articulate a rationale for disagreement.

Second and more basically, citizens both encounter and recognize disagreeable information. They do not exercise complete control over the stream of incoming information and, at least in Mr. Barkley's case, they recognize that the information is at odds with their own choices and rationales. This point may seem obvious, but a great many arguments lead us to expect otherwise. Economists tell us that people will select information sources to coincide with their own interests and predispositions, and social psychologists tell us that people interpret and reinterpret information to coincide with these predispositions. A synthesis of these views suggests that citizens are able to control incoming information with the one–two punch of control and misinterpretation. The expected end result would thus be very low levels of perceived disagreement among people who exchange political information through social interaction.

How, then, can we account for both the reality and perception of disagreement? People encounter disagreeable information because the incoming stream of information is environmentally contingent, and environments do not come made-to-order according to the specifications of the people living within them. We choose a job for the pay and the work, a neighborhood for the house and the schools, and we tolerate the politics of neighbors and co-workers. Like Mr. Barkley, we select associates and friends for a variety of reasons: their lack of skill at poker, a shared interest in professional basketball, their tolerant personalities, a shared location in the same family or workplace or neighborhood. Some of us screen potential associates on the basis of political criteria, but none of us exercise complete control over even the most intimate of environments – the environment of friendship and friendship groups.

To what extent and under what circumstances do people recognize disagreement when it occurs? An adequate response to this question takes us beyond the purposes of the present chapter. It is sufficient for present purposes to observe that, like Mr. Barkley, many but not all citizens know when they are talking politics with a wrongheaded associate. Moreover, and as we will see, the conditions that give rise to the accurate perception of incoming information do not lie wholly within the head of the person who is perceiving the information.

Finally, it is important to observe that we do not really know whether friends and other intimates are the most efficacious and widely used sources of political discussion and socially obtained information. At least in the case of Mr. Barkley, we see a citizen who may talk politics with his family and friends, but who certainly does not allow even intimate associates to dictate his own political choices. Would Mr. Barkley be more likely to rely on political discussion with people he perceived as sharing his own interests, even if these people were not family members, good friends, or close associates?

These are the types of questions we begin to address in the present chapter. With a primary focus on isolated and independent individuals, political science research has taught us surprisingly little regarding the information received through social interaction, the characteristics of the relationships through which political information is conveyed, and the types of people who serve as political communicators. We begin by focusing on the types of relationships that serve as vehicles for the transmission of political information.

TYPES OF RELATIONSHIPS

All relationships in the main respondent–discussant data matrix involve discussion dyads, but they differ in a number of important ways. Perhaps most important, the relationships differ in terms of their structural locus. Taken together, social relationships between individuals go a long way toward defining social structure, but social structure is not subsumed by these networks of social relationships. Rather, the networks are laid over, and configured by, important structural properties: marriage, family, workplace, neighborhood, church, and so on. A particular individual finds herself in a particular marriage, with a particular family, working at a particular job, living in a particular neighborhood. We conceive of social relationships as being, in some sense, subsidiary to these structural locations. Opportunities and constraints operating on the formation of social relationships are imposed on the individual by important structural elements.

A first question naturally arises: How is political discussion affected by the structural locus of a relationship? The main respondents were asked whether each of their three discussants were family members – whether the discussant was related to them by either blood or marriage. On the basis of their responses for each discussion partner, we consider three types of dyadic relationships: (1) relationships between spouses, (2) relationships between relatives who are not spouses – other relatives, and (3) relationships between individuals who are not related by blood or marriage – nonrelatives.

The response of the main respondents to this question are cross-tabulated in Table 6.1 by the order in which the discussant was named within the sequence of three discussants. First notice that the marginal distribution indicates that more than half of the discussants are nonrelatives, 28 percent are other relatives, and only 17 percent are spouses. These figures must be seen from the perspective of the procedure we have designed to identify discussants. Our respondents have, at most, only one spouse, and thus even if everyone was married and discussed politics with a spouse, only one-third of discussants would be marriage partners. Moreover, the table also shows that the relative frequency of spouses is quite high among first-named discussants, but drops off dramatically thereafter. In short, the relative role of the spouse in political discussion is partially dictated by the format of these questions.

Even viewed in this context, the importance of nonrelative discussants is quite dramatic. Nonrelative is the modal category among first-named discussants, and the ratio of nonrelatives to other relatives – relatives other than the spouse – is consistently two-to-one across the columns of the table. In summary, Table 6.1 suggests that personal discussions of politics, and hence this aspect of social interaction in politics, should not simply be viewed as a family affair.

Table 6.1. *Type of relationship by order in which discussant is named*

	First	Second	Third	Total
Nonrelative	41.8%	61.4	60.8	54.6
Spouse	36.2	7.9	6.9	17.2
Other relative	22.0	30.7	32.3	28.2
N	1,422	1,389	1,364	4,175

Source: Perception data.

Not surprisingly, the frequency of social contact varies considerably across the different types of relationships. As panel A of Table 6.2 shows, almost every marriage relationship produces daily discussion, and the frequency of contact drops off dramatically among other relatives and nonrelatives. This pattern of interaction frequency may not be surprising to most readers, but several other features of the table are perhaps more interesting. First, the frequency of contact among other relatives and nonrelatives is virtually the same. Second, the frequency of contact is relatively high for both: About 80 percent of the main respondents report either daily contact or contact one or more times per week with both nonrelatives and other relatives. Thus, our main respondents report more extensive contact with the political discussants to whom they are married, but the frequency of contact is still relatively high for other relatives and nonrelatives. In short, the political discussants tend to be people with whom contact is regular and recurring.

In contrast to the frequency of social contact, the frequency of political discussion, *given a social contact,* is relatively constant across the different types of relationships. Panel B of Table 6.2 suggests that our main respondents are equally likely to discuss politics with any one of the three types of discussants. This helps to define more fully the potential influence of a spouse as a political discussant. The influence of a marriage partner is probably less related to the relative frequency of political discussion than it is to the relative frequency of social interaction in general. The power of a marriage partner rests in frequent and repeated contact – a fact consistent with a classic learning theory interpretation of social interaction and its consequence for politics (McPhee 1963; Sprague 1982). Given a social contact, people are only slightly more likely to discuss politics with discussants who are spouses than they are with any other discussants. But the important point is that social contact is more frequent among spouses.

Citizens do not choose their political discussion partners on the basis of free choice alone. The formation of this and every other relationship is subject to the constraints of social structure. People do the best they can, subject to available alternatives. Thus it follows that some people evaluate

Table 6.2. *Perceptions of discussant and relationship by type of relationship*

	Nonrelative	Spouse	Other relative	Total
A. How often do you talk with (discussant)?				
Every day	38.8%	97.2	31.3	46.8
Once or twice a week	45.7	2.1	48.3	38.9
Once or twice a month	12.1	.0	17.2	11.4
Less than once a month	3.4	.7	3.2	2.9
N	2,267	718	1,176	4,161
B. When you talk with (discussant), about how often do you discuss politics?				
Most times	7.0	7.0	6.9	6.9
Fairly often	18.3	34.3	20.3	21.6
Only once in a while	67.8	57.5	67.7	66.0
Never	6.9	1.3	5.2	5.4
N	2,273	717	1,179	4,169
C. About how much of the time does (discussant) follow politics?				
Most of the time	39.8	41.6	39.4	40.0
Some of the time	42.8	42.4	44.2	43.1
Not much at all	17.4	16.0	16.4	16.8
N	2,084	713	1,118	3,915
D. And generally speaking, how much do you think (discussant) knows about politics?				
A great deal	33.4	36.2	34.6	34.2
An average amount	56.9	58.6	54.7	56.6
Not much at all	9.7	5.2	10.7	9.2
N	2,209	715	1,152	4,076
E. When you discuss politics with (discussant), how often do you disagree?				
Often	14.4	10.0	13.3	13.3
Sometimes	44.3	46.8	40.7	43.7
Rarely	26.6	34.5	32.1	29.6
Never	14.6	8.8	13.9	13.4
N	2,110	708	1,114	3,932

Source: Perception data.

their discussion partners favorably, whereas others view them unfavorably. Panels C and D of Table 6.2 show the main respondents' evaluations of their discussion partners across two dimensions – the extent to which discussants follow politics and the extent of their knowledge about politics. In both instances there is a nearly imperceptible tendency to evaluate marriage partners more favorably, but the tables are more notable for the uniformity that they reveal across relationship types rather than for the differences that they expose. Clearly, respondents generally perceive their discussion partners as both alert to current politics and politically knowledgeable.

This analysis is extended in panel E of Table 6.2 to examine the frequency of disagreement between discussion partners across the different types of relationships. The frequency of disagreement varies quite modestly across the three types of relationships, with only a very slight tendency for disagreement to be higher among nonrelatives than among spouses, and among nonrelatives more than among other relatives. At the same time, however, disagreement is not at all uncommon across all three types of relationships. The main respondents characterize more than half of all relationships as having disagreement that occurs often or sometimes, and thus it would appear that Mr. Barkley is not the only one who perceives political disagreement with his associates. This feature of the relationships, disagreement, should be kept in mind as we address political convergence and divergence between discussion partners in the chapters that follow. Disagreement between political discussion partners is a phenomenon of great interest in determining the dynamics of citizen preference because disagreement furnishes the occasion for new information search – it furnishes an engine to drive political change.

Thus far we have only examined the perceptions of the main respondents regarding their discussants, but we are also able to compare the self-reported social and political characteristics of the main respondent to those of the discussion partner because, in more than 900 instances, both were interviewed. We must, however, issue a word of caution regarding the marginal distributions of spouses, nonrelatives, and other relatives in the network data. This typology of relationships served as a main criterion for the network sampling design. Given limited resources – insufficient funds were available to interview all the discussants for whom we had identifying information – we decided to interview as many nonrelative discussants as possible. As a result, the marginal distribution of spouses, other relatives, and nonrelatives in these network data cannot be interpreted as the relative density of corresponding relationship types among political discussants.

Selected characteristics of main respondents and their discussion partners are compared across relationship types in Table 6.3. The table displays mean values for difference measures obtained by subtracting the main respondent's score on a variable from the score of the discussant, and thus a mean closer to zero indicates convergence between discussion partners.

Table 6.3. *Mean values (N in parentheses) for discussant-main respondent difference scores, by type of relationship*

	Nonrelative	Spouse	Other relative
Campaign participation	.50	.21	.26
	(516)	(175)	(222)
Partisanship	-.15	.02	-.10
	(495)	(167)	(217)
Schooling	.25	.11	.36
	(585)	(178)	(227)
Income	.31	-.10	.39
	(448)	(153)	(197)
Age	.58	-.18	-2.41
	(515)	(176)	(226)
Union	.02	.00	.08
	(517)	(177)	(224)

Note: Each difference score is calculated by subtracting the main respondent's score on a variable from the discussant's score on the same variable: discussant score − main respondent score. The variables are defined as follows, for both discussants and main respondents: campaign participation = number of campaign activities performed, range is from 0 to 4; party identification = six point scale (0 = strong Democrat); years of schooling = actual years (17 = beyond college diploma); income = measure of family income, range is from 1 to 8; union = 1 if some family member is a union member, 0 otherwise; age = age in years.

Source: Network data.

Several features of the table merit attention. First, for each of the measures considered here, spouses are (on average) more similar to the main respondent than either nonrelatives or other relatives. In short, the convergence of social and political characteristics among discussants is most pronounced among marriage partners, reflecting both the selection process *into* the marriage and continued social interaction *within* the marriage. In contrast, the pattern of differences between other relatives and nonrelative discussion partners is not as consistent.

A second interesting feature of Table 6.3 is that it gives us several direct checks on measurement error among marriage partners. We asked main respondents and discussants whether anyone in their households belonged to a union, as well as asking for an estimate of family income. These responses should correlate perfectly for marriage partners, and the table shows very minimal differences, with mean differences that are quite negligible.

Third, the difference measures are formed by subtracting the main respondent's score on a measure from that of the discussant, and thus the direction of the difference score has a direct interpretation. In particular, main respondents tend to choose discussion partners who are both better educated and more active in campaign politics. In short, these data are consistent with the argument that social interaction tends to enhance the civic capacity of the electorate because citizens turn to others who are more likely to be competent and engaged in political affairs.

THE STRUCTURAL LOCUS OF NONRELATIVE DISCUSSANTS

The structural factors that tie together marriage partners and relatives are fairly clear, but the loci of the relationships between discussants unrelated by blood or marriage are open to examination. On the basis of the main respondent's own report, panel A of Table 6.4 shows whether discussants live in the same neighborhood as the main respondent, cross-classified by whether they work at the same job. Nearly 70 percent of the relationships share one environment or the other, with the workplace being marginally more important as a locus of relationships among nonrelatives.

A separate but related question involves not the locus but rather the source of the relationship. To say that discussants share an environment is not to say that the environment was responsible for the relationship. Panel B of Table 6.4 considers the source of the relationship among nonrelative discussants, first for discussants who live in the same neighborhood, second for discussion partners who work together, and finally displaying the pattern for all the nonrelative discussants.

In terms of discussants who share the same neighborhood, only 46 percent of the main respondents reported that the relationship originated in the neighborhood. Indeed, 22 percent originated at the workplace and 8 percent at church. Thus it would appear that the neighborhood is important not simply as a direct source of relationships, but also as an enabling factor that sustains and nurtures social contacts that originated elsewhere. Stated differently, an employee is likely to have contact with a number of co-workers, any one of whom who might become a more important acquaintance. The choice among these possibilities is likely to be influenced by ease of interaction, and residential proximity is one of the factors that makes interaction easier.

A very different pattern emerges among discussant pairs who work together. Nearly 90 percent of these relationships also *originated* at the workplace, and only minuscule percentages originated elsewhere. The importance of the workplace as a staging ground for social relationships emerges quite clearly in the third column of Table 6.4B: Nearly half of all nonrelative discussants come from the workplace, about 19 percent come from the neighborhood, and about 8 percent come from church. This is not to say that neighborhoods or churches are unimportant. Indeed, as Table 6.4A shows, the workplace and the neighborhood are roughly equivalent in importance when we ask where discussants are located with respect to the main respondent. Rather, Table 6.4 indicates the relatively specialized roles of various social structural elements as sources and support for the origination and

Table 6.4. *Location and source of nonrelative discussion partners*

A. *Location of nonrelative discussion partners*

	Do you work with (discussant)?		
	Yes	No	Total
Does (discussant) live in			
your neighborhood?			
Yes	6.4%	27.1	33.5
No	33.7	32.8	66.5
Total	40.1	59.9	$N = 2,275$

B. *Source of nonrelative discussion partners, by location*

	Discussant lives in same neighborhood	Discussant works at same location	Total nonrelative discussants
Work	22.5%	88.5	48.0
Church	7.9	2.2	8.2
Neighborhood	46.0	2.9	18.9
Family	4.0	1.0	4.4
Republican party	.4	.1	.4
Democratic party	.4	.1	.3
Other organization	.3	.0	.2
Politics (in general)	.4	.1	.6
School	4.0	1.3	3.8
Children in school together	.5	.7	.8
Friend of a relative	5.3	1.0	5.4
Casual social situation	8.3	2.2	9.3
N	756	910	2,244

Source: Perception data.

sustenance of social relationships with political import. Quite simply, the workplace is especially important as a source of these relationships, while the neighborhood is important for sustaining such relationships.

DISCUSSANT ASSESSMENTS AND THE FREQUENCY OF POLITICAL DISCUSSION

The importance of individual discretion in obtaining political information is most apparent between discussion partners who are not members of the same family. It may be quite difficult for a wife to escape political discussion with a husband, even if he is misguided, uninformed, and wrong-headed! Alternatively, a citizen's political assessment of someone who does not belong to the same family may indeed be an important factor in stimulating political discussion. At least if we can help it, most of us are less likely to choose someone as a discussant whom we judge to be politically incompetent.

As panels A and B of Table 6.5 show, the main respondent's assessment of the nonrelative discussant's political sophistication plays an important role in stimulating political discussion. Political discussion is more likely to occur frequently when the main respondent believes that the discussant knows more about politics (panel A) and when the main respondent believes that the discussant follows politics more regularly (panel B). This coincides with the conclusion reached on the basis of Table 6.3: Main respondents tend to report discussants who are, relative to themselves, better educated and more involved in politics.

An alternative explanation for these patterns of association is that they are simply by-products of social intimacy. That is, we may discuss politics with people whom we admire and trust – people with whom we have more intimate relationships. And because these people are trusted intimates, we might also have a high degree of respect for their political competence and expertise. Such an argument suggests, in turn, that discussion should be more frequent among nonrelatives who are more intimate – recall the discussion habits of Mr. Barkley – but such a pattern is not sustained in panel C of Table 6.5. Indeed, panel C shows that the intimacy of a relationship has *very little* to do with the relative frequency of political discussion. Nearly half of nonrelative discussants are less than close friends, and intimacy is unrelated to the frequency of political discussion.

The intimacy of the social ties through which political information is communicated becomes an important issue in our analysis. As Granovetter (1973) has argued so persuasively, weak ties are important because they lead to the widespread diffusion of information, whereas strong ties lead to recirculated information that does not travel far. We build on his insight by using intimacy as an indicator of relationship strength. If socially conveyed political information was only communicated through strong ties, then the structural implications for democratic politics and for political analysis would be less profound, indicating that we should merely replace our focus on individuals with a slightly wider focus on small intimate groups and cliques of relatives and close friends. In other words, political information that is conveyed through strong ties will not travel far, and thus a socially disjointed view of democratic politics and political life is not seriously threatened or called into question. Alternatively, if political information is also conveyed through weak ties and casual acquaintances, public opinion is *truly public* and it becomes problematic to consider the individual citizen apart from the public opinion of which she is a part. Panel C of Table 6.5

Table 6.5. *Frequency of political discussion with nonrelative discussants as a function of various factors: When you talk with (discussant), about how often do you discuss politics?*

A. *Political discussion frequency by "And generally speaking, how much do you think (discussant) knows about politics?"*

	Great deal	Average amount	Not much
Most times	13.0%	4.6	1.9
Fairly often	29.3	14.3	8.4
Only once in a while	55.0	75.8	74.0
Never	2.7	5.3	15.8
N	738	1,254	215

B. *Political discussion frequency by "About how much of the time does (discussant) follow politics?"*

	Most of the time	Some of the time	Not much at all
Most times	13.3%	3.6	3.6
Fairly often	30.9	14.0	7.2
Only once in a while	54.5	79.1	71.8
Never	1.3	3.2	17.4
N	829	891	362

C. *Political discussion frequency by "Would you say (discussant) is a close friend, a friend, or just someone that you regularly come into contact with?"*

	Close friend	Friend	Just regular contact
Most times	7.2%	5.7	8.5
Fairly often	20.7	15.4	15.6
Only once in a while	66.1	72.9	65.3
Never	6.0	6.1	10.6
N	1,256	671	340

Source: Perception data.

only speaks to the communication of information as it is affected by the intimacy of relationships, and later analyses must address the influence of information as a function of relationship intimacy, but there is no other table in this book that is more crucial to the message we are attempting to convey.

In summary, it would appear that a combination of access, opportunity, and instrumental behavior plays an especially important role in the social transmission of political information. Citizens are likely to identify political discussants with whom they share important life spaces – neighborhoods, workplaces, churches. Some of these discussants are intimate friends and valued relatives, but others are only casual acquaintances. Finally, citizens are not without discretion and control in the communication process. In particular, they act on the basis of their own evaluations of these associates as sources of political information.

SOCIAL CORRESPONDENCE BETWEEN DISCUSSANTS

In this section we examine more carefully the social correspondence between discussants along several different dimensions: class membership, religious preference, and ethnic identification. We are particularly concerned with discussion partners who are not related, but some attention will be given to relatives and spouses as well.

Contemporary South Bend is built on the edifice of an earlier industrial city, and it maintains the reputation of being a union stronghold. This reputation is called into question by panel A of Table 6.6. Only 12 percent of the nonrelative discussant pairs in our sample involve individuals who are both from union families. Furthermore, this dilution of union strength within discussant relationships occurs regardless of high levels of selectivity on the part of union family members. The marginals of the table place the ratio of nonunion families to union families at roughly 3 to 1 among both main respondents and discussants. For nonunion main respondents, the ratio of nonunion to union discussants is roughly 4 to 1 – a fairly accurate reflection of the population composition. In contrast, among main respondents from union families, the ratio is approximately 1 to 1, and thus it would appear that union members are much more likely to turn (or to be turned) inward in the selection of discussion partners. In other words, either because of structurally limited choices, or because of individual preference, or because of some other factor, members of union families are much more likely to talk politics with other people who are also from union families. (This result can be compared usefully to the empirical findings of Finifter [1974] for Republican autoworkers in Detroit.)

The tendency toward social introversion helps to maintain political cohesion among union family members, but it does not help much. Assuming for the moment that our sample is an adequate representation of union densities in the South Bend area, random association would result in only about 6 percent of the discussant pairs being composed of two people from union families. The increase from 6 to 12 percent is important on theoretical grounds, but it is probably not important as a practical matter. We see a pronounced tendency toward introversion among the members of union families, but this tendency is overwhelmed by the minority status of union members.

Table 6.6. *Social characteristics of discussants and main respondents,*
for nonrelatives

A. *"Does anyone in your household belong to a labor union?"*

	Main respondent union membership		
	No	Yes	Total
Discussant union membership			
No	60.9%	12.6	73.5
Yes	14.3	12.2	26.5
Total	75.2	24.8	$N = 517$

B. *Self-identified class membership*

	Main respondent class membership		
	Middle	Working	Total
Discussant class membership			
Middle	40.9	19.6	60.6
Working	17.1	22.4	39.4
Total	58.0	42.0	$N = 474$

Source: Network data.

Note: Each cell entry is a percentage of the respective table.

Much the same pattern is produced in panel B of Table 6.6 when we consider the subjective class identification of main respondents and discussants. Once again, the minority group – in this instance self-identified workers – is more selective in its associational patterns, but as before the practical significance is not huge. Random association would result in about 16 percent of the relationships being homogeneously working class. Instead, given a relatively high level of introversion among workers, 22 percent are homogeneously working class. In summary, it is not that we are witnessing random patterns of association, but rather that decidedly non-random patterns do not have much consequence. They are overwhelmed by structurally imposed opportunities and constraints operating on social interaction. (We will return to this issue in Chapter 8.)

In Table 6.7 we turn to a consideration of religious preference within discussant pairs. Panel A of the table shows modest evidence of social introversion within denominational boundaries: 65 percent of Protestants associate with other Protestants, and 56 percent of Catholics associate with other Catholics. In both instances these figures are only modestly higher than the marginal density of the denomination in the sample. Furthermore, the success of introversion tends to decline as the size of the group in the

Table 6.7. *The extent of shared religious preference among nonrelative discussion partners*

A. *Whether the discussant has a matching religious preference by the main respondent's religious preference*

| Main respondent's religious preference | Does the discussant have a matching religious preference? | | | |
	Yes	No	N	Sample %
Protestant	64.8%	35.2	293	56.9
Roman Catholic	56.0	44.0	175	34.0
Jewish	20.0	80.0	5	1.0
Orthodox	0.0	100.	2	.4
Something else	4.2	95.8	24	4.7
No religion	37.5	62.5	16	3.1

B. *Church attendance frequency by whether discussant shares religious preference, for nonrelatives*

| | Discussant's religious preference | |
	Different	Same
Every week	29.3%	55.4
Almost every week	15.1	9.7
Once or twice a month	11.7	7.6
A few times a year	34.6	22.8
Never	9.3	4.5
N	205	289

Source: Network data.

sample declines, with the important exception of the small group that claims no religion. Thirty-eight percent of their discussants *also* claim no religion, even though it appears that the group makes up a very insignificant portion of the population.

Panel B of Table 6.7 provides evidence to suggest that not only nominal affiliations but also activity levels are important in determining the likelihood of social contacts within and between religious groups. People who have discussion partners with the same religious preference were much more likely to be active participants, where participation is measured as the frequency of attending religious services. We do not pretend to separate the chicken from its egg. Certainly it is the case that active participation produces an increase in the incidence of social ties between the individual and the group, and these social ties produce more active participation. The important point is that relationships within the group are intimately tied up with group activity and commitment, and thus the political significance of

Table 6.8. *Whether discussants who are nonrelatives have matching ethnic identifications, for selected ethnic identifications*

	Does the discussant have a matching ethnic identification?			
	Yes	No	*N*	Sample %
Main respondent's ethnic identification				
Polish	22.0%	78.0	59	12.1
Hungarian	13.0	87.0	23	4.7
German	23.7	76.3	118	24.2
Irish	29.0	71.0	38	7.8
English	11.4	88.6	44	9.0
Scandinavian	5.6	94.4	18	3.7
American	15.8	84.2	19	3.9

Source: Network data.

group membership is inherently sociological rather than being merely psychologically or individually based.

Table 6.8 parallels Table 6.7A, but it focuses on ethnicity rather than religion. Once again, the extent of social introversion is fairly modest, but in this instance it does not vary so directly as a function of relative group size. German ethnics appear to be the largest ethnic group, but they fall behind the Irish – a much smaller ethnic group – in terms of maintaining social contacts within the group. This is important because it suggests that minority standing can, at least in some instances, be overcome. And it pushes toward further consideration of the factors that maintain the social integrity of ethnic groups and other groups as well.

POLITICAL DIVERSITY AS A FUNCTION OF SOCIAL DIVERSITY

A primary focus of this chapter has been on the social composition of discussion networks – particularly on the extent to which discussants share the same social characteristics and the degree to which they are located in the same groups, organizations, families, and workplaces. The relationship between social diversity and political diversity within discussant networks is problematic, however. On one hand, social homogeneity does not necessitate political homogeneity, but even more important, social diversity does not necessarily imply political diversity. Indeed, to the extent that individuals use their own idiosyncratic political criteria in the selection of political discussion partners, or to the extent that discussion partners influence one another, we would expect political diversity to be extinguished regardless

Table 6.9. *Heterogeneity of abortion attitudes within discussion dyads as a function of social heterogeneity within discussion dyads, for all discussant pairs*

	Coefficient	t-value
Constant	.66	.90
Sex of main respondent	.65	2.55
Sex difference	.56	2.58
Education of main respondent	-.055	1.11
Education difference	-.10	2.02
Church attendance of main respondent	-.13	1.50
Attendance difference	-.53	6.87
Discussant is a spouse	.36	1.38
Discussant is a relative	.30	1.19
N	586	
R^2	.09	

Note: Sex: 1 if male, 0 if female; sex difference: discussant sex – main respondent sex; education: years of schooling; education difference: discussant years of schooling – main respondent years of schooling; church attendance: index of frequency of attendance, ranging from 1 (every week) to 5 (never); attendance difference: discussant attendance – main respondent attendance; discussant is a spouse: spouse = 1, otherwise = 0; discussant is a relative: discussant is a relative but not a spouse = 1, otherwise = 0.

Source: Network data.

of social diversity. In other words, an individual's location in the social structure might be irrelevant because self-selection and social influence combine to insure political homogeneity *independent of social diversity.*

In this concluding section the focus begins to shift in an effort to consider the factors that minimize and maximize political diversity within discussion networks. In particular, to what extent can political diversity between discussion partners be predicted on the basis of social diversity? This question has far-reaching consequences regarding the nature of social influence in politics. Does social heterogeneity translate directly into political heterogeneity, or are political discussion partners chosen to maximize political agreement regardless of social diversity? Discussion partners can do little to produce social homogeneity within discussion groups once they have chosen their discussants, but do processes of social influence tend to increase levels of political homogeneity, thereby weakening the relationship between social and political diversity?

Providing answers to these questions provides much of the focus for the subsequent four chapters, but a preliminary examination is undertaken in Table 6.9 that considers differences in prolife attitudes on the part of discussion partners. The table incorporates all three types of dyads – spouses, other relatives, and nonrelatives – but includes two dummy-variable controls for whether the relationships are between spouses or other relatives, with the baseline category thus being nonrelative pairs. The type of relationship appears to have little consequence for the level of agreement regarding abortion between discussants, but several other factors appear to be quite important. Gender diversity, educational diversity, and religious diversity within discussion networks all seem to have consequences for levels of political agreement. Among these respondents, men are more prolife than women, people with less education are more prolife than people with more education, and people who attend church are more prolife than people who do not. More important for this analysis, differences in these social characteristics between main respondents and discussants translate into higher levels of political diversity and disagreement within discussant relationships. Social homogeneity breeds political homogeneity, and social heterogeneity breeds political heterogeneity.

These preliminary analyses raise a number of questions. If political agreement cannot be taken for granted between discussion partners, what is the role of social influence and how does it operate? If social heterogeneity translates into political heterogeneity, what are the factors that produce social heterogeneity? What are the criteria that guide the choice of political discussants? How are these criteria imbedded within a particular set of opportunities and constraints that are structurally imposed? We address these questions in the chapters that follow.

7

Networks in context:
The social flow of political information

This chapter examines the social transmission of political information as it is affected both by individual political preference and the distribution of political preferences surrounding the individual. We address several questions. First, to what extent do individuals purposefully construct informational networks corresponding to their own political preferences, and to what extent do they selectively misperceive socially supplied political information? Second, how are these individual-level processes conditioned by constraints that arise due to the distribution of political preferences in the social context? In other words, to what extent is individual control over socially supplied political information partial and incomplete? In answering these questions we argue that information transmitting processes interact with the social context in a manner that favors partisan majorities while undermining minorities.

Politics is a social activity, imbedded within structured patterns of social interaction. Political information is not only conveyed through speeches and media reports but also through a variety of informal social mechanisms: political discussions on the job or on the street, campaign buttons on a co-worker's shirt, even casual remarks. Such political information is not processed and integrated by isolated individuals but rather by interdependent individuals who conduct their day-to-day activities in socially structured ways – individuals who send and receive distinctive interpretations of political events in a repetitive process of social interaction. Thus political behavior may be understood in terms of individuals who are tied together by, and located within, networks, groups, and other social formations that largely determine their opportunities for the exchange of meaningful political information (Eulau 1986).

In short, the environment plays a crucial role in affecting the social flow of political information. People often choose their associates and the content of their conversations, but each of these choices is, in turn, bounded by an environment that for many purposes must be taken as given rather than chosen. This chapter explores the ramifications of these two-way streets between individually selected associates and discussion content on the one hand, and the socially structured supplies of possible associates and conversation content on the other. Hence our focus is on the content and perception of political information, and the influence of the social context within which such information is exchanged. We turn initially to an examination of individual control over the social flow of political information before considering the role of the environment in limiting such control.

INDIVIDUAL CONTROL OVER INFORMATION

Political information is conveyed through social interaction, but does political preference determine the supply of information, or does the supply of information determine political preference? The direction of influence undoubtedly runs both ways. People choose information sources subject to their own preferences, but they also take what is available. They consume what social structure and social situations supply, albeit guided in acceptance by individual perceptual mechanisms. Thus, several different individual-level processes might account for the high levels of political homogeneity so frequently reported in studies of associated individuals.

High levels of correspondence between individual preference and the surrounding preferences of associated individuals might arise from discretion in the choice and use of associates. Individuals certainly choose to associate with some individuals and to avoid others, and they talk politics with some associates but avoid discussions with others. To the extent that these choices are motivated by a priori political preference, a high level of homogeneity in the politics of associates is the consequence of preference rather than its cause.

Indeed, the dominance or precedence of political preference over social influence corresponds well with a choice-theoretic perspective on political behavior. In his *Economic Theory of Democracy,* Anthony Downs argues (1957: 229) that it is fully rational for individuals to reduce information costs by obtaining political information from personal contacts. Among the benefits of socially obtained information is the ability of the receiver to choose the information source, and thus to select a set of biases and viewpoints on the part of the source that the receiver finds congenial: "It is often relatively easy for a man to find someone he knows who has selection principles like his own."

A second source of reported political homogeneity within informational networks arises from measurement procedures. The level of correspondence between a respondent and his associates is often determined on the basis of the respondent's own report. A single respondent provides information not only on his own political preferences, but also on the political preferences of his associates. Thus, if individuals selectively screen the political information they receive through social interaction, they may also systematically misperceive its content (Lauman 1973). Political homogeneity produced in this fashion is, from a purely technical perspective, a measurement artifact. Notice, however, this is a measurement artifact with significant theoretical consequences. It indicates that disagreeable interactions can be reinterpreted (misperceived) in an agreeable light. Even if individuals are unable to control the objective content of socially transmitted political information, they are still able to control the interpretation of that content in a manner that reduces political dissonance and thereby minimizes the impact of social influence.

Finally, additional subtleties may operate as well. An individual who is well aware of an associate's political preferences, and also knows they are at variance with her own beliefs, may very well misrepresent, or not fully communicate, or deliberately make ambiguous her own preferences, precisely because she wishes to reduce dissonance in the relationship (Macoby, Matthews, and Morton 1954). Hence, a discussion partner may be quite prepared to misperceive political information when, simultaneously, the transmitter is prepared to obfuscate the message (Jones 1986), and thus it is not only political elites or candidates for public office (Shepsle 1972) who may have motives to heighten communication ambiguity in democratic politics (MacKuen 1990; Calvert 1985).

In summary, three individual-level factors undermine the potential impact of socially transmitted information. Citizens choose with whom to discuss politics, they reinterpret dissonance-producing information, and they may deliberately misrepresent their true opinions. These individual-level capabilities bring us full circle. Political information is conveyed through social interaction, but individuals choose with whom to interact, and they also suppress dissonance-producing information if it is not already rendered politically inoffensive by the transmitter. On these premises, socially transmitted political information becomes, wholly and completely, an extension of individually based political preference. The potential influence of socially transmitted information is explained away on the basis of choice, misperception, and misrepresentation: Sociology gives way to economics and individual psychology.

SOCIAL CONSTRAINTS ON INFORMATION

The emphasis on individual control over information flow may be juxtaposed against a view which makes a case for the significance of social structure in determining the transmission of political information. Not only is it worthwhile to inquire into the structural factors that motivate people to conform or to misrepresent their positions, but one might also examine the manner in which social structure determines interaction opportunities, or even imposes interactions. The case for social influence might be made on either theoretical or empirical grounds. In anticipation of empirical support for social influence to be offered later, is there a theoretical basis from which to build an expectation for the influence of socially transmitted information?

First, to argue that the selection of information sources takes precedence over social influence is to assert that political preferences dominate social influence processes running in the other direction. It is a gross simplification to assume that individually defined interests translate directly into individual preferences (Lewis-Beck 1986: 342–4) for preferences must be informed, and information arrives through socially structured channels. In particular, as McPhee (1963) persuasively argues, political preferences are sustained within particular structural locations, and they are configured by the multiple interactions of the individual within those structural locations. Thus, to the extent that political preferences are dependent on (socially supplied) information, they are inherently dynamic and responsive to social influence. Preference is not only inflicted on socially transmitted information, but socially transmitted information is inflicted on preference. Mutual causation between social contexts and individual preferences is inherent in this view of mass political information processing.

Second, it is often difficult for political scientists to remember that politics is not at the forefront of most choices that most individuals make. If one assumes for the moment that individuals do indeed choose their own locations within social and political structures, the choices are likely to be predicated on matters other than politics and political preference (Brown 1981). People choose a job because it pays better or because they need work. People choose a neighborhood because they can afford one of the houses. People choose a church because their parents raised them in it. The point to be emphasized is that politics and political preferences are ancillary to most of the significant life choices people make, the choices that locate individuals within the social structure. But these choices, made largely on apolitical grounds, may nevertheless impinge mightily on politics. Particular locations within the social structure expose citizens to particular social contexts and the information biases such contexts inevitably provide. These social contexts circumscribe the opportunities for social interaction. And thus individual choice regarding associational patterns and political discussions may be seen as operating within the opportunities and constraints imposed by a given social context.

These processes are stochastic. It is possible to buy into an upper-class neighborhood and find oneself surrounded by Democrats, but it is not as likely as a preponderance of Republican neighbors. Individuals probably reason over these bundles of probabilities in a similar fashion: If I buy into this neighborhood the chances are my daughter will date good Catholic boys (and ultimately marry one), the reasoning might run. But recognizing the contingent nature of the processes of living does not make the (stochastically determined) impact of events any less. Indeed, events that are not certain are more effective conditioners than those which occur regularly, as Skinner (1938) demonstrated long ago.

This is not to say that individuals are powerless in deciding with whom to discuss politics. In her study of a predominantly Democratic automobile plant, Finifter (1974) demonstrated that Republican autoworkers became socially introverted, resisting association with the numerically superior Democrats. In his study of a working-class suburb, Berger (1960) demonstrated that the middle-class minority was excluded and withdrew from community life. It is not that choice is absent but rather that associational choice is contingent – a locationally specific response to a particular social mix.

The role of the mass media may be deceptive in regard to these social processes. The nationalization of political information sources achieved through the disappearance of multiple-newspaper cities and the dominance of television may very well enhance the coercive power of informationally biased social contexts. If individuals are to acquire second opinions about their beliefs in one-newspaper and three-look-alike-network cities, the most likely recourse is probably socially transmitted new information. But this will be biased by its social location – that is, by the social context. Hence, readily available political information from the modern mass media may, because of its increased uniformity and homogeneity, increase rather than decrease the political influence potential of the social context.

NETWORKS AND CONTEXTS IN SOUTH BEND

As a first step in analyzing the social flow of political information, it is crucial to draw an important, if abstract, theoretical distinction between contexts and networks: *Contexts are structurally imposed whereas networks are individually constructed.* Contexts are external to the individual, even if the composition of the context depends on the makeup of individuals contained within it. In contrast, networks represent the product of myriad choices made by people who compose the net, but these choices are circumscribed by the opportunities and constraints imposed by the context. To present an extreme example, a Mondale voter will be unable to discuss politics with another Mondale voter if she resides in a context where all other individuals support Reagan. As a practical matter this distinction between networks and contexts may blur, but it provides a useful analytic tool with which to consider the issues just raised.

The analyses of this chapter are based primarily on the postelection survey of main respondents to the South Bend study in conjunction with a subsequent snowball survey of discussion partners named by the main respondents. The South Bend study was designed with a particular motive: to locate mass political behavior – political attitudes, candidate preferences, party preferences, policy positions, and political activities – within the structures and patterns of everyday life. Two structural ingredients are especially germane here: the informational *networks* through which individuals send and receive political information, and the larger but still very immediate *contexts* within which individuals reside. Both networks and contexts are observed and measured as part of the South Bend study, and it is important in understanding our results to be clear about measurement procedures.

The main respondents to the survey lived in sixteen different South Bend area neighborhoods purposefully selected to maximize social homogeneity within the neighborhoods, and social heterogeneity between the neighborhoods. These neighborhoods constituted the primary sampling units, and a high rate of random sampling was achieved in each neighborhood. Approximately equal numbers of respondents were randomly selected within each of the neighborhoods and interviewed at each of the three survey waves. Intensive sampling within neighborhoods produces two distinct advantages. First, any survey item can be aggregated to produce a measure of the neighborhood context, and in this chapter survey-derived estimates of neighborhood support for Reagan in the 1984 election are constructed. Second, intensive sampling makes it possible to employ the procedures developed by Boyd and Iversen (1979) for the analysis of contextual data, and a variation of the Boyd and Iversen centering procedure is employed here to produce approximately orthogonal explanatory variables.

In summary, contexts are measured at the level of the neighborhood using an aggregated survey item to provide the contextual measure, and the relevant individual–contextual property is voting behavior in the 1984 election. Thus the context of political behavior, as distinguished from the network of political discussion, is defined geographically and socially on a priori grounds and measured directly by aggregating survey responses within neighborhoods. Although our measure of context is the geographically based neighborhood, the social context is clearly a much broader concept that encompasses wider domains such as religious affiliation, recreational activities, and social organizations. The neighborhood measurement device employed here is narrower and more conservative than the theoretical construct it represents. Indeed, more comprehensive measures of social contextual experience would likely demonstrate even larger effects than those reported in our tables.

Networks are measured from two vantage points: first, that of the main respondent to the survey and, second, that of the political discussant named by the main respondent. Respondents to the third-wave survey, conducted shortly after the 1984 election, were asked to give the first names of three people with whom they were most likely to have discussions about politics. Again, the nature of the probe is very important because it was intentionally structured around a clear political reference point. We did not ask our main respondents to give us a list of their best friends or their close associates. Rather, we asked them to tell us with whom they discussed politics – their social sources of political information. Not surprisingly, many of the main respondents named discussants who were spouses and other relatives. For the purposes of this chapter, however, all relatives by either blood or marriage are omitted, and our focus is entirely on nonrelative discussants.

Notice that our definitions of contexts and networks do not require that the two overlap territorially. That is, a network may lie wholly outside the context, but this fact would not negate interdependence between these two elements of social structure. A person who lives in a context surrounded by Reagan voters may come to assume that everyone votes for Reagan, even when encountering individuals outside that context. Furthermore, a person imbedded in a Reagan context may have a higher likelihood of encountering Reagan voters, even when the encounter occurs beyond the context. Contexts create opportunities for social interaction that are not necessarily bounded by the original context.

A series of follow-up questions in the third-wave, postelection survey asked main respondents for information and perceptions regarding their discussants, including the presidential candidate for whom the discussant voted in 1984. A final question asked for the last name and street address of each discussant so that we could ask the discussants "a few short questions regarding the last election." Our interviewing budget allowed us to conduct a fourth interview with more than 900 discussants. In addition to these interviews, 55 main respondents reported a discussant who had also been interviewed in the third wave. This was not wholly unexpected since the neighborhoods were relatively small in size with a great deal of social integrity, and the sampling rate within the neighborhoods was accordingly high. After the relationships between spouses and other relatives are removed, the resulting dyadic data set includes about 500 conversational relationships. Twenty-two percent of the relationships in the analyses of this chapter involve repeated use of a main respondent – instances when a main respondent has more than one relationship presented in the data matrix.

CONGRUENCE AND DISSONANCE BETWEEN DISCUSSION PARTNERS

The resulting data set offers a unique opportunity to examine political choices as they are imbedded within the social flow of political information. As a first step we examine (1) the objective correspondence between the preferences of main respondents and their discussants, (2) the perceptions of the political preferences of discussants held by main respondents, as well as (3) the accuracy of these perceptions. Table 7.1 summarizes this information for the relationships included in this analysis.

Table 7.1. *Proportion of main respondents who correctly perceive discussant's voting behavior (omits relatives)*

	Discussant		
	Nonvoter	Reagan	Mondale
Main respondent			
Nonvoter	.222	.790	.818
	(9)	(19)	(11)
Reagan	.400	.912	.662
	(20)	(170)	(65)
Mondale	.333	.547	.922
	(15)	(53)	(90)

Percent of voters' relationships that produce agreement
Reagan voters $170/(20 + 170 + 65) = 67\%$
Mondale voters $90/(15 + 53 + 90) = 57\%$

Voters with similarly voting discussants show a remarkably high level of accuracy in their perception of discussant behavior: 91 percent of Reagan voters with Reagan discussants correctly identified discussant behavior, and 92 percent of Mondale voters with Mondale discussants made similarly correct identifications. Accuracy is reduced somewhat within relationships that produce disagreement. Both Reagan and Mondale voters have considerably more difficulty in correctly identifying nonvoting discussants, but 66 percent of Reagan voters correctly identify discussants who voted for Mondale, and 55 percent of Mondale voters correctly identify discussants who voted for Reagan. This general pattern changes among the nonvoting respondents: They do not accurately identify fellow nonvoting discussants (22 percent), but they are fairly accurate in their identification of Reagan voters (79 percent) and Mondale voters (82 percent). Finally, Table 7.1 shows the general levels of agreement within relationships: 67 percent of the Reagan voters' relationships involve discussants who voted for Reagan, and 57 percent of the Mondale voters' relationships involve discussants who voted for Mondale.

In summary, Table 7.1 demonstrates several features regarding the political content of these relationships. First, the relationships are not overwhelmingly homogeneous in terms of voting preference. They include substantial levels of political disagreement measured in the metric of reported votes. Second, although perceptual accuracy generally increases in politically congruent relationships, clear majorities of voters in dissonant relationships recognize the disagreement.

What factors are responsible for objectively defined congruence and dissonance within the relationships? What factors are responsible for accurate and inaccurate perceptions?

THE STRUCTURAL BASIS OF POLITICAL INFORMATION

In the analysis that follows we consider the preferences of discussion partners from two different perspectives: the perceptions of those preferences
by the main respondents, and the objective reality of those preferences as
they are measured by the discussants' own self-reports. The analysis comes
in three stages. First, are the perceptions of discussion partners affected by
the political preferences of, and by the political preferences surrounding,
the main respondents? Second, are main respondents likely to have discussion partners whose objectively defined (self-reported) preferences correspond to the political preferences of, and the political preferences surrounding, the main respondents? In this instance the social context becomes
important as it affects the supply of particular political preferences, and
thus the opportunities for discussion with people holding particular preferences. Finally, do the main respondents systematically *misperceive* discussant preferences as a function of their own preferences and as a function
of the preferences surrounding them?

The relationships between networks, contexts, and individual preference
are estimated using a logit model for microdata (Hanushek and Jackson
1977). The model is appropriate to these data where the dependent variables are binary – Reagan discussant or not, perceived Reagan discussant
or not. An otherwise straightforward analysis is complicated by two factors. First, the choice and perception of discussion partners constitute one
part of an inherently simultaneous social influence process. A citizen's own
political preferences influence the choice of a discussion partner, but this
choice has subsequent consequences for the citizen's preference. These two
phenomena are inherently dynamic and interdependent. The resulting technical problem is simultaneity which leads to identification problems in the
statistical models to be estimated. Discussant choice may be a function of
individual preference and individual preference may be a function of discussant choice. Although we do not carry out the analysis for the implicit
full simultaneous system, it is appropriate to take the simultaneity into
account in estimation.

The simultaneity problem is addressed in the analysis that follows
through the construction of two instruments that measure the likelihood
that any individual (1) voted for Reagan, and (2) did not vote. Each instrument is constructed from the logistic regressions shown in Table 7.2. Thus,
rather than using dummy variables to represent the main respondents'
voting behavior, we employ the probabilities estimated by the instruments
(Maddala 1983). The instruments avoid the measurement bias due to simultaneity. They are constructed to correlate highly with reported behavior
but to be (relatively) independent of discussant behavior (Wonnacott and
Wonnacott 1979).

The second estimation problem arises due to the danger of potentially

Table 7.2. *Construction of instruments for main respondents' voting behavior*

	A. Probability of Reagan vote	B. Probability of no vote
Constant	-4.46	.92
	(4.66)	(.67)
Age	.012	-.049
	(1.38)	(3.89)
Education	.13	-.32
	(2.37)	(3.72)
Party identification	.83	—
	(12.12)	
Partisan loyalist	—	.49
		(2.68)
Interest	—	1.50
		(6.32)
N	506	506

Note: Logit model.

Age = main respondent's age in years; education = education of main respondent (years of schooling); party identification = seven-point party identification scale (0 = strong Democrat); partisan loyalist = 0 is strong partisan, 1 is weak partisan, 2 is independent leaning toward a party, 3 is independent; interest (in election) = 1 is a great deal, 2 is some, 3 is only a little, 4 is none at all.

omitted explanatory factors. Beginning at least with the work of Hauser (1974), critics of contextual research have demanded that alternative, individual-level explanations be taken into account before asserting a contextual effect. In principle this is a laudable practice, but in practice it has often meant the inclusion of long lists of correlated individual-level control variables (Kelley and McAllister 1985). It should come as no surprise that the inclusion of highly correlated explanatory variables often proves to weaken statistical purchase. That is, additional individual-level controls run the very real danger of producing excessive colinearity and, thus, a misplaced willingness to accept null hypotheses.

The research design for the South Bend study provides at least a partial solution to this second problem. By centering the individual-level variable around its mean within contexts, and by centering contextual means around the mean for the sample as a whole, orthogonality is produced between the centered individual measure, the centered neighborhood mean, and their multiplicative interaction. This does not guarantee orthogonality between these variables and the additional individual-level controls, but it decreases colinearity to a degree sufficient for the present analyses. (See the appendix for technical details.)

To summarize, the main respondent's voting behavior is measured through the use of two instruments that measure the likelihood of voting for Reagan and the likelihood of not voting. This removes the taint, technically, of causation from the discussion partner's behavior in statistical estimates of coefficients. A mean likelihood of voting for Reagan is then calculated within the neighborhood and for the sample as a whole. The individual-level Reagan vote instrument is centered around the respective neighborhood mean, the mean Reagan vote likelihood within neighborhoods is centered around the overall sample mean, and an interaction variable is formed from the product of these two variables. Finally, two demographic controls for income and education are included in each model as well.

These procedures are all well-understood and straightforward applications of statistical technique. They have the unfortunate side effect of appearing as a great deal of hocus-pocus, and thus we include a second model in each analysis that uses simple and straightforward procedures: no instruments, no centering, no interaction, no individual-level controls, where the main respondent's right-hand-side explanatory voting behavior is measured through the use of dummy variables. This simplified model corresponds to Alwin's formulation for estimating the effects of social context (Alwin 1976). We are not surprised (and the reader should be reassured) to find that the results are much the same for both models.

The centering procedure is best accomplished by calculating neighborhood means from the sample that is employed for a particular analysis. This means that, on average, neighborhood means are calculated from approximately twenty-four interviews within each neighborhood. The reliability of the neighborhood means is supported by their very high correlation ($r = .95$) with the proportion of the entire third-wave sample in each neighborhood voting for Reagan. And in this latter case the average sample size in each neighborhood is more than eighty-five. The general reliability of the survey-derived contextual measures is further supported by the correlation of third-wave neighborhood demographic means with demographic measures for the neighborhoods taken from the 1980 census. Once again, the survey measures do quite well, correlating with the census measures at the .9 level.

A final measurement issue involves response bias in the survey. Our respondents report a level of voting turnout that is in excess of the true population value. This is due in part to common overreport problems, but it is also due to the panel design. People who agree to participate repeatedly in a panel study concerned with politics are more likely to be upper-status people, and they are also more likely to be voters. Thus the question arises whether using neighborhood means provides a reliable measure of Reagan support within the neighborhoods. If the measure is intended to provide a precise estimate of neighborhood Reagan support to the base of all eligible voters, then it certainly fails the validity test because turnout is undoubtedly overestimated. But this bias does not render the measure useless for present purposes. What is central to the analysis is variation in Reagan support across neighborhoods, and the measure is appropriate for such use. As we showed, survey-derived measures of neighborhood social demographics compare very well with the census-derived measures of social demographics, and there is no reason to expect that survey-derived measures of political demographics would compare any worse. Thus, in spite of the overreport bias, there is strong reason to believe that it provides a good relative measure of Reagan support across neighborhoods.

Perhaps more important, the measure of neighborhood Reagan support has an additional virtue: It provides an estimate of Reagan support to the base of the *politically active* neighborhood population – the population that should matter both substantively and theoretically. That is, the survey ends up, de facto, being a survey of politically engaged citizens, and politically active citizens tend to be surrounded by other active citizens. Thus, from a substantive standpoint, the bias in the neighborhood means corresponds well to the bias in the sample. In terms of anticipated effects from the social context this is a desirable design feature because the politically active population is the theoretically correct population to sample.

THE PERCEPTION OF INFORMATION

Does the perception of a discussant's preference continue to vary as a function of the main respondent's own preference when the social context is taken into account? Does the perception vary as a function of Reagan support in the main respondent's context?

Table 7.3A displays the results for the logit model, which estimates the main respondent's perception of the discussant's vote as a function of both the main respondent's voting behavior and the level of Reagan support in the main respondent's neighborhood. Reagan support at both the individual and contextual levels generates coefficients that lie in the expected direction and which possess respectable t-values. Respondents who support Reagan and, to a lesser degree, respondents who are less likely to vote are more likely to perceive their discussants as Reagan voters than the respondents who support Mondale. Furthermore, respondents who live among Reagan voters are also more likely to perceive their discussants as Reagan voters.

The magnitude of these effects is characterized in Table 7.3B, where the probability of perceiving a discussant as a Reagan voter is computed from the model estimates reported in Table 7.3A, across main respondent preferences and across the observed range of neighborhood Reagan support. In order to arrive at main respondent preferences, the mean value of both instruments is calculated within the three possible behavior categories of Reagan voter, Mondale voter, and nonvoter. The two demographic controls are held constant at the sample means. (See the appendix to this chapter for details.)

Table 7.3A. *Projected Reagan vote for discussant by vote of main respondent and by Reagan support in main respondent's neighborhood, for discussants who are not relatives*

	Instruments with controls[a]	Original data
Constant	-.40	-3.15
	(.52)	(5.96)
Main respondent Reagan support	2.79	1.82
	(7.97)	(7.78)
Nonvoting main respondent	.80	1.31
	(1.08)	(3.51)
Neighborhood Reagan support	4.58	4.04
	(4.69)	(4.10)
Individual/context interaction	3.88	—
	(1.48)	
Education of main respondent	.0033	—
	(.06)	
Income of main respondent	.084	—
	(1.06)	
N	444	468

Note: Logit model. Dependent variable is projected Reagan vote. *t*-values are shown in parentheses.

Projected Reagan vote = 1 if main respondent *thinks* discussant voted for Reagan, 0 otherwise; main respondent Reagan support: original variable equals 1 if main respondent voted for Reagan, 0 otherwise (the instrument varies from .05 to .98); nonvoting main respondent: original variable equals 1 if main respondent did not vote for president, 0 otherwise (the instrument varies from .001 to .92); neighborhood Reagan support = mean level of Reagan support in main respondent's neighborhood, calculated from survey (mean instrument in left column; proportion Reagan voters in right column); individual/context interaction = main respondent Reagan support multiplied times neighborhood Reagan support; education of main respondent = years of school completed by main respondent (possible range = 0-17; approximate mean = 13); income of main respondent = family income (possible range = 1-8; approximate mean = 5, or 20 to 30 thousand dollars per year).

[a]In this column main respondent Reagan support, neighborhood Reagan support, and their interaction are centered variables.

Table 7.3B shows that, regardless of context, Reagan voters are most likely to perceive their discussants as Reagan voters and Mondale voters are least likely to do so. The table also shows that main respondents who reside among Reagan voters are more likely to perceive their discussants as Reagan voters, regardless of individual preference. This latter effect is substantial and it compares quite favorably to the effect of individual prefer- ence. Differences of 17 and 30 points are shown between the perceptions of Mondale and Reagan voters, and the difference between main respondents

Table 7.3B. *Probability that main respondent perceives discussant as a Reagan voter by main respondent's vote and by the proportional Reagan vote in the main respondent's neighborhood*

	Neighborhood Reagan support [a]	
	.31	.78
Main respondent's vote		
Reagan	.38	.87
Nonvoter	.32	.76
Mondale	.21	.57

[a] These levels represent the range on the neighborhood proportions who reported voting for Reagan, for 1,390 nonmissing third-wave respondents. The corresponding centered neighborhood means for the Reagan support instrument, upon which the estimates are based, were -.21 and .24.

Source: Estimates of Table 7.3A logit model (first column).

living in Reagan and Mondale neighborhoods ranges between 36 and 49 points.

It is important to realize that the table displays something other than marginal effects. In an 80 percent Reagan neighborhood, if all that was involved was the increased supply of Reagan voters, then the expected value should be the same: .8 for all three classes of voters. It is not. Indeed, the table shows either a discussant selection bias based on individual party preference – a consequence of personal preference imposed on social structure (Finifter 1974) – or it shows some form of misperception that is perhaps complex (Jones 1986), or it shows both.

A common question looms behind both sets of effects. Do individual preferences and contextual properties affect the perception or the reality of the socially transmitted information? Put another way, are these perceptions rooted in an accurate assessment of discussant preferences, or in an interpretation that distorts discussants' actual (self-reported) preferences? We divide this problem into two components by (1) investigating the discussants' self-reported preferences before (2) examining the main respondents' perceptions in light of discussants' self-reported preferences.

THE CONTENT OF INFORMATION

Is the objective content of socially transmitted information affected by individual preference? Is it affected by the social context? These questions are attacked indirectly by considering the discussant's self-reported vote (interpreted here as the objective political content of socially transmitted information) as a function of the main respondent's vote and the level of Reagan support in the main respondent's neighborhood. Our concern is

Table 7.4A. *Self-reported Reagan vote for discussant by vote of main respondent, and by Reagan support in main respondent's neighborhood, for discussants who are not relatives*

	Instruments with controls[a]	Original data
Constant	.28	-1.69
	(.41)	(3.72)
Main respondent Reagan support	2.11	1.03
	(6.43)	(4.91)
Nonvoting main respondent	1.03	.52
	(1.48)	(1.56)
Neighborhood Reagan support	2.72	2.34
	(3.04)	(2.68)
Individual-context interaction	2.84	—
	(1.13)	
Education of main respondent	-.076	—
	(1.46)	
Income of main respondent	.16	—
	(2.19)	
N	466	491

Note: Logit model. Dependent variable is discussant Reagan vote. *t*-values are shown in parentheses.

Discussant Reagan vote = 1 if discussant reports voting for Reagan, 0 otherwise.

[a]In this column main respondent Reagan support, neighborhood Reagan support, and their interaction are centered variables.

not with the conditions that affect perceptions of discussant preferences, but rather with the conditions that affect the reality from which these perceptions are developed.

The logit model of Table 7.4A estimates the choice of a Reagan-voting discussant as a function of the main respondent's voting preference and the main respondent's social context. Essentially the table answers the question: How powerful are your preferences, and the preferences that surround you, in determining the likelihood that you will have a discussion partner who reports a particular preference? The coefficients of central interest lie in the expected direction and each possesses a satisfactory *t*-value. Reagan supporters are more likely to have discussants who voted for Reagan, and main respondents living among Reagan voters are more likely to have discussants who voted for Reagan. The table provides evidence for the selective choice of discussants based on the preferences of main respondents, and also evidence for social coercion arising from the partisan supply available in the social context of the main respondents. It is not only the perception of discussant preferences that is affected by the context, but the reality underly-

Table 7.4B. *Probability that discussant voted for Reagan by main respondent's vote and by the proportional Reagan vote in the main respondent's neighborhood*

	Neighborhood Reagan support	
	.31	.78
Main respondent's vote		
Reagan	.46	.79
Nonvoter	.44	.71
Mondale	.31	.53

Source: Estimates of Table 7.4A logit model (first column).

ing these perceptions as well. It is not merely that citizens who live in contexts dominated by Reagan supporters are more likely to perceive their discussion partners as Reagan voters, but it is also the case that these citizens are more likely to have discussion partners who *are* Reagan voters.

The magnitudes of these effects on the probability of having a self-reported Reagan voter for a discussant are displayed in Table 7.4B. As before the effect of context compares favorably to the effect of individual preference, but the effects are somewhat less pronounced than those demonstrated in Table 7.3B. Reagan voters are 15 and 26 points more likely than Mondale voters to have a discussant who voted for Reagan. And in comparison with main respondents living among Mondale voters, main respondents who live among Reagan voters are between 22 and 33 points more likely to have a discussant who voted for Reagan. Thus the objective political content of socially transmitted information (the true partisanship of the discussant) depends both on associational choice exercised by the receiver and on the constraints on supply arising from the political composition of the social context that circumscribes the choice.

Note that there is no reason to expect the partisan behavior of discussion partners to reflect the contextual distribution of partisanship if discussion partners are chosen only on the basis of the selector's individual partisanship. The latter condition predicts the same cell entries in both columns of a given row in Table 7.4B, which manifestly is not the case. In summary, then, the objective content of the partisan signal in the political discussion process is a function of both the individual's preferences and the preferences in his surroundings. But does this make any difference? If misperception is sufficiently systematic and sufficiently strong, then objective content may not matter. We now turn to an investigation of this final issue.

THE PERCEPTION AND MISPERCEPTION OF INFORMATION

Is the misperception of socially transmitted information affected by the political preferences of the receiver? Is it affected by the social context?

Table 7.5A. *Projected Reagan vote for discussant by vote of main respondent, self-reported vote of discussant, and by Reagan support in main respondent's neighborhood, for discussants who are not relatives*

	Instruments with controls[a]	Original data
Constant	-2.33	-4.39
	(2.40)	(6.52)
Discussant Reagan vote	2.81	2.94
	(9.52)	(10.17)
Nonvoting discussant[b]	.49	.46
	(1.11)	(1.08)
Main respondent Reagan support	2.10	1.77
	(4.95)	(6.00)
Nonvoting main respondent	.62	1.39
	(.66)	(2.97)
Neighborhood Reagan support	4.20	3.45
	(3.59)	(2.93)
Individual-context interaction	3.26	—
	(1.02)	
Education of main respondent	.072	—
	(1.01)	
Income of main respondent	-.011	—
	(.11)	
N	428	450

Note: Logit model. Dependent variable is projected Reagan vote. t-values are shown in parentheses.

[a] In this column main respondent Reagan support, neighborhood Reagan support, and their interaction are centered variables.

[b] Nonvoting discussant = 1 if discussant did not vote, 0 otherwise.

More important, does misperception reinforce individual political preference in the choice of discussion partners and thereby offset the potential of the social context to expose individuals to sources of dissonant information?

To address these issues it is necessary to take account of the objective (self-reported) voting behavior of both the discussant and the main respondent when examining the main respondent's perception of the discussant's vote. The logic of the analysis is to investigate the main respondent's perception of the discussant's vote while controlling for the discussant's objectively defined (self-reported) vote. With objective content controlled, it is possible to assess whether individual misperception overwhelms the effect arising from information exposure to partisan distributions in the individual's social context.

Table 7.5B. *Probability that the main respondent perceives discussant as a Reagan voter by main respondent's vote, and by the proportional Reagan vote in the main respondent's neighborhood*

Vote of the		Neighborhood Reagan support	
Main respondent	Discussant	.31	.78
Reagan	Reagan	.68	.95
Reagan	Nonvoter	.18	.65
Reagan	Mondale	.12	.53
Nonvoter	Reagan	.64	.91
Nonvoter	Nonvoter	.15	.51
Nonvoter	Mondale	.10	.39
Mondale	Reagan	.54	.84
Mondale	Nonvoter	.10	.34
Mondale	Mondale	.07	.24

Source: Estimates of Table 7.5A logit model (first column).

Table 7.5A displays the logit model that is obtained when the main respondent's perception is treated as the left-hand-side dependent variable, and the self-reported voting behavior of both the main respondent and the discussant, as well as Reagan support in the neighborhood, are treated as right-hand-side explanatory variables. The explanatory variables of central interest produce coefficients that lie in the expected direction with crisp *t*-values. In general, main respondents are more likely to perceive a discussant as a Reagan voter if the discussant voted for Reagan (objective reality), the main respondent resides among Reagan supporters (social reality), and the main respondent supported Reagan (subjective reality). The table shows that controlling for the discussant's objective partisanship does not eliminate either individual preference effects or social context effects on perception.

These results become more provocative when the magnitudes of effects are considered in Table 7.5B. This table is striking for the probability differences it reveals between objectively homogeneous versus objectively dissonant dyads, and similarly between politically supportive and nonsupportive social contexts. These results can be made even more vivid by focusing on only the dyads of central theoretical interest and by transforming the dependent variable. In Table 7.5C the dependent variable has been transformed into the probability of correctly identifying whether the discussant is a Reagan voter. Thus a main respondent who perceives a Mondale voter as a Reagan voter is incorrect, as is a main respondent who perceives a Reagan voter as a nonvoter, and so forth.

Table 7.5C is worth some study. It shows, first, that voters tend to be accurate in their perceptions of discussion partners who agree with their own preferences. Reagan voters tend to recognize other Reagan voters,

Table 7.5C. *Probability that the main respondent correctly perceives whether or not the discussant is a Reagan voter by main respondent's vote, the discussant's vote, and by the proportional Reagan vote in the main respondent's neighborhood (for main respondents and discussants who voted for Reagan or Mondale)*

Vote of the		Neighborhood Reagan support	
Main respondent	Discussant	.31	.78
Reagan	Reagan	.68	.95
Reagan	Mondale	.88	.47
Mondale	Reagan	.54	.84
Mondale	Mondale	.93	.76

Source: Estimates of Table 7.5A logit model (first column).

and Mondale voters tend to recognize other Mondale voters. This is especially the case when surrounding preferences are supportive of the voter's preference. In both instances the social context has at least a modest effect on perceptual accuracy. But now examine disagreeing dyads.

Clearly, the greatest opportunity for contextual effects on perceptual accuracy arises in discussion dyads that involve heterogeneous preferences. This is consistent with theory about the dynamics of the political discussion process (McPhee 1963; Sprague 1982; Huckfeldt 1986; MacKuen and Brown 1987). Reagan voters are more likely to perceive Mondale discussants accurately in Mondale contexts, and they are less likely to perceive them accurately in Reagan contexts. Similarly, Mondale voters are more likely to perceive Reagan discussants accurately in Reagan contexts, and they are less likely to perceive them accurately in Mondale contexts. Thus, majority versus minority status for a particular political preference in the social context emerges as a crucial consideration in cases where there is objective political disagreement between discussion partners (Noelle-Neumann 1984).

Finally, notice that the holders of a *minority* preference are more likely to perceive the *majority* preference accurately: They are more likely to perceive their discussion partner's political preference correctly if *disagreement* is present within the dyad. Thus, the social context transforms the nature of discussion dyads even between discussion partners who share the same preference. Members of the minority evidently come to expect political dissonance during social encounters, and they frequently fail to recognize political agreement even when it is present.

INTERPRETATION

Two interpretive comments are central to understanding these results. First, a politically supportive social context sustains the receiver's misper-

ception of dissonance-producing, socially transmitted, political information. Second, members of the political minority accurately perceive members of the majority, whereas members of the majority do not accurately
perceive members of the minority.

More analysis is necessary to sort out the nature of these contextual
effects, but the substantive political consequences seem clear. Minorities
are debilitated (Miller 1956) because they are often acutely aware of their
own minority status. They are likely to recognize the variance between
their own preferences and those of their surroundings. In contrast, and for
whatever reason, dissonant information is frequently ignored by members
of the majority.

In summary, the majority enjoys a double benefit while the minority
suffers a double liability. Not only are members of the minority more likely
to encounter dissonance-producing information, they are also more likely
to recognize it as such. Not only are members of the majority less likely to
encounter dissonance-producing information, they are also less likely to
recognize it as such.

CONCLUSION

These empirical analyses emphasize the interdependence of private preference and politically relevant distributions in the individual's social context.
The interesting conditions, as expected on the basis of theory, are those of
dissonance – either between the main respondent and the discussant, or
between the main respondent and the preponderance of political opinion in
her social context. It is clear, especially from Table 7.5C, that these conditions interact.

It would appear that individuals do purposefully attempt to construct
informational networks corresponding to their own political preferences.
This exercise of choice, however, is not independent from socially determined conditions of supply – from the contextually imposed opportunity
(or lack of opportunity) for social interaction with people who hold various
political preferences. Similarly, selective misperception is apparent in the
analyses, and it too is socially conditioned.

The most interesting feature of the empirical work, perhaps the most
surprising result, and certainly the most significant for the operation of
democratic politics, is the asymmetry in choice and perception arising from
majority or minority political status in one's social context. Political majorities are able to ignore dissonant information. Political minorities, in contrast, suffer from a heightened level of vulnerability for the simple reason
that their members accurately perceive the incoming flow of dissonant
information. This analysis reveals, then, the informational coercion of political minorities achieved through mechanisms of social interaction, and

the next chapter's analysis gives more deliberate attention to the process through which such coercion is realized.

APPENDIX

The analysis conducted here benefits greatly from the statistical framework for contextual analysis set forth by Boyd and Iversen (1979), but it also marks a departure from their model. They develop their argument within the general framework of the linear model, but we adapt part of their centering procedure to this analysis using the nonlinear logit model. (Also see Iversen 1991.) The differences are sufficient to warrant a brief explanation.

First, a great virtue of the Boyd and Iversen approach is that variance may be partitioned between individual effects, contextual effects, interaction effects, and error. Because the logit model has no error term, this is impossible in the current application.

Second, Boyd and Iversen develop some useful techniques to check for appropriate model specification that cannot be used in this instance. The root cause of this inability is, once again, the lack of an error term. In particular, we are unable to check for homogeneity of error across contexts, or to check for correlation between explanatory variables and error across contexts. An especially crucial test in the Boyd and Iversen model is the ability to recover equivalent coefficients for the two-equation and the single-equation specifications, but the two-equation specification cannot be estimated using the logit model. Thus, while we cannot carry out this check using the logit model, we have carried it out with the South Bend data for other specifications of the linear model with different dependent variables (see Chapter 5), and these tests have been uniformly successful.

Our inability to carry out the Boyd and Iversen tests for misspecification is unfortunate, but it is not crippling, at least by contemporary standards. The vast majority of contextual studies, and indeed every empirical study, make assumptions regarding the behavior of error terms. The utility of Boyd and Iversen's approach is that it offers a way to check many of these assumptions, but few empirical studies are able to employ such a technology.

Finally, the Boyd and Iversen centering procedure not only transforms the explanatory variables, but the dependent variable as well, in order to maintain the original metric on the estimated coefficients. This cannot be done in the current instance, and thus the metric for coefficients is transformed. This is not a serious problem, however, because the metric for coefficients in a nonlinear model, such as the logit model, offers little interpretive insight. Instead of interpreting the magnitudes of coefficients, we use the logit model to calculate change in probabilities across values of one explanatory variable while other explanatory and control variables are held constant. As was stated in the text, social demographics are controlled at their sample means, and the instruments are controlled at their mean

Table 7.6. *Technical matters*

A. Centering procedure

Centered Reagan support

At the individual level = $R_{ij} - R_j$

Within neighborhood = $R_j - R$

where:

R_{ij} = the score of the ith respondent in the jth neighborhood on the Reagan support instrument

R_j = the mean score on the Reagan support instrument in the jth context

R = the mean score on the Reagan support instrument for the sample

B. Control values used to generate estimated probabilities in Tables 7.3B, 7.4B, 7.5B and 7.5C

Demographic means:

Education = 13

Income = 5

Means for instruments across reported vote categories:

		Reported vote	
	Reagan	No vote	Mondale
Centered Reagan vote probability	.18	-.08	-.26
Nonvote probability (not centered)	.06	.36	.09

Range on centered neighborhood Reagan support:

(calculated from the entire third wave)

Highest neighborhood level of Reagan support = .24

Lowest neighborhood level of Reagan support = -.21

levels for the respective reported vote categories. The range on centered neighborhood means for Reagan support is calculated on the basis of the entire third-wave survey in order to take advantage of the larger sample size. Table 7.6 shows the values for the controlled variables, as well as providing the central formulas for the centering procedure.

8

Choice, social structure, and the informational coercion of minorities

To what extent do people impose their own political preferences on the search for political information? To what extent is such an effort limited by the availability of alternative information sources? This chapter develops a model of discussant choice that incorporates individual political preferences as they operate within the boundaries and constraints of the social context. Special attention is given to the consequences attendant on minority and majority preference distributions in the local social milieu. We argue that rational voters exhibit rational information search behavior, but the outcome of rational search is a compromise between individual political preference and socially structured discussion opportunities.

Citizens in a democracy exercise free choice when they obtain political information. They avoid some information sources and they seek out others based on their own political preferences and viewpoints. Indeed, the availability of informational alternatives is one of the defining characteristics of democratic politics. Liberals are free to read liberal newspapers and conservatives are free to read conservative newspapers. More important for this analysis, Democrats are free to seek out other Democrats as political discussion partners, and Republicans are free to seek out other Republicans. While this sort of free informational choice is central to democracy, it is also constrained by social structure. Free choice operates within opportunities and constraints that are imposed by the social context, and the central issues pursued here are two. First, how is informational choice circumscribed by the structurally determined opportunities for social interaction, interaction that carries political content? Second, what are the consequences of these opportunities and constraints for majority and minority political preferences?

PREFERENCE AND SOCIAL INFLUENCE

Anthony Downs (1957: 229) argues that socially obtained political information is a valuable resource because it is "often relatively easy" to find sources of information that coincide with the receiver's own political preferences. That is, rational actors are well served to obtain information from other actors similarly situated because the bias and content of such information is controlled more easily than the bias and content of information obtained, for example, from television or newspapers. If one assumes the truth of Downs's proposition, how is this behavior guided by social structure?

The role of social structure in politics (social influence) depends fundamentally on two issues. First, does the choice of an information source precede or antecede the formation of a preference? Second, to what extent is the imposition of informational choice problematic in its effectiveness? At one extreme, if political preference precedes informational choice, and if informational choice is powerfully invoked, then social influence is nothing but a mirror image of an individual citizen's prior inclination. Alternatively, if informational choice precedes preference or if informational choice is incomplete, then the potential for social influence arises.

In terms of the first issue, it is clearly the case that political preference and informational choice are coupled, simultaneously, in their movement through time. Preference affects informational choice, and informational choice affects preference. This simultaneity was addressed in the previous chapter, and it is considered again here, but the primary focus of this chapter rests on the second issue: the extent to which political preferences are imposed on informational choice. That is, does the social context impose limits on the effectiveness of individual control over political information?

In the analysis that follows, two different types of effects due to the social context are considered: effects on the content of socially transmitted political information, and effects on the resistance to disagreeable, dissonance-producing information. The central argument of this chapter is that, if informational choice is made subject to available alternatives, then choice must be invoked in systematically different ways across social contexts because the availability of informational alternatives varies across contexts. In particular, minorities will be forced to invoke choice more vigorously than majorities in order to obtain the same mix of socially transmitted political information. Thus, either (1) the flow of information must be circumscribed by the supply of political information in the social context, or (2) the level of dissonance resistance must respond to these varying conditions of supply, or (3) both.

METHODS OF CONTROLLING INFORMATION

This chapter depends primarily on the third wave, postelection survey interviews of approximately 1,500 main respondents living in sixteen South Bend area neighborhoods. As part of the interview, respondents were asked the first names of the "three people you talked with most about the events of the past election year." The analysis reported here depends primarily on the main respondents' perceptions of voting preferences among discussion partners who are not relatives.

Two preliminary issues naturally arise: First, to what extent are discussion partners in agreement regarding candidate choice in the election? Second, to what extent do the main respondents systematically misperceive the voting behavior of their discussion partners? As we saw in the previous chapter, two-thirds of Reagan voters have discussants who reported voting for Reagan, and 57 percent of Mondale voters have discussants who reported voting for Mondale. This is strong evidence in support of informational choice operating in the selection of discussion partners. The self-reported voting behavior of discussion partners tends toward agreement, even though their political preferences fall far short of uniformity.

We also know from Chapter 7 that the South Bend respondents systematically misperceive the voting behavior of their discussants. They are 90 percent accurate when the discussant shares the same preference, but accuracy diminishes for discussants with opposite preferences, and it diminishes even further among nonvoting discussants. The net effect of misperception on the part of the main respondents is, of course, to overestimate the level of political agreement between themselves and their discussion partners.

In summary, political preference is impressed on the choice of a discussion partner in two ways: (1) Voters are more likely to discuss politics with people who share their preferences, and (2) voters who discuss politics with people not sharing their preferences frequently misperceive discussant preferences in a manner that is biased toward agreement. In the analysis that follows we combine both mechanisms for enforcing preference on associational choice – selective choice and selective misperception – by focusing on respondent perceptions without concern for perceptual accuracy. Our present interest is not with objective content but rather with perceived content, and with the manner in which these perceptions respond both to the biased distribution of political information in the social context, and to individual resistance in choosing discussion partners with whom preferences are perceived to be in conflict.

A MODEL OF DISCUSSANT CHOICE

An excessive focus on individual choice in the selection of discussion partners produces two problems. First, it does not take into account the varying opportunities available for discussion with politically like-minded individuals. Members of political majorities and members of political minorities choose discussion partners subject to dramatically different sets of opportunities and constraints, but a focus on individual control ignores these environmental contingencies. Second, a failure to isolate choice from supply in the formation of a politically agreeable discussion network results in a failure to examine the contribution of each and, perhaps more important, a failure to examine the manner in which *choice responds to supply* in the flow of political information.

In order to address these issues we reinterpret the logic set forth by Coleman (1964) to construct a model of discussant selection (Huckfeldt 1983b). The logic of this model is portrayed in Figure 8.1. When a citizen considers whether to discuss politics regularly with another individual, the choice is predicated on her agreement or disagreement with the potential discussant. If agreement is present, the person is accepted as a discussant, but if disagreement is present the citizen must either look for a new discussant or accept a politically disagreeable discussant, and hence a politically dissonant relationship.

The social context is important in this model because the supply of discussants with various preferences is environmentally circumscribed. People living among Republicans, *ceteris paribus,* have fewer opportunities to choose political discussants who support Mondale. Thus the expression of political preference in the choice of associates is imbedded within a set of opportunities and constraints imposed by the social context. As a limiting case, the last Mondale supporter in an otherwise homogeneously Reagan supporting environment will be unable to find a politically like-minded discussant.

The expression of choice as it is incorporated within the model must be correctly understood. Some structural settings allow little choice regarding political discussants: Husbands and wives often have little choice regarding whether they will discuss political matters, and therein lies the motive behind the high levels of political homogeneity within families (Macoby et al. 1954; McCloskey and Dahlgren 1959). Many other settings, however, severely constrain choice without necessarily producing agreement between discussion partners. Sons-in-law and fathers-in-law provide an extreme example of these sorts of relationships, but co-workers and nosey next-door neighbors with repugnant political viewpoints provide others. In short, choice is best seen as operating probabilistically. Whether a citizen continues to discuss politics with a disagreeable associate depends on numerous factors: the structural setting of the relationship, the extremity of disagreement, the intensity of viewpoints, and, as we will show, majority–minority standing on the part of a political preference.

THE LOGICAL STRUCTURE OF THE MODEL

The logic of Figure 8.1 is readily translated into an algebraic representation. We demonstrate this translation for Reagan preferences, but the same principles apply for Mondale preferences as well. Let the ith preference be for Reagan and define:

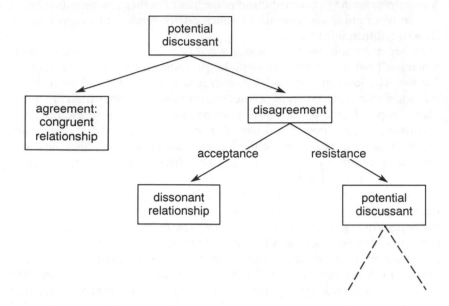

Figure 8.1 A model of discussant selection.

P_{ij} = the probability that a Reagan voter in the *j*th context has a discussant who is also a Reagan voter;

S_j = the probability of encountering another Reagan voter, or the probability that a population member in the *j*th context is a Reagan voter; and

r_{ij} = the probability that a Reagan voter in the *j*th context resists political discussion with someone who is not a Reagan voter.

After one opportunity for choosing a discussant, the probability of a Reagan voter selecting someone with a Reagan preference is the probability of encountering a Reagan supporter, if one assumes random encounters. After two opportunities, the probability is (1) the probability of randomly encountering someone who supports Reagan at the first encounter, plus (2) the product of the probability of encountering a non-Reagan voter at the first opportunity $(1 - S_j)$ multiplied times the probability of resisting discussion (r_{ij}) multiplied times the probability of encountering a Reagan supporter at the second opportunity (S_j). This logic proceeds indefinitely, and is expressed as:

$$P_{ij}[k] = S_j[1] + (1 - S_j)[1]r_{ij}S_j[2] + \ldots \quad (1)$$

where *k* indexes the probability after *k* opportunities, and where the bracketed number specifies a particular opportunity measured from some arbitrary starting point.

Several assumptions are necessary to utilize this logic, but none of them are particularly heroic. First, we are assuming that opportunities for obtaining information are contextually structured, but that individuals exercise discretion regarding whether to make use of the opportunities. In other words, the model is not deterministic. The structural setting imposes opportunities and constraints by determining supply, but people are free to make choices within that setting. The social context determines social encounters, but individuals invoke choice in deciding whether to turn an encounter into a relationship.

Second, we are assuming that the choice of a political discussant is based on political criteria, and that people do not reject politically like-minded discussants when they invoke political criteria. Other criteria might certainly be used to reject politically like-minded discussants, but the purpose of this exercise is not to incorporate the full range of motives used by individuals in selecting associates. Rather, the model is an abstraction that will help to untangle the interplay of choice and supply in the flow of political information.

Third, we are treating preferences as fixed, and thus S_j is constant across opportunities. This assumption allows the deletion of the bracketed index on discussion opportunities, and the model simplifies to:

$$P_{ij}[k] = S_j + (1 - S_j)r_{ij}S_j + \ldots + (1 - S_j)^{k-1}r_{ij}^{k-1}S_j. \tag{2}$$

Treating this geometric series as infinite, it may be rearranged into the closed form:

$$P_{ij}[k] = [S_j - r_{ij}^k(1 - S_j)^k]/[1 - r_{ij}(1 - S_j)]. \tag{3}$$

As the number of opportunities grows large, k becomes large and thus the model approaches the following equilibrium:

$$P_{ij}^* = S_j/(1 - r_{ij}(1 - S_j)). \tag{4}$$

Notice that if dissonance resistance is complete ($r_{ij} = 1$), discussion partners are politically homogeneous ($P_{ij}^* = 1$). Conversely, if people are politically indiscriminate in their choice of discussion partners ($r_{ij} = 0$), then the probability of a like-minded discussant is the same as the supply of like-minded discussants (S_j).

ESTIMATING THE MODEL

Equation 4 may be manipulated to derive a representation of dissonance resistance, or information choice:

$$r_{ij} = (P_{ij} - S_j)/(P_{ij}(1 - S_j)). \tag{5}$$

And this form of the model offers potential for better understanding the nature of minority information search. The resistance parameter (r_{ij}) is unobservable, but measures for S_j and P_{ij} are readily available. Thus r_{ij} can be estimated once a pair of values for P_{ij} and S_j are obtained.

As a first step, Table 8.1 sets forth results from a logistic regression model (Hanushek and Jackson 1977) estimating the contextually contingent probabilities that Reagan voters *believe* their discussant voted for Reagan, and that Mondale voters *believe* their discussant voted for Mondale. The social context is defined as the proportions of the neighborhood population that voted for Reagan and for Mondale in the November election. These measures are obtained directly from the third-wave survey by aggregating respondents within neighborhoods, and calculating the proportion of the neighborhood sample that voted accordingly. The regressions are carried out separately for Mondale voters and Reagan voters, and demographic controls for income and education are introduced in each equation (Hauser 1974). The analysis only includes discussants who are not relatives. If a respondent mentions more than one discussant who is not a relative, the analysis is carried out for the first mentioned nonrelative discussant.

We have also undertaken analyses of these data which incorporate the simultaneity of informational choice and political preference. This is accomplished through a two-stage estimation procedure, where the first stage constructs instruments for political preference that are (relatively) independent from the effects of informational choice. These instruments are, in turn, used in the subsequent estimation of contextual effects on informational choice. These more complicated techniques do not alter conclusions reached through the more straightforward procedures presented here.

Two features of Table 8.1 merit reader attention. First, coefficients operating on context produce crisp *t*-values and appropriate signs. Second, the magnitude of the context coefficients are remarkably similar, in spite of the fact that they are estimated independently in separate regressions. The significance of this fact will become apparent later in the analysis.

As a second step, the probability that Reagan voters perceive their discussants as Reagan voters, and the probability that Mondale voters perceive their discussants as Mondale voters, are shown across the observed range of contextual support levels in Figure 8.2A, with income and education controlled at sample means. The horizontal axis is measured according to two different but corresponding dimensions: The Reagan support proportion varies across an observed range of .3 to .8, and the Mondale support proportion is estimated as a linear function of the Reagan proportion. (A nonlinear, logistic transformation produced virtually identical results, and thus the linear function was employed.) This allows us to observe Mondale and Reagan voters in the same contexts. In other words, neighborhoods that are 30 percent Reagan are 50 percent Mondale, and we can

Table 8.1. *Perceived discussant voting behavior in the 1984 presidential election, for discussants who are not relatives (logit models)*

A. *Reagan voters' perceptions of Reagan voting on the part of their discussants by the proportional Reagan vote in the Reagan voters' neighborhoods, controlling for the Reagan voters' income and education levels (the dependent variable is perceived Reagan vote)*

	Coefficient	*t*-value
Intercept	-.13	.17
Neighborhood Reagan support	3.53	3.14
Individual education	-.07	1.21
Family income	.04	.51
N	449	

B. *Mondale voters' perceptions of Mondale voting on the part of their discussants by the proportional Mondale vote in the Mondale voters' neighborhood, controlling for the Mondale voters' income and education levels (the dependent variable is perceived Mondale vote)*

	Coefficient	*t*-value
Intercept	.10	.10
Neighborhood Mondale support	3.55	2.12
Individual education	-.03	.51
Family income	-.08	1.02
N	303	

Note: Perceived Reagan vote = 1 if main respondent thinks discussant voted for Reagan, 0 otherwise; perceived Mondale vote = 1 if main respondent thinks discussant voted for Mondale, 0 otherwise; neighborhood Reagan support = proportion of respondents in main respondent's neighborhood who voted for Reagan; neighborhood Mondale support = proportion of respondents in main respondent's neighborhood who voted for Mondale; individual education = respondent's years of school (range: 4-17; mean: 13); family income = respondent's family income (range: 1-8; mean: 5).

observe the consequences of such a context for information flow among both sets of voters.

Figure 8.2A shows clearly that perceptions of discussants march with the social context. As we have seen in Chapter 7, this is the result of two facts: Objective content is structured by the distribution of political preferences in the social context, misperception is structured by the same conditions, and both move in the same direction. That is, people are more likely to have like-minded discussants if they live in contexts with higher densities of other like-minded people, and independently of this first fact, they are more likely to perceive their discussants as like-minded if they live in contexts with higher densities of other like-minded discussants. For the voter, however, the only reality that matters is the reality that is

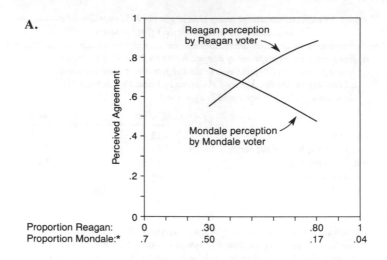

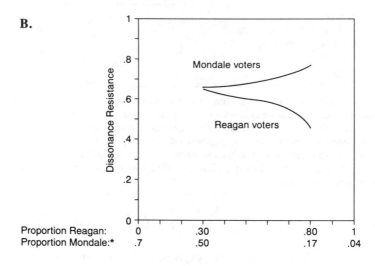

Figure 8.2. Perceived agreement and resistance to dissonance across observed neighborhood contexts.

Top: Probability that voters perceive discussant preferences as being the same as their own.

Bottom: Dissonance resistance probability among Reagan and Mondale voters.

*For both parts of the figure, the proportion Mondale is estimated as:
$$.7-.66 \times (\text{proportion Reagan}).$$

perceived, and thus the entire analysis here is performed in terms of voter perceptions.

Figure 8.2A shows something else. The range of Reagan support is higher overall than the range of Mondale support, and the probability that a Reagan voter's discussant is also a Reagan voter is higher overall than the probability that a Mondale voter's discussant is a Mondale voter. In short, Reagan voters are in a majority, and thus they have greater opportunities to locate like-minded discussants. Contextual support for Reagan varies approximately from .3 to .8, while estimated support for Mondale varies approximately from .17 to .5. Thus, at best, Mondale voters found themselves in a neighborhood context that was evenly divided between supporters and nonsupporters of Mondale.

The plots of Figure 8.2A are used to obtain estimates of dissonance resistance (see equation 5), which are in turn plotted in Figure 8.2B for both Reagan voters and Mondale voters. The resulting picture is quite striking: For both groups of voters, greater majority status produces less resistance to disagreeable discussion partners. As voters come to occupy a more extreme minority status they become more resistant to discussion partners with opposite preferences. In other words, minorities are more likely to turn inward by resisting opposing preferences. In keeping with their minority status, Mondale voters show a higher overall level of dissonance resistance. Indeed, their lowest level of dissonance resistance is about the same as the highest level of dissonance resistance among Reagan voters. What do these results mean?

THE UPHILL STRUGGLE OF POLITICAL MINORITIES

The chief lessons to be learned from Figure 8.2B are that (1) political minorities turn inward in an effort to avoid a flood of disagreeable information, but (2) their efforts are doomed to failure. This is readily seen in two different ways. Mondale voters are more likely than Reagan voters to resist dissonance, but they are also more likely to experience dissonance. Both Reagan voters and Mondale voters are more likely to resist dissonance if they occupy minority status, but they are also more likely to experience dissonance if they occupy minority status. Political minorities face an uphill struggle as informational choice is overwhelmed by informational supply, and supply is determined by the political distribution in the local social context.

These results are consistent with a literature pointing out that minority-status social groups turn inward in the face of majority dominance (Noelle-Neumann 1984). Finifter (1974) studied Republican autoworkers at an automobile factory and showed that they avoided association with the majority-status Democrats. Berger (1960) studied middle-class residents of a working-class suburb, and found that they were socially isolated, and likely to have moved away. Gans (1967) studied a middle-class suburb and found that a range of minority-status social groups – the working class, Jews, old people – did not fit in with the dominant social life. Our own results suggest that increased resistance to interaction outside the group is a natural consequence of minority status, but so is increased contact outside the group.

The theoretical, as opposed to empirical, comparison of dissonance resistance among Mondale and Reagan voters is furthered by observing information flow across the entire theoretical range of variation. That is, how do Reagan voters and Mondale voters compare when both are lo-cated in contexts where, say, 20 percent of the population holds compati-ble vote preferences. This is accomplished in Figure 8.3. Information flow and dissonance resistance are virtually identical across the two groups of voters. At theoretically comparable levels of contextually determined con-ditions of supply, Reagan and Mondale voters are equally likely to reject discussants with opposite preferences, and thus they are equally likely to have discussants with the same preferences. Thus, the higher level of attempted introversion among Mondale voters is wholly a function of minority status.

Once again, Figure 8.3B must be seen in light of Figure 8.3A. At the same time that Reagan voters become more resistant to dissonant informa-tion as the supply of dissonant information increases, so they are simulta-neously more exposed to dissonance! It is not that choice is absent, but rather that it is ultimately doomed to failure. Even high levels of resistance cannot insulate minorities from exposure to majority preference.

South Bend neighborhoods may, of course, be important elements of social structure in a way that Phoenix neighborhoods or Houston neighbor-hoods are not. (For contrary evidence on this issue, see Huckfeldt and Sprague 1990.) The possibility of such variation does not compromise our analysis. The important point is not that informational choice is circum-scribed by the neighborhood, but rather that it is circumscribed by social structure. The structural specifics, and their political significance, undoubt-edly vary from place to place and from time to time, but this does not call into question the importance of social structure more generally. If the locus of social interaction changes, then the political significance of structural elements will change as well. Indeed, many of these structural elements march together: Residents of working-class neighborhoods are more likely to drink at working-class bars, worship at churches with high densities of working-class parishioners, and come into contact with more working-class employees at their place of work. Our goal is not to make a compelling case for the importance of neighborhoods, but rather to offer empirical support for the ways in which individual choice is circumscribed by important struc-tural elements.

A.

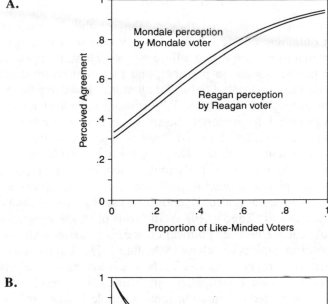

B.

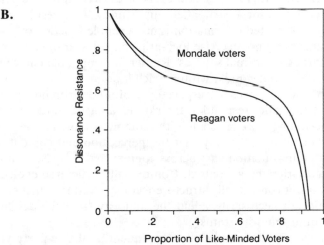

Figure 8.3. Perceived agreement and resistance to dissonance across the full possible range of theoretically comparable contexts.

Top: Probability that voters perceive discussant preferences as being the same as their own.

Bottom: Dissonance resistance probability among Reagan and Mondale voters.

CONCLUSION

Voters are certainly rational, and they exhibit sensibly rational search procedures in obtaining political information. Voters seek to control socially transmitted information in two different ways: They attempt to locate politically compatible discussion partners, and they reinterpret dissonant information in a more favorable light. Taken alone, however, these facts tell us little regarding the flow of socially transmitted information. The crucial fact regarding informational choice is not that it is rational, but rather that it is structurally imbedded. Few people intentionally expose themselves to repugnant political views, but many people have no other alternative. Thus rational individuals make their choices at particular times, in particular places, subject to particular constraints. Informational choice may be rational, but it also depends on a particular configuration of structural circumstances (Boudon 1986). In terms of this analysis, the expression of political preference (political choice) is fundamentally dependent on the political choices of others (Schelling 1978). On the argument and analysis offered here, rational political choice is a compromise between private preference and socially supplied opportunity. As a result, the content of socially transmitted information is not a simple function of political preference. Citizens do not exercise lock-grip control over the information they acquire through informal sources. Rather informational choice is circumscribed by the social context within which it occurs.

The political consequences are especially profound for minority preferences. Political minorities respond to their disadvantaged status by turning inward – by becoming more resistant to the communicators of disagreeable preferences. Thus it is not simply that the perception and content of socially transmitted information vary across context, but it is also that informational choice varies across context. Contextually structured choice does not, however, offset contextually structured supply. And thus higher levels of resistance do not necessarily shield the minority from the debilitating consequences of its minority status.

In his classic work on the minority consequences of one-party voting, Warren Miller (1956) showed that the image of cohesive minorities failed to account for the political disorganization and disarray of those who hold minority preferences. Our analysis suggests that minorities may be both cohesive and in disarray. At the same time that they are resistant to contacts with the majority, they are also unable to control such contacts, and thus they are bombarded with dissonance-producing information.

In the chapter that follows we shift our focus from the acquisition of information and the logic of information search to the consequences of that information for individual behavior. What are the consequences of socially supplied information for the preferences of individual voters?

9

Discussant effects on vote choice: Intimacy, structure, and interdependence

Political discussion during an election campaign is an important vehicle of social influence – a means whereby the preferences of individuals are brought into correspondence with political surroundings. Correspondingly, the study of discussion effects is not simply an examination of dyadic information flows. Rather, it is one part of a more thorough explication of the political linkages that lie between individuals and groups within the society, and of the manner in which individual politics is imbedded within the larger community. This chapter addresses a series of questions related to the influence of political discussion. To what extent are political preferences affected by discussion? What types of discussant relationships are most likely to foster political influence? What types of discussants are most influential?

One important arena of social influence in an election campaign is the person-to-person transmission of political opinion and preference that occurs during political discussion. When one citizen discusses politics with another citizen, the stage is set for the politics of one or both discussion partners to be affected. Indeed, these dyadic encounters provide the most common characterization of social influence – the model of two citizens engaged in earnest political discourse. The characterization is, of course, often divorced from reality. Political discussion is typically unstructured, episodic, and frequently unsustained. More important, political discussion is not the only or even the most important form of social influence (Eulau 1986; Przeworski 1974). Many mechanisms of social influence bypass discussion entirely – yard signs, bumper stickers, lapel pins, and so on. Furthermore, in many social settings, particular political preferences are rendered unthinkable, much less being topics of rational discourse. How many blacks tried to influence their discussion partners to vote for Ronald Reagan in 1984? How many Mississippi whites tried to influence their discussion partners to vote for Walter Mondale? Thus, when social influence is exceptionally potent, the influence due to the particular mechanism of political discussion becomes problematic.

Nevertheless, political discussion becomes an important vehicle of social influence in many political environments – a means whereby the preferences of individuals are brought into correspondence with social surroundings. Furthermore, the transmission of political preference through informal discussion is not simply the product of structurally arbitrary citizen pairings, produced as the result of idiosyncratic associational choice (Huckfeldt 1986). Rather, the choice of a discussion partner is structurally bounded and circumscribed by available alternatives. Political discussion thus becomes the vehicle through which dominant preferences within the larger community are transmitted to the individuals who are members of that community (R. Putnam 1966).

The study of discussant effects is not simply an exercise in understanding dyadic information flows. Rather, it is one part of a more thorough explication of the linkages that tie individuals to groups within the society, and of the manner in which individual politics is structurally imbedded within larger social aggregates (Cox 1974; Orbell 1970; MacKuen and Brown 1987; Weatherford 1982). Several issues become crucial: the conception and measurement of discussant influence, the extent to which political influence occurs between discussion partners, the characteristics of participants and relationships that encourage and inhibit the flow of influence, the macro-consequences of various micro-influence models.

SOURCES OF SOCIAL INFLUENCE IN POLITICS

A first question immediately arises: What are the factors that encourage and inhibit the political influence of one citizen on another? Who is affected by whom, under what circumstances? Answers to this question have been offered from the perspectives of several research traditions: public choice theories of citizen information processing, social network analyses of behavioral interdependence, social psychological assessments of personal influence, examinations of the political socialization process.

Perhaps the most significant studies of interpersonal political influence have been these latter examinations of socialization within families (Jennings and Niemi 1968, 1974, 1981; Tedin 1974; Dawson, Prewitt, and Dawson 1977). As a result of these socialization studies, the family has been widely recognized as a preeminent agent of social influence with long-lasting political consequences, not only for the individual but also for the political system (P. Beck 1974). Indeed, the family frequently becomes the standard by which other sources of social influence are evaluated, and thus socialization research has not only established the role of the family, it also has served to define implicitly the mechanisms through which social influence is realized.

One frequently drawn conclusion from socialization research is that personal influence is a product of the intimacy and access within primary social groupings (Dawson et al. 1977: 115–16). Within this general context, several efforts have aimed explicitly at identifying the factors that minimize and maximize the family's influence. Tedin (1974) demonstrates that the effect of parental viewpoints on children is greatest when (1) children accurately recognize the parents' preferences and (2) the attitudinal object is of high salience. Jennings and Niemi (1974) also show that the parental effect on partisanship is stronger when (1) the parents' preferences are correctly perceived and when (2) the level of attention devoted to politics is higher within the family. Ironically, socialization research has not offered consistent support for the importance of intimacy within families – the effect of parent on child is not necessarily maximized within families that are more cohesive. Indeed, Tedin (1974: 1587–8) and Jennings and Niemi (1968, 1974: 80–1) find only mixed evidence to support the argument that the transmission of parental preference is affected by modes of interaction within the family.

Most of the political socialization studies lie within a broader social-psychological tradition that emphasizes particular features of personal influence settings. In proposing a theory of personal influence to account for the impact of social sources on a target individual, Latane (1981: 344) identifies strength, immediacy, and number as the important properties of sources. He argues that social influence is more effective when the source of influence is salient and intense, when contact between the source and the target is both direct and close in time and space, when the target has multiple contacts with sources sending the same message.

Burt (1987) refers to this general framework as a social cohesion model in his analysis of the Coleman et al. (1966) medical innovation study. As it is defined by Burt (1987: 1289), "The cohesion model focuses on socialization between ego and alter. The more frequent and emphatic communication is between ego and alter, the more likely that alter's adoption will trigger ego's."

It is not difficult to understand why this model has appealed to so many political scientlsts. First, it accounts for the influence of families. Second, it builds on an intellectual tradition that sees democratic citizenship rooted in well-informed citizens engaged in earnest discourse, attempting to persuade one another of their own viewpoints. Indeed, some variant of this general model has provided the basis for nearly every investigation of social influence in politics, including the seminal studies of the Columbia school (Lazarsfeld et al. 1948; Berelson et al. 1954).

As an alternative, Burt suggests a structural equivalence model to account for patterns of personal influence. According to a structural equivalence explanation, people base their behavior on models provided by others who are similarly situated – people in like structural circumstances. Alter's influence on ego depends on the extent to which alter occupies a structural location that is similar to ego, and it is independent of the qualitative dimensions of the relationship between alter and ego. Furthermore, structural equivalence is not simply a matter of people sharing the same characteristics as other individuals – it is rather the result of people sharing the same patterns of social relationships and social interaction patterns.

Given a complete mapping of social networks, individuals are structurally equivalent when they exhibit identical patterns of social ties.

The distinction between social cohesion and structural equivalence models might be further clarified in terms of exemplary discussant dyads. A dyad is marked by social cohesion to the extent that the relationship is characterized by intimacy, trust, respect, access, and mutual regard. In contrast, a dyad is marked by structural equivalence to the extent that individuals share the same social relationships. Once again, a rigorous operational determination of structural equivalence requires a comprehensive mapping of relevant social relationships. Such network data are extremely rare, but it is possible to identify some of the conditions that might give rise to structural equivalence: Individuals are more likely to be structurally equivalent if they live in the same neighborhoods, drink at the same bars, worship at the same churches, work at the same places of employment, and so on. Relationships marked by social cohesion are often characterized by structural equivalence as well, but they need not be, and thus it is important to maintain the distinction.

Applying the structural equivalence model to politics suggests that traditionally defined efforts at persuasion are irrelevant – social influence is a blunter instrument than persuasive argumentation among friends based on the political merits of a particular case. In other words, social influence in politics might be divorced from discussion, argumentation, and debate. Rather, it would depend on a shared social location on the part of the sender and the receiver of informal political messages.

The interpretative justification for structural equivalence provided by Burt is social-psychological in its underpinnings. In the context of the medical innovation study (Burt 1987; Coleman et al. 1966), doctors realized status anxiety when other doctors in similar structural circumstances adopted a new medicine. "Once the occupants of his status begin adopting, ego is expected to follow suit rapidly in order to avoid the embarrassment of being the last to espouse a belief or practice that has become a recognized feature of occupying his status" (Burt 1987: 1294).

The structural equivalence argument might also be considered in light of a rational choice perspective toward the acquisition of political information. Given the potentially high cost of political information, it is eminently reasonable for citizens to obtain such information at a discounted price through discussion with other individuals. Rational citizens are not indiscriminate, however, in their social search for information. Rather, they choose as informants people with political biases that are congenial to their own (Downs 1957).

How does the search for a congenial bias take place? To the extent that people act rationally in politics, they are likely to pay more attention to advice from people who are similarly located within the social structure. Thus, even if ego and alter are friends, ego might be more likely to take alter's advice if she perceives that alter has similar interests arising out of a similar structural location. Thus we end up at a similar end point, from a strikingly different theoretical perspective. The important theoretical proposition for present purposes is a threefold denial. Structural equivalence, as an interpretation of politically significant social influence, does not assume (1) that the influential transmission of political information necessarily occurs between friends, or (2) that political argumentation is the primary vehicle of political influence, or (3) that the dynamics of persuasion are central to the political influence process.

In a reconsideration of the famous Asch experiments, Ross, Bierbrauer, and Hoffman (1976) provide a microsociological basis for this general viewpoint. Social influence is less likely to occur if an individual has a compelling rationale for dismissing a divergent viewpoint – a rationale that is more likely to be present in ambiguous settings. In the Asch experiments, such a rationale was absent. If everyone says that the longer line is shorter than the shorter line, how can an individual quickly dismiss these judgments? Alternatively, if alter says that Ronald Reagan is the better candidate, ego might be able to dismiss this judgment either because alter has interests that diverge from ego, or because alter has engaged in a questionable analysis of a complex and ambiguous subject. Thus, perhaps ironically, the lack of ambiguity in the Asch experiments *heightens* the potential for social influence. Along these same lines, when ambiguity *is* present, ego is more likely to accept alter's judgment to the extent that ego and alter occupy a common structural location that is perceived as creating common interests and viewpoints.

In summary, we see two very different conceptions of social influence. In one instance, influence is a function of intimacy and respect – social cohesion. In the other, influence is a function of a shared location in social structure. As we shall see, these explanations are not only important for understanding the nature of social influence between individuals, but also for understanding aggregate political consequences of social influence processes. In the analysis that follows we consider factors that might explain the influence that occurs within politically relevant social relationships, and the extent to which these factors coincide with these two different perspectives. A full and complete test of the two explanations lies beyond the bounds of this chapter, but they provide a useful framework from which to address the analysis of social influence in politics that follows.

MEASURING SOCIAL INFLUENCE

An analysis of the effects that arise from political discussion in an election campaign is rendered problematic by several sources of simultaneity (Berelson et al. 1954). First and most important, influence flows in two directions, and thus showing a strong correlation between the political preferences of discussant pairs does not isolate the unique effects that are due to each discussion partner. Are the voting preferences of egos and alters coincidental because alters affect egos, or because egos affect alters?

Second, do the preferences of discussion partners correspond because discussion is influential, or because discussants tend to share common sets of attributes that translate directly and unambiguously into individually coincidental understandings of social and political life? The same structural factors that bring individuals together in social and political relationships also tend to create social and political homogeneity within relationships. Thus, showing that political preferences correspond within relationships does not provide sufficient evidence to support the claim that preferences are predicated on social interaction – they may be simply the products of shared attributes.

Third, in order to argue that discussion affects preference, we must take account of each discussant's own prior partisan commitment. In this way we attempt to separate short-term discussant effects on vote choice from the more diffuse, long-term effects on party loyalty (Segal and Meyer 1974). The standard measurement procedure for such an undertaking is to incorporate party identification as a surrogate for the citizen's standing political commitment, but Franklin and Jackson (1983) show that current political preference (in the form of vote choice) affects partisan orientation at the same time that partisan orientation affects vote choice. Thus, the simultaneity problem is further compounded.

In summary, discussion partners might affect one another in two ways: by a short-term effect on vote choice and by a long-term effect on basic partisan orientations. Furthermore, the partisan orientation of each partner affects that individual's vote choice, and vote choice reinforces partisan orientation. Finally, each individual's own social attributes produce independent exogenous effects, both on vote choice and on partisan orientation. And thus, to the extent that these attributes are shared by discussion partners, it is entirely possible to exaggerate the direct effects of alter on ego by failing to take account of ego's own characteristics and predispositions.

OBSERVING SOCIAL INFLUENCE

The observational data that would be necessary to disentangle each of these component parts fully and directly are unavailable, and very nearly unimaginable. Some analysis is possible, however, using South Bend network data. A battery of questions was included in the third, postelection survey, which asked main respondents to provide the names of the three people with whom they "talked with most about the events of the past election year." A fourth-wave, one-stage snowball survey was conducted subsequently with more than 900 discussants identified in this manner. On the basis of these third- and fourth-wave interviews, we are able to construct a data matrix of relationships between our third-wave main respondents and their fourth-wave discussants. Each observation in the data matrix is a relationship that includes self-report information from both the main respondent and the discussant, as well as the main respondent's perception of various discussant characteristics. Especially in the case of main respondents, individuals are frequently included in more than one relationship, and thus in more than one observation within the data matrix. Each dyad is, of course, unique and independent.[1]

This data base does not alleviate all problems of measurement posed earlier, however, and thus we must turn to several statistical procedures for assistance. First, in order to take account of the main respondent's social attributes and political predispositions, we consider a range of political, social, and demographic information: income, education, age, union membership, religion, partisan identification. We also consider a contextual measure for each main respondent's neighborhood – the proportion of respondents in the neighborhood who report that a household member belongs to a union. (Neighborhood union membership is measured on the basis of the third-wave main respondent sample, with an approximate n-size of ninety-four respondents in each neighborhood.) By taking account of these various factors, we hope to guard against the possibility that the appearance of shared preferences between discussion partners is actually a spurious by-product of shared attributes and predispositions, rather than the result of social influence.

Second, in order to take account of the simultaneity between the main respondent's partisan orientation and the main respondent's vote choice, we employ a modified, three-category party-identification measure that minimizes the reciprocal effect of 1984 vote choice on partisanship. This modified party-identification measure is based on two dummy variables derived from the initial party-identification question, which asks people whether they are Democrats, Republicans, or independent. One dummy variable measures whether the respondents are independent, and another measures whether they are Republican identifiers, with the excluded baseline category being Democratic identification. Most evidence suggests that short-term movement in party identification lies within partisan categories: from weak to strong, strong to weak, true independent to an independent leaning toward a party, and so on. Thus the dummy-variable procedure should allow us to take account of the main respondent's partisan orientation without introducing major contamination due to short-term simultaneous effects on partisan orientation.

1 We base this assertion of independence on the weakness of ties that will be demonstrated among nonrelative discussants and, in particular, on the low level of reciprocity between discussion partners (see Table 9.2).

Including even this modified form of party identification potentially creates problems, of course. To the extent that the main respondent's partisan orientation is influenced endogenously, either by the main respondent's vote choice or by the discussant, we run the risk of contaminating other estimates. Thus, the analyses that are discussed here have been replicated using both the full seven-category party-identification measure and using an instrument for partisan orientation that is purged of these simultaneous endogenous effects. None of these procedures compromises the central findings of this chapter.

Finally, we must also take account of the simultaneity that is inherent in the vote choices of the main respondent and the discussant (Maddala 1983; Wonnacott and Wonnacott 1979). Our goal is to produce a vote instrument for the discussant that is purged of the reciprocal influence due to the main respondent. This will allow us, in turn, to estimate the independent effect of the discussant on the main respondent. The estimation of the instrument is shown in Table 9.1, using a logistic regression of vote choice on the various demographics as well as the modified three-category form of party identification. The parameters used in constructing the discussant vote instrument are estimated on the basis of the third-wave, postelection interview with main respondents in order to make use of the larger sample that was interviewed at this wave of the study.

On the basis of this logistic regression, a Reagan vote probability is assigned to each of the discussants in the matrix of discussion dyads. Each discussant's score on each of the regression's right-hand-side variables is weighted by the coefficient estimated from the third-wave survey to produce an assigned score on the vote instrument. The end product of these procedures is an estimated probability of Reagan support for each discussant that varies from .072 to .985. A probability is thus assigned to each discussant and treated as a vote instrument – the likelihood of a Reagan vote apart from the effect of the main respondent's influence.[2]

Once again, in order to maximize sample size, the parameters for the discussant vote instrument are estimated on the basis of the entire third-wave, postelection survey of main respondents, including only main respondents who are white and reported voting in the presidential election. The instrument is constructed for each discussant on the basis of these parameter estimates and the discussant's own characteristics. All other analyses in this chapter are based on the matrix of discussion dyads, for main respondents who are white and reported voting. These combined procedures allow us to estimate the independent effects of the main respondent's

2 We have made a slight modification and correction in the construction of the instrument from procedures used in an earlier analysis (Huckfeldt and Sprague 1991). The two versions of the instrument are correlated at .96, but the range of the new instrument is somewhat larger.

Table 9.1. *Construction of instrument for discussant vote choice*

	Coefficient	*t*-value
Constant	-.74	1.05
Union member	-.75	3.89
Education	-.02	.35
Income	.05	.84
Age	-.01	1.98
Religion	.28	1.62
Independent	2.04	11.35
Republican	4.90	13.18
N	1,064	

Note: Logit model estimated on the basis of the third-wave, postelection survey of main respondents.

Vote (dependent variable): 1 = Reagan, 0 = Mondale; union membership: 1 = someone in household belongs, 0 otherwise; education: schooling in years (17 = post college graduate); income: household income scale varies from 1 to 8; age: age in years; religion: 1 = Protestant, 0 otherwise; Independent identifier: 1 if respondent identifies as an Independent, 0 otherwise; Republican identifier: 1 if respondent identifies as a Republican, 0 otherwise.

partisan orientation and the discussant's vote choice on the vote of the main respondent.[3]

BASELINE DISCUSSANT EFFECTS

According to Lasswell (1948: 37), communication can be conveniently described according to: "Who, says what, in which channel, to whom, with what effect." This chapter is concerned with the "who" of discussion partners, and the "whom" of those who identify the discussion partners. This distinction is an important one, because the level of reciprocity within these dyads is quite low. As Table 9.2 shows, the level of reciprocity is especially low among dyads involving discussion partners who are not relatives. Only about 15 per-

3 In summary, an estimate of each discussant's vote is constructed that extracts and eliminates the reciprocal flow of influence from the main respondent to the discussant. This estimate is derived in two steps. First, the model parameters of Table 9.1 are obtained using data from our main respondents in order to exploit the larger main respondent sample. Using a logit model, the *main respondent's* vote is expressed as a function of several exogenous factors: the *main respondent's* union membership, education, income, age, religion, and partisanship. We treat the Table 9.1 parameters as estimates of the relationship between the vote and these exogenous factors for both the main respondents and discussants. As a second step, a probability of Reagan support is assigned to each *discussant* based on the Table 9.1 parameters for the *main respondent* and the same set of exogenous information obtained in interviews with the *discussant*. Once again, we are assuming that these factors relate to vote choice among discussants in the same way as for main respondents. In this manner a vote instrument is derived which estimates the discussant's vote wholly as a function of the discussant's own exogenously determined characteristics, apart from main respondent influence.

Table 9.2. *Levels of reciprocity between discussion partners by type of relationship*

	Type of relationship		
	Not a relative	Spouse	Other relative
Did discussion partner choose main respondent?			
Yes	15.0%	50.0	20.7
No	85.0	50.0	79.3
N	472	160	208

Note: Discussant interviews were undertaken in an effort to maximize the number of interviews with nonrelatives. Thus, the marginals do not reflect the actual incidence of relationship types among political discussants.

cent of all the nonrelative dyads involve an identified discussion partner who, in turn, named the main respondent as a discussion partner. Thus, at least in this sense, being a discussion partner tends to be a one-way street. These analyses concern the impact of a discussant named by the main respondent on the preference of the main respondent, and this is most certainly not symmetric with an examination of the reciprocal pathway of influence.

We are interested in a particular channel of informal social communication – political discussion – but we have no way of knowing "what" was actually said in these discussions. Indeed, absent a highly abstracted experimental design, such knowledge would be impossible to obtain. We are, however, able to characterize the nature of relationships on the basis of various pieces of information obtained from the main respondent and from the discussant. In terms of the particular content of the discussion, we make the assumption that Reagan voters send cues favorable to Reagan, and Mondale voters send cues favorable to Mondale. This assumption greatly simplifies reality. A discussant's vote preference is much more likely to be perceived accurately in an environment where more people hold the same preference. Thus the transmission of information between discussion partners, and the nature of the social influence process, must inevitably be seen in terms of the larger social structures within which the relationship is imbedded (E. Katz and Lazarsfeld 1955).

This chapter is devoted to an examination of "what effect" discussion has on the main respondent. Our basic procedure is to estimate a logit model that regresses vote choice (among main respondent voters) against the vote preference instrument for the discussant while controlling for the partisan orientation of the main respondent, a series of main respondent demographics, and neighborhood union membership. This model is then used to consider the magnitude of the discussant effect by holding all other variables constant while the discussant vote preference is varied, subject to various contingencies. Most of the other variables are held constant at mean values,

Table 9.3. *Main respondent vote by main respondent partisanship, main respondent demographics, and discussant vote*

	All pairs	Spouses	Nonrelatives
Intercept	-3.95	.19	-3.55
	(3.40)	(.06)	(2.32)
Independent	1.66	1.31	1.46
	(7.02)	(1.89)	(4.73)
Republican	4.51	11.89	4.16
	(9.10)	(.55)	(6.48)
Union membership	-.68	-1.94	-.84
	(2.68)	(2.17)	(2.50)
Neighborhood union	-.30	-6.94	.03
membership	(.24)	(2.06)	(.02)
Education	.08	-.11	.06
	(1.41)	(.66)	(.84)
Income	.12	-.11	.20
	(1.49)	(.51)	(1.72)
Age	.006	-.004	.01
	(.67)	(.15)	(1.15)
Religion	.55	1.23	.44
	(2.44)	(1.83)	(1.47)
Discussant preference	1.49	4.72	.50
	(4.09)	(3.75)	(1.04)
N	643	126	354

Note: The model is estimated separately for all discussant pairs, married discussant pairs, and nonrelative discussant pairs. Logit model; t-values are in parentheses.

Neighborhood union membership: proportion of third-wave respondents in each neighborhood who report that someone in their household belongs to a union (approximate sample in each neighborhood is 94 respondents); discussant preference: this instrument measures a probability of Reagan support that varies from .072 to .985.

but union membership is held constant at nonmember, religion is held constant at Protestant, and party identification is held constant at independent.

These procedures are employed in Table 9.3 and Figure 9.1 to consider the political effect of discussants according to the nature of the relationship that ties together the discussant pairs. A general discussant effect is demonstrated within all the discussant pairs, but this general effect is greatly magnified among spouses, and greatly attenuated among nonrelatives. Indeed, the effect of nonrelative discussants fails to generate a satisfactory t-value, and its magnitude is quite small. In contrast, the vote of a married main respondent is very sensitive to the preference of a spouse who is named as a discussant: The probability of a Reagan vote by the main respondent varies

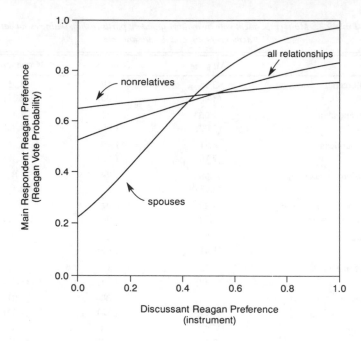

Figure 9.1. Discussant effects by type of relationship. *Source:* Table 9.3 logic estimates.

from less than .1 to more than .9 across a range of zero to unity for the discussant preference. In summary, some relationships matter more than others, and the discussant who is a spouse is particularly influential.

The analysis of political influence between spouses is worthy of extended attention, and it is treated separately using these data in the next chapter. The remainder of this chapter's analysis focuses explicitly on the political influence that occurs among nonrelatives. As Figure 9.1 demonstrates, the influence of these nonrelative relationships does not appear to be impressive – at least in the aggregate when compared with the effects that occur within families. As we shall see, however, under some circumstances such relationships become extremely influential at the microlevel, and their significance for democratic politics at the macrolevel cannot be overstated.

THE IMPORTANCE OF CORRECT PERCEPTION

In addressing levels of influence among nonrelative discussion partners, it is important to consider the level of perceptual accuracy that occurs within the dyads. A consistent finding within the family socialization studies is

Table 9.4. *Main respondent vote by main respondent partisanship, main respondent demographics, and discussant vote, for nonrelative discussant pairs*

	Correct perception	Incorrect perception
Intercept	-5.30	.87
	(2.58)	(.26)
Independent	1.67	.85
	(4.07)	(1.25)
Republican	3.99	9.79
	(5.74)	(.47)
Union membership	-1.04	.52
	(2.38)	(.67)
Neighborhood union membership	1.82	-8.59
	(.87)	(1.79)
Education	.12	.07
	(1.23)	(.43)
Income	.12	.20
	(.79)	(.80)
Age	.02	-.01
	(1.58)	(.48)
Religion	-.14	.03
	(.36)	(.05)
Discussant preference	1.62	-1.58
	(2.55)	(1.39)
N	245	76

Note: The model is estimated separately for main respondents who correctly perceive the discussant vote and for main respondents who incorrectly perceive the discussant vote. Logit model; *t*-values are in parentheses.

that influence is predicated on correct perception. What is the consequence of misperception on the flow of influence within a discussion dyad?

Table 9.4 and Figure 9.2 consider nonrelative dyads, sorted according to whether the main respondent correctly perceives the discussant's vote choice. This is accomplished with two separate models, one measuring the effect of discussants whose vote preferences are correctly perceived by the main respondents, and the other measuring the effect of discussants whose vote preferences are incorrectly perceived. In comparison to the baseline nonrelative effect of Table 9.3 and Figure 9.1, the magnitude of the discussant effect increases among main respondents who correctly perceive the discussant's preference. In contrast, while the *t*-value for the coefficient is not of satisfactory magnitude, the effect among those who perceive incorrectly lies in a reversed (negative) direction. This means that, among main

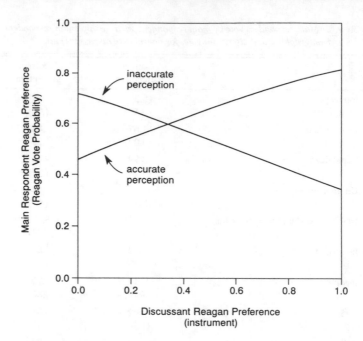

Figure 9.2. Discussant effects among nonrelatives, by accuracy of perception regarding discussant's vote. *Source:* Table 9.4 logit estimates.

respondents who incorrectly perceive, a strong Reagan preference on the part of the discussant might be related to a strong Mondale preference on the part of the main respondent. What do these divergent effects suggest?

First and most important, correct perception is a precondition for the exercise of influence within discussion dyads. This is important because our earlier analyses of these data show that misperception is systematically encouraged by several factors. First, objective disagreement encourages higher levels of misperception – discussants with conflicting political preferences are more likely to misperceive. Second, misperception is also the result of minority standing because people project environmentally dominant views on their discussion partners. Thus the structural obstacles to a political minority become apparent (Miller 1956). Members of a political minority are less likely to encounter supportive preferences, their preferences are less likely to be accurately perceived, and this lack of an adequate perception undercuts the influence that minority viewpoints might be able to register.

Temporarily ignoring the weak *t*-value, how can we explain the reversed discussant effect among main respondents who incorrectly perceive discussant preferences? One explanation points to some form of obfuscation on the part of the discussant. Strong Democrats who discuss politics with strong Republicans are perhaps more likely both (1) to obscure their own position in an effort at being politically tactful, and (2) to misperceive their partner's preference. Alternatively, or simultaneously, perhaps a reversed effect is exactly what we should *expect* to see on the part of misperceived discussants. What does it matter, for these purposes, if Joe is actually a Mondale supporter when Tom thinks he is a Reagan voter? In such an instance, it is the *perception* that is important, and therein lies the reversal of effect.

COMPETENCY JUDGMENTS AND DISCUSSANT EFFECTS

What are the characteristics of discussants and main respondents that serve to inhibit and encourage the flow of political influence within discussion dyads? Although we have no direct evidence regarding the nature and quality of political interaction between the main respondent and the discussant, we can assess the main respondents' evaluations of their discussion partners, and the main respondents' characterizations regarding the nature of political discussion. (More direct evidence could only be obtained by direct observation of interaction within dyads, and thus it is nearly unobtainable, at least outside the confines of a laboratory setting.)

First, the interviewers asked main respondents "about how much of the time does (the discussant) follow politics?" In the first column of Table 9.5 we compare discussant effects within those dyads where the main respondent said "most of the time" against those discussant effects where the main respondent said "some of the time" or "not much at all." Two interaction variables are included to take account of the potential interdependence between (1) the influence of the discussant and (2) the main respondent's perception of the extent to which the discussant follows politics. One variable is set equal to the discussant preference for main respondents who believe that the discussant follows politics, and it is set to zero for main respondents who believe that the discussant does not follow politics. The other variable is set equal to zero for the main respondents who believe that the discussant follows politics, and it is set to the discussant's preference for main respondents who believe that the discussant does not follow politics. The t-values shown in the table for these variables' coefficients can be used to assess whether each coefficient is different from zero.

The important comparison lies between the first-column coefficients (1.22 and 1.79) operating on the two-discussant preference variables. Thus the analysis shows only a minimal difference in the magnitude of discussant effects, lying in an unexpected direction, and this difference is not sustained by a statistical test (not shown) for the difference in coefficients.

Interviewers also asked the main respondents a question regarding the discussant's level of knowledge regarding politics: "And generally speaking, how much do you think (the discussant) knows about politics?" A

Table 9.5. *Main respondent vote by main respondent partisanship, main respondent demographics, and discussant vote, for accurately perceived nonrelative discussant pairs*

| | Discussant effect according to main respondent's perception | |
	How regularly does the discussant follow politics?	How much does the discussant know about politics?
Intercept	-5.34	-5.34
	(2.57)	(2.58)
Independent	1.75	1.68
	(4.15)	(4.06)
Republican	4.04	4.03
	(5.69)	(5.66)
Union membership	-.98	-1.03
	(2.23)	(2.34)
Neighborhood union membership	1.51	1.80
	(.72)	(.85)
Education	.12	.12
	(1.20)	(1.25)
Income	.12	.12
	(.78)	(.77)
Age	.02	.02
	(1.48)	(1.58)
Religion	-.12	-.15
	(.31)	(.38)
Follows most of time/knows a great deal	.35	.07
	(.47)	(.10)
Discussant preference (most of time/great deal)	1.22	1.42
	(1.31)	(1.36)
Discussant preference (some, not much/average, not much)	1.79	1.70
	(2.17)	(2.23)
N	239	245

Note: In each model the discussant effect is measured separately according to the main respondent's judgment of the discussant's political competency. Logit model; t-values are in parentheses.

Follows most of the time: 1 = main respondent believes that the discussant follows politics "most of the time," 0 if "some" or "not much"; discussant preference (most of time): discussant preference for main respondents who believe that discussant follows politics most of the time, 0 otherwise; discussant preference (some, not much): discussant preference for main respondents who believe that discussant follows politics some or not much, 0 otherwise; knows a great deal: 1 if main respondent believes that the discussant "knows a great deal" about politics, 0 if "average" or "not much"; discussant preference (great deal): discussant preference for main respondents who believe that the discussant knows a great deal, 0 otherwise; discussant preference (average, not much): discussant preference for main respondents who believe that the discussant knows an average amount or not much, 0 otherwise.

further analysis of discussant effects is carried out in the second column of Table 9.5, comparing those who feel their discussants know "a great deal" to those who feel their discussants know "an average amount" or "not much at all." As before, two interaction variables are calculated – one measuring the discussant preference among main respondents who believe that the discussant knows a great deal, and the other measuring the discussant preference among main respondents who believe that the discussant knows an average amount or not much at all. In keeping with the previous results, main respondents who evaluate their discussants' levels of political sophistication more favorably register a discussant effect that is slightly smaller than the effect among those evaluating their discussants less favorably. And once again, a statistical test for the difference in coefficients (not shown) fails to sustain the differential.

In summary, judgments of political competency appear to have little consequence for the influence of discussion partners. Discussants who are judged positively appear to have roughly the same effect as discussants who are judged less positively.

DISAGREEMENTS WITHIN DYADS

If judgments regarding political competency do not enhance or diminish the flow of influence, what are the consequences of political discord within discussion dyads? This is a complex question. In one sense, influence cannot truly be said to occur when discussion takes place between like-minded discussion partners. At the same time, the presence and persistence of disagreement are prima facie evidence that influence has not occurred – that opinions and preferences have not been brought into harmony.

Our interviews asked the main respondents: "When you discuss politics with (the discussant), how often do you disagree?" The conditional effects of discussants are considered in Table 9.6 and Figure 9.3, for main respondents who report that they disagree "often" or "sometimes" and for main respondents who report that they disagree "rarely" or "never." Two interaction variables are calculated: The first measures the discussant preference for main respondents who report disagreement with the discussant, and the second measures discussant preference for main respondents who report agreement.

The results are clear. Main respondents who report substantial disagreement are unaffected by the politics of their discussants, whereas the main respondents who report an absence of disagreement demonstrate some of the largest effects we have seen in the analysis. Furthermore, the *t*-value for the difference in effects shown in Figure 9.3 supports the argument that the effect of the discussant is contingent on the level of agreement perceived by the main respondent. What does this suggest regarding the effects of disagreement between discussion partners?

Table 9.6. *Main respondent vote by main respondent partisanship, main respondent demographics, and discussant vote, for accurately perceived nonrelative discussant pairs*

	Discussant effect according to how often the main respondent disagrees with the discussant
Intercept	-6.57
	(2.99)
Independent	1.42
	(3.28)
Republican	3.78
	(5.30)
Union membership	-1.09
	(2.41)
Neighborhood union membership	2.43
	(1.12)
Education	.07
	(.70)
Income	.12
	(.74)
Age	.03
	(1.66)
Religion	-.34
	(.83)
Disagree often or sometimes	2.86
	(3.14)
Discussant preference (often, sometimes)	.40
	(.54)
Discussant preference (rarely, never)	4.58
	(3.41)
N	240

Note: The discussant effect is measured contingent to the main respondent's perceived level of disagreement. Logit model; *t*-values are in parentheses.

Disagree often or sometimes: 1 if main respondent believes disagreement occurs "often" or "sometimes," 0 if main respondent believes "rarely" or "never"; discussant preference (often, sometimes): discussant preference for main respondents who believe that disagreement occurs often or sometimes, 0 otherwise; discussant preference (rarely, never): discussant preference for main respondents who believe disagreement occurs rarely or never, 0 otherwise.

First, what does it mean when a main respondent reports substantial disagreement? It means, quite simply, that the main respondent rejects the politics of the discussant. Joe understands the preferences of Dick, and he finds those preferences wrongheaded. Does influence occur in such a relationship? Not in the way we have defined influence for the purposes of this

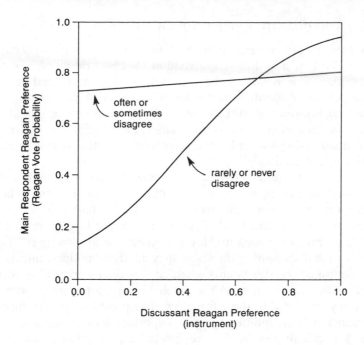

Figure 9.3. Effects of accurately perceived nonrelative discussants, by the main respondent's perception regarding the level of disagreement. The *t*-ratio for the difference in discussant effects is 2.81 (228 d.f.). *Source:* Table 9.6 logit estimates.

analysis. By defining influence more broadly, we might be able to assert that influence does indeed occur. Encountering the preferences of a wrong-headed discussion partner might reinforce Joe's original preferences, and it would almost certainly encourage Joe to rethink his own preferences (McPhee 1963). But those are subtler effects than the ones we are examining here. When a main respondent correctly perceives a discussant's preference and reports substantial disagreement with the discussant, we see a clear rejection and negation of those preferences.

What does it mean when a main respondent reports substantial agreement? It does not simply mean that the main respondent was able to locate a politically agreeable discussion partner. If such was the case, we would not expect to see the strong discussant effects in Figure 9.3. Rather, the report of agreement would be better interpreted to suggest that the discussion partners have been able to accommodate one another's preferences. Disagreements undoubtedly occurred along the way, but the end product of the interaction process was accommodation rather than conflict.

A RECONSIDERATION OF THE TWO-STEP FLOW

How do these results correspond to the "two-step flow" of political communication? The two-step flow (Lazarsfeld et al. 1948) provided one of the earliest explanations regarding the importance of informal social communication in politics. According to this formulation, most citizens do not obtain political information directly from the original source – politicians' speeches, media reports, and so on. Rather, information is socially mediated by other individuals who intercept political stimuli and provide a distinctive interpretation.

This classic conception of a two-step flow corresponds well with the asymmetrical nature of network ties within our sample – the relatively small proportion of discussants who named a main respondent as one of their discussants. This low level of reciprocity may in large part be a function of the demanding measure for reciprocity being employed. Rather than asking the discussants with whom they discussed politics, interviewers might have asked the discussants whether they discussed politics with the relevant main respondents, and a much higher proportion would have undoubtedly answered in the affirmative. The point still stands, however, that respondents' perceptions regarding important discussion partners demonstrate a decidedly low level of reciprocated perceptions, and thus the two-step flow takes on additional meaning.

We should not push the two-step flow too far, however. In particular, we should not overrate the importance of political expertise in determining the political influence of citizens who are sending and receiving information through the social influence process. Perhaps inadvertently, the two-step flow seems to suggest a social and political elite who informs the rest of the electorate (Katz 1957). Our own analysis, shown earlier in Table 9.5, does not support such a view.

An alternative approach to this problem is to consider the political interest levels of both discussion partners. Four different comparisons are possible between discussion partners, each of whom reports being more or less interested in the campaign.[4] We do not possess a sufficient sample to analyze all four pairings separately and simultaneously, but we have analyzed all four in turn. The pairing that shows the largest divergence in the size of discussant effect is the combination of a disinterested main respondent and an interested discussant. In Table 9.7, one interaction variable measures the discussant preference for dyads with a disinterested main respondent and an

---

4 The main respondents to the postelection survey report "a great deal," "some," "only a little," or "none at all" when asked how much interest they had in the election. The discussants report being "very interested," "somewhat interested," or "not too interested" when asked how interested they were in following the "political campaign this past year." Unfortunately, the authors have no one to blame but themselves for failing to use the same question in both interviews.

Table 9.7. *Main respondent vote by main respondent partisanship, main respondent demographics, and discussant vote, for accurately perceived nonrelative discussant pairs*

	Discussant effect according to the levels of interest within the dyad
Intercept	-5.61
	(2.56)
Independent	2.14
	(4.60)
Republican	4.38
	(5.99)
Union membership	-1.39
	(2.87)
Neighborhood union membership	2.18
	(.99)
Education	.08
	(.74)
Income	.21
	(1.30)
Age	.03
	(1.75)
Religion	-.01
	(.03)
Disinterested main respondent and interested discussant	-.45
	(.52)
Discussant preference (disinterested MR and interested D)	4.81
	(3.05)
Discussant preference (all other dyads)	.94
	(1.26)
N	245

Note: The discussant effect is measured contingently by levels of political interest within the dyad. Logit model; *t*-values are in parentheses.

Disinterested main respondent and interested discussant: 1 if main respondent reports "some" interest in the election, "only a little," or "none at all" and if discussant reports being "very interested" in the campaign, 0 otherwise; discussant preference (disinterested MR and interested D): discussant preference for dyads with disinterested main respondents and interested discussants, 0 otherwise; discussant preference (all other dyads): 0 for disinterested main respondent and interested discussant, discussant preference for all other dyads.

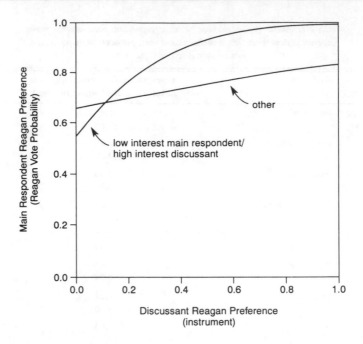

Figure 9.4. Effects of accurately perceived nonrelative discussants, by levels of interest for discussant and main respondent. The *t*-ratio for the difference in discussant effects is 2.21 (233 d.f.). *Source:* Table 9.7 logit estimates.

interested discussant. The other interaction variable measures the discussant preference for all other dyads. The discussant effect is magnified considerably among these dyads, and, for the display in Figure 9.4, the difference in discussant effects is sustained by a standard statistical significance test.

It would be a mistake to assume that social influence only affects those who are in some sense marginal to the political process. Politically interested citizens as well as politically disinterested citizens are subject to the influence of their discussants. However, these results do suggest a qualification in the socialization research argument that influence is magnified where politics is more salient to the relationship. This argument is undoubtedly true – we are, after all, only examining relationships where at least one of the participants has identified politics as being an important dimension of interaction. At the same time, where levels of interest vary between discussants, the more interested citizen is likely to exercise more influence in the relationship.

CLOSE FRIENDS, FRIENDS, AND REGULAR CONTACTS

We have already seen that discussant influence is more pronounced in some types of relationships than in others. For instance, the effect of a spouse is more pronounced, in general, than the effect of a discussant who is not a relative. What can be said regarding different types of relationships among nonrelatives? If it is the intimacy of marriage partners that leads to their greater influence as discussion partners, then we might expect more intimate relationships among nonrelatives to yield stronger effects than less intimate relationships.

In the case of nonrelative discussants, interviewers asked the main respondents: "Would you say (the discussant) is a close friend, a friend, or just someone that you regularly come into contact with?" The analysis shown in the first column of Table 9.8 and in Figure 9.5 considers the effects of accurately perceived nonrelative discussants among two groups of main respondents – one interaction variable measures the discussant effect in dyads where the main respondent identifies the discussant as a close friend, and the other measures the discussant effect in dyads where the main respondent identifies the discussant as only a friend or a regular contact. The results, which might be surprising for some readers, offer some evidence to suggest that discussant effects are stronger within the less intimate relationships, for discussion partners who are just friends or regular contacts. The t-value for the difference in discussant effects fails to achieve an adequate t-value for the display in Figure 9.5, however.

How could this pattern of effects be explained? First, it would seem that the influence of a nonrelative discussant might not be based on intimacy, but perhaps instead on immediacy and regularity of contact. Learning theory points to the efficiency of reinforcement that is immediate, recurring, and sustained through time (Sprague 1982). Along these same lines, the source of spouse and familial influence might also be reconsidered. A spouse is often able to administer this sort of efficient reinforcement, and thus it is not surprising from this standpoint alone that the influence of spouses is greater, on average, than the influence of nonrelative discussants.

Neither is it surprising that close friends have less influence than the less intimate but more frequent encounters that occur between casual associates who share common structural locations and roles. Other analyses of these data show that the frequency of reported contacts between the main respondent and the correctly perceived, nonrelative discussant varies inversely with the intimacy of the relationship. Thirty-five percent of the main respondents report that they interact daily with discussants who are close friends. But 47 percent interact daily with friends, and 55 percent interact daily with the regular contacts.

This discussion could be brought to a neat and satisfying conclusion if we could show that the influence of correctly perceived, nonrelative discussants increases as a function of more regular contact. The second column of Table 9.8 does not support such a conclusion, however. We asked the main respondents a question regarding their overall frequency of interaction with the discussant: "How often do you talk with (the discussant)?" In the Table 9.8

Table 9.8. *Main respondent vote by main respondent partisanship, main respondent demographics, and discussant vote, for accurately perceived nonrelative discussant pairs*

	Discussant effect according to main respondent's perception	
	Is the discussant a close friend, a friend, or just a regular contact?	How often does the main respondent talk with the discussant?
Intercept	-6.18	-5.00
	(2.83)	(2.41)
Independent	1.74	1.64
	(4.14)	(3.87)
Republican	4.10	4.01
	(5.78)	(5.73)
Union membership	-1.00	-1.02
	(2.30)	(2.32)
Neighborhood union membership	1.75	1.86
	(.83)	(.88)
Education	.13	.12
	(1.36)	(1.24)
Income	.12	.12
	(.77)	(.80)
Age	.02	.02
	(1.69)	(1.50)
Religion	-.14	-.19
	(.37)	(.47)
Close friend/frequent talk	.96	-.56
	(1.25)	(.75)
Discussant preference (close friend/frequent talk)	.95	1.90
	(1.21)	(2.10)
Discussant preference (friend, contact/infrequent talk)	2.61	1.38
	(2.61)	(1.65)
N	245	245

Note: In each model the discussant effect is measured separately, according to the main respondent's perceived level of discussant of intimacy in the first model, and the main respondent's reported frequency of interaction in the second model. Logit model; *t*-values are in parentheses.

Close friend: 1 if main respondent reports that discussant is a "close friend," 0 if "friend" or "just regular contact"; discussant preference (close friend): discussant preference for main respondents who report that discussant is close friend, 0 otherwise; discussant preference (friend, contact): discussant preference for main respondents who report that discussant is friend or regular contact, 0 otherwise; frequent talk: 1 if main respondent reports talking with the discussant "everyday," 0 if "once or twice a week," "once or twice a month," or "less than once a month"; discussant preference (frequent talk): discussant preference for main respondents who report daily discussion, 0 otherwise; discussant preference (infrequent talk): discussant preference for main respondents who report discussion less than daily, 0 otherwise.

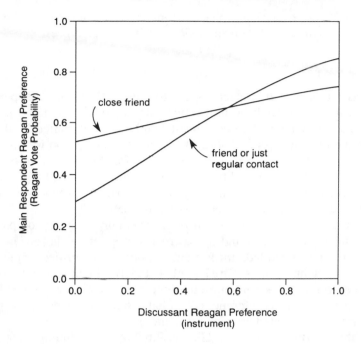

Figure 9.5. Effects of accurately perceived nonrelative discussants, by the main respondent's assessment of relationship intimacy. The *t*-ratio for the difference in discussant effects is 1.34 (233 d.f.). *Source:* Table 9.8 (first column) logit estimates.

analysis, one interaction variable measures the discussant effect in dyads where the main respondent reports daily discussion, and the other interaction variable measures the discussant effect in dyads where the main respondent reports less frequent discussion. The results show a discussant effect that is only marginally greater among discussants who interact more regularly – a difference that is not sustained by standard statistical tests. In summary, although frequency of contact is not a fully satisfying explanation for the influence of discussion partners, it is still the case that intimacy does not serve to enhance influence: "Close friends" probably have less influence than "friends" and "regular contacts." What does this suggest regarding intimacy and its relationship to personal influence in politics?

Close friends are, by definition, those people we choose to be near when we exercise choice. In many circumstances, however, citizens lack the necessary discretion to control their agenda of social contacts. Thus the people who are strategically located to affect political preferences and choices are not necessarily close friends, but rather the structurally provided associates with whom we share a common life space (Huckfeldt 1986). Furthermore, most citizens choose their close friends on some basis other than politics.

And hence, close friends may be close friends in spite of their wrongheaded views, and regardless of their obnoxious political preferences.

STRUCTURE, DISCUSSION, AND INFLUENCE

Whereas intimacy and respect appear to have little to do with personal influence in politics, we have shown that correct perception (Table 9.4) and the absence of perceived disagreement (Table 9.6) are related fundamentally to the influence process. Indeed, without exaggeration we might say that these two factors serve as preconditions for the exercise of personal influence. Are these preconditions the by-products of individually idiosyncratic associational choice, or are they better seen as the products of individual choice constrained by particular structural settings?

Earlier analyses have shown that both the supply of discussion partners with particular viewpoints and the correct perception of those viewpoints are structurally imbedded. In particular, political minorities – defined at the level of neighborhoods – are less likely to have discussion partners who share their preferences, and more likely to perceive correctly their discussion partners' political preferences. To what extent are citizens' perceptions of disagreement affected by minority standing?

As Table 9.9 (first column) and Figure 9.6 show, surrounding preferences in the neighborhood have much to do with the perception of disagreements, at least among Mondale voters. Two interaction variables measure the effect of surrounding voting preferences in the main respondent's neighborhood: One variable measures the neighborhood Reagan vote for main respondents who voted for Reagan, and a second variable measures the neighborhood Reagan vote for main respondents who voted for Mondale. Mondale voters are much more likely to perceive disagreement with their discussion partners if they live among Reagan voters. In contrast, the estimated effect among Reagan voters is nearly imperceptible.[5]

Can we put these observations together in a way that will allow us to relate micro-influence patterns to larger structural factors? If accurate perception and a lack of perceived disagreement are preconditions to personal influence, what conditions encourage the simultaneous presence of both attributes within relationships? Table 9.9 (second column) and Figure 9.7 employ a logit model to consider the probability that both conditions are simultaneously present as a function of several factors, including the respondent's vote preference and the preferences of the surrounding neighbor-

5 In the analyses of Figures 9.6 and 9.7, the main respondent's interest level is held constant at a "great deal"; the reported frequency of interaction with the discussant is held constant at "once or twice a week," "once or twice a month," or "less than once a month"; intimacy is held constant at "friend" or "just regular contact"; and perceptions of political competence are held constant at follows politics "most of time" and knows a "great deal" about politics.

Table 9.9. *Preconditions for political influence by main respondent vote, neighborhood vote, and other main respondent and discussant characteristics, for nonrelative discussant pairs*

	The dependent variable is	
	Perceived disagreement	Perceived agreement and correct perception
Intercept	-1.46	1.35
	(1.17)	(1.01)
Reagan voter	2.92	-3.75
	(2.39)	(2.84)
Neighborhood Reagan vote for Reagan voters	-.33	.39
	(.26)	(.28)
Neighborhood Reagan vote for Mondale voters	4.76	-6.73
	(2.18)	(2.82)
Education	-.009	.06
	(.18)	(1.08)
Income	.15	-.16
	(1.92)	(1.80)
Age	-.02	.01
	(2.00)	(1.36)
Great deal of interest	-.54	.66
	(2.25)	(2.44)
Frequent interaction	.05	-.13
	(.21)	(.54)
Close friend	-.07	.18
	(.32)	(.75)
Regularly follows	.03	.29
	(.11)	(1.16)
Knows a great deal	-.34	.31
	(1.42)	(1.24)
N	416	377

Note: Logit model; *t*-values are in parentheses.

Perceived disagreement (dependent variable): 1 = respondent disagrees with discussant "often" or "sometimes," 0 = respondent disagrees with discussant "rarely" or "never"; perceived agreement and correct perception (dependent variable): 1 = respondent disagrees with discussant "rarely" or "never" and respondent accurately perceives discussant's vote choice, 0 otherwise; Reagan voter: 1 = voted for Reagan, 0 = voted for Mondale; neighborhood Reagan vote for Reagan voters: proportion of all third-wave respondents in neighborhood who voted for Reagan, if the main respondent voted for Reagan, 0 otherwise (approximate *n*-size in each neighborhood is 94); neighborhood Reagan vote for Mondale voters: proportion of all third-wave respondents in neighborhood who voted for Reagan, if the main respondent voted for Mondale, 0 otherwise (approximate *n*-size in each neighborhood is 94); great deal of interest: 1 = main respondent reports "a great deal of interest" in the election, 0 otherwise.

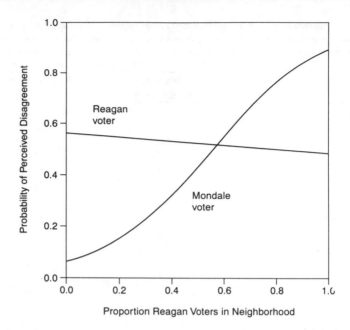

Figure 9.6. Probability that the main respondent perceives disagreement with discussant, for Mondale voters and Reagan voters, by the level of Reagan support in the neighborhood. (Nonrelatives only.) The *t*-ratio for the difference in neighborhood effects is 2.10 (404 d.f.). *Source:* Table 9.9 (first column) logit estimates.

hood population. Once again, the composition of neighborhood voting preferences is measured separately for main respondents who voted for Reagan and for main respondents who voted for Mondale. As before, the neighborhood effect is quite strong among Mondale voters but entirely absent among Reagan voters.

These results point toward a political minority that is insulated from social influence or, viewed from a different perspective, a minority that does not enjoy social support. At least among Mondale voters, the conditions that lead to influence are less likely to be present to the extent that Mondale voters live surrounded by Reagan voters. Why is the same pattern not present among Reagan voters? Quite simply, support for Reagan in 1984 was sufficiently widespread in the South Bend area that Reagan supporters rarely found themselves in socially isolated circumstances. Neighborhoods with the highest levels of Mondale support still demonstrate significant levels of Reagan support as well. In contrast, neighborhoods with the highest levels of Reagan support demonstrate nearly nonexistent

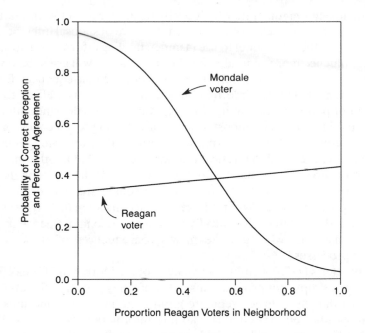

Figure 9.7. Probability that the main respondent accurately perceives discussant's vote preference *and* perceives agreement, for Mondale voters and Reagan voters, by the level of Reagan support in the neighborhood. (Nonrelatives only.) The *t*-ratio for the difference in neighborhood effects is 2.67 (365 d.f.). *Source:* Table 9.9 (second column) logit estimates.

levels of Mondale support. Thus, the Reagan voters are less likely to be socially isolated and lacking in social support for their preferences.

INTIMACY, WEAK TIES, AND POLITICAL COMMUNITY

Two empirical results of this chapter are especially important. First, if the political preferences of nonrelative discussion partners are correctly perceived, they are capable of producing sizable effects on voting behavior. Second, the magnitudes of these discussant effects are, at the very least, not affected positively by the strength and intimacy of the relationships. Even if these results can be readily reconciled with a structural equivalence perspective, they are nonintuitive and quite surprising viewed from the social cohesion framework that is more typically used to consider social influence in politics.

Has this analysis stacked the deck against social cohesion models by focusing on nonrelatives? Certainly we should expect to see, on average, much higher levels of cohesion among relatives and especially spouses, and we have previously demonstrated high levels of influence between marriage partners. But even if social cohesion lies at the core of spousal influence, it is not necessarily the best model to use in understanding information flows and political influence more generally. Furthermore, as we will argue below, the mechanism of extrafamilial influence has profound consequences for the dissemination of political information and preference as well as for the definition of political community. In short, this analysis does not intend to suggest that intimacy is unimportant, but only that (1) social cohesion may not be the crucial factor in determining political influence among nonrelatives, (2) there are good theoretical reasons to expect that another model – structural equivalence – may be appropriate, and (3) the two models have very different consequences for the nature of democratic politics.

The bigger question is, What difference does this all make? Why should we care whether intimacy is centrally related to personal influence in politics? In particular, what are the macro consequences of these micro-influence processes?

Granovetter's (1973) well-known analysis of the "Strength of Weak Ties" is based on a simple but profound insight: weak ties play an influential role in bridging the gap between separate groups and networks, and thus they are strategically well located to spread new information. So long as all ties are strong ties, society will be highly segmented into families, cliques, and friendship groups characterized by introverted information patterns. The strength of weak ties is that they further the diffusion process by tying these groups together. In terms of politics, weak ties might be influential in creating a political community – in creating a public opinion that is genuinely more than the aggregation of opinions held among component individuals and socially cohesive subunits.

As Weimann (1982) argues, the concept of "weak ties" provides new insight regarding the "two step flow" of information and the role of opinion leaders. Properly understood, the two step flow might be reinterpreted in terms of weak ties. That is, weak ties have a tendency toward intransitivity which furthers their dissemination effectiveness. Pushing this position a bit further, the "opinion leader's" influence may in part be a function of the weakness of relationships, and her position external to the intimate patterns of social interaction.

The analysis of this chapter speaks directly to these issues. Not only are reciprocity levels quite low among nonrelative discussion partners, but our main respondents report discussion with regular contacts as well as with close friends, with people whose opinions are trusted as well as with people whose opinions are suspect. Furthermore, these factors of intimacy and respect do not affect the magnitude of influence in normally expected ways. Thus, at least defined in these ways, discussion partners are frequently weak ties, and therein may lie their strength for the definition and sustenance of political community.

CONCLUSION

The political preferences of citizens have important consequences for the vote choices of other citizens who look to them as political discussants. Even when the partisan orientation and social attributes of a voter are taken into account, the influence of the discussion partner continues to emerge. This is an important finding because it shows, in conjunction with earlier analyses, that individual vote choice is imbedded within, and influenced by, a social context that emits, sustains, and perhaps amplifies some partisan cues while it submerges, attenuates, and eliminates others. People exercise discretion in the choice of a discussion partner, but that choice is circumscribed by the structurally determined availability of like-minded individuals. These structurally supplied discussion partners, in turn, have important effects on vote choice.

Discussion partners do not always present a convincing case, however, and they do not always register political influence. We have located a number of factors that inhibit and encourage the flow of influence within discussion dyads. Among discussants who are not relatives, the correct perception of a discussion partner's preference is crucial to the flow of influence. In relationships between nonrelatives, where the discussion partner's preference is accurately perceived, influence is greater when the relationship is perceived to be marked by political agreement. These are not trivial matters because both conditions of influence are socially structured – *the conditions of micro-influence are contingent on macro-circumstance.*

In contrast, ego's judgment regarding the political competence of alter has no consequence for the extent of influence exercised by alter. Furthermore, relatively few of the relationships among nonrelatives are reciprocated – very few alters choose egos as discussion partners. Finally, among accurately perceived nonrelative discussion partners, friends and regular contacts appear to have political effects that equal or surpass the effects of close friends – a pattern that further coincides with a view that discounts respect and intimacy in determining personal influence.

This chapter offers no definitive test of social cohesion and structural equivalence models of social influence in politics. Neither do we intend to dismiss social cohesion as a potentially important factor in explaining many forms of political influence. Rather, we have shown that intimacy and respect between discussion partners fail to offer a satisfactory explanation for varying degrees of influence. Alternatively, several preconditions for political influence are related to structural factors in important ways. In particular, minority–majority status has major implications for the flow of social influence in politics.

In summary, this analysis shows that vote preferences are socially structured, not only by the characteristics of the voter, but also by the characteristics and preferences of others with whom the voter discusses politics. The mix of people with whom a voter interacts is, in turn, influenced by the social contexts where the voter resides, and thus we are left with a multilayered view of social influence in an election campaign. The vision of politics that emerges is one in which individual voters are the constituent elements, but the constituent individuals are tied together in politically significant ways. These ties of interdependence between voters, which are the systematic products of particular social contexts and structural locales, make it possible to understand the formation and survival of preferences on the basis of a model that takes account of the multiple structural levels within which the individual resides.

In the chapter that follows we examine one additional characteristic of individuals and relationships that conditions the flow of information between citizens. Our analysis turns to gender and the role it plays in structuring political communication.

10

Gender effects on political discussion: The political networks of men and women

This chapter examines the political significance of gender by focusing on its consequences for politically relevant social interaction among South Bend respondents during the 1984 presidential election campaign. What is the extent of political discussion between men and women? Between husbands and wives? How do husbands and wives evaluate their spouses as political discussion partners? What are the implications for the transmission and diffusion of political information?

The political significance of gender extends beyond its relevance to political issues and appeals, and thus the role of gender in politics is not fully captured by differences in attitudes and opinions between men and women. Gender is important because it is a primary element in the structure of social interaction, and processes of social interaction are central to political life. Citizens do not formulate their political preferences or exercise their political choices in a social vacuum, but rather in response to a multitude of political messages, many of which are conveyed through personal communication. For these reasons, the political significance of gender is directly related to its potential for structuring social interaction, thereby affecting the transmission and diffusion of political messages. And thus, before turning to an analysis of organization effects on the transmission of political information, this chapter examines gender effects on political discussion.

The conventional tools of political science are not well suited for the study of gender in politics. The most common method for studying the political consequences of an individual-level characteristic is to treat the characteristic as a factor that operates on the behavior of the individual who possesses the characteristic in question. Blacks support Democratic candidates because there is something about being black that encourages Democratic support. Bankers support Republican candidates because there is something about being a banker that encourages Republican support. We are fully prepared to argue that this general framework for under-

This chapter was coauthored with Bettina Brickell, who died in the fall of 1991, and it relies on our earlier collaboration with her (see Brickell, Huckfeldt, and Sprague 1988).

standing politics may be inadequate and misleading, but our goal in the present chapter is more modest in scope. This chapter addresses the political significance of gender by focusing on its consequences for politically relevant social interaction. Gender is important not simply because being a woman or being a man leads individuals to different assessments of political issues or appeals. Gender is important because it is an important structural element imposed on politically relevant social interaction.

Several questions guide our effort. How does gender affect the politically relevant interaction patterns of men and women? What is the extent of political discussion between men and women? Between husbands and wives? How do husbands and wives evaluate their spouses as political discussion partners?

THE POLITICS OF GENDER

Gender, to the extent that it is considered in studies of politics, is typically viewed as one more background variable – as another factor potentially affecting political attitudes and behavior (Goot and Reid 1984). The typical comparison is between men and women on some political measure such as efficacy, participation, or conservatism. The usual goal of the scholar is to discover how and why women differ from men. Sex differences, when found, are usually attributed to characteristics that uniquely and consistently inhere to females or to female social roles. For example, the fact that women are slightly more likely to mention personal attributes in candidate evaluations is taken by many to indicate the lack of a rational, issue-oriented approach to politics. Women are believed to personalize the political system at the cost of in-depth, analytical reasoning, perhaps because of their socialization. An alternative explanation is certainly available: Women as a group simply may be less impressed by the differences in the two party platforms, and so may employ another method to adjudicate between them (Bourque and Grossholtz 1984).

Underlying this manner of viewing gender differences is the male-as-norm assumption. In gender research, the two comparison groups are often not considered on equal footing. Male political attitudes and behaviors are accepted, at least implicitly, as the standard against which women's attitudes and behaviors are measured (Sapiro 1983; Siltanen and Stanworth 1984). More strongly stated, the male-as-norm assumption accepts, without question, the existing power relations and the way those in power structure and define the political world. Gender is significant for politics only when female responses and actions deviate from those of males, in which case the females are seen as deficient, not just different (Bourque and Grossholtz 1984). Subsequently, women whose political characteristics differ from men's are labeled either apolitical or politically unsophisticated (Bourque and Grossholtz 1984). In political science as well as the political world itself, politics is twice-over a man's world: Not only are male actors dominant in the political arena, but males define politics and things political.

An alternative approach to studying the political significance of gender is to focus on social structure and social relations rather than on women and their so-called deficiencies relative to men (Rakow 1986). This approach suggests we examine underlying power relations and the political environment that structures the interactions between men and women. Given the premise that social interactions are central to political life, the significance of gender manifests itself in male–female political relationships, *not* in the characteristics of women alone. If the importance of gender does indeed lie in relationships, then an excessively individualistic focus will miss the significance of gender.

Male–female relationships occur in a political context that is not gender neutral. Politics is oriented around male activity such that political issues, and the way we think about and pursue them, rise out of male experience (Siltanen and Stanworth 1984). That is, "those characteristics and enthusiasms which supposedly sway men (war, controversy, electoral manipulation) are defined as specifically political, while those characteristics and enthusiasms which supposedly sway women (human needs for food, clothing and shelter, adherence to consistent moral principles, the preemption of national by human concerns, a rejection of war as rational) are simply not considered political" (Bourque and Grossholtz 1984: 118). The political arena, in short, is designed by and for men. Women's issues, such as childcare, are normally relegated to the private, or apolitical, sphere.

The very nature of this private–public split is determined by power relations in which men are dominant. This is a crucial issue because, as Schattschneider (1960) teaches us, the location of the division between the (1) public/political and the (2) private/apolitical is a central contest in politics and should not be taken as a given. Men, by virtue of a dominant position, have more influence over what is considered political and appropriate for public attention and what is apolitical and thus appropriate to remain in the private realm. By being the master of the political game, men can determine the rules of the game and what it takes to be a winner; and "in politics as in everything else it makes a great difference whose game we play" (Schattschneider 1960: 47). Women are not necessarily excluded, but when they enter the realm of politics, they enter with a handicap because they play by male-set rules.

The structure of the political world is necessarily biased (Schattschneider 1960), and with respect to male–female interactions, it is significant that the political world is biased in favor of men. The nature of the political world will set the stage for male–female interactions. Because of the home-court advantage enjoyed by males, we expect political interactions between men and women to be asymmetrical. First, men will not turn to women (or report that they turn to women) for information and ideas about politics if women's perspectives are different and constantly devalued. In this light, women are not considered worthwhile discussion partners. Women, however, will not be as segregated in their political interactions because they are members of a less powerful political group and they have learned that they must abide by male rules to play the political game. Second, if men do turn to women for political discussions, they will be more likely to question women's political competence because women may deviate from the accepted, male-defined standards and thus appear to the males to be out of touch with politics. We turn, then, to an empirical examination of the asymmetrical political relationships between men and women.

GENDER EFFECTS IN SOUTH BEND

Most investigations of gender effects in politics focus on differences in preferences, opinions, and activity levels. We wish to focus instead on patterns of political interaction among men and women, and the South Bend study is well suited for such an undertaking. The analyses reported here are based primarily on the third-wave, postelection survey of main respondents in combination with the subsequent snowball survey of a subset of the people with whom these main respondents report political discussion.

Individuals form their social networks on the basis of many considerations, and an important design feature of the South Bend study was built around the need to ascertain, at least partially, the structure of the social network that furnished political discussion and thus socially derived political information to the respondents. Information regarding the political discussants of our third-wave survey respondents was obtained in a straightforward fashion. We asked for the first names of the three people with whom third-wave respondents "talked with most about the events of the past election year." Respondents were told that "these people might be from your family, from work, from the neighborhood, from church, from some other organization you belong to, or they might be from somewhere else." Notice once again that the question does not ask about wives, husbands, best friends, bridge partners, or any other social relationship. Our goal is to determine where people turn for political discussion, and for these purposes we self-consciously avoid any prior definition of relationships. As it turns out, this design feature is crucial to the purposes of the present chapter.

Subsequent to obtaining these first names of discussants, we asked a battery of questions that gathered information from the main respondent about each political discussant. After this battery of questions was completed, we made an attempt to obtain more complete identifying information regarding the discussants, and on the basis of this information, a fourth-wave snowball survey was conducted with more than 900 discussants. Some of the analyses of this chapter depend on the discussant interviews and some do not. For many purposes, the main respondent perceptions speak quite loudly to the issues at hand.

In summary, these data collection procedures yield two different informational bases for judging gender effects on political discussion. First, for the vast majority of our 1,500 main respondents to the third-wave survey, we are able to analyze information provided by the main respondents regarding the people with whom they report discussing politics. For each discussant named by the main respondent, we asked a battery of questions regarding characteristics of the discussant. This practice results in information regarding more than 3,600 discussion partners. Most of the analysis in this chapter focuses on the information provided in this data set. (It is identified in the tables as the *perceptual data*.)

Second, for a subset of these discussion partners, somewhat in excess of 25 percent, we were able to interview the discussant as well. Thus, using this data set, we are able to compare the self-report and the perceptions of the main respondent with the self-report and the perceptions of the discussant. (This data set is identified in the tables as the *network data*.) Both data sets are considerably reduced in size for the present analyses due to the focus of our research. We are only interested in cross-gender discussion partners, but it turns out that political discussion tends to be a sexually segregated activity, and thus we have relatively few cross-gender discussion partners to analyze.

SEXUAL SEGREGATION IN POLITICS

To what extent does gender underlie the structure of political discussion networks? Previous analyses of these data have shown that discussion patterns are structured by both choice and availability. Citizens are more likely to choose discussion partners with whom they agree, or at least discussion partners with whom they perceive agreement. But choice operates within the constraints of structurally circumscribed supply. Citizens with the same political preferences are more or less likely to have politically agreeable discussion partners to the extent that they reside in a neighborhood context populated by other residents who are politically agreeable.

Certainly these are not the only factors that structure opportunities for social interaction. Ethnic affiliations, group memberships, organizational involvements, membership in the labor force, the nature of the workplace, and gender might all have important effects on the configuration of associational opportunities. Table 10.1 considers discussion partners who are not relatives. As this table shows, the sexual segregation of political discussion among nonrelatives is extensive. Indeed, for men it is nearly complete. In these nonrelative discussion dyads, 84 percent of men report that they discuss politics only with other men, and 64 percent of women report that they discuss politics only with other women. The barriers imposed by gen-

Table 10.1. *Number of main respondent's discussants who are of the opposite sex, for discussants who are not relatives*

Number of opposite sex discussants	Categories of main respondents			
	All men	All women	Women who work outside home	Women who are housewives
None	83.9%	64.0	58.4	74.2
One	14.6	27.9	31.8	21.2
Two	1.0	7.2	8.0	4.6
Three	.4	.8	1.8	.0
N	492	612	286	151

Source: Perceptual data.

der are lowered among women who work outside the home and increased among women who are housewives: 74 percent of housewives and 58 percent of women who work outside the home report no males as nonrelative discussants.

It is important to place Table 10.1 in a somewhat broader perspective. Jennings (1983), Welch (1977), and others have drawn attention to the importance of structural, situational, and socialization explanations for male–female participation differences. A situational explanation sees lowered levels of political involvement being rooted in the particular roles and life spaces occupied by women. Women might be less politically engaged because of competing demands and role expectations as mothers, housewives, and so on. Alternatively, a structural explanation looks toward social institutions that have differential consequences for the participation opportunities of males and females – party organizations, for example, that severely limit the leadership positions that are available to women. Finally, a socialization explanation focuses on preadult learning experiences that teach boys and girls that they are destined to occupy different political roles at the same time that they nurture different political aspirations.

These explanations are not, of course, mutually exclusive. Moreover, and as Table 10.1 shows, they may provide a pernicious triple threat that compromises the ability of women to engage in political life on an equal footing with men. Women who work outside the home are better able to break through the gender barriers imposed by the sexual segregation of politics. The crucial fact is, however, that while women who are exposed to the world outside the home engage in political conversation across gender boundaries, their involvement serves to highlight political introversion among males. In other words, removing the situational boundaries to political engagement among women reveals more fully the asymmetries that are present in the gender stratification of political discussion. Sorting out the respective contributions of structural and socialization factors lies beyond the aim of this chapter, but it is clear in the present instance that removing situational impediments is insufficient to the task of fully incorporating women into politics.

In summary, that great mass of political discussion occurring among nonrelatives takes place within the boundaries of gender. And thus, as a source of cross-gender political discussion, the potential importance of relatives and especially marriage partners looms large. What is the source of gender segregation in political discussion? First, the mores of American marriage may make it difficult for many men and women to develop cross-gender relationsips. Not a few individuals feel uncomfortable discussing *anything* regularly with people of the opposite sex to whom they are not married. Second, the sexual segregation of everyday life may produce far more discussion opportunities within the boundaries of gender than across the boundaries of gender. In this sense the sexual segregation of political discussion is derivative from the sexual segregation of everyday life. Finally, the pattern of segregation shown in Table 10.1 may be simply the result of sexual stereotypes and sexism on the part of men – men are, after all, more introverted in their patterns of political discussion.

DISCUSSION AMONG SPOUSES

We can at least partially evaluate the worthiness of these explanations for the sexual segregation of politics by restricting our attention to political discussion among marriage partners. If husbands report that they discuss politics with their wives at a lower rate than wives report discussing politics with their husbands, then the source of sexually differentiated discussion patterns can credibly be attributed to sexist attitudes regarding politics.

As Table 10.2 shows, 76 percent of wives name their husbands as a political discussant, but only 55 percent of husbands name their wives as a political discussant. Moreover, the rate at which wives name husbands is not appreciably affected by whether the women are employed outside the home. These figures are interesting from two perspectives. First, quite clearly, husbands would appear to be less trusting of wives than wives are of their husbands. In this sense then, politics tends to be defined as a man's activity. Second, the overall level of political discussion between spouses is not particularly high, given the availability of a spouse as a discussion partner. Even among married women, nearly one-fourth of the sample ignore their husbands when naming political discussion partners. Some of this may, of course, be a measurement artifact. Our respondents may have assumed that we wanted them to name discussants other than their spouses, but there is nothing in the probe to suggest that spouses be ignored.

Is it possible that the results of Table 10.2 might be altered if we take into account the political sophistication of both marriage partners? A useful surrogate for political sophistication is educational attainment. We plead

Table 10.2. *Percentage of married main respondents who name their spouses as political discussants*

	Categories of main respondents			
	All men	All women	Women who work outside home	Women who are housewives
Does not name spouse	44.6%	24.4	21.6	20.7
Does name spouse	55.4	75.6	78.4	79.3
N	534	544	255	188

Source: Perceptual data.

no special case for the value of education as a measure of sophistication; it quite clearly taps a variety of factors in addition to sophistication that are directly related to class and status. But for present purposes such a control is beneficial for assessing any systematic discrepancies between marriage partners that might account for the results of Table 10.2. That is, it might be that husbands tend to be better educated than their wives, and this may be the factor that accounts for the gender discrepancy in the reported rates of discussion between spouses.

Table 10.3 reports a logit analysis where the dependent variable is whether a married respondent chooses her or his spouse as a discussion partner, and where the explanatory variables are the education of the main respondent, the education of the discussant, and the sex of the main respondent, as well as the main respondent's age and attitude toward the women's movement. These last two variables are included as controls to assess whether gender stratification persists when relevant attitudes and age-related factors are taken into account. The model produces statistically discernible effects for gender, the education of the spouse, and the age of the main respondent, but the magnitudes of effects in a logit model must be assessed relative to particular values of the independent variables (Hanushek and Jackson 1977).

This is done in Table 10.4, where the logit model is used to predict the probability that a husband chooses a wife as a discussion partner, and the probability that a wife chooses a husband as a discussion partner, subject to four different educational-level pairings between husbands and wives.[1] (We include the education of the main respondent in Table 10.4 even though it produced a marginal *t*-value in Table 10.3.) The table shows quite clearly that gender has a pronounced effect on the choice of discussion partners by husbands and wives. Regardless of the marriage partners' educational levels, husbands are less likely than wives to choose their spouses as discussion

[1] Age is held constant at 48 years. The opinion toward the women's movement is held constant at 3 – "neither close nor far."

Table 10.3. *Political discussion between spouses,[a] by sex, education, age, and opinion of women's movement*

	Coefficient	*t*-value
Constant	-0.551	-0.94
Main respondent sex (1 = male, 0 = female)	-0.917	6.54
Education of main respondent	0.059	1.62
Education of spouse	0.098	2.68
Age of main respondent	-0.011	2.12
Main respondent's opinion of women's movement[b]	0.056	1.04
N	1,053	

Note: Logit model.

[a]Dependent variable is whether the main respondent names his or her spouse as a political discussant: 0 = no, 1 = yes.

[b]This variable measures how close the respondent feels to the women's movement: 1 = very close, 2 = somewhat close, 3 = neither close nor far, 4 = somewhat far, 5 = very far.

Source: Perceptual data.

partners. We are, of course, only measuring perceptions. From one standpoint, husbands and wives *must* discuss politics with their spouses at equal rates. The significant point for our analysis is the relative importance of this discussion for each spouse. Many husbands evidently fail to value such discussion highly because they do not acknowledge the discussion by naming their wives as discussion partners.

A closely related issue is the extent to which husbands and wives correctly communicate their preferences to one another with respect to important political choices. First, to what extent do married discussion partners agree regarding their political choices? As part A of Table 10.5 shows, the political correspondence between married discussion partners is quite high: 90 percent of Reagan voters have a spouse who voted for Reagan, and 77 percent of Mondale voters have a spouse who voted for Mondale. This level of correspondence is considerably higher than the previously examined correspondence that exists between discussion partners who are not relatives. (The comparable levels of corresponding preferences for nonrelative discussants are 67 percent for Reagan voters and 57 percent for Mondale voters.)

Married discussion partners not only demonstrate a high level of correspondence in their political preferences, but they are also very accurate in their perceptions of each other's preferences. As part B of Table 10.5

Table 10.4. *Predicted probability that main respondent names spouse as a discussion partner, by sex for specified educational levels*

Educational level of the		Probability that	
		Husband	Wife
Main respondent	Spouse	chooses wife	chooses husband
High school	High school	.51	.73
College	High school	.57	.77
High school	College	.61	.80
College	College	.66	.83

Source: Table 10.3 logit estimates.

Table 10.5. *Correspondence and perception of voting behavior between spouses*

A. *Correspondence between spouses' self-reported votes, for main respondents who reported voting*

	Main respondents' votes	
	Reagan	Mondale
Discussant spouses' votes		
Nonvoter	3.2%	4.7
Reagan	90.4	18.8
Mondale	6.4	76.6
N	94	64

B. *The percentage of main respondents who accurately perceive their spouse's vote preference, for main respondents who both report voting and report that their spouse is a political discussant*

	Sex of main respondent	
	Male	Female
Married discussion partners	92.1%	95.5
N	63	89

Source: Network data.

shows, wives who report their husbands as discussion partners correctly perceive the husbands' preferences more than 95 percent of the time. Similarly, husbands who report their wives as discussion partners correctly perceive the wives' preference 92 percent of the time. Once again, these levels compare quite favorably with levels achieved between discussion partners who are not relatives.

In summary, and as we might have expected, these data show that married discussion partners are more likely to agree, and they are more likely to perceive each other's preferences accurately. Not all marriage partners report one another as discussion partners, but when marriage partners do discuss politics, and perhaps even when they do not, the stage is set for a powerfully invoked mechanism of social influence.

POLITICS AS A MALE ACTIVITY

Finally, what is the nature of political discussion between marriage partners? In particular, how do marriage partners assess each other's political competence? We have already seen that husbands are less likely to report discussing politics with their wives than wives are to report discussing politics with their husbands. Do gender effects disappear once political discussion occurs?

We asked our respondents two questions regarding the competence of their discussion partners: "How much of the time does (discussant) follow politics?" and "How much do you think (discussant) knows about politics?" The responses for the main respondents who chose their spouses as discussion partners are shown in Table 10.6. Once again, a gender-specific pattern of effects emerges. Husbands are less likely than wives to believe that their spouses follow politics regularly, and husbands are less likely than wives to believe that their spouses know much about politics. Thus it is not simply that men are less likely than women to choose their marriage partners as political discussants, but it is also the case that when men do choose wives as discussion partners, they tend to evaluate their political competence less favorably.

Once again, it is at least possible that this pattern of gender differentiation is produced by different levels of political sophistication between marriage partners. In order to consider this argument, we construct an index of perceived political competence by summing the responses to the two questions, such that a score of one signifies a main respondent who believes her or his spouse both follows politics "most of the time" and knows "a great deal" about politics. At the other extreme, a score of five indicates a main respondent who believes that his or her spouse follows politics "not much at all" and believes that the spouse knows "not much at all" about politics. Thus *higher* numbers indicate a *higher* level of perceived *in*competence.

In Table 10.7 this index is regressed on the gender of the main respondent, the education of the main respondent, the education of the spouse, the age of the main respondent, and the main respondent's attitude toward the women's movement. Quite clearly, the gender effect persists. In comparison to wives, husbands evaluate the political competency of spouses less favorably. A person's own education has no discernible effect on his or her own judgment regarding the political competence of the spouse, but the spouse's education has a decided effect lying in the expected direction.

Table 10.6. *Main respondents' perceptions of spouses' political competence, for main respondents who name their spouse as a discussion partner, by sex of main respondent*

	Men	Women
How much of the time does (discussant) follow politics?		
Most of the time	25.9%	52.8
Some of the time	50.5	36.7
Not much at all	23.6	10.5
N	293	409
How much do you think (discussant) knows about politics?		
A great deal	27.6%	42.6
An average amount	65.6	53.5
Not much at all	6.8	3.9
N	294	411

Source: Perceptual data.

Table 10.7. *Main respondent's evaluation of spouse's political competence,[a] for main respondents who name their spouses as political discussion partners*

	Coefficient	*t*-value
Constant	4.71	13.74
Main respondent education	.02	.89
Spouse education	-.15	7.62
Main respondent sex (1 = male, 0 = female)	.52	6.37
Age of main respondent	-.02	-5.36
Main respondent's opinion of women's movement	.05	1.53
N	689	
R^2	.17	

Note: Ordinary least squares model.

[a]Dependent variable is a perceived competency index formed by summing the criterion variables of Table 10.7, such that: 1 = main respondent believes spouse is extremely competent; 5 = main respondent believes spouse is extremely incompetent.

Source: Perceptual data

Most important, neither individual educational levels nor age nor politically relevant opinions serve to diminish the gender differentiation of political competency evaluations among married political discussion partners.

How can we explain these effects? It would appear that politics is frequently defined as a male activity. Even when husbands choose to discuss politics with wives, they often downgrade their wives' political competence. Thus we are probably seeing the end result of a process that reinforces gender differentiation in politics. Men are perceived as being more politically competent and, as a result, men tend to be more gender introverted in their political discussion habits. Even when men do discuss politics with women, they tend to downgrade the political capacities of women. And thus the process continues, with men controlling the agenda inside countless discussion environments across the nation.

CONCLUSIONS

How does gender affect politically relevant social interaction? Earlier work has indicated that social interaction is structured by choice and availability. People are more likely to choose discussion partners with whom they agree, yet this choice is obviously constrained by the availability of like-minded people. This chapter shows that, among nonrelatives, men overwhelmingly identify other men as political discussants. Under similar circumstances, women identify other women as political discussants more often than they identify men, but they are not nearly as segregated in their choices as are men. These findings could either indicate a gender-specific effect operating through the *choice* of a discussion partner, or a more generalized sexual segregation of everyday life that serves to limit *availability*. Since the bulk of cross-gender discussions are between married couples, we examined discussion patterns between husbands and wives in order to increase our leverage on this problem.

If the findings among nonrelatives were primarily attributable to sex segregation, then we should have expected spouses to choose each other with about the same frequency, both because availability is high and because agreement between marriage partners is likely to be high. Alternatively, if gender-specific effects explain the sex-segregation findings among nonrelatives, then we might have expected a similar outcome to occur within married couples. Indeed, as we have seen, husbands identify their wives as discussion partners less often than wives identify their husbands. Moreover, among men who do identify their wives, a gender-specific pattern is still evident in that husbands are more likely than their wives to devalue their spouses' levels of political competence. Clearly, then, gender has a pronounced effect on the choice (and evaluation) of discussion partners by men and women. Even when availability and like-mindedness are high, the choice of politically relevant social interaction is structured by gender.

What is the mechanism by which gender affects choice for politically relevant interaction? We have suggested that women and men interact in a gender-biased world. Not only are men the main power brokers in the political arena, they also define the nature of politics. Gender differentiation in political discussions may be more profitably analyzed in terms of male–female interactions embedded in this biased political context, rather than in terms of female deficiencies. Men choose other men for political discussions, and devalue the competence of women, because political issues and activities have come to be equated with male political issues and activities.

This research is significant because gender differentiation may be part of a self-perpetuating system. The patterns of political discussion we observed between men and women may serve to reinforce gender differences. Women identify men as political discussants more often than men identify women. It may be, therefore, that women are more likely to learn the views of men than men are to learn the views of women. Men are not likely to see, and accept as valid, female political agendas or perspectives. Consequently, the male orientation toward politics is perpetuated, which in turn reinforces gender stereotypes, gender differentiation, and power relationships. Thus gender differentiation is not only a significant political causal force, but it may very well be an important outcome of politically situated social interactions between men and women (L. Putnam 1982; Rakow 1986).

In subsequent chapters we move away from the focus on dyads and networks to examine the consequences of organizational structures for the social communication of political information and influence. In particular, our attention turns to political parties and churches as primary elements of social and political structure that are responsible for the communication of important political messages.

IV

The organizational locus of social communication

11

One-party politics and the strategic and behavioral bases of partisanship

What are the consequences of one-party politics for the behavior of individual citizens? How do these individual-level consequences serve to perpetuate one-party dominance? One important mechanism of this self-perpetuation is the institutionally disadvantaged position of the minority party, particularly with respect to the participatory incentives attached to primary election participation. Our argument is as follows: (1) The best way for a minority partisan to maximize her influence in a primary election is often to vote the majority party's primary ballot. But (2) as a result of such crossover voting the minority party loses an important manifestation of support – participation in its own primary election. And thus (3) the minority party demonstrates a level of support that greatly exaggerates the extent to which it is a minority. Furthermore, (4) many individuals who participate in majority party affairs by voting in majority party primaries are likely to develop loyalties to the majority party.

What are the consequences of local one-party politics for the behavior of individual citizens? How do these individual-level consequences serve to perpetuate one-party dominance? These questions are as important today as when they were first addressed by V. O. Key (1949), Alexander Heard (1952), Warren Miller (1956), and Robert Putnam (1966). Arguments to the contrary notwithstanding, American politics has not been fully nationalized, and American citizens do not reside in local communities that are politically indistinguishable. Indeed, relatively few of us live in communities that are genuinely competitive in local political contests. In their analysis of party competition within the American states, Bibby et al. (1983) classify only twenty-two states as being two-party competitive, and one-party dominance within particular locales is even more widespread. Moreover, increased levels of split-ticket voting have meant that local one-party politics can survive even when one-party control runs in an opposite direction from state and national trends, and Gibson et al. (1985) show that the organizational vitality of state party organizations is independent of the organizational vitality of local party organizations. Hence it is not uncommon for American voters to live, for example, in one-party dominant Democratic cities that lie within one-party-dominant Republican states.

For all these reasons, the causes and consequences of one-party politics merit renewed attention.

A crucial ingredient of one-party dominance is its self-perpetuating property. Our own thesis is that a major mechanism of this self-perpetuation is the institutionally disadvantaged position of the minority party. Having once become a minority party in local affairs, citizens face institutionalized disincentives for participating in the affairs of the minority party. In particular, there is little incentive to vote in the primary election of the minority party because there is little instrumental reward or emotional gratification in selecting the designated loser at the subsequent general election. This simple fact and its attendant behavioral consequences go quite far in explaining the perpetuation of one-party dominance.

A full empirical evaluation of our thesis is demanding because it requires a cumulative record of individual behavior that does not depend on self-report. Only rarely in the study of mass political behavior are we presented with direct measures of political behavior rather than self-reports. This chapter reports one such happy instance – an instance in which an individual, behavioral record of participation in primary elections is accumulated over time and combined with responses from interview protocols on a one-to-one basis. The behavior of interest is participation in primary elections: Who votes in the primaries of which parties under what circumstances? And most important for one-party politics, what are the partisan consequences of these patterns of primary participation?

We begin with a review of several arguments regarding the causes and consequences of one-party politics, as well as considering the role of primary elections and the choices of primary voters within one-party dominant communities. Our attention then turns to the analysis of data collected as part of the South Bend study.

THE SELF-PERPETUATION OF ONE-PARTY POLITICS

As Key observed in his postwar study of southern politics (1949: 407), the "Democratic primary in the South is in reality the election." The overwhelming dominance of the southern Democracy, particularly in state and local politics, meant that the general election was little more than a formality required by law. For all practical purposes, the outcome of the Democratic primary determined the outcome of the general election. Although one-party control was crucial to white racial dominance in the politics and society of the South, Key was much too astute to argue that one-party politics survived because white racial dominance required it. Rather he pointed to two factors. First, one-party control depended on the creation and manipulation of distinctive electoral institutions: white primaries, literacy tests, and poll taxes. While these institutional mechanisms served to explain the exclusion of black citizens from the southern electorate, they did not explain why all white people voted for the Democrats, and thus a second argument pointed to social pressure among whites. According to Key (1949) and Heard (1952), informal social sanctions were employed against whites who dared to vote for Republican candidates or who participated in Republican affairs. And these two arguments in tandem have been generally accepted as the decisive mechanisms creating the solid white Democratic south: black disenfranchisement and social pressure among white citizens.

The persistence of one-party control is not unique to the history of southern politics. At the same time that Key was engaged in field research in the South, several Columbia University sociologists were engaged their own research programs – first in Erie County, Ohio (Lazarsfeld, Berelson, and Gaudet 1948), and then in Elmira, New York (Berelson et al. 1954) – and their efforts address the issue of one-party politics quite directly. They argued that people could shield themselves from the biased partisan signal of the larger community, but only if they were located in a personal environment that supported an alternative preference. According to their articulation of the breakage effect, Berelson et al. (1954: 99–101) argued that people who received conflicting personal cues from their personal environments were more likely to vote in line with the larger community, and thus mechanisms of social influence emerge as the means by which one-party politics is sustained.

The focus on one-party politics outside the South continued in the work of Miller (1956) and R. Putnam (1966). Miller's (1956) analysis of the individual consequences of one-party politics constituted a breakthrough. One might have inferred from the Columbia studies that a political minority should be cohesive and resolute – those people who are embedded within a politically homogeneous environment that supports a minority preference. But Miller demonstrated that the political minority is lacking in cohesion and resolve, and thus that the minority party receives less than its fair share of support. Miller's argument is important because it points toward the self-perpetuating properties of one-party politics that arise due to the disorganized quality of minority preference. R. Putnam (1966) builds on Miller's (1956) work by focusing on the mechanisms through which the influence of the larger community is realized. In line with the earlier work of Heard and Key and the Columbia studies, he isolates the importance of political influence exercised through environmentally structured patterns of social interaction. Perhaps most important, he helps to explain why the minority is less cohesive than the majority – a function of the necessarily stochastic structure of social interaction that works to the disadvantage of political minorities even when personal choice and political preference are being exercised in the selection of associates (also see Finifter 1974 and Huckfeldt 1983b).

Our goal in this analysis is not to take issue with arguments regarding the importance of social influence mechanisms in politics. Indeed we find such arguments to be quite congenial. Rather, our primary interest lies in addressing the institutional and organizational consequences of one-party politics for the minority party. In other words, we are interested in the political structure underlying one-party dominance – a political structure that is complemented by the social structural influences identified previously. This focus on partisan organization has not been altogether lacking in earlier work on the perpetuation of one-party politics. Key (1949) gives detailed attention to electoral laws and their consequences, and R. Putnam (1966) considers (and rejects) a party-activity explanation for the influence of local communities. Finally and fundamentally, however, the political structure of one-party dominance remains underarticulated.

We return to Key (1949: 407) for our primary insight – "the Democratic primary in the South is in reality the election." The heightened significance of the majority party's primary is a fundamental consequence of one-party politics, but might it not also be an important perpetuating factor? Even absent mechanisms of social influence, why would anyone have bothered to vote in a Republican primary in Alabama during the 1940s? More contemporaneously, under what circumstances would it be reasonable for anyone to bother voting in a Republican mayoral primary in Cook County? (The 1983 answer was, of course, only when the Democratic primary chooses a black mayoral candidate and white voters embrace whomever the handful of Republican primary voters happened to nominate.) Exceptions aside, the typical end product of a minority party primary is the selection of a loser for the next general election. But what are the organizational consequences of this fact for the minority party? And what are the behavioral consequences for the likely supporters of minor parties?

STRATEGIC VOTING AND ONE-PARTY POLITICS IN SOUTH BEND

The particular concern of this chapter is with participation and ballot choice in party primaries as mechanisms that are responsible for the perpetuation of one-party politics, but these are issues that relate directly to the nature and extent of voting that may be seen as strategic – as individual efforts to maximize political influence through the vote. Such voting is generally thought to be rational, purposive, sophisticated behavior, and the objective of this chapter is to show that such rational, goal-oriented behavior is profitably seen within the opportunities and constraints that are imposed not only by particular institutional settings, but also by particular partisan settings. Our thesis is that citizens choose between alternatives that are environmentally imposed, and thus purposive, goal-oriented political behavior is contingent on particular configurations of alternatives – alternatives that are tied to specific political, social, and historical settings (Boudon 1986).

The political behavior that serves as our focal point is party crossover voting in primary elections – the practice whereby self-identified Democrats choose a Republican ballot, or self-identified Republicans choose a Democratic ballot, or any citizen chooses both ballots through time. The South Bend study included a three-wave panel survey of approximately 1,500 respondents, where the second and third waves were supplemented with new respondents to offset panel attrition. The first two waves of the survey were taken prior to the general election, and they provide the data base for most of the analyses undertaken here. In this way we avoid the stimulating effect of the election – a stimulus that is not relevant to the purposes of this chapter.

Several features of South Bend and the South Bend study deserve special attention for the purposes of this chapter. First, the 1,500 respondents were chosen to be equally distributed across sixteen neighborhoods, and thus we have random samples of more than 90 respondents in each neighborhood – samples that can be used to obtain point estimates of neighborhood characteristics. Second, the survey information is augmented by public record data regarding voter registration and primary participation for individual citizens. This individual-level, public, and behavioral information is used to determine (1) whether respondents are registered to vote, (2) whether they voted in past elections, and (3) which party's primary ballot they requested when voting in a primary election. We emphasize that these data were obtained apart from the interview and thus provide a direct measure of behavior that does not depend on self-report (Traugott and Katosh 1979; Katosh and Traugott 1981). Finally, the Democrats realize a distinct advantage in the local politics of South Bend and St. Joseph County, and thus our entire study must be understood within the context of one-party dominance.

As a matter of law, Indiana voters are not entitled to take the primary ballot of a political party unless they intend to support the party in the next general election. Technically, voters are subject to challenge if they request the ballot of a party they do not support. As a practical matter, such challenges are virtually nonexistent, and few people – including the officials who are responsible for conducting primary elections – are even aware that they might be issued.[1] The reason is simple. If a voter is challenged, she can defeat the challenge by signing an affidavit promising support for the party at the next election. Because such a pledge of support cannot be verified within the requirements of a secret ballot, the challenging procedure is rendered ineffectual. Thus, as a practical matter, voters may request different primary ballots at different elections.

---

1 In the course of determining Indiana practice regarding voter challenges in primary elections, we contacted several local government officeholders who were unaware that a challenge might be issued. One of them, however, directed us to a longtime Republican party activist who holds a clerical position in county government. She was not only able to explain the procedure to us, but she also directed us to the appropriate section of the Indiana Code.

The public record registration data make it possible to construct a direct behavioral measure of cross-party voting in primary elections. The registration record for each voter contains a participation history, including information on which party's primary ballot the voter chose in past primary elections. Thus it is possible to determine not only whether a respondent voted in a particular primary election, but also the primary ballot chosen by the voter in that same election. According to these public record data, which provide participation and ballot choice in as many as eight previous primary elections for each voter, more than 10 percent of our third-wave respondents have at some time taken the primary ballots of both parties. Viewed from a different perspective, of those who have participated in a primary election, approximately 20 percent have voted in the primaries of both parties (Ranney 1972; Hedlund and Watts 1986). These data indicate that a significant if not overwhelming portion of the sample has voted in the primary elections of both parties, and the natural question becomes, who are the crossover primary election voters?

PARTISAN IDENTIFICATION AND BALLOT CHOICE

A highly purposive or strategic voter in the context of Indiana elections would be an individual who chooses a primary ballot based on the salience and competitive nature of a particular race (Farquharson 1969; Abramowitz, McGlennon, and Rapoport 1981; Jewell 1984). If voters are rational, attentive, instrumental, and highly sophisticated in their choice of a primary ballot, some predictions are possible. In particular, one would expect crossover voting to occur more frequently among those who have the most cause for calculation. We might look for crossover voters among the highly partisan or, alternatively, among those for whom crossing over might have instrumental value politically. For example, a naive set of predictions based on common qualitative characteristics of the presidential primaries in 1980 and 1984 goes like this. In 1984, when it was virtually certain that Ronald Reagan would be renominated, rational Republicans should have fled to the hotly contested Democratic primary where they might have engaged in strategic allocations of their vote. Cross-party voting was less likely in 1980 among Democrats because the incumbent, Jimmy Carter, was being challenged in Democratic primaries by Ted Kennedy. But certainly we would expect Republicans to vote in their own 1980 primary due to the competitive nature of the Republican primary in that year. Observation is at sharp variance with these speculations.

Table 11.1 displays the relationship between partisan primary ballot choice and self-reported partisanship in primary elections from 1980 through 1984. Two of these years' primaries, 1980 and 1984, involved the selection of both presidential and gubernatorial candidates. The 1982 primaries involved a midterm congressional race as well as a senatorial race,

Table 11.1. *Primary ballot selection by self-reported partisanship, for the four previous primary elections, 1980 to 1984*

	Strong Dem.	Weak Dem.	Ind. Dem.	Ind.	Ind. Rep.	Weak Rep.	Strong Rep.
1984 primary							
Democratic	55.1%	48.9	42.9	19.0	16.8	11.5	3.9
Republican	0.3	0.8	1.0	2.7	13.5	14.9	32.0
No vote	44.6	50.2	56.2	78.2	69.7	73.6	64.0
N	303	235	203	147	185	174	203
1983 primary							
Democratic	51.8%	45.5	31.5	17.0	16.8	8.6	5.9
Republican	0.3	1.3	2.5	2.7	11.9	16.1	34.5
No vote	47.8	53.2	66.0	80.3	71.4	75.3	59.6
N	303	235	203	147	185	174	203
1982 primary							
Democratic	39.6%	31.9	29.6	12.9	11.9	6.3	3.9
Republican	0.7	0.4	1.5	3.4	13.5	11.5	26.6
No vote	59.7	67.7	69.0	83.7	74.6	82.2	69.5
N	303	235	203	147	185	174	203
1980 primary							
Democratic	44.2%	36.2	32.0	11.6	11.4	5.2	6.9
Republican	0.7	2.1	5.9	4.8	22.7	17.2	38.9
No vote	55.1	61.7	62.1	83.7	66.0	77.6	54.2
N	303	235	203	147	185	174	203

Source: Preelection surveys.

and senate candidates were also chosen in the 1980 primaries. The 1983 primaries involved the selection of nominees for local offices. Thus, Table 11.1 allows a comparison of cross-party voting across different historical circumstances: presidential year primaries with very different configurations of partisan alternatives, midterm primaries, and local primaries.

Perhaps it is important to emphasize the temporal ordering of the various measures in the table. The row variables are historical records of participation in past primaries, *all of which occurred prior in time to the respondent's self-report of partisan identification.* We are not, of course, making a causal argument that current partisanship has changed subsequent to the behavior. Indeed, later in this chapter we will make that precise argument – that partisan loyalties are subject to redefinition in terms of partisan behavior. But these preliminary analyses are more limited in scope. Our initial descriptive goal is simply to compare past primary participation histories among currently defined partisan categories.

What does Table 11.1 show? Not surprisingly, Republican identifiers are more likely to have voted in Republican primaries, Democratic identifiers are more likely to have voted in Democratic primaries, and primary nonvoting reaches its highest levels among independents. At the same time, Table 11.1 displays a pronounced asymmetry in the rates and patterns of participation among Democrats and Republicans that persists across the primaries (see Adamany 1976). In comparison with Democrats, Republicans are (1) much less likely to have participated in their own party's primary, (2) more likely to have voted in the opposite party's primary, and (3) at least somewhat less likely to have participated in primaries overall. Why?

A first potential explanation for these partisan asymmetries points toward factors idiosyncratic to particular primary elections, and although there are certainly variations across the elections, these idiosyncratic factors do not entirely explain the partisan asymmetry. The 1984 Republican primary was a dreary affair with an incumbent Republican president, an incumbent Republican governor, an incumbent Republican congressman, and no senate race. In contrast, the 1980 Republican primary was more interesting – the party had no incumbent in its nominating races for president, governor, the House, or the Senate. Correspondingly, primary turnout drops off among Republicans between 1980 and 1984, and the level of cross-party voting among Republicans increases slightly, *but the partisan asymmetry is present in both years.* Moreover, in both the midterm and local primaries we continue to see that Republicans were less likely to have participated in their own party's primary, more likely to have engaged in cross-party voting, and more likely not to have voted at all.

Second, the evidence forcefully contradicts a naive strategic voting hypothesis. Accumulated evidence indicates that the most highly motivated and sophisticated voters are likely to be the strong partisans, and thus we might expect crossover voting within a particular partisan category to be highest among the strong identifiers. In fact, the pattern runs in an opposite direction. Among Republican identifiers in general, strong identifiers are *least* likely to vote in the Democratic primary, for all four primary elections.

Two other explanations for the partisan asymmetry can also be dismissed. There is no evidence to suggest that South Bend–area Democrats take their citizenship duties more seriously than South Bend–area Republicans – other analyses show that Democrats are *not* more likely than Republicans to participate in general elections. Indeed, in keeping with a finding replicated in many other places at many other times, general election turnout is higher among Republicans than among Democrats at corresponding levels of partisan asymmetry in the organizational activity of South Bend–area party organizations. Our respondents report rates of contact by Democratic and Republican campaign organizations that are

Table 11.2. *Perceived partisanship of respondent's discussants by self-reported partisanship of respondent*

Perception of discussants' partisanship	Strong Dem.	Weak Dem.	Ind. Dem.	Ind.	Ind. Rep.	Weak Rep.	Strong Rep.
-3 (All Dem.)	37.7%	18.0	8.4	1.2	1.6	1.6	1.2
-2	19.0	14.5	15.1	9.5	4.2	1.5	1.2
-1	20.6	26.5	29.5	14.3	15.1	11.8	8.3
0	14.5	24.0	25.9	56.0	29.7	31.6	16.1
1	6.1	13.5	14.5	14.3	27.1	24.3	22.7
2	1.6	1.5	4.8	3.6	9.4	9.6	18.2
3 (All Rep.)	.3	2.0	1.8	1.2	13.0	19.8	32.2
N	310	200	166	84	192	136	242

Source: Postelection survey.

virtually identical – a result that is in keeping with R. Putnam's (1966) analysis showing that rates of contacting by a particular party do not vary as a function of that party's electoral strength in particular areas. Most party contacting probably occurs after the primary is over, but this does not change the fact that we fail to find any enormous disparity in the organizational capacities of the party organizations.

Finally, although Democrats are dominant in the partisan composition of the South Bend area, we cannot easily explain the participation differential of Table 11.1 on the basis of an argument regarding social influence and the microenvironments of social support. In the third wave of the survey, after the general election, we asked the respondents to provide the "first names of the three people you talked with most about the events of the past election year." And then, as part of a larger battery of questions, we asked respondents whether each of their discussants "supports political candidates who are Republicans, Democrats, both, or neither." These questions provided us with measures of respondent perceptions regarding social support for Republican and Democratic preferences.

The respondents' perceptions regarding their discussants' political loyalties are cross-classified by respondent partisanship in Table 11.2. A Democratic discussant is scored "−1," a Republican discussant is scored "1," and other discussants are scored "0." The discussant scores for each respondent are then summed, providing an index of partisan support that ranges from homogeneously Democratic (−3) to homogeneously Republican (+3). As Table 11.2 demonstrates, there is at most only a modest partisan asymmetry in the respondents' perceptions of social support for their own preferences, and thus it is difficult to argue that the partisan asymmetry in primary participation is a function of social support differences in the political discussion networks between partisan categories. We do not intend to suggest that social support for political loyalties is inconsequential. Indeed, Table 11.2 supports the argument of the Columbia sociologists that minority preferences are able to survive when they are imbedded within politically supportive microenvironments. Our only point is that these microenvironments of political support do not explain the *partisan asymmetries in participation and ballot choice in primary elections.*

REPUBLICAN VOTERS IN A DEMOCRATIC ENVIRONMENT

In our search for an explanation of the participatory asymmetry between Democrats and Republicans, we are inevitably drawn toward the unique features of the political environment in St. Joseph County. What is there about this environment that might explain the lower rates of participation among Republicans? Most important, the city of South Bend has been a Democrat stronghold, where most of the action in local politics takes place within the Democratic party. While Republicans have been able to secure countywide and citywide offices, such successes can usually be explained in terms of an internally fractured Democratic party rather than in terms of emerging Republican competitiveness in local politics (Stabrowski 1984).

Democratic dominance has important consequences for Republican voters and the ballot choices they make. At least in local affairs, Republican primaries are less likely to be consequential contests – they are more likely to be exercises in the selection of a designated loser for the next general election.[2] Thus locally structured incentives to participate would be higher, on average, for the Democratic primary. How might we expect reasonable citizens to respond in such an environment? Table 11.1 has already shown that cross-party voting tends to be lower among strong partisans while overall participation tends to be higher, but these results were derived from analyses of particular primary elections and their attendant idiosyncrasies. Thus it becomes important to reconsider cross-party voting and turnout within the context of a longer time horizon.

South Bend–area respondents who were thirty years of age and older at the time of the interview are categorized across the rows of Table 11.3 according to a summary measure of past participation. The registration data record the ballot chosen by each respondent in as many as eight previous primary elections, and on this basis the following summary categories are constructed: no record of primary participation, only participation in Democratic primaries, only participation in Republican primaries, and participation in the primaries of both parties.[3] These participation histories

2 There are, of course, exceptions. The smaller community of Mishawaka lies adjacent to South Bend and is included in our study. The Republicans do better in Mishawaka, and indeed the current mayor is a Republican.
3 The marginals of Table 11.3 should be read with some care. The sixteen sample neighborhoods were chosen to maximize social status variation across the South Bend area and thus

Table 11.3. *Cumulative participation record in primaries by partisan self-identification, for respondents who are thirty years of age and older*

	Strong Dem.	Weak Dem.	Ind. Dem.	Ind.	Ind. Rep.	Weak Rep.	Strong Rep.	Total
Primary history								
Never voted	33.6	34.9	40.5	61.8	41.1	50.0	38.7	41.2
Only Democratic	62.9	56.9	45.8	23.7	16.7	10.7	5.9	35.7
Only Republican	0.0	1.4	1.6	6.1	14.9	24.0	36.6	10.9
Both	3.5	6.7	12.11	8.4	27.4	15.3	18.8	12.3
N	283	209	190	131	168	150	186	1,317

Source: Preelection surveys.

are cross-classified according to self-identified partisanship, and thus, as in Table 11.1, we are comparing past behavior across subsequently measured partisan categories. Notice first that exclusive partisanship in Republican and Democratic primaries varies monotonically as a function of partisanship, but it is much lower for Republican primaries. Only 37 percent of strong Republicans voted exclusively in Republican primaries compared with 63 percent of strong Democrats who voted exclusively in Democratic primaries. Furthermore, the rate at which respondents have voted in both parties' primaries is decidedly higher among Republicans than among Democrats, by 10 to 15 points in comparable partisan categories. Finally, the rate of nonparticipation is also somewhat higher among Republicans, due in large part to the relatively high rate of nonparticipation among weak Republicans.

These participation histories are reconsidered in Table 11.4, where two logit models are estimated to consider the likelihood of participation and cross-party voting in primary elections as a function of several factors: (1) the strength of partisan identification, (2) self-identification as a Republican, (3) individual education, and (4) attentiveness to electoral politics. These models are, once again, only intended to describe past partisan behavior across various social and political characteristics, all of which are measured subsequent in time to the behavior. The first model considers the likelihood of having participated in a primary among all citizens who are thirty years of age and older. The second model considers the likelihood of cross-party voting among those citizens, aged thirty and over, who have ever participated in a primary election. (For these purposes, a cross-party voter is defined as either a self-identified partisan who has taken the opposite party's ballot, or an independent who has taken both party ballots.)

they do not comprise a random sample of South Bend neighborhoods. At the same time, these marginals are unlikely to be biased in a manner affecting our basic conclusion.

Table 11.4. *Cumulative primary voting record by individual partisanship with individual education controlled, for those respondents who are thirty years of age or older*

	Respondent has voted in a primary election	Respondent has engaged in cross-party voting, for respondents who have voted
Constant	-1.55	-.91
	(4.60)	(1.56)
Education	.10	.003
	(4.04)	(.07)
Partisan intensity	.25	-.65
	(4.29)	(6.58)
Republican partisan (dummy coded)	-.31	2.32
	(2.53)	(11.56)
Campaign attentiveness (dummy coded)	.46	.16
	(3.83)	(.75)
N	1,311	771

Note: Logit models with coefficient *t*-values in parentheses.

Primary participation = 1 if the respondent is recorded as having participated in a primary election, 0 otherwise; cross-party voting = 1 if respondent has voted in both party primaries or if a self-identified Republican partisan has voted in a Democratic primary or if a self-identified Democratic partisan has voted in a Republican primary, missing for nonvoters in primaries, 0 otherwise; partisan intensity = strength of self identified partisanship: 0 for independents, 1 for independent partisans, 2 for weak partisans, 3 for strong partisans; education = years of school; Republican partisan = 1 if respondent self-identifies as a strong Republican, weak Republican, or independent leaning toward the Republicans, 0 otherwise; campaign attentiveness = 1 if respondent is "interested in following the political campaigns this year," 0 if not.

Source: Preelection surveys.

The first model suggests that all four factors are related to the likelihood of participation: Stronger partisans, people with higher levels of education, non-Republicans, and citizens who are more attentive to politics are more likely to have participated. In contrast, the second model suggests that only two of these factors are related to cross-party voting: Less committed partisans and self-identified Republicans are more likely to have engaged in cross-party voting, but neither education nor attentiveness produce *t*-values that support the presence of statistically discernible relationships.

The estimated magnitude of the relationships to partisanship and attentiveness are shown in Table 11.5. The first part of the table considers the probability of having participated in a primary election, and the probability of cross-party voting is considered among primary voters in the second part. The previously observed partisan asymmetry is preserved in both instances, although it is more pronounced in the case of cross-party voting.

Table 11.5. *Predicted turnout and cross-party voting in primary elections by partisanship and campaign interest, for respondents who are thirty years of age and older*

	Strong Dem.	Weak Dem.	Ind. Dem.	Ind.	Ind. Rep.	Weak Rep.	Strong Rep.
Probability that respondent has voted in primary election							
Interested	.72	.67	.61	.55	.54	.60	.66
Disinterested	.62	.56	.50	.44	.42	.48	.55
Probability that respondent has engaged in cross-party voting[a]							
Interested	.06	.12	.20	.33	.72	.57	.42
Disinterested	.06	.10	.18	.30	.69	.54	.38

Note: Individual schooling is held constant at the mean, thirteen years.

[a] Only for respondents who have ever voted in a primary election.

Source: Table 11.4 estimates.

In contrast, attentiveness is quite important for turnout, but even if we ignore the small *t*-values, the effect of attentiveness on cross-party voting is quite weak.

In short, these results do not support an interpretation of cross-party voting as primarily a response that is characteristic among sophisticated and attentive citizens – it would rather seem to be a more typical behavior among Republicans and weaker partisans. And in the context of South Bend–area politics, it is certainly reasonable for such people to engage in cross-party voting. Tables 11.4 and 11.5 do not compromise the rationality of cross-party voting in a one-party dominant region – they merely call into question the nature of cross-party voting as being predominantly a sophisticated and attentive response on the part of highly strategic voters.

CROSS-PARTY VOTING AS A MULTILEVEL STRATEGY

When is cross-party voting most likely to occur? One answer to this question might be that Republican crossover voting in Democratic primaries is most likely to occur in local contests. In short, we may be seeing a northern variant of the dual partisanship that is widely acknowledged to be present in the South. Many South Bend–area voters identify themselves as Republican, but they take an interest in Democratic primary politics at the local level because that is frequently the most important game in town (Key 1949).

If Republican loyalists were implementing such a federal or multilevel strategy, they would typically vote in the Democratic primary for local races and the Republican primary for national races. In Indiana, local primaries are held in the spring prior to the presidential election year, and thus local primaries were held in the South Bend–area during the springs of 1979 and 1983. An important question thus becomes: How did the ballot choices of the Republican respondents compare between 1979 and 1980 and between 1983 and 1984? To the extent that a multilevel strategy is widely operational, we should expect to see a common pattern in which many self-identified Republicans switch from a Democratic ballot to a Republican ballot between local and national primary elections.

The primary election behavior of self-identified Republicans is isolated in Table 11.6: Primary ballot choice in the 1984 presidential primary is cross-classified by ballot choice in the 1983 local primary, and ballot choice in the 1980 presidential primary is cross-classified by ballot choice in the 1979 local primary. The table provides only limited evidence of systematic, multilevel strategic voting. In both 1979 and 1983, a significant minority of Republican primary voters voted in the Democratic primary: 22 percent in 1983 $(27/(27 + 98))$ and 40 percent in 1979 $(32/(32 + 48))$. Among these self-identified Republicans who had voted in the local Democratic primary, 26 percent chose a Republican ballot in the 1984 presidential primary and 44 percent chose a Republican ballot in the 1980 presidential primary.

In summary, these results suggest that, among self-identified Republicans in 1984, approximately 6 percent had implemented the multilevel strategy in 1983–4, and approximately 18 percent had implemented it in 1979–80. Thus, even in 1980, and even ignoring the large numbers of nonvoters, only a relatively small proportion of these self-identified Republicans could be defined as acting strategically in a way that reflects a sophisticated and attentive response to minority status.

These Table 11.6 results are in keeping with the evidence of Table 11.1 where we failed to see dramatically higher levels of cross-party voting in a local primary (1983) than in presidential preference primaries (1980 and 1984). In short, it would appear that one-party politics at the local level has important consequences for primary participation, but the effects extend beyond local races. Once again, these data fail to sustain cross-party voting as a highly attentive, sophisticated, and strategic behavior. Rather, it would appear to be an entirely reasonable response on the part of weak partisans and people who find themselves as members of a political minority – a response based on a very rough calculation regarding the average reward of voting in the minority party's primary.

What are the political costs associated with crossover partisan activity? As Table 11.3 shows quite clearly, Republican participation rates suffer along a variety of dimensions. Most important, the level of regular and consistent participation in past Republican primaries among Republican partisans is much lower than the comparable level of participation in past Democratic primaries among Democratic partisans. Faced with a Republi-

Table 11.6. *Ballot choice in subsequent local and national primaries, for self-identified Republicans*

	1983 ballot choice in local primary		
	Democratic	No vote	Republican
1984 ballot choice in presidential primary			
Democratic	40.7%	4.4	6.1
No vote	33.3	87.3	29.6
Republican	25.9	8.3	64.3
N	27	252	98

	1979 ballot choice in local primary		
	Democratic	No vote	Republican
1980 ballot choice in presidential primary			
Democratic	34.4%	4.0	0.0
No vote	21.9	78.4	10.4
Republican	43.8	17.5	89.6
N	32	297	48

Note: Self-identified Republicans are defined to include strong Republicans, weak Republicans, and independents who lean toward the Republican party.

Source: Preelection surveys.

can primary election that often has little consequence, some Republicans evidently stay home on a habitual basis. And although there is little evidence of highly strategic, highly sophisticated crossover voting, other Republican partisans have regularly voted in Democratic primaries. Thus we see further evidence of the debilitating consequences of minority political status (Miller 1956). Republican voters in a Republican state[4] are put at a decided disadvantage when they reside in a Democratic city. Moreover, at least for these respondents, it is not politics at the state or national level

4 It is probably safe to say that Indiana is a Republican state, but Hoosier voters are sometimes difficult to classify. The state regularly gives large landslide votes to Republican presidential candidates, both of its U.S. senators are Republicans, and until recently the Republicans controlled both houses of the state legislature as well as the governor's mansion. Indeed, at the time of the South Bend study, the Republicans also controlled the congressional delegation. Currently, however, the Democrats control one house of the legislature, the governor's mansion, and the congressional delegation, and this latter feat occurred in spite of a notorious Republican gerrymander following the 1980 census. Why have these reversals occurred? Certainly it is not due to any Hoosier warming trend toward the national Democratic party. One Republican congressman received new 1982 district boundaries that assured him of keeping the seat unless, as the story goes, he got drunk, ran his car into a tree, and tried to deny the fact shortly before an election. That is, of course, exactly what happened.

that structures turnout in party primaries, but rather politics at the local level.

At this point it is important to (1) review our results and (2) establish a procedure for considering their political, behavioral consequences. We have shown that weak partisans and Republicans – the partisan minority in South Bend – are less likely to have voted in primaries but more likely to have engaged in cross-party primary voting. Our argument is that such behavior tends to weaken individual partisan loyalties, thereby perpetuating the minority status of the Republican party. But how can we support such an argument empirically? How can we show that weak partisan ties are the consequence rather than the cause of a failure to participate in a particular party's primary elections? If our observations of individual behavior were limited to a single point in time, or even to a short period of time, such a problem might well produce an irresolvable conundrum. But this is where the individual-level, primary-election participation histories become indispensable. Quite simply, we are able to observe individual behavior over the relatively long haul, and such an observational capacity is central to the argument we are making.

The crucial question becomes: What are the individual consequences of one-party politics? In particular, what are the long-term partisan consequences of voting or not voting in particular party primaries at different elections? If partisan politics is a learned behavior that is reinforced and nurtured through time (Beck 1974), then participation in party primaries may be an important learning device with lasting consequences for the strength of partisan attachment (Finkel and Scarrow 1985). If partisanship is a standing decision (Key and Munger 1959), then this decision is either ratified or reversed as a function of individual behavioral choices in time.

How might we think of this problem? First, define a unit of time as beginning at the moment after a primary ballot is chosen and suppose that a citizen's partisan loyalty at one time period, $t + 1$, is influenced by his immediate preceding primary ballot choice at t, as well as by the residue of his prior partisan loyalty at t (Franklin and Jackson 1983). Further assume that his primary ballot choice at $t + 1$ is a simultaneous function of his loyalty at $t + 1$ and a residual function of his preceding ballot choice at t. These assumptions are written in equation form as:

$$L_{t+1} = aL_t + bB_t \tag{1}$$

$$B_{t+1} = fL_{t+1} + gB_t, \tag{2}$$

where L indexes partisan loyalty on an abitrary scale from -3 (strong Democrat) to 3 (strong Republican); B indexes primary ballot choice on a scale of -1 (Democratic ballot), 0 (no vote), 1 (Republican ballot); the residue parameters (a,g) lie within the 0,1 interval; and the effects of previous ballot choice (b) as well as contemporaneous loyalties (f) are positively valued.

On the basis of equations 1 and 2, and given that the initial condition lies at $t = 0$, any successive partisan loyalty is written as:

$$L_n = a^n L_0 + b[B_{n-1} + aB_{n-1} + a^2 B_{n-3} + \ldots + a^{n-1} B_0] \tag{3}$$

and any successive primary ballot choice is written as:

$$B_n = g^n B_0 + f[L_n + gL_{n-1} + g^2 L_{n-2} + \ldots + g^n L_0] \tag{4}$$

In words, a citizen's loyalty at a point in time is a function of (1) a decreasingly weighted sum of past ballot choices and (2) a temporally discounted initial loyalty (cf. McPhee 1963; Converse 1969; and Fiorina 1981). A citizen's ballot choice at a point in time is a function of (1) a decreasingly weighted sum of current and past loyalties and (2) a temporally discounted initial ballot choice.

When equation 2 is incorporated into equation 1, the following reduced form can be obtained:

$$L_{t+1} = [b + a/f]B_t - [ag/f]B_{t-1} \tag{5}$$

And thus it is possible, even if potentially misleading, to express partisan loyalty wholly as a function of the past two ballot choices. The problem with such an alternative is that the operator on $B_t - [b + a/f]$ – indexes not only the effect of behavior on loyalty (b) but also the effect of loyalty on behavior (f) as well as loyalty residue (a), and thus statistical estimation would generate an underdetermined mapping from statistical coefficients to model parameters. If the effect of loyalty on behavior (f) is very large and (or) the loyalty residue (a) is absent, this operator simply reduces to b. Alternatively, if the effect of loyalty on behavior is absent, the problem disappears because the original substitution would not be possible. The difficulty arises because we lack strong prior arguments regarding the size of these parameters. As a result, our strategy is to return to equation 3 where loyalty is expressed as the decreasingly weighted sum of past behavior as well as a temporally discounted initial loyalty. Equation 3 is probably best understood in the context of equation 4 (Engle, Hendry, and Richard 1983; Harvey 1989: chap. 7), and this means that past ballot choices are weakly exogenous to current loyalties. The presence of weak exogeneity assures us that, if we can obtain measures of past ballot choices, the estimates of their effects will be statistically efficient. In most settings such measures would be impossible to obtain, but the presence of individual-level, historical participation records makes it possible to exploit the form of equation 3.

As a matter of measurement, we do not intend to press equation 3 to its logical long-term consequence – we will not argue that current loyalty is but the residue of past ballot choices. Indeed, by successive substitutions it can be shown that current loyalty is merely the temporally discounted residue of initial conditions for both behavior and loyalty (B_0 and L_0). But such a measurement strategy pushes the deterministic logic of these equations too far – a logic that is, in reality, subject to both the systematic and random bumps and shocks of politics and real life. Rather, we will adopt a measurement strategy that considers the effects of past behavior, while at the same time taking account of factors relating to past and initial loyalties.

THE BEHAVIORAL BASIS OF PARTISANSHIP

In the analyses that follow, respondents' current loyalties are regressed on a behavioral record of their participation in past primary elections – whether they chose a Democratic ballot, a Republican ballot, or did not vote. In addition, a number of control variables are included as regressors. One set of these variables is included to take account of the social circumstances of the respondent that condition the development of contemporaneous partisan loyalty – education, income, religion, ethnic loyalties and so on – and thus should be predictors of partisan loyalty apart from the reinforcing effects of past behavior. Three additional controls are included to serve as a combined proxy for the respondent's initial party loyalty (L_0): the respondent's recall regarding his or her mother's partisanship, father's partisanship, and the social class of the respondent's family of origin. These control variables provide only imperfect measures of the reality we would like to consider. Indeed, several of them are undoubtedly biased according to the respondent's partisanship – Democrats, for example, are more likely to believe that their parents were Democrats. For present purposes, this bias lies in a conservative direction, assigning too much explanatory purchase to parental partisanship and thus not enough to the respondent's past behavior.[5]

The first column of Table 11.7 displays a regression model with the two sets of controls, as well as a set of six variables that directly measures the respondents' participation in the previous six primaries on the basis of public report: the presidential preference primaries of 1984 and 1980, the local primaries of 1983 and 1979, and the midterm primaries of 1982 and 1978. Each variable is scored "−1" for a Democratic ballot, "0" for nonparticipation, and "1" for a Republican ballot. The coefficients for these variables display an order of magnitude that is generally consistent with the expectation of equation 3: The coefficients for more recent primaries tend to be larger than those for earlier primaries.

5 These procedures constitute a conservative estimation strategy, but some readers might argue that the list of control variables is excessive. To the extent that equation 3 provides the correct specification, controls for contemporaneous social location should be excluded. Reestimating the model with all control variables excluded except for the respondent's recall of his parents' partisanship and his childhood family's social class does not alter any conclusion drawn from the results displayed in Table 11.7.

Table 11.7. *Party identification by primary participation and assorted control variables*

			Dem. primary[a]	Rep. primary[a]
Constant	6.34		6.47	
	(1.55)		(1.58)	
Mean education in neighborhood	-.67		-.68	
	(1.94)		(1.97)	
Education	.04		.04	
	(1.50)		(1.34)	
Family income	.19		.19	
	(6.12)		(6.09)	
Union family[a]	-.50		-.52	
	(4.17)		(4.32)	
Ethnic loyalty[a]	-.27		-.27	
	(2.60)		(2.58)	
Protestant[a]	.27		.26	
	(2.49)		(2.38)	
Age	.01		.01	
	(3.02)		(2.73)	
Mother's partisanship[b]	.37		.36	
	(4.03)		(3.87)	
Father's partisanship[b]	.30		.30	
	(3.30)		(3.30)	
Family of origin's social class[c]	-.03		-.02	
	(.51)		(.34)	
1984 primary[d]	.62	1984	-.71	.45
	(5.20)		(4.43)	(1.87)
1983 primary[d]	.59	1983	-.39	.93
	(4.88)		(2.35)	(3.99)
1982 primary[d]	.35	1982	-.23	.55
	(2.58)		(1.26)	(2.26)
1980 primary[d]	.36	1980	-.29	.38
	(3.01)		(1.67)	(1.74)
1979 primary[d]	-.05	1979	-.01	.04
	(.36)		(.07)	(.16)
1978 primary[d]	.20	1978	-.21	.29
	(1.45)		(1.19)	(1.01)
R^2	.49		.49	
N	986		986	

Note: t-values are in parentheses.

[a]Dummy coded.

[b]Coded as: -1 = Democrat, 0 = independent, 1 = Republican.

[c]Coded as -1 = working class, 0 = neither, 1 = middle class.

[d]Coded as: -1 = Democratic, 0 = no vote, 1 = Republican.

Source: Preelection surveys.

The same basic model is displayed in the second column of Table 11.7, but in this instance ballot choice in the previous six primaries is dummy coded. These estimates show a different pattern of effects for Democratic and Republican primary participation. Participation in Democratic primaries generally produces the expected pattern of temporal decline in magnitudes of effect. In contrast, Republican primary participation produces its biggest effect in the 1983 election and declines thereafter. In comparison, the 1984 Republican primary produces only a modest effect with a marginal t-value. Why do we see these divergent patterns?

It may be that the 1984 Republican primary was simply too inconsequential (and poorly attended) to produce a reinforcing effect on partisan loyalty. Alternatively, recall that the incentive for Republican loyalists to engage in cross-party primary voting should be highest in local races. Thus, among South Bend–area voters, the most important self-defining behavior of a Republican may be to participate in a local Republican primary. In either case, we are pushed beyond the simple representation of equation 1 to recognize that some primaries may be more important than others in their potential to reinforce partisanship.

In summary, these data support the argument that, for many voters, cross-party primary voting inhibits the development of strong partisan ties. A strong commitment to the Republican party is enhanced by participation in Republican primaries, and it is inhibited by participation in Democratic primaries. Such a problem is not relevant for most Democrats – they have the luxury of limiting their partisan activity to the Democratic party, and thereby Democratic loyalties are consistently reinforced.

Thus, in Table 11.7 we see one of the mechanisms that perpetuates one-party politics. Lacking an opportunity to behave like Republicans in a consistent fashion, many voters fail to develop a strong commitment to the Republican party. The menu of choices available to voters reinforces a particular constellation of preferences, which, in turn, tends to perpetuate the limited menu of choices.

CONCLUSION

The unifying theme of this chapter is the environmentally contingent basis of party support and involvement. This theme manifests itself in a number of ways. Supporters of the majority Democratic party are more likely to have participated in primary elections than are supporters of the minority Republican party. Even when they did vote in a primary, Republican supporters were more likely to have engaged in cross-party voting. Moreover, partisan loyalty is in part contingent on past ballot choices in primary elections, and thus cross-party voting tends to undermine the position of the minority party further – a conclusion that flows directly from the second column of Table 11.7. These patterns of differential primary turnout and cross-party voting tend to perpetuate, in turn, the dominance of the Democratic party in the South Bend area. And thus it is not only the ballot choices of individual voters that must be understood as being environmentally contingent, but also the successes and failures of party organizations.

Our argument complements the work of Jewell (1984: 192) who shows that primary turnout within states corresponds to the respective party votes in general elections – turnout in a particular party's primary tends to be higher in states where that party is more dominant in general elections. Our own effort expands this finding in two ways. First, not only states but also localities are relevant in this regard: If the South Bend pattern is general, turnout in party primaries appears to vary across localities as a function of local partisan dominance. Second, it is not only the overall level of primary turnout that is affected by partisan dominance, but also the rate of turnout among natural party constituencies. Democrats in the South Bend area are more likely to vote in a Democratic primary than are Republicans to vote in a Republican primary.

Citizens act reasonably and purposefully in their choice of a primary ballot, and some of their choices can be understood from the perspective of strategic voting, but the boundaries on their efforts are tightly drawn. In general, they do not carefully monitor each primary election campaign in an effort to determine the ballot choice that will maximize their influence. Rather, most of them would appear to adopt the entirely reasonable strategy of long-run habit – or, alternatively, long-run "judgmental heuristics" (Ottati and Wyer 1990: 200) – rather than a strategy of short-run analysis (and reanalysis) of highly complex and ambiguous decision-making opportunities. For some Republican identifiers in the South Bend area, this means not voting in primary elections. For others it means consistently voting in Democratic primaries. For still others it means cross-party voting, but cross-party voting that typically lacks any highly attentive and sophisticated underlying strategy.

None of these results should be interpreted as compromising the rational, purposive basis of mass politics. The Achilles heel of strategic voting is not the rationality required of individual actors, but rather the attentiveness. In order to fulfill the model of a strategic voter, an individual must invest substantial resources in monitoring and keeping up-to-date on the course of electoral politics. A voter need not only decide on a course of action that is consistent with his or her political preferences, but the voter must also engage in complex calculations regarding the likely behavior of other voters and the consequences of other voters' behavior for the maximization of the voter's own influence. Faced with such a daunting challenge – referred to by Downs (1957) as the "maze of conjectural variation" – it is not surprising that voters choose consistent shortcut guides to behavior (Lodge and Hamill 1986). And it is in the context of such shortcuts that the participation patterns of political minorities in primary elections can be usefully reconstructed.

Neither do we mean to suggest that highly strategic, sophisticated, attentive voters do not exist, but only that their numbers are small (Abramowitz et al. 1981). Moreover, their numbers are considerably smaller than the number of people who engage in some form of cross-party voting, and this fact is quite important. For the highly motivated, strategic, and attentive cross-party voter, ballot choice is unlikely to have major consequence for the development of partisan identity because the choice of a ballot is an entirely instrumental act predicated on a careful calculus. For the less attentive and strategic citizen who engages in cross-party voting, ballot choice is likely to play a larger role in political self-identification, and, as we have seen, it appears that cross-party voting thus further erodes the position of the minority party.

Indeed, the unforeseen consequence of minority participation in majority primaries is to maintain one-party dominance within the community. The logic is as follows: (1) The best way for a Republican voter to maximize her influence in a Democratic environment is often to vote the Democratic primary ballot. But (2) by voting the Democratic ballot the Republican party loses an important manifestation of support – participation in its own primary election. And thus (3) the minority party demonstrates a level of support that greatly exaggerates the extent to which it is a minority. Furthermore, (4) many individuals who participate in Democratic party affairs by voting in Democratic primaries are likely to develop Democratic loyalties.

Thus, at both the individual and corporate levels we see a tendency for one-party politics to be self-perpetuating, for reasons that are rooted in entirely reasonable choices on the part of individual citizens. The irony is, of course, that short-term rationality on the part of Republican participants in Democratic primaries produces an end result that is not in their own best interests – the further deterioration of their own party's ability to compete effectively (Schelling 1978).

12

Political parties and electoral mobilization: Political structure, social structure, and the party canvass

As agents of electoral mobilization, political parties occupy an important role in the social flow of political communication, and this chapter addresses several questions regarding party mobilization efforts. Whom do the parties seek to mobilize? What are the individual and aggregate characteristics and criteria that shape party mobilization efforts? What are the intended and unintended consequences of partisan mobilization, both for individual voters and for the electorate more generally? In answering these questions we make several arguments. First, party efforts at electoral mobilization inevitably depend upon a process of social diffusion and informal persuasion, and thus the party canvass serves as a catalyst aimed at stimulating a cascading mobilization process. Second, party mobilization is best seen as being environmentally contingent upon institutional arrangements, locally defined strategic constraints, and partisan divisions within particular electorates. Finally, the efforts of party organizations generate an additional layer of political structure within the electorate that sometimes competes with social structure and often exists independently from it.

One of the major good works of political parties is to engage citizens in the political process. Parties play an important role in democratic politics when they mobilize the electorate to turn out and vote, thereby involving citizens in democratic governance. These efforts on the part of parties are not unbiased attempts aimed at encouraging diffuse system support – they carry an explicitly partisan message. But in the necessarily free market of democratic electoral competition, such self-interest is a virtue because it serves to educate and inform the electorate in a politically meaningful manner. Modern treatments of American political parties often focus on parties as formal secondary organizations that publish platforms, endorse and support candidates, and provide officeholders with a framework for coalition formation (Mayhew 1986). At the same time it is important to remember that, as agents of electoral mobilization, parties occupy an important role in the social flow of political communication. And thus, inevitably, party politics and partisan efforts at electoral mobilization include a heavy dose of social influence. When a party worker knocks on a citizen's door, or calls a citizen on the telephone, or affronts him with a yard sign, an effort is being made by one individual to provide information that will influence the behavior of another individual.

Moreover, the motivation for such contact resides in a set of implicit assumptions regarding the manner in which voters make their political choices. Successful efforts at voter mobilization do not enlist party supporters in single-file fashion. Even at the height of the so-called machine era in party politics, jobs and favors and assistance were not distributed on a tit-for-tat basis – one job for one vote. Such an enterprise would have bankrupted even the wealthiest party organization. Rather, party efforts at electoral mobilization inevitably depend upon a process of social diffusion and informal persuasion. If a party worker can succeed in convincing Sally to vote Democratic, then Sally might be able to convince Bill, and so on. The investment of party resources becomes more potent to the extent that the votes of individuals are interdependent because the initial contact has cascading consequences in the collective deliberations of democracy.

This chapter is organized around a set of questions regarding the role of party organizations as agents of mobilization in contemporary American politics. First, whom do the parties seek to mobilize, and what are the individual and aggregate characteristics and criteria that shape party mobilization efforts? Second, what are the intended and unintended consequences of these mobilization criteria – are the parties able to identify and contact appropriate portions of the electorate? Finally, what impact do party mobilization efforts have upon citizens who are contacted, and does this impact reach beyond the point of contact to affect the electorate more generally? Before turning to these questions, we address several antecedent issues related to the environmentally contingent nature of organized partisan efforts at electoral mobilization.

PARTIES AND MOBILIZATION

Any analysis of partisan mobilization in the context of American politics must address a seeming discrepancy: At the same time that political scientists have developed a general skepticism regarding the mobilization potential of party organizations, party activists continue to invest heavily in the effort. Indeed, the reported incidence of party contacts among the electorate is higher now than it was in the early 1950s (Krassa 1985), a period of time during which political parties are generally thought to have been more vibrant.

Skepticism regarding the mobilization potential of party organizations is rooted in several lines of argument. Many scholars and journalists agree that party organizations have weakened dramatically over time, and from this perspective it is difficult to see how party mobilization efforts could be important. Further, viewed from the perspective of national surveys, party contacts are seen as having generally consistent but modest effects on turnout, with little or no effect on the direction of the vote (Kramer 1970–1; Krassa 1988, 1989).

How can the discrepancy be understood? Why would party organizations continue to invest so heavily in undertakings that yield so modest a reward? First, it is important to remember that even modest effects in a statistical sense may be consequential to the outcome of an election, thereby making party efforts worthwhile. Second, the demise of party organizations, particularly at the local level (Gibson et al. 1983, 1985) may have been seriously overstated. Third, most analyses that point toward weak parties are narrowly focused to exclude candidate-centered organizations, perhaps the dominant form of partisan electoral organization in American politics. If we include the mobilization efforts of candidate-centered organizations as party activity – a wholly appropriate practice in the organizationally fractured world of American political parties (Beck 1992: chap. 1) – locally organized party efforts can be quite substantial. Finally, and perhaps most important, more recent efforts at understanding party mobilization are typically undertaken from the vantage point of the national sample survey. But is it appropriate to judge the impact of party mobilization efforts based simply on the votes of contacted respondents? Or should we look beyond the reports of individual voters to examine the environment of party mobilization, both as it affects the strategy and consequence of mobilization efforts?

THE ENVIRONMENT OF PARTY MOBILIZATION

The efforts of parties and their candidates to mobilize the electorate are located geographically and socially within the context of particular structural and institutional settings. Political party organizations in Indiana face a different set of opportunities and constraints than party organizations in California or Illinois (Jewell and Olson 1982; Jewell 1984). Some of these constraints are legal and institutional. The advent of the direct primary revolutionized the conduct of party politics, but the revolution occurred along very different lines in different settings depending upon the particular shape of the reform. These reforms, coupled with later national reforms, produce a synergism with truly profound consequences that are still unfolding (Shafer 1983, 1988). Electoral reforms in many states were designed with the explicit purpose of creating an environment hostile toward organized parties and their efforts, effectively divorcing electoral participation from partisan involvement (Hawley 1973). In other states an environment was created that proved to be much more congenial to organized party politics, maintaining a crucial and visible role for party organizations and partisan attachments (Bledsoe and Welch 1987).

It is not only the various legal and institutional settings of American electoral politics that create the unique environments of party mobilization. As P. Beck (1974) and others have shown, party mobilization efforts must also be seen within the existing partisan balance of particular locales (also see Hofstetter 1973; Miller 1956; R. Putnam 1966). The perpetuation of one-party dominance in state and local politics creates a variegated partisan landscape with important and variable consequences for the mobilization efforts of partisan organizations in particular states and locales. If less than half of the American states maintain competitive two-party electoral environments (Bibby et al. 1983), and if one-party dominance is even more characteristic of local politics, then local and state partisan environments become especially relevant to the success or failure of organized mobilization efforts. Taking account of the partisan environment becomes even more important if the vitality and direction of local partisan organization is independent of the vitality and direction of state partisan organization (Gibson et al. 1985). It thus becomes commonplace for American voters to live, for example, in Democratic cities that lie within Republican states, and configurations such as these will be shown to have important political consequences.

Both environmental features loom especially large with respect to the present analysis: (1) the institutional environment of party activity, particularly as it affects the availability of information that parties might use in their mobilization efforts, and (2) the partisan balance that exists within a particular locale. Both features are part of the inescapable context within which party efforts are formulated, and both have substantial consequences for the strategies of party organizations.

STUDYING PARTISAN ORGANIZATION IN SOUTH BEND

South Bend proves to be an advantageous site for studying the strategies and consequences of partisan mobilization. First, the city possesses a political environment that is relatively congenial to political organization and the conduct of partisan politics (Stabrowski 1984). While the state of Indiana does not possess a closed primary system, voters go on record as party supporters when they choose a party's primary ballot, and party organizations are able to identify the voters who participate in their primaries.[1] Second, the Democratic party has traditionally possessed an advantage in South Bend politics, and thus we are able to examine the organizational and institutional implications of majority and minority standing. Third, the study of partisan mobilization is hampered by an exclusive focus on presidential politics, but important gubernatorial and congressional campaigns

1 Indiana voters may not legally vote in the primary of a party whose candidates they do not intend to support in the subsequent general election, but as a practical matter this law is virtually unenforceable. Moreover, there is nothing in the law that would restrict voters from shifting their allegiances through time, and hence voters might be expected to request the primary ballots of different parties at different elections.

were also being waged in South Bend during the fall of 1984, and we will consider partisan mobilization with respect to these campaigns as well.

The argument we develop here does not depend upon the selection of South Bend as a study site, and a skewed partisan environment does not make South Bend atypical of other American cities. The short answer to those remaining skeptical is this: Everyone lives in some South Bend. The compelling reality of urban and suburban politics today is that almost all of us live and work as part of political majorities or minorities because few environments maintain a genuine political balance. Our neighborhoods are tilted one way, our workplaces another, and our cities perhaps another. The aggregation of microenvironments to the typical levels of party organization is unlikely to create politically competitive units – indeed the continuing efforts of political elites are aimed at avoiding just such competition. But just because the partisan bias of an environment is highly skewed, it does not follow that party organization and political mobilization become irrelevant. A major proposition advanced here is that important and systematic political consequences flow from these normal and typically skewed partisan distributions.

The analysis of this chapter relies most heavily on information taken in the third-wave, postelection survey, and two features of the South Bend study design merit special attention for purposes of this analysis. First, the 1,500 main respondents were equally distributed across the sixteen study neighborhoods, thereby providing random samples of more than 90 respondents in each neighborhood. Any question included in the survey can either be used as an individual measure or aggregated to provide a neighborhood measure. This means that the analysis can operate either at the individual level, or at the aggregate level, or at both levels simultaneously; and such a capability is crucial to this chapter's analysis.

Second, the survey information is augmented by public record data regarding voter registration and primary participation for individual citizens. This information is used to determine (1) whether respondents are registered to vote, (2) whether they voted in past elections, and (3) which party's primary ballot they requested when voting in a primary election. Thus we are able to consider the citizens' self-reported behavior relative to the official record of the behavior (Traugott and Katosh 1979; Katosh and Traugott 1981), and all this within a particular political and social setting. Such information is particularly important to our analysis in this chapter.

In summary, this chapter is necessarily aimed at the analysis of a particular party system, particular party organizations, and a particular institutional setting. What relevance does such an analysis have for American politics more generally? A major weakness of modern research on parties and party systems is that it is typically and implicitly predicated on the unsustainable myth that the relationship between parties and voters can be understood *apart* from a particular setting. The argument underlying this chapter lies in an exactly opposite direction: The relationship between parties and electorates is environmentally contingent and must be understood in that light. Only by appreciating the relationship between parties and voters in South Bend (and Los Angeles and Schenectady and Walla Walla) can we begin the task of making meaningful statements in more general terms (Boudon 1986).

THE STRATEGIC BASIS OF THE PARTY CANVASS

Perhaps the most important form of encounter between parties and citizens, and certainly the most widely studied, is the party canvass – the effort of party workers contacting individual citizens. About one-third of our South Bend respondents report being contacted by at least one of the parties, with 22 percent reporting contact by each of the parties and 10 percent reporting contact by both of the parties.[2] If party organizations are successful at targeting their potential supporters for contact, we should expect to see a strong negative relationship between the likelihood of being contacted by the Democrats and the likelihood of being contacted by the Republicans. But the South Bend data demonstrate a level of mutual contacting (.10) that is double the proportion that would be expected by chance alone (.22 × .22 = .046), and this raises an important issue. Whom *do* each of the parties contact? What criteria do the parties use in deciding whom to contact? Are the parties ignorant, or perhaps naive?

The most readily available source of information that most parties can use in their efforts to mobilize voters is the official list of registered voters within a particular governmental jurisdiction. State-to-state variations in voter registration arrangements are enormous, but in many states the record-keeping operations of the registrar provide a valuable source of information for political party efforts. First, registration records identify that part of the citizenry that is currently eligible to participate in an election. Second, in many states, registration records provide at least indirect evidence regarding the partisan loyalties of citizens. In some states voters must register with a particular party in order to participate in that party's primary. In other states, such as Indiana, voters do not register with a party, but they go on record as party supporters when they request that party's ballot at a primary election.

How useful is this information as a guide to the predicted political behavior of a voter? Participation in St. Joseph County primaries is a less than perfect indicator of partisan loyalty (also see Finkel and Scarrow 1985). More significant for the conduct of electoral politics, the choice of

2 The text of the contacting question was as follows: "As you know, the political parties try to talk to as many people as they can to get them to vote for their candidates. Did anyone from one of the political parties call you up, or come around and talk to you about the campaign this year? Which party was that?"

a party's ballot is a *biased* measure of partisanship because an asymmetrical relationship exists between partisanship and primary ballot choice. The dominance of the Democratic party in local politics creates a situation in which the winner of the Democratic primary is frequently the winner of the general election as well, and thus the stakes are often higher in the Democratic primary (Farquharson 1969; Key 1949). As we have seen (in Table 11.1 of Chapter 11), many Republican loyalists have voted in Democratic primaries, but Democratic loyalists have seldom voted in Republican primaries. Although this sort of cross-party primary voting is substantial, it has not reached epidemic proportions, and thus knowing which ballot a voter takes at a particular election still provides a useful indicator of partisan preference.[3] At the same time, ballot choice is a biased indicator, and the bias has important consequences for political organization and partisan mobilization.

CRITERIA FOR PARTY CONTACT

To what extent does information regarding primary participation affect the likelihood that a voter will be contacted by a party? We employ public record data regarding cumulative primary participation histories to address this question among our respondents. These cumulative histories provide information on as many as eight previous primaries for individuals who are registered to vote, and this information is used to determine frequency of participation and ballot choice among our respondents.

Among those respondents who have never voted in a primary, approximately 25 percent report being contacted during the campaign. In contrast, the rate of reported contact increases to about 40 percent among other respondents. Not surprisingly, party organizations focus their contacting efforts on their own primary voters. Thirty-two percent of those who vote only in Democratic primaries report being contacted on behalf of Democratic candidates, and only 19 percent report a Republican contact. Among Republican primary voters, 34 percent report a Republican contact and only 15 percent report a Democratic contact. Significantly, the Democrats demonstrate a rate of contacting among the citizens who have voted in both parties' primaries (23 percent) that is nearly equal to that of the Republicans (29 percent), even though we have seen (in Table 11.1 of Chapter 11) that these voters are almost entirely Republican in their professed political sympathies. It would appear that the Democrats are either misperceiving, miscalculating, or unable to repair a situation in which they contact voters who are likely to be Republican loyalists.

What other information might the party organizations use in their con-

---

3 For example, two-thirds of the respondents who voted in the 1984 Democratic primary report voting for Walter Mondale, and 94 percent of the respondents who voted in the 1984 Republican primary report voting for Ronald Reagan.

tacting efforts? South Bend politics is structured by local geography in some very pronounced ways. For example, the proportion of our survey respondents voting for Reagan within the sixteen sampled neighborhoods varies from .18 to .59, and the proportion voting for Mondale varies from .14 to .38.[4] Political strategists within the city are certainly aware of these patterns, and thus it is reasonable to expect that they use zone of residence as an indicator of likely political sympathies. Such a measurement device is especially useful because it allows the party to organize its efforts on a geographic (door-to-door) basis rather than on the basis of a list of individuals. But how should parties decide *which* neighborhoods might provide a fruitful focus for their activity? Several criteria might be used: (1) They might select neighborhoods where the turnout for the party's primary was heaviest; (2) they might select neighborhoods that are high (or low) in terms of social status, (3) they might have complex, historically idiosyncratic reasons for selecting particular neighborhoods, and so on.

We have experimented with a variety of different aggregate measures that might potentially explain the individual incidence of party contact within our sample. The results of these efforts are shown in part A of Table 12.1, which displays logit models for the probabilities that a respondent is contacted by each of the parties. Party contact by a particular party is the criterion variable. The explanatory variables are cumulative participation records in Democratic and Republican primaries, and the neighborhood property that was found to be most influential in explaining each party's contacting efforts. The magnitude of effects predicted by the models of Table 12.1(A) are shown in part A of Figure 12.1. As this figure shows, the probability of Republican contact among our respondents is enhanced both by Republican primary participation and by living in a neighborhood with a higher turnout in the Republican party primary. Several neighborhood properties provided nearly equivalent statistical purchase in explaining Republican contact – the closest competitor being the mean level of education attainment within the neighborhood. In other words, citizens are more likely to be contacted by the Republican party if they participate in Republican primaries. Independent of their own participation, they are also more likely to be contacted if they live among others who vote in Republican primaries, and this tends to occur in higher-status neighborhoods.

The Democrats exhibit a different pattern of contacting, at least with respect to aggregate neighborhood effects. Figure 12.1(A) shows that those who participate in Democratic party primaries are more likely to be contacted by Democrats, but the only neighborhood property that helps to explain Democratic contact is simply the proportion of neighborhood

4 All measures of the vote used in this chapter are validated with registration data. Respondents who do not appear on the registration list are counted as nonvoters. Respondents who appear on the registration list *and* who reported voting for Mondale or Reagan are counted accordingly.

Table 12.1. *Republican and Democratic contact by primary election participation and selected neighborhood characteristics, with and without controls for party identification and education*

	Democratic contact	Republican contact
A. How do the parties decide whom to contact?		
Constant	-2.25	-1.70
	(8.93)	(10.99)
Cumulative participation in Democratic primaries (range: 0-8)	.17	-.04
	(7.76)	(1.42)
Cumulative participation in Republican primaries (range: 0-8)	-.03	.16
	(.74)	(4.30)
Neighborhood proportion contacted by Democrats[a]	2.73	—
	(2.69)	
Neighborhood proportion voting in 1984 Republican primary	—	4.09
		(2.86)
B. Whom do the parties contact?		
Constant	-2.70	-3.24
	(5.96)	(8.29)
Cumulative participation in Democratic primaries	.15	.01
	(6.46)	(.45)
Cumulative participation in Republican primaries	-.01	.08
	(.23)	(1.96)
Neighborhood proportion contacted by Democrats[a]	2.77	—
	(2.72)	
Neighborhood proportion voting in Republican primary	—	1.94
		(1.29)
Individual education (years of school)	.05	.09
	(1.72)	(3.09)
Individual party identification	-.06	.16
	(1.56)	(4.39)

Note: Logit model with coefficient t-values in parentheses. N-size is 1,446 respondents for all models.

[a]The respondent's own contacting experience is excluded in the calculation of this neighborhood proportion for that respondent.

respondents who report being contacted. Thus, people who live in neighborhoods with high levels of Democratic contact are more likely to be contacted, even after the individual criteria for contacting are taken into account.

Is it tautological to say that people living in high-contact areas are more likely to be contacted? We have removed the respondent's own experience

A.

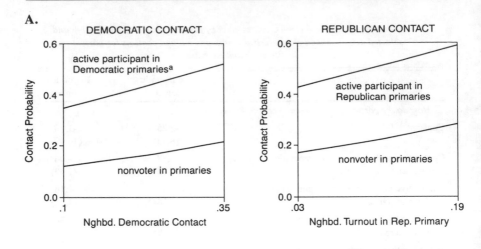

B.

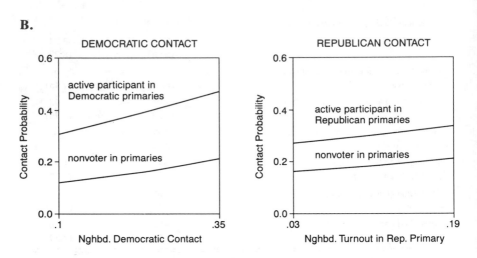

Figure 12.1. Party contacts and primary election participation. (An active participant is defined as someone who has voted in eight primaries.)

Top: How do the parties decide whom to contact? Table 12.1A estimates without controls for education or partisanship.

Bottom: Whom do the parties contact? Table 12.1B estimates with controls for education and partisanship: education is controlled at 12 years and party identification is controlled at independent.

when calculating the proportion of neighborhood respondents who were contacted by the Democrats, and thus the relationship is not tautological. For example, if a respondent lives in a neighborhood where 20 percent of the people were contacted by the Democrats, this means that 20 percent of all *other* respondents living in the neighborhood were contacted. Indeed, the individual probability of being contacted by the Republicans is *not* significantly affected by the level of neighborhood contacting after the individual contacting criteria are taken into account.

In one sense this account of Democratic contacting is not entirely satisfactory because it does not provide a rationale for the higher incidence of contacting in some neighborhoods. For some reason – perhaps related to traditional areas of Democratic strength (Stabrowski 1984) – the Democratic party tends to concentrate its resources within particular neighborhoods. At the same time, our inability to explain this concentration of effort is revealing in another respect. *It shows that political structure as well as social structure is a significant element in political affairs.* Political outcomes cannot be explained wholly in terms of class and status; they must also be explained in terms of party. Indeed, in the sense we are defining it here, political structure provides a separate level of meaning and experience that is imposed on social structure (Key and Munger 1959).

THE EFFECTIVENESS OF THE PARTY CONTACTING CRITERIA

Thus far we have addressed the factors that serve as criteria for party contact – information that the parties use to locate and mobilize their supporters. This information provides only an indirect measure of partisan orientation, but it is the best that the parties can do because it is, in essence, all the information that is available. In other words, the party is not able to interview all the voters prior to contacting them! If they *were* able to conduct such interviews, they might obtain a more direct measure of partisan orientation that left less room for doubt regarding political intentions.

Although such information is unavailable for the entire electorate, it *is* available for the respondents who participated in the survey. Thus we can assess the success of each party in locating its supporters. Part B of Table 12.1 replicates the analysis of Table 12.1(A), but it includes individual level controls for self-reported partisanship (party identification) and for individual educational attainment. This table allows us to address the following question: To what extent do the contacting criteria serve as valid indicators of party support? If the introduction of a control for each respondent's partisanship diminishes the explanatory power of the contacting criteria, then the contacting criteria can be assumed to be doing a good job for the party.

The introduction of these controls produces very different consequences for the analysis of Democratic and Republican contacting efforts. In terms of Democratic contact, neither individual education nor party identification produces particularly strong, statistically discernible effects, and Figure 12.1(B) shows that the originally estimated effects of Democratic primary participation and Democratic contacting in the neighborhood are essentially maintained. In contrast, for Republican contact, both individual education and party identification produce strong, statistically discernible effects, and the originally estimated effects are substantially reduced in magnitude (see Part B of Figure 12.1).

What does this suggest? It would seem that the Republicans are doing a better job than the Democrats in contacting their supporters. When we hold primary participation constant, the probability of being contacted by the Democrats is, at most, only modestly affected by class and party. Under the same conditions, the probability of being contacted by the Republicans is dramatically affected by class and party. Why is this the case? Part of the answer lies in the partisan pattern of cross-party primary voting. When the Republicans contact a participant in Republican primaries, they can rest assured that they have contacted a voter with Republican sympathies. Even when the Republicans contact a voter who is a switch-hitter in primary voting, they can still be relatively confident that they have made connection with a Republican sympathizer. In contrast, even when the Democrats contact a voter who participates exclusively in Democratic primaries, they still cannot be confident that they have located a voter with Democratic loyalties.

Ironically, this set of circumstances is generated by the *strength* of the Democratic party in the South Bend area. Democratic dominance in local politics has produced a situation in which Republican primaries frequently become only a sideshow in local political affairs (Key 1949). As a result, many Republicans regularly participate in the affairs of the Democratic primary. But this produces a situation in which it is often difficult to tell the players apart – it becomes difficult, especially for the Democrats, to identify supporters. And thus the majority party is placed at an institutional disadvantage (see Katz and Eldersveld 1961).[5]

THE AGGREGATE STRUCTURE OF THE PARTY CANVASS

If we adopt the premise that citizens' political choices are socially interdependent – that the behavior of one individual is affected by the behavior of other individuals who share the same social space – then the aggregate pattern of party contact becomes at least as important as the micropattern.

5 A methodological possibility is that partisanship works well for the Republicans because much of partisan identification is a simultaneous function of vote choice. This alternative interpretation seems unlikely in light of the very strong education effect for Republican contacts. Whatever else this class measure may proxy, it is certain that vote does not determine education. Substantive rather than methodological interpretations are more persuasive.

When the Republicans contact a voter who lives in a particular neighbor-hood, works at a particular office, and bowls in a particular league, then the party has potentially gained access to the neighborhood, the office, and the bowling alley. The ripple effect of social interaction produces conse-quences that lie beyond the initial contact and extend more generally to the social space that is inhabited by the contacted individual (Eulau 1986; Huckfeldt 1986).

We have already seen that parties and candidates impose a political structure upon the electorate that is distinct from important social struc-tural elements. We cannot easily predict the individual likelihood of con-tact simply with reference to aggregate social structural properties within the individual's environment. Much of this is undoubtedly due to the indi-viduation of party contacting strategies – to the use of voter registration lists – but it does not follow that individualized strategies are lacking in aggregate consequences, even if the consequences are unforeseen. Rather, a new layer of aggregate organization is imposed upon an already complex set of well-organized aggregate properties. Perhaps the best evidence for this politically imposed structure is the range of variation in the level of contacting between the neighborhoods included within our sample. The proportion of neighborhood respondents who report being contacted var-ies from .12 to .36 and from .11 to .34 for the Republicans and Democrats respectively. A natural question thus arises: How does the aggregate struc-ture of party mobilization relate to other structural characteristics within the community?

Table 12.2 displays the correlations between neighborhood patterns of party contacting and a number of other, neighborhood-level social and political characteristics. This table provides an aggregate picture of the political and social structure of party mobilization efforts during the elec-tion campaign. The neighborhood characteristics are measured by aggregat-ing survey responses within each of the sixteen study neighborhoods, thereby providing a point estimate within each neighborhood based on an average sample of approximately ninety respondents.

These correlations are revealing on several counts. First, the aggregate patterns of Democratic and Republican contacting efforts are only weakly related to each other. In the context of individual contacting, we have already seen that the probabilities of being contacted by the Republicans and Democrats are slightly correlated in a positive direction. Now, in the case of aggregate patterns of contacting, we see a pattern of near indepen-dence with a slightly *negative* relationship between Democratic and Repub-lican efforts. In both instances, however, the relative independence of mobilization efforts is more striking than the presence of any weak relation-ship. Once again, if both parties were efficiently contacting their potential supporters, we might expect to see a strong negative relationship between the mobilization efforts.

Table 12.2. *Correlations between neighborhood patterns of party contacting and various political and social characteristics*

	Proportion contacted by Democrats	Proportion contacted by Republicans
Proportion contacted by Democrats	1.000	-0.080
Proportion contacted by Republicans	-0.080	1.000
Mean education (school years)	-0.220	0.564
Mean party identification	-0.378	0.685
Proportion voting in Democratic primary	0.274	-0.364
Proportion voting in Republican primary	-0.106	0.631

Note: The N-size for each correlation is sixteen neighborhoods. Neighborhood characteristics are measured on the basis of 1,446 interviews sorted by sixteen neighborhoods.

Much of the independence between party mobilization efforts is due to the very ambiguous structure that underlies Democratic mobilization. Using aggregate party identification as an invisible criterion of contacting success – invisible at least to party strategists – the neighborhood-level relationship between mean party identification and proportion contacted is much stronger for the Republicans: .68 compared with $-.38$. This means that 46 percent of the aggregate pattern of Republican mobilization effort covaries with neighborhood partisanship, whereas only 14 percent of Democratic mobilization effort similarly covaries – the Republicans are more than three times as efficient as the Democrats at this crucial discriminatory task. If the goal of mobilization is to activate the party's friends, then the Republicans are much more effective at this effort.

Finally, Table 12.2 also provides information regarding the class basis of party mobilization efforts. The aggregate structure of party contacts is more closely related to the aggregate structure of educational attainment (our measure of social class) for the Republicans than for the Democrats: .56 compared to $-.22$. In words, Republican mobilization efforts are more strongly oriented toward upper-status locales than are Democratic efforts oriented toward lower-status locales. In terms of explained variation, this presents a sixfold difference (.05 compared with .31) in the ability of class to account for aggregate variations in party mobilization effort. Why is this the case?

Even though the Democrats' natural constituency is located among lower-status citizens, the *class structure* of mobilization runs at least partially counter to the *political structure* of mobilization. When the Democrats focus their mobilization efforts on those citizens who have indicated Democratic sympathies by voting in Democratic primaries, they are introducing a mobilization criterion with an upper-status bias because primary participants are more likely to be upper-status citizens (see Krassa 1985). This is seen in the aggregate correlations between education and participation in each of the party primaries. The correlations lie in the expected opposite directions, but the relationship between education and Republican primary participation is considerably stronger.

In summary, this examination of the aggregate structure of party mobilization points once again to the dilemma of the majority party. The Democrats are unable to impose a cohesive structure on their efforts for two separable reasons. First, Democratic primary participation is an especially ambiguous criterion of party support. Many Democratic primary voters are not loyal Democrats, and thus the party has a difficult time identifying its supporters. In this light it is not surprising that the pattern of Democratic contacting is less closely linked to the pattern of Democratic primary voting. Second, the political criterion for identifying supporters tends to run in an opposite direction from the class basis of party support. Primary participation is more widespread among upper-class citizens, and contacting primary participants thus tends to dilute the class basis of Democratic organization. Stated somewhat differently, social structure tends to lose out to political structure. Particularly for the Democrats, it thus becomes clear that *the unintended consequence of party mobilization activity is an aggregate structure of contacting that is only weakly related to the social structure underlying party support.*

AGGREGATES AND INDIVIDUALS

To reiterate our earlier argument, the aggregate distribution of these behaviors is just as important as the individual distribution. That is, it is just as important to recognize the aggregate consequences of individual behavior as it is to recognize the individual consequences of aggregate behavior (Sprague 1976). Party strategists adopt a set of strategies that determine the individual likelihood of contact. As we have seen, however, these individualized strategies do not translate unambiguously into aggregate consequences.

This imperfect match between politics at the individual level and politics in the aggregate extends to other forms of electoral involvement as well. Consider a very visible manifestation of individual involvement with important aggregate manifestations – the placement of bumper stickers and yard signs. Such behavior is important in the aggregate because it sends a signal regarding appropriate behavior to others who are exposed to these signs. Moreover, exposure is selective. The people who are most likely to see the yard signs and bumper stickers are those who share the same living space. Thus, a confluence of individual interest and socially transmitted influence is produced. People who live around me – people who are like me and share many interests in common with me – send a very visible aggregate message regarding appropriate political behavior. As a result, I receive a cumulative signal regarding the political preferences of those whom I am likely to perceive as sharing my own interests and viewpoints (Downs 1957; Burt 1987).

How should we expect the distribution of signs and bumper stickers to vary across neighborhoods? A first response might be that Democratic yard signs should be more prevalent in Democratic neighborhoods, and Republican yard signs in Republican neighborhoods. Fair enough, but part A of Table 12.3 suggests that this is only part of the picture. Neighborhood partisanship appears to be important for the distribution of Democratic signs and stickers, but not for Republican. Republican variation is better explained by the aggregate pattern of Republican contacting.[6]

Finally, Table 12.3(A) also suggests a symbiotic effect: The presence of Democratic signs and stickers tends to stimulate Republican signs and stickers, and the presence of Republican signs and stickers tends to stimulate Democratic signs and stickers. Why might this cross-stimulation occur? Some individuals are, undoubtedly, goaded into action by visible signs of support for a candidate they oppose. Just as likely, the distribution of yard signs in particular may be strategically controlled. The placement of signs may be calculated as a response to a higher density of signs in a particular area of town. Along these same lines, it is interesting to note the stronger effects on the distribution of Republican signs and stickers that occur as the result of both party contact and the opposite party's signs and stickers. If Republicans perceive themselves as a minority in South Bend, and particularly if they perceive themselves as a minority within a neighborhood, then they may behave more strategically than Democrats, as the rate of primary crossover already indicates (Farquharson 1969). In particular, confronted by excess Democratic yard signs and bumper stickers, they may well contact their known supporters to put up yard signs in response. In short, we may be seeing further evidence of the value that accrues to the political minority as a result of intense party activity (D. Katz and Eldersveld 1961).

The distribution of yard signs and bumper stickers reflects the complex interplay of partisan support, party strategy, and party competition. While we do not possess the precise menu that yields the aggregate result, we are

---

6 In order to determine whether a respondent displayed a Democratic or a Republican yard sign or bumper sticker, their presidential vote is used as an indicator. For example, we assume that self-reported Reagan voters who also report putting up a yard sign or a bumper sticker did in fact put up a Republican sign or sticker. They might have, of course, put up a sign or a sticker for a Democratic candidate running for some other office. Indeed, in view of the election results, where many Democratic identifiers voted for Reagan, we probably overestimate Republican signs and stickers and underestimate Democratic signs and stickers. The resulting bias is not likely to compromise our analysis to any serious extent. Split-ticket voters are less likely to display signs and stickers and thus the bias is not likely to be profound. Indeed, these data show that (using our measure) less than 1 percent of self-identified Democrats put up a Republican sign or sticker, and not a single self-identified Republican put up a Democratic sign or sticker. Alternatively, none of the Democratic signs or stickers were put up by Republicans, and only 6 percent of the Republican signs and stickers were put up by Democrats.

Table 12.3. *Neighborhood distribution of yard signs and bumper stickers*

A. *Proportion of Democratic and Republican signs and stickers as a function of neighborhood partisanship, party contacts, and opposite party's yard signs and bumper stickers*

	Democratic yard signs and bumper stickers	Republican yard signs and bumper stickers
Constant	.10	-.14
	(4.29)	(2.83)
Neighborhood partisanship	-.021	.02
(mean party identification)	(4.23)	(1.30)
Neighborhood proportion contacted	-.02	.32
by party	(.26)	(2.36)
Opposite party's signs	.27	1.39
and stickers (proportion)	(2.88)	(3.25)
R^2	.65	.65
N	16	16

B. *Neighborhood ratio of Democratic signs and stickers to Republican signs and stickers by Republican and Democratic contact in the neighborhood*

Constant	1.46
	(2.52)
Neighborhood proportion contacted by Democrats	8.03
	(4.55)
Neighborhood proportion contacted by Republicans	-9.05
	(5.23)
R^2	.80
N	16

Note: Least squares models with coefficient *t*-values in parentheses.

able to identify many of the crucial ingredients. They are displayed in part B of Table 12.3, where the ratio of Democratic to Republican signs and stickers is regressed on the levels of Democratic and Republican contacting in the neighborhoods. Quite clearly, party activity makes a decided difference: 80 percent of the variation in the ratio can be explained in terms of party effort.

CONSEQUENCES OF PARTY EFFORTS

What are the consequences of party mobilization efforts for the citizens who are contacted? Do organized partisan efforts have results that extend beyond the point of contact? These are crucial questions that speak directly to the role of political parties in democratic politics, and to the potential for a politically organized electorate. We address them here in the context of extensive previous work showing (1) generally moderate but consistent effects on levels of turnout and (2) mixed evidence regarding effects on the direction of the vote (Krassa 1988, 1989; Kramer 1970–1; D. Katz and Eldersveld 1961; Pimlott 1972, 1973; Cutright 1963; Cutright and Rossi 1958; Crotty 1971; Wolfinger 1963; Gosnell 1927).

As we have seen, South Bend party organizations tend to pursue contacts among those citizens who have voted in previous party primaries and thus have a record of party support. This is an important fact to take into account when judging the individual consequences of party contact. South Bend primary voters participated in the subsequent general election at an extraordinarily high rate – more than 98 percent of respondents who voted in the primary also voted in the general election. In contrast, nonparticipants in the primary were equally likely to vote or stay home at the general election. Thus, if an analysis ignores the high level of participation among primary voters, the importance of party contacting might easily be exaggerated because party contacting is keyed to primary participation.

In keeping with the importance of primary participation, the consequences of party contact are analyzed separately among primary election voters and nonvoters. The effects of party contacts on turnout, presidential voting, gubernatorial voting, and congressional voting are considered among primary election nonvoters in part A of Table 12.4. In the first column, nonvoting is the reference condition, and the coefficients predict the probability of voting in the general election. In the remaining columns, voting for the Democratic candidate is the reference condition, and the coefficients predict the probability of voting for the Republican candidate. Thus, we can use the first model to consider the effect of contact on turnout. And for those who *do* vote in the general election, we can employ the other models to consider the effect of contact on the two-party division of the vote. Table 12.4(A) shows, at most, weak effects due to party contacting among nonvoters in the primary election. Both Republican and Democratic contacts fail to generate statistically discernible effects at even the .05 level for any of the voting behaviors, although the respective coefficients all lie in the expected directions. In general, the more impressive effects in these four models are due to self-identified partisanship[7] and, in the case of turnout, to individual and contextual education.

The estimated effects of individual and contextual education on turnout, based on the first model of Table 12.4(A) with all other variables

7 In light of work showing reciprocal causation between vote choice and party identification measured as a seven-point scale (Franklin and Jackson 1983), we have restricted our measure of partisanship to three categories: Democratic, Republican, and independent (the baseline category). This practice is based on the assumption that people are much more likely to shift the strength of their attachment within categories than they are to switch their actual attachment during the campaign – an assumption that is sustained by the South Bend data.

Table 12.4. *Voting choices in the 1984 general election*

	Turnout	Republican president	Republican governor	Republican congressman
A. Primary nonvoters				
Constant	-3.16**	-.51	-4.91*	-3.87
Democratic identifier[a]	-.49**	-2.77**	-1.84**	-2.17**
Republican identifier[a]	.26	2.10**	1.96**	1.45**
Age	-.02**	.02	.01	.02
Education (years of school)	.09*	.01	.02	-.06
Neighborhood education (mean school years)	.24**	.08	.32	.31*
Democratic contact in neighborhood[b]	-.78	-.61	1.69	-.76
Republican contact in neighborhood[b]	-.89	.36	-.03	.40
Democratic contact[a]	.35	-.73	-.12	-.44
Republican contact[a]	.23	.19	.27	.33
N	853	373	374	374
B. Voters in the primary				
Constant		.70	-2.49	-.42
Democratic identifier[a]		-1.35**	-2.14**	-1.69**
Republican identifier[a]		4.13**	1.70**	2.23**
Age		-.01	.00	.00
Education (years of school)		.04	.03	.06
Neighborhood education (mean school years)		-.06	.14	-.14
Democratic contact in neighborhood[b]		.44	2.64	.59
Republican contact in neighborhood[b]		.33	-.60	2.87
Democratic contact[a]		-.49	-.85**	-.83**
Republican contact[a]		.46	.62*	.10
N		539	557	552

Note: Logit models.

[a]Dummy coded.

[b]Proportion contacted.

*Two-tailed *p*-value < .05; ** two-tailed *p*-value < .01.

held constant, are shown in Figure 12.2. Respondents with higher levels of schooling are more likely to vote, regardless of the educational level of the surrounding neighborhood population. Conversely, respondents who live among a more highly educated population are more likely to vote regardless of their own educational levels (Tingsten 1963). Recall once again that Table 12.4(A) is estimated on the basis of respondents who did not vote in the previous spring's primary election. For these individuals lying outside the boundaries of conventional party involvement, political structure has little effect on turnout in the general election. In contrast, social structure has a decided effect on whether they vote. For the other respondents – those who *did* vote in the primary election – the level of participation in the general election is so high that *both* social structure *and* party contact are rendered irrelevant. This is not to say that partisan contacts and social structural influences are immaterial to their involvement, but the focus of this effort is necessarily upon the activation process during the campaign, and primary voters did not need to be activated.

If party contacting is immaterial to general election turnout among primary voters, does it have any effect on the two-party division of the vote? Part B of Table 12.4 shows that, at least in terms of the presidential vote, the contacting coefficients for party contact lie in the substantively appropriate directions, but they fail to satisfy the .05 level of significance. A very different situation occurs with respect to the gubernatorial and congressional elections. In three of four instances, the coefficients not only lie in the expected directions, but they also satisfy at least the .05 level of significance. Both of these elections produced highly visible campaigns. The incumbent Republican governor took advantage of a significant statewide organization to ensure his reelection, and South Bend's popular and well-known Democratic county prosecutor mounted an aggressive but unsuccessful challenge against the incumbent Republican congressman.[8] These results, which show an effect due to party activity in subnational elections, are in keeping with a stream of research documenting the importance of parties and party activities particularly at the state and local level (Wolfinger 1963; D. Katz and Eldersveld 1961; Patterson and Caldeira 1983; Caldeira, Patterson, and Markko 1985; Caldeira, Clausen, and Patterson 1990).

How large are the estimated effects due to party contacts? Table 12.5 uses Table 12.4(B) coefficient estimates to illustrate the effect of party contact on the predicted probability of a Republican gubernatorial vote, across categories of party identification. The effect of the partisan contact

---

8 The incumbent congressman, John Hiler, was one of House Speaker Tip O'Neill's "Reagan robots," originally winning office in the 1980 election. He had only narrowly hung on to his seat in the 1982 midterm election, but in 1984 he took advantage of Reagan's coattails to win more easily (Mondak 1990).

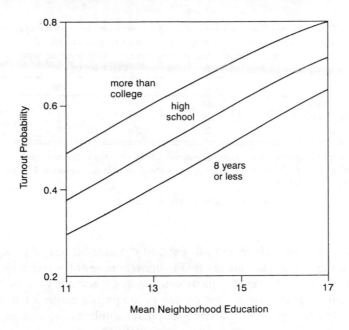

Figure 12.2. Turnout probability in the general election by individual and neighbor-hood education, for nonvoters in the primary election. Age is held constant at 45 years, neighborhood proportions contacted by Democrats and Republicans are held constant at .10, partisanship is held constant at independent, and Republican and Democratic contact are held constant at no contact. *Source:* Table 12.4A estimates.

is especially pronounced among independents and Republicans. This is not to argue that contacting is always important, but only that it can be. And these results suggest that it is more likely to be important in state and local contests, among those citizens who participate in party primaries.

Thus the irony of party contacting deepens. In terms of turnout, politically marginal citizens – citizens who failed to vote in the primary election – appear to lie beyond the reach of partisan organization. Conversely, politi-cally engaged citizens – citizens who vote in party primaries – are over-whelmingly likely to vote in the general election *whether they are contacted or not.* The effectiveness of organized partisan effort is most pronounced among these citizens who vote in the primaries, but the effect lies in altering the two-party division of the vote in state and local contests. And thus it would appear that partisan contact is less important as a vehicle to get out the vote than it is a means of swaying the preferences of voters who are already likely to vote.

We could end the analysis here with the conclusion that party contacting only has an effect on the direction of the vote among some citizens in some

Table 12.5. *Predicted Republican percentage of two-party vote for governor in general election among primary voters, by party contact and party identification*

| | Contacted by | | | |
	Democrats	Republicans	Neither	Both
Democratic identifier	.04	.15	.08	.07
Republican identifier	.65	.89	.81	.77
Independent	.25	.59	.44	.38

Note: Other variables are held constant at intermediate values: age = 45 years, education = 12 years, neighborhood education = 12 years, neighborhood Democratic contact = .10, neighborhood Republican contact = .10.

Source: Table 12.4(B) estimates for gubernatorial election.

contests. But does such an analysis exhaust the possibilities? Are we looking in the right places to understand the consequences of partisan mobilization? Should we only view the party canvass as a direct instrument of mass mobilization enlisting voters one by one to the party's cause, or should we also view the canvass as a catalytic agent that stimulates voter mobilization by enlisting additional party workers in the effort?

OTHER FORMS OF ELECTORAL INVOLVEMENT

Voting in an election is only one form of electoral involvement that is susceptible to the influence of party mobilization efforts. A whole range of gladiatorial activities are central to the electoral process and dependent upon party organizational activities. We consider four of these activities here, based on the following questions asked in the third-wave, post-election survey.

1. Did you work for any candidate in this election?
2. Did you go to any political meetings, rallies, dinners, or things like that?
3. Did you put up a political yard sign or bumper sticker during the campaign?
4. Did you give any money to a political party or candidate?

Each of these activities considered singly is, of course, a rare event when compared with the frequency of voting. But taken together they point toward involvement that is perhaps surprisingly widespread. A summary index is formed by counting the number of activities in which each respondent reported participating. A score of zero indicates no involvement in any of the activities (71 percent of the third-wave respondents), and a score of four indicates involvement in each of the four activities (2 percent of the third-wave respondents). Thus nearly 30 percent of the sample reported engaging in at least one of these activities.

As Table 12.6 suggests, the structure of political life looms large with

Table 12.6. *Partisan electoral involvement as a function of various factors, including party contact*

	Coefficient	*t*-value
Constant	-.24	.77
Democratic identifier[a]	.24	4.38
Republican identifier[a]	.21	3.42
Voted in Democratic primary[a]	.07	1.25
Voted in Republican primary[a]	.30	3.48
Democratic contact[a]	.24	4.08
Republican contact[a]	.19	3.26
Democratic contact in neighborhood (proportion contacted)	-.44	1.22
Republican contact in neighborhood (proportion contacted)	1.19	2.92
Individual education (years of school)	.04	3.98
Neighborhood education (mean school years)	-.02	.86
N	1,439	
R^2	.08	

Note: Ordinary least squares model.
[a]Dummy coded.

respect to these other forms of electoral involvement. In particular, party contacts play an important role, but there is also evidence to suggest that partisan identification, primary participation, and the level of party contacting within neighborhoods – at least by Republicans – may make a difference as well.[9] In contrast, although the effect of individual education is substantial, the neighborhood educational level has no effect at all. *Unlike the case of general election turnout among nonvoters in the primary, political structure rather than social structure goes much farther in explaining levels of activation and involvement.*

SECOND-ORDER CONSEQUENCES OF THE PARTY CANVASS

The party canvass has substantial consequences for activating the activists, but does it serve to stimulate a more widespread mobilization process? One

9 An alternative analysis of these data was undertaken in which electoral involvement was truncated to a binary variable: those who had participated in *any* of the activities versus those who had participated in *none* of the activities. This variable was, in turn, the criterion variable in a logit regression with the same explanatory variables as in Table 12.6. The results were wholly consistent with the Table 12.6 analysis.

opportunity to address this question lies in examining the consequences that derive from simple, grass-roots partisan activity – displaying a political yard sign or bumper sticker. Does the aggregate distribution of yard signs and bumper stickers have any measurable consequence for the individuals who are exposed to them? At the second-wave interview, during the heart of the campaign, we asked our respondents a question regarding which presidential candidate they thought would win the most votes in their neighborhood. We also asked whether they thought it would be a close race, and thus a four-point index can be constructed that measures the respondents' expectations regarding voting behavior among neighborhood residents. (Higher values correspond to Republican expectations.)

How might partisan activity alter these expectations? In the first column of Table 12.7 the expectation regarding the neighborhood is regressed on respondents' preelection candidate preferences and the neighborhood distribution of yard signs and bumper stickers, and the results show that the distribution of yard signs and bumper stickers is quite clearly related to neighborhood expectations. The problem is, of course, that while Democratic yard signs and bumper stickers *do* tend to be located in Democratic neighborhoods, they are not the only ways in which residents of a neighborhood form judgments regarding the political tendencies of other residents. We have no method for sorting out the extent to which signs and stickers are responsible for these judgments, but we can examine the extent to which respondents' expectations are misinformed – the extent to which yard signs and bumper stickers have effects that are not attributable to the actual distribution of support.

The respondents' expectations are considered once more in the second column of Table 12.7, but controls are included for the *actual* distribution of votes in the respondents' neighborhoods. Our strategy is to reconsider yard signs and bumper stickers, but to subject their effect on respondent perceptions to a control for reality. Do visible manifestations of support continue to affect respondent perceptions once we simultaneously take into account the reality upon which the perceptions are based? It must be emphasized that this is a very stringent test. Our new question becomes: Do yard signs and bumper stickers have an effect on perceptions of support when we control the actual levels of support on which the perceptions are based? Thus we are ignoring yard signs and bumper stickers as vehicles for communicating the reality of these support levels and focusing instead on their potential to produce alternative perceptions of the same underlying reality.

This new test is accomplished by aggregating the reported votes of respondents from the third-wave, postelection survey within each of the neighborhoods. Treating the resulting measures as the actual distributions of support within the neighborhoods, we are able to isolate the independent informational effect due to visible demonstrations of support – the

Table 12.7. *Expectations of election outcomes in neighborhood by respondent's preference and neighborhood yard signs and bumper stickers, with and without controls for actual levels of support in the neighborhoods*

No control for actual support levels in neighborhoods		Controls for actual support levels in neighborhoods	
Constant	3.41	Constant	2.24
	(32.63)		(8.28)
Mondale supporter[a]	-.41	Mondale supporter	-.36
	(4.97)		(4.51)
Reagan supporter[a]	.15	Reagan supporter	.11
	(1.91)		(1.42)
Democratic signs and stickers	-22.54	Neighborhood Mondale vote	-1.92
(neighborhood proportion)	(14.13)	(proportion)	(3.26)
Republican signs and stickers	8.48	Neighborhood Reagan vote	2.77
(neighborhood proportion)	(10.75)	(proportion)	(8.34)
		Partisan difference	-4.11
		signs and stickers[b]	(4.88)
R^2	.29	R^2	.36
N	939	N	939

Note: Ordinary least squares models. Coefficient *t*-values are in parentheses.

[a]As is the case with the dependent variable, these dummy variables are measured at the second wave of the survey, prior to the general election. Only the neighborhood variables are taken from the third-wave postelection survey. Only respondents participating in both the second and third waves are included in this table.

[b]The partisan difference in signs and stickers is measured as the neighborhood proportion with Democratic signs and stickers minus the neighborhood proportion with Republican signs and stickers.

yard signs and bumper stickers. A single measure for the distribution of signs and stickers has been constructed that provides the difference in the proportions of neighborhood residents displaying Democratic versus Republican yard signs and stickers – the proportion Democratic minus the proportion Republican. As the table shows, this variable measuring the distribution of yard signs and bumper stickers produces a statistically discernible effect with an appropriate sign for neighborhood expectations.

Contextual theories of politics often assert that citizens surrounded by a particular preference are more likely to adopt the preference. The empirical support for such an argument is substantial and widespread, e.g., Segal and Meyer 1974. But the enduring critique of such an argument is an alleged failure to document the mechanisms whereby the aggregated preferences of a population are translated into a source of influence for individuals (Hauser 1974). This chapter supplies one part of the response to this critique: An important mechanism of contextual influence is party effort.

Table 12.8. *Individual party identification as a function of neighborhood partisanship and other individual-level factors*

	Without controls for presidential vote choice	With controls for presidential vote choice
Constant	-0.68	.09
	(1.55)	(.24)
Individual education	0.10	.08
(years of school)	(3.60)	(3.29)
Family income	0.15	.09
(range: 1-8)	(4.11)	(3.00)
Age	0.01	.01
	(2.08)	(2.75)
Ethnic attachment[a]	-0.45	-.30
	(3.99)	(3.18)
Union member in family[a]	-0.71	-.25
	(5.54)	(2.28)
Protestant[a]	0.90	.63
	(7.95)	(6.56)
Neighborhood party	0.36	.26
identification[b] (mean)	(3.89)	(3.34)
Mondale voter[a]	—	-1.66
		(14.12)
Reagan voter[a]	—	1.31
		(11.47)
N	1,326	1,285
R^2	.20	.46

Note: Ordinary least squares models. Coefficient t-values are in parentheses.

[a]Dummy coded.

[b]The respondent's own party identification is excluded in the calculation of the neighborhood mean for that respondent.

People know their neighbors' politics, and one reason they know is party organization aimed at informing them.

Viewed somewhat differently, party organization is designed to exploit social organization. The first column of Table 12.8 displays a regression of party identification among the South Bend respondents on a range of different measures: education, income, age, the strength of the respondent's ethnic attachment,[10] union membership, religion, and the partisan composition of the respondent's neighborhood. As this regression shows, individual partisan orientations are subject to the influence of the individ-

10 The strength of a respondent's ethnic attachment is measured with the following question: "How important would you say your ethnic background is to you?" Possible responses are: "very important" or "somewhat important," coded 1; and "not too important," coded 0.

ual's partisan surroundings, even when we include controls for a wide range of individual-level characteristics (Hauser 1974). In particular, the mean partisanship of the neighborhood has important consequences for the partisanship of individuals who live within the neighborhood. Even when we take account of short-term factors affecting partisanship (Franklin and Jackson 1983) by controlling for presidential vote choice in the second column of Table 12.8, the effect of the partisan context on individual loyalties is still substantial. In short, individual partisanship is contingent upon partisan surroundings. Party organization is not the only mechanism that ties individual preference together with the politics of the larger community, but it is certainly one of the ways.

These data demonstrate that party activity matters. The seemingly ordinary act of putting up a yard sign sends a message to others who are exposed to the sign. But the yard sign is only one part of a more complex, highly structured process of political mobilization. Organizations make contact with potential activists who in turn make contact with the population at large. Huge amounts of slippage occur along the way. Organizational contacts often fall on deaf ears – or, still worse, misdirected contacts serve to mobilize supporters of the other party. But the significance of the contact does not end once the contact is made. Rather, the contact serves as a catalyst that sets into motion a series of events that, in the end, has important consequences for ordinary citizens – concerned bystanders who pass judgment on the electoral contests of democratic politics.

CONCLUSION AND IMPLICATIONS

How should we view the efforts made by party organizations to mobilize the electorate? Most important, as long as we focus primarily upon the direct individual consequences of party contacts for voting behavior, we will continue to see the party as playing a marginal role in American politics, and we will consistently underestimate the consequences of party activity. Kramer's (1970–1) work on party contacting deservedly became a watershed event in the analysis of party mobilization efforts, but it also led to a subtle but important redefinition of the expected consequence that derives from party activity. An earlier tradition of analysis, perhaps represented best by the D. Katz and Eldersveld effort (1961), addressed the aggregate pattern of party activity and its consequence for the aggregate distribution of party support. Kramer's analysis turned toward an individual-level analysis of these phenomena, an approach that was readily embraced by social scientists with a heightened sense of skepticism regarding any aggregate data.

The problem remains: Partisan mobilization is best understood at two levels of analysis – the individual and the aggregate. In the general context of American politics it is unreasonable to expect that party contacts should produce dramatic consequences for the voting behavior of those individuals who are contacted. Rather, party contacts are most important as a means of mobilizing potential activists. Most people do not give money and put up yard signs unless someone asks them to do so, and thus we see a catalytic function of party activity. Party organizations mobilize the faithful, and the activity of the faithful sends a message to the rest of the public.

It is ironic that political scientists have become so skeptical regarding party activity and its consequences. If party activity is so ineffective, why do parties and candidates continue to invest their resources in the activity? Gibson et al. (1983, 1985) investigate the vitality of party organizations at both the state and local levels, and they show that state and local party organizations started to become more active during the 1960s and 1970s. Krassa (1985: 5–6) uses national survey data to show that the incidence of party contacting has generally increased during the post–World War II period. It is possible, of course, that academics understand something that activists have missed, but in this instance it is doubtful.

There are, of course, limits on the ability of party organizations to mobilize the electorate, and the limits are more pronounced today than they were fifty years ago. The effectiveness of Chicago's Mayor Daley (the elder) and his precinct runners and precinct captains was genuinely impressive, but organizations such as these have always been the exception rather than the rule. Absent such an organization, an organization that presents an impossible standard of effectiveness, we should not assume that political organization is absent.

Finally, the biggest challenge to any political organization is strategic – developing methods of mobilization that are efficient and effective. As we have seen, numerous obstacles inhibit this sort of effectiveness, and the majority party is perversely vulnerable to its own special strategic constraints. The lesson to be drawn from this analysis is that the parameters determining the relationships between parties and voters, and thus determining the success of partisan mobilization, are environmentally contingent. They cannot be understood from afar.

This chapter and the previous one show that partisan organization matters. Party is not only something that resides in the heads of voters. Indeed, what does reside in the heads of voters may very well be a residue of party organization. But parties are not the only organizations with political consequences. In the next chapter we shift our focus to another form of organization – the church and its consequences for the opinions and behavior of its members.

13

Alternative contexts of political preference

This chapter examines the political consequences that arise due to multiple and simultaneous bases of social experience. Two alternative contexts – those of neighborhoods and churches – provide an empirical setting for the effort; and the analysis focuses on two different political attitudes – policy preferences regarding abortion and partisan self-identification. Several questions are addressed: In what manner are the alternative contexts of politics different and in what manner are they similar? To what extent are churches and neighborhoods reinforcing in the political messages they convey, and to what extent do they serve as independent bases of social experience? How do individual differences and individual discretion mediate and deflect the impact of these alternative sources of political influence?

South Bend citizens live simultaneously in a variety of social worlds, any and all of which might have important political consequences. At one and the same time they are rooted socially in neighborhoods, workplaces, churches, clubs, and associations. Indeed, every citizen lies at the center of a social experience produced by a series of intersecting, overlapping, layered environments. Each of the environments, in turn, has potentially important consequences for politics because each serves to modify and deflect the opportunities and constraints that circumscribe social interaction – social interaction that serves as a vehicle for the transmission of political information and guidance.

Individuals and individual differences are important too – they are not simply artifacts of larger social forces. Citizens pay heed to some aspects of social experience and they reinterpret others. They are attracted to some environments while they seek to avoid others. In these and other ways, individually motivated choice becomes an important element of the structural basis underlying democratic politics. And thus, political preference can be seen as the product of interdependent citizens making choices and decisions within a range of contexts over which they have only partial control.

This chapter is motivated by a concern with the political consequences of

This chapter builds on an earlier collaborative effort with Professor Eric Plutzer (Huckfeldt, Plutzer, and Sprague 1993).

the multiple and simultaneous bases of social experience. Two alternative contexts provide the focal point for the present effort – churches and neighborhoods. And two attitudes are examined – policy preferences regarding abortion and partisan self-identification. Several questions are addressed: What are the political consequences of parish and neighborhood contexts? Which context matters most for what behavior, under what circumstances? How do individual differences mediate the impact of both parishes and contexts?

DEFINING SOCIAL STRUCTURE

Contextual theories of politics build upon the argument that individual political preference is not a simple function of individual characteristics alone, but rather the complex product of an individual's own characteristics in combination with the characteristics and predispositions of other surrounding individuals. Thus, the political consequences of being an Irish Catholic might differ dramatically between Massachusetts and New Hampshire, not due to variation in individual characteristics, but rather due to variations in social experience (Ennis 1962; Sprague 1982). Correspondingly, the political significance of *being* an Irish Catholic could only be understood relative to a particular place and time. The central motivation for contextual theories of politics is the idea that patterns of social interaction are influenced by surrounding population distributions (McPhee 1963). To push the previous example somewhat farther, if there are proportionally more Democrats in Massachusetts than in New Hampshire, Massachusetts Democrats might have a much better chance of encountering other Democrats. And thus the likelihood of receiving social support for a Democratic preference, and socially supplied information compatible with a Democratic loyalty, would be higher in Massachusetts.

In practice, the demonstration of such contextual effects on political behavior is a complex undertaking, at least in part due to the difficulty of identifying relevant social boundaries. In terms of sustaining Democratic loyalties, is it more important to live in a Democratic neighborhood, to worship at a Democratic church, or to drink at a Democratic bar? Correspondingly, some might argue that the demonstration of neighborhood effects is not plausible because modern citizens are not tied to their neighborhoods any longer; or the study of parish effects might be called into question because people do not go to church any longer; and so on.

One way out of these difficulties is to adopt an egocentric definition of social structure. That is, a social structure might be defined relative to each individual that is unique to that individual's idiosyncratic life space (Eulau 1986; Burt 1987). Such a procedure underlies many efforts at social network analysis, where social structure is often defined according to the individual's own report of social relationships. Such an approach has many virtues and advantages, but it includes shortcomings as well. Most important, it runs the conceptual risk of reducing social structure to a manifestation of individual choice by creating a model of individually manufactured patterns of social interaction. Our own analyses suggest that such control over social interaction is far from complete: Individuals exercise choice during processes of social interaction, but the logic of choice operates probabilistically rather than deterministically. Put another way, decisions to take a job or join a church are not retaken every day, but rather evaluated only periodically. In the meantime and on an everyday basis, citizens make do with what goes on at work, at church, in the neighborhood, and so on.

Incomplete individual control over patterns of social interaction points toward the virtue of a multilevel understanding of social structure and the political behavior of individual citizens. The premise of a multilevel contextual analysis is that social structure is imposed upon individuals. This does not mean that individuals fail to exercise discretion over social interaction, but only that such control is constrained and bounded by a set of interaction probabilities that are contingent upon contextually determined supply (McPhee 1963; Huckfeldt 1986). Such a perspective requires that individual preference, including preferences regarding social interaction alternatives, be considered in light of surrounding populations and the distribution of various characteristics and preferences within the population.

The problems thus remain: How should the relevant populations be identified? Which population boundaries are most important? In short, how should social structure be defined relative to politics and political behavior? In the analyses and discussions that follow, we consider two separate contexts – those of the parish and the neighborhood. These two sets do not, of course, exhaust the list of politically relevant contexts, but they provide a useful comparison for purposes of the underlying questions of theory and measurement.

ALTERNATIVE CONTEXTS

The political consequences of religious affiliation and local residential settings have been well established by some of the earliest systematic studies of mass political behavior. In the previously discussed work of Tingsten (1963) on Swedish politics, Stockholm workers were more likely to vote if they lived among other workers, and Tingsten offered persuasive evidence to suggest that the probability of a worker voting socialist was contingent upon residential working-class densities as well. In their early and influential efforts at locating the political preferences of individuals within social structure, sociologists from Columbia University (Lazarsfeld et al. 1948; Berelson et al. 1954) demonstrated the importance of religious affiliation first in Erie County, Ohio, and then in Elmira, New York. In 1948, for example, Protestants in Elmira were more likely to support Dewey, and

Catholics in Elmira were more likely to support Truman, even after the influence of class backgrounds was taken into account. Other and more recent efforts continue in these same traditions. The importance of religion and parish contexts is demonstrated by Wald et al. (1988, 1990) and by Leege and Welch (1989). Elaboration of the political significance of religion in South Bend is given by Gilbert (1993). The importance of neighborhoods, counties, communities and states has been shown by Segal and Meyer (1970), Wright (1976, 1977), Huckfeldt and Kohfeld (1989), and many others.

The importance of religion in Erie County and Elmira contrasts well with the importance of neighborhood (or its facsimile) in Stockholm, but few would suggest, at least on the basis of these results, that religion or neighborhood matter more or less in Sweden or America. The focus upon religion or residence or any other element of social structure is largely dictated by the particular features of research design. The efforts of the Columbia sociologists revolved around survey data, and religion – at least religion defined as a characteristic of individuals – is readily studied with such information. In contrast, Tingsten exploited the rich supply of aggregate political and social data available for Stockholm precincts, and such data push in the direction of aggregate (neighborhood) analyses. In general, research design tends to dictate the elements of social structure that can be examined as possible sources of political influence. The notable work of Finifter (1974) concerning workplace contexts, with workplaces as primary sampling units, is yet another example of this general tendency.

As a practical matter, this close relationship between research design and the possibility of studying various aspects of social structure has tended to fragment studies of social influence and politics. Very little serious comparison occurs between the alternative contexts of politics because very few studies are equipped to support such a comparison. Instead we see the development of a neighborhood clique, a workplace clique, and a parish clique among scholars interested in contextual theories of politics.

This is not to say that comparison never occurs, but only that it serves as a sideshow to the main event. Indeed, significant progress has taken place when scholars have been forced to engage in a comparison of contextual effects across different types of environments. In his study of American Jews, Fuchs (1955) observed that Jewish wives, rather than Jewish husbands, were more likely to demonstrate political preferences coincidental with the dominant views held by Jews as a group. He argued that Jewish men were more likely to leave the neighborhood during the day and were thus more likely to be exposed to non-Jewish influences – a comparison that forces us to address the structurally contingent nature of contextual effects.

Similarly, one of the lasting contributions of the Columbia studies has been the demonstration of cross pressures upon American voters. It was, as they show so well, the middle-class Catholics and the working-class Protestants who had difficulty making up their minds for whom to vote. As Berelson et al. (1954: 131) argue, "such people, by being subject to the influence upon social minorities of different majorities, have more 'freedom of choice' as to which group they will side with. . . . But this freedom – which helps give the community a certain flexibility of political change – is purchased only at the price of high turnover or individual instability." In terms of this discussion, political preference is thus seen as a complex product of competing structural elements – religion and class – as well as their underlying contexts of support.

An implicit assumption underlies most such comparisons: Social structural elements are judged, a priori and by default, to be equivalent in affecting political preferences. That is, the possibility is seldom considered that social structure might be specialized in terms of its effects on politics, or that individuals might selectively and differentially control their own exposure to various contexts and settings. In other words, people might manipulate one social setting versus another, depending on their own preferences and predispositions. But if citizens are rational and purposive in their search for political information from social sources (Downs 1957: 229), they probably look to different social arenas for cues and information regarding different areas of concern. In particular, associates from the church or synagogue or parish might be more influential regarding matters that touch on issues of spirituality and conscience, whereas associates from other domains might be more relevant as sources of information and guidance affecting other areas of concern. Alternatively, people might depend more heavily upon voluntary forms of social organization when they are located in involuntary settings where the distribution of opinion runs counter to their own political preferences. Possibilities such as these lead us to expect variations in the effect of various contexts upon various political opinions and preferences.

ALTERNATIVE CONTEXTS IN SOUTH BEND

The data that serve as the basis for this chapter's analysis were taken primarily from information obtained during the third, postelection interview of the main respondents. As in previous chapters, the sampling design provides a double measurement benefit: Any survey item can be used as a measurement device both at the level of individuals and at the level of environments. By aggregating at the level of neighborhoods, any question included in the survey can be used to measure neighborhood population composition.

In addition, one of the survey questions asked each respondent, "When you go to services, where do you usually go?" More than twenty parishes were named by ten or more respondents, and the respondents choosing one of these parishes provide the subset of the survey used for most analyses here. Such a practice introduces two biases into the sample. First, Catholic parishes tend to be larger than those of other denominations, and thus Catholics are overrepresented in the resulting data set. Second, all the respondents in these analyses name a particular congregation, even if they also report attending infrequently, and thus a major portion of the population – those who do not name a congregation – is unrepresented.[1]

The benefit of the resulting data set is that it can be used to obtain aggregate measures of parishes as well as neighborhoods. Thus the data set provides observation at three distinct levels – the neighborhood, the parish, and the individual. The bulk of the analysis is conducted in terms of individuals, but for each individual we are able to estimate the attitudinal composition of the parish and the neighborhood contexts with respect to both partisanship and abortion attitudes. Several contextual measures are central to the analysis: the mean scores for party identification and abortion attitudes within the neighborhoods and parishes, as well as the standard deviations for these means. For instance, we are able to locate each respondent within a neighborhood and within a parish, and in each parish and neighborhood we know the mean abortion attitude and the standard deviation around that mean. In summary, the resulting data set presents a rare opportunity to address the issues and questions posed earlier.

COMPARING THE CONTEXTS OF PARISHES AND NEIGHBORHOODS

In what ways are the contexts of neighborhoods and parishes different? In what ways are they the same? They are certainly different in terms of their overt purposes. We choose a neighborhood for its schools, its services, the house or apartment we find within its boundaries. We choose a church because it is convenient to the neighborhood, because we like the pastor or priest or rabbi, because our parents raised us in its tradition, because it offers a shared community of faith. In this sense the neighborhood is an instrumentally oriented social aggregate whereas the church is a value-oriented social aggregate.

This chapter is less concerned with the overt functions of parishes and neighborhoods than it is with an important latent consequence – the role each of these contexts plays in structuring opportunities and constraints that act upon social interaction, and thus the role each plays in structuring social influence upon politics (Wald et al. 1988). Of course, overt functions and latent consequences inevitably become intertwined, and thus it is im-

---

1 The first question asked: "When you go to services, where do you usually go?" The following question was: "Would you say you go to church/synagogue every week, almost every week, once or twice a month, a few times a year, or never?" A relatively small number of respondents provide an answer to the first question but then report that they never attend.

portant to consider their relationship. This inevitably means that we consider the role of individual choice as it affects the location of individuals within various contexts.

When people select a church, they are *by definition* locating themselves within a community of like-minded individuals along some unspecified dimension. No claim is being made to suggest that people exercise free and unfettered choice in the selection of a congregation or a parish, even though few people locate themselves intentionally in situations where they feel ill at ease. Rather, people choose a congregation or a parish on the basis of criteria that are more or less incomplete – criteria that lie at least partially beyond their own control. Parishes do not come tailor-made to individual specifications, and in this sense alone individual choice is less than complete. Even if they cared, few people conduct political surveys of parishioners when choosing a parish, and thus they make their choice on some other basis, accepting whatever else happens to come along with the choice.

The general point becomes more obvious in relationship to the social construction of neighborhoods (Suttles 1972). Few people select a neighborhood based on any direct calculation regarding the political or moral belief systems that are likely to be dominant. At the same time, the sorting and mixing process of residential location produces a tendency toward homogeneous values in urban neighborhoods. Perhaps the most common example occurs when middle-class parents choose neighborhoods on the basis of school quality, but at a closely related latent level they are selecting a neighborhood where most residents are also more likely to value better schools (Ostrom 1972), as well as holding related systems of values and beliefs.

In summary, when citizens locate themselves in churches and in neighborhoods they make choices with important consequences for the political preferences that surround them, but these are latent consequences that flow from different choice criteria. Few people choose neighborhoods and churches based on the abortion attitudes and partisan orientations of parishioners and neighborhood residents, but even though these locational choices are predicated on other bases, they carry along important implications for a whole range of surrounding preferences – including abortion attitudes and partisan orientations.

This raises an important issue: Which choice – neighborhood or parish – translates most directly into an attendant political bias? Some locational choices carry immediate and direct political consequences even if they are produced as a latent result of the primary selection criteria. Other choices translate much less directly into a political bias.

One way to address this issue is to determine the relative level of diversity between and among parish and neighborhood contexts. To the extent that locational choice translates directly and unambiguously into political bias, we would expect to see a high level of homogeneity within a single context and a high level of diversity among contexts. In other words, to the

Table 13.1. *Diversity within contexts: the mean of the standard deviations within neighborhood and parish contexts, for party identification and abortion attitudes*

	Party identification	Abortion attitudes
Mean standard deviation within neighborhoods	2.08	2.11
Number of neighborhoods	16	16
Mean standard deviation within parishes	1.99	2.02
Number of parishes	23	23

extent that people are sorted into contexts on the basis of political criteria, we should expect to see contexts that are internally homogeneous and externally differentiated. The reader should recall that the dice are loaded in favor of the neighborhood. The study's sampling frame was purposefully chosen to maximize social class variation between the sixteen neighborhoods. Thus, to the extent that political beliefs are class-based, we might expect to see politically differentiated neighborhoods.

The level of efficiency in the translation of locational choice into a political bias is addressed in Tables 13.1 and 13.2. The level of diversity *within* neighborhood and parish contexts is assessed in Table 13.1, for both partisanship and abortion attitudes. As this table shows, the level of diversity within contexts varies little, either by the attitude being considered or by the level of observation. A slight tendency is present for parishes to be more internally homogeneous than neighborhoods, but the differences fall short of being dramatic. (See Wald et al. 1990 regarding variations in religious cohesiveness.) Thus, our analysis fails to present a picture in which value-oriented aggregates (parishes) extinguish internal diversity while instrumentally oriented aggregates (neighborhoods) sustain diversity. Rather, in both instances, the average distance between the group's central tendency and the attitude of group members is similar, at least to the extent that this distance is measured by the standard deviation.

A different picture emerges in Table 13.2, where the external diversity among the respondents' contexts is considered. Part A of the table shows that the extent to which contexts are differentiated from one another – measured in terms of the standard deviation among the respondents' contexts – varies both as a function of the attitude and as a function of the observational level. The diversity among contexts is considerably greater for churches than for neighborhoods, and it is also considerably greater with respect to partisan orientation rather than abortion attitudes. Part A of the table is replicated in parts B and C, but separately for Catholics

Table 13.2. *Diversity among contexts: standard deviations for the respondents' contexts*

	Party identification	Abortion attitudes
A. Catholics and non-Catholics combined		
Neighborhood contexts	.72	.36
	(635)	(512)
Parish contexts	.96	.69
	(635)	(512)
B. Catholics only		
Neighborhood contexts	.74	.37
	(474)	(387)
Parish contexts	.67	.45
	(474)	(387)
C. Non-Catholics only		
Neighborhood contexts	.53	.26
	(161)	(125)
Parish contexts	.91	.87
	(161)	(125)

Note: Respondent *N*-size is in parentheses.

and non-Catholics. Much of the pattern of variation in neighborhood abortion attitudes and partisan orientations is sustained for Catholics and non-Catholics. Perhaps the most important point of divergence lies in the pattern of variation across parish contexts. Particularly in terms of abortion attitudes at the parish level, much less variation is present among Catholics. Indeed, parish variation among Catholics on abortion attitudes is roughly half the level of parish variation among non-Catholics.

Several preliminary conclusions are warranted. (1) The translation of location and choice into political bias is far from complete. Significant within-context variation remains both for parishes and for neighborhoods. (2) While the level of internal variation is roughly equivalent across attitudes and levels of aggregation, the level of differentiation across contexts is extremely sensitive to both. (3) For the combined sample, variation in abortion attitudes among parishes is considerably less than variation in partisan attitudes, and in both instances neighborhoods vary less than parishes. (4) Levels of parish differentiation are modified when Catholics and non-Catholics are considered separately. In particular, Catholics realize much less variation in abortion attitudes across parishes than do non-Catholics.

A final point of comparison between parishes and neighborhoods lies in the extent to which they serve as surrogate and reinforcing sources of

Table 13.3. *Correlations between parish and neighborhood contextual measures*

	X1	X2	X3	X4
X1: neighborhood party identification	1			
X2: neighborhood prochoice	.60	1		
X3: parish party identification	.60	.53	1	
X4: parish prochoice	.22	.22	.53	1

Note: N-size is 518 respondents.

influence. In other words, do individuals typically find themselves in circumstances where the political composition of the parish and the neighborhood are in agreement, and thus where the social and political cues emanating from both sources are compatible? Alternatively, do individuals typically find themselves in circumstances where the political and social cues are in conflict – where the political and social composition of the neighborhood and the parish are at variance with each other?

These questions are addressed in Table 13.3, which displays the Pearson correlation coefficients between each compositional property at each level of aggregation. If we restrict our attention to partisanship, we see a relatively high correlation between the central tendencies of the neighborhood and the parish among our respondents. Parish partisanship and neighborhood partisanship correlate at a level of .6, and thus more than one-third of the variation at each level is shared with the opposite level ($R^2 = .36$). Further, abortion attitudes in the neighborhood show a relatively high level of correlation with parish partisanship and neighborhood partisanship. The point of departure comes in terms of parish abortion attitudes, which show much lower levels of shared variation with the neighborhood measures. Indeed, parish abortion attitudes are nearly independent from the two neighborhood compositional measures ($R^2 = .05$).

Thus, along the partisanship dimension our respondents are more likely to find themselves in politically compatible, mutually reinforcing life spaces. But this political compatibility of life-space dimensions is not always the case. Particularly in terms of abortion attitudes, the signal coming from the parish is only weakly related to the signal coming from the neighborhood. In summary, the life space of citizens in a democracy is multidimensional, and in some instances the dimensions are politically independent and diverse.

AGGREGATES, INDIVIDUALS, AND METHODOLOGICAL IMPERATIVES

Thus far the focus of attention has been upon the compositional properties of aggregate units, and the manner in which these compositional properties vary as a function of various attitudes and levels of observation. In the following analysis we pursue the political consequences of these compositional properties for the behavior of individuals. Particular attention focuses upon the individual-level consequences that arise due to the aggregate distribution of political attitudes. How do the aggregate distributions of abortion attitudes and partisan orientations within parishes and neighborhoods affect the abortion attitudes and partisan orientations of individuals within those parishes and neighborhoods? Is the parish or neighborhood most important? For which individuals and which behaviors? Under what circumstances?

The theoretical premise being considered is that the behavior of individuals is contingent upon the behavior of others within an individual's life space. But this theoretical premise generates several methodological complications. First, it is potentially tautological to argue that individuals are more likely to be Democrats or prolife in environments where more people are Democratic or prolife. This is an especially severe problem when the sample within contexts is small, and when such a sample is used to infer both the behavior of individuals and the aggregate patterns of behavior within the contexts. In such an instance the behavior of the individual – the phenomenon being explained – has a pronounced effect upon the construction of the compositional property. Part of the problem is resolved if we can be assured that, *as a matter of construction,* the behavior of the individual is independent of the behavior of the aggregate. In the analyses conducted here, the aggregate measures are constructed to insure such independence. In calculating the mean abortion attitude within a respondent's parish, for example, the respondent's own attitude is excluded from the calculation, and the resulting measure is precisely and only an estimate of the opinions surrounding the respondent within the parish.

Moreover, we take the additional precaution in our analyses of including controls for a variety of individual-level factors (Hauser 1974). Thus, for example, we do not simply examine the relationship between holding a prolife opinion and attending a church where others hold prolife opinions. Rather, we ask whether people who attend prolife churches are more likely to be prolife when we take account of their religious affiliations, their frequencies of church attendance, their incomes, and their educations. As we shall see, including controls such as these makes it problematic whether such a relationship holds.

A second problem in the analysis is less easily resolved. The insights of the Columbia school of political sociologists lead us to expect that the effects of various dimensions of social experience upon political behavior should be interdependent (Lazarsfeld et al. 1948; Berlson et al. 1954). Thus the effect of the parish should depend upon the neighborhood, and the effect of the neighborhood should depend upon the parish. Unfortunately, such interdependent effects are sometimes difficult to sort out as an empirical matter due to excessive collinearity among the various measures. The standard procedure used to test for such a contingent effect is to calculate a simple multiplicative interaction term for the contextual measures and enter it as a regressor in the estimation procedure. Unfortunately for these purposes, the interaction variable is often highly correlated with one or the other of the component contextual variables, thereby making the analyses problematic. A major culprit in the production of such collinearity is a lack of variation in one or the other of the component variables. These statistical problems are not without substantive corollaries. The variation in partisanship and especially abortion attitudes[2] is particularly limited across the Catholic parishes of our sample, and thus it is sometimes difficult to sort out the importance of being Catholic as opposed to the importance of being among other Catholics – a problem of truly ancient lineage in the social sciences (Durkheim 1951). Our general practice here is to include such an interaction term in models where the evidence supports it.

Finally, to what extent, and on what basis, do individuals control their locations in churches and neighborhoods? How do people resolve the conflicting information they receive from politically disparate environments? Most citizens do not choose neighborhoods or churches on the basis of explicitly political preferences, but even though these choices are predicated on other bases, they bring implications for a whole range of surrounding preferences – including abortion attitudes and partisan orientations. At the same time, and perhaps more important, individual control does not end once an environment is chosen. Rather, individuals are able to control their exposure to many of the environments within which they are located, and thus social influence is rightfully seen as an ongoing give-and-take between the source and the recipient of a particular political message (Finifter 1974). This interplay will provide an important focus for the present chapter.

PARTISANSHIP IN PARISH AND NEIGHBORHOOD

The social basis of partisanship is well established in the literature of political science and sociology. Jennings and Niemi (1968), Dawson et al. (1977),

---

2 Partisan orientations are measured on the familiar 7-point party identification scale, where 0 is strong Democrat and 6 is strong Republican. Abortion attitudes are measured on a 7-point scale formed by summing the responses to six questions soliciting whether a respondent believes that abortion should be legal or illegal in particular circumstances. A score of 0 indicates that the respondent feels abortion should never be legal. A score of 6 indicates that the respondent feels abortion should always be legal. The complete battery of questions follows: "There has been a great deal of talk about abortion in this election campaign. Under which of the following conditions do you think abortion should be legal? First, if a woman is married and doesn't want any more children. Should abortion be illegal in this situation? If a woman is not married and doesn't want to marry the man. If a family has very low income and cannot afford any more children. If there is a strong chance there is a serious defect in the baby. If the woman became pregnant as a result of rape. If the woman's own health is endangered by the pregnancy." A slightly different version of this question asked the clerics to provide the positions of their church regarding whether abortion should be legal in each of the same six circumstances.

and others have uncovered its roots in the relationships between parents and children. Lipset (1981), P. Beck (1976), and others demonstrate its relationship to cleavage structures and political epochs. Network and contextual studies show the correspondence between compositional properties and the partisan choices of individuals who compose the context (Eulau 1986).

In the analyses that follow, we consider the partisan orientation of individuals within the contexts of parishes and neighborhoods. Thus our effort falls within this latter body of work – an attempt to relate individual choice to the choices of other individuals who share a common life space. In the analyses that follow, we consider the partisan orientations of individuals within the contexts of parishes and neighborhoods. In view of the attitudinal homogeneity across the Catholic parishes of our sample, we have chosen to conduct analyses separately for Catholic and non-Catholic respondents, as well as for both groups combined.[3]

Table 13.4 considers the effects of neighborhood and parish contexts on individual partisanship, controlling for individual income and education,[4] and the results of the Catholic regression are shown in the first column of the table. Two things are especially noteworthy regarding the regression among Catholics. First, the model does not explain a high proportion of the variation in partisanship among Catholics with an R^2 of only .12. Second, the only contextual attribute that produces an effect among Catholics is neighborhood partisanship.

Does this mean that parish partisanship is unimportant to the individual partisan attitudes of Catholics? Perhaps, but an alternative interpretation might be that the minimal variation in the strongly Democratic partisan signal coming from Catholic parishes is not sufficient to explain variation in individual partisanship. Viewed from one perspective this would mean that the level of partisanship among parishioners has little consequence for the partisanship of Catholics when only Catholics are considered. Viewed from another perspective, the high level of Democratic identification among the Catholics in our sample may be due in part to the uniformly high level of Democratic support within parishes.

These results for Catholics contrast sharply with the results obtained in

3 By conducting these analyses separately for Catholics and non-Catholics, and by restricting attention to respondents within parishes where ten or more respondents attend, the sample size for non-Catholics in particular grows quite small. Thus, the results of this chapter have been confirmed using all respondents who attend parishes with more than three respondents attending. This reanalysis was conducted using ordinary least squares as well as weighted least squares to reflect the small parish N-sizes (Hanushek and Jackson 1977), and these reanalyses produced estimates generally in keeping with the results reported in this chapter. For all the analyses of Tables 13.4 and 13.5, the neighborhood measures are taken on the basis of the entire third wave of the survey, and thus are based on nearly 1,500 interviews equally spread across the sixteen neighborhoods.

4 Education is measured according to the years of schooling, to a maximum of seventeen years. Family income is measured according to a scale that ranges from 1 to 8.

Table 13.4. *Partisanship in parishes and neighborhoods*

	Catholics	Non-Catholics	Both
Constant	-1.09	6.36	-.94
	(1.94)	(1.77)	(1.50)
Education	.08	.28	.12
	(1.72)	(3.16)	(2.78)
Income	.15	-.06	.11
	(2.38)	(.55)	(1.89)
Mean neighborhood	.55	-2.90	.21
partisanship	(2.79)	(2.62)	(1.28)
Mean parish	.005	-1.76	.47
partisanship	(.03)	(1.78)	(3.48)
Parish mean X	—	.80	—
neighborhood mean		(2.61)	
Catholic	—	—	-.51
			(1.99)
R^2	.12	.20	.18
N	430	142	572

Note: Ordinary least squares; coefficient *t*-values are in parentheses.

the second column of Table 13.4 where only non-Catholics are considered. Indeed, all three of the contextual measures – neighborhood and parish partisanship as well as their interaction – yield at least marginal *t*-values. Furthermore, the R^2 for this model is increased, explaining 20 percent of the variation in partisanship among non-Catholics. The best way to understand the pattern of effects suggested by the non-Catholic model of Table 13.4 is to portray the effects in the three dimensional graphs of Figure 13.1. The two graphs provide alternative perspectives on the same pattern of effects, where the individual-level factors are held constant at intermediate values, and mean partisanship levels in the neighborhood and the parish are allowed to vary across their observed ranges. We emphasize that the two parts of Figure 13.1 provide alternative perspectives of the same three-dimensional space. The only difference is that the ordering of the neighborhood partisanship axis is reversed, thereby providing two different vantage points from which to view the three-dimensional surface.

As Figure 13.1 shows, the highest level of Republican support is found among respondents who are located in Republican parishes and Republican neighborhoods. Perhaps less intuitively, the highest level of Democratic support is found among respondents who are located in Democratic parishes and Republican neighborhoods. In such a situation it would appear that the parish shields the individual from the neighborhood and even sustains a reaction to it (Huckfeldt 1986). If we can assume that people

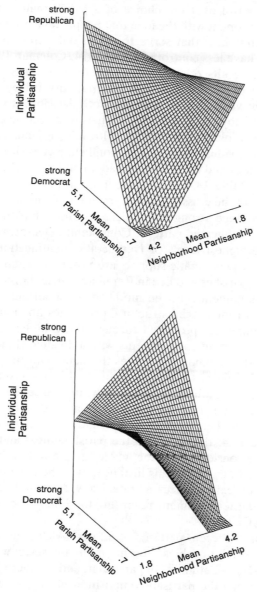

Figure 13.1. Individual party identification by mean party identification in the neighborhood and in the parish, for non-Catholics. *Source:* Estimated for non-Catholics from regression estimates of Table 13.4.

exercise more control over the choice of a parish than a neighborhood, these data are consonant with the idea that people take refuge in protective environments (churches) that serve to shield them from political signals over which they have less control (Finifter 1974; Coleman 1964).

How do these results relate to the literature on cross pressures? Although the cross-pressures argument was put forward by the Columbia school to explain various aspects of the vote decision, it can be applied readily to partisan loyalty as well. Individuals who receive consistent cues should tend to be resolute in their political loyalties as Democrats or Republicans, whereas individuals who receive conflicting cues should be ambivalent in their loyalties and more likely to adopt an independent orientation.

The results of Table 13.4 and Figure 13.1 do not fully support such a direct translation of the cross-pressures argument. Consistently Republican contexts do encourage strong Republican loyalties, but the other results present a more complicated pattern. Consistently Democratic contexts do not produce the highest levels of Democratic identification. Indeed, the strongest levels of Democratic support are produced when individuals attend Democratic parishes and live in Republican neighborhoods. Thus, the cross-pressures argument must be modified by important asymmetries in the influence of various social structural properties upon various political behaviors – asymmetries produced through the complex intersections of multiple and overlapping environments with individual choice.

The problem still remains: Why does the same pattern of effects fail to appear among Catholics? One might argue that it is a mistake to separate the Catholic and non-Catholic analyses in the first place, but the problem is not easily or neatly resolved by combining Catholic and non-Catholic respondents in a single regression. In an alternative model, shown in the third column of Table 13.4, the effects of the parish context and the neighborhood context are considered for the whole sample with a dummy-variable control for being Catholic. In this instance, only the regression coefficient for the parish context produces a statistically discernible effect, perhaps supporting the earlier argument regarding the importance of Democratic parishes among Catholics.

Why do we see different patterns of effects? A clue lies in the range of variation and interrelationships present among the social worlds inhabited by Catholics and non-Catholics. In particular, and as Figure 13.2 shows, the relationship between the partisan composition of the two contexts is very strong among Catholics, but virtually nonexistent among non-Catholics. In short, the Catholics in our sample are less likely to experience neighborhoods and parishes that emit divergent political signals, and hence it is more difficult to uncover the pattern of interdependent effects present among non-Catholics.

The level of diversity in the social worlds of Catholics and non-Catholics is not simply a methodological issue. Being Catholic (or not being Catholic)

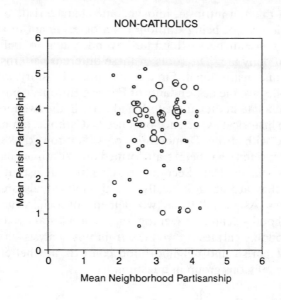

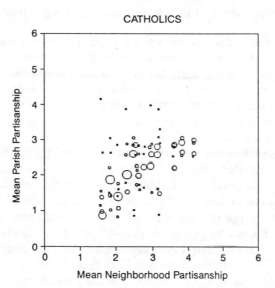

Figure 13.2. Parish partisanship by neighborhood partisanship among Catholics and non-Catholics. The area of each bubble is proportional to the number of respondents lying at that point. *Source:* 1984 South Bend study.

Top: y = 3.0 + .18*x*   *R*² = .01   *N* = 161

Bottom: y = .48 + .64*x*   *R*² = .50   *N* = 474

is much more than an intrinsic, idiosyncratic characteristic of individuals. Being Catholic (or not being Catholic) is a determinant of social experience, and the consequences extend far beyond systems of belief to include the realities of daily life. The roots of these different patterns of existence are historical and institutional. First, as a matter of history, many of South Bend's Catholics are the descendants of Eastern European immigrants who came to Indiana late in the nineteenth and early in the twentieth centuries. That common historical experience produced a Catholic, ethnic community in South Bend with strong Democratic roots (Stabrowski 1984), and even though the community has been transformed on a continual basis, a historical residue is still evident. Second, as a matter of institutional design, Catholic parishes are geographically based – individuals are assigned to nearby parishes. As a result these two elements of social structure – parish and neighborhood – tend to travel together. The substantive (and theoretical and methodological) lesson we take from this analysis is that the partisan effects of parish and neighborhood contexts are better understood relative to the religious group in question.

ABORTION ATTITUDES IN PARISH AND NEIGHBORHOOD

The political reach of social influence extends far beyond partisanship. In the following analyses we consider the consequences of neighborhoods and parishes for the abortion attitudes of individual respondents. The initial question thus becomes: Does the structure of social influence vary as a function of the behavior being influenced? If citizens live simultaneously in a variety of social worlds, do all these social worlds have similar political consequences across different behaviors?

Using Table 13.4 as a point of reference, a different pattern of contextual effects is demonstrated when the neighborhood and parish effects on abortion attitudes are considered in Table 13.5(A). In this instance no contextual effect is present among Catholics. The neighborhood effect among non-Catholics disappears, but a parish effect is sustained – non-Catholic respondents who attend prochoice parishes are more likely to hold prochoice attitudes. Both models demonstrate an effect for church attendance that is especially pronounced among Catholics: People who attend more frequently appear to be more prochoice in their attitudes.

In summary, the evidence suggests that the neighborhood is relevant for some behaviors but not for others, among some respondents but not among others. In a similar vein, parish effects are present for both partisanship and abortion attitudes among some people but not among others. At least among non-Catholics, it would appear that social influence is specialized and structured by the multidimensional nature of social experience. People look to different places for different cues regarding different behaviors. Coreligionists may be more influential regarding political issues that

Table 13.5. *Abortion attitudes in neighborhoods and parishes*

	Catholics	Non-Catholics	Both
A. Effects of neighborhood and parish contexts			
Constant	4.12	5.32	3.97
	(3.17)	(1.76)	(3.23)
Party identification	-.07	-.07	-.07
	(1.31)	(.76)	(1.43)
Church attendance	-.66	-.29	-.58
	(7.85)	(2.02)	(7.96)
Education	.07	-.01	.06
	(1.34)	(.01)	(1.30)
Income	-.01	.08	.004
	(.18)	(.69)	(.07)
Mean neighborhood attitude	.31	-.59	.16
	(1.03)	(.82)	(.58)
Mean parish attitude	-.07	.53	.23
	(.30)	(2.42)	(1.43)
Catholic	—	—	-.53
			(2.01)
R^2	.16	.14	.18
N	348	108	456
B. Contingent effects of parish contexts, depending on attendance			
Constant	4.58	13.72	9.18
	(1.56)	(4.42)	(5.08)
Party identification	-.06	-.02	-.07
	(1.17)	(.25)	(1.54)
Church attendance	-.57	-2.99	-1.69
	(.86)	(4.12)	(4.43)
Education	.08	.003	.06
	(1.46)	(.04)	(1.21)
Income	-.002	.12	.02
	(.04)	(1.13)	(.36)
Mean parish attitude	.09	-2.22	-1.08
	(.10)	(2.94)	(2.28)
Attendance X parish attitude	-.03	.67	.33
	(.14)	(3.77)	(2.97)
Catholic	—	—	-.76
			(2.80)
R^2	.16	.24	.20
N	348	108	456

Note: Ordinary least squares; coefficient *t*-values are in parentheses.

involve faith and morality. Secular settings may be more important as sources of influence regarding secular matters – politics and partisanship.

When the model is estimated for a combined sample of Catholics and non-Catholics with a dummy variable for Catholics (third column of Table 13.5(A)), the non-Catholic pattern of effects is maintained but the magnitudes of the parish effect and its corresponding t-value are substantially reduced. And thus adding Catholics to the analysis tends to attenuate the parish effect. Why do we fail to find a parish effect among Catholics. Or *do* we fail to find an effect? Recall that the variation in abortion attitudes is restricted across Catholic parishes. In other words, to attend a Catholic parish is to be exposed to a context where prolife attitudes prevail. The difference among Catholic parishes may not be sufficient to provide statistical purchase, but this is not the same as saying that the parish does not matter.

An alternative way to address the importance of the parish is in terms of individual exposure. Recall the strong effect of church attendance among Catholics. At least two interpretations might account for this effect. First, it may simply be the case that regular attenders are more religious, and religious people are more prolife. Alternatively, it may be the case that regular attenders expose themselves more frequently to the normative stance of their congregations regarding abortion (Sprague 1982). We cannot easily choose between these two alternatives for Catholics because there is so little parish variation in abortion attitudes. That is, we cannot observe the consequence of Catholics attending a prochoice Catholic parish.

A far different situation exists among non-Catholics, however. The composition of their parishes with respect to abortion attitudes shows much more variation, and thus a direct test is available for the two previously stated alternatives. If attendance is important because it exposes church members to the climate of opinion within the parish, then we should expect that: (1) The effect of the climate of opinion should depend upon attendance, and (2) the effect of attendance should depend upon the climate of opinion.

These expectations are set against evidence in Table 13.5(B), where a simple multiplicative interaction variable is included in the regression models. This interaction variable is calculated as the product of individual church attendance frequency and the mean parish abortion attitude. Not unexpectedly, given the restricted range of mean abortion attitudes among Catholic parishes, this additional variable fails to provide explanatory purchase among Catholics. Among non-Catholics, in contrast, all three variables – church attendance, parish abortion attitudes, and the interaction – produce crisp t-values and substantial coefficients. A similar pattern is present for the sample as a whole in the third column of the table, but the magnitude of the coefficients and their t-values are diminished.

Once again, the interaction effect among non-Catholics is best considered through the use of three-dimensional projections (see Figure 13.3). As be-

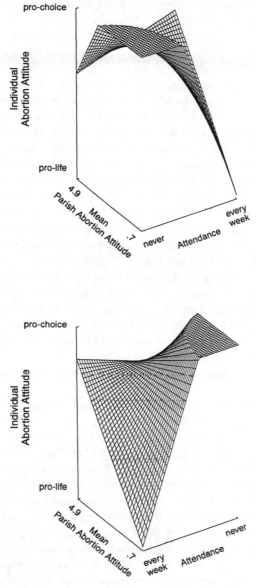

Figure 13.3. Individual abortion attitude by mean abortion attitude in parish and individual attendance frequency, for non-Catholics. *Source:* Estimated for non-Catholics from regression estimates of Table 13.5B.

fore, the figure is displayed from two different perspectives, in this instance according to alternative orderings of the attendance frequency axis. Careful examination of Figure 13.3 shows that: (1) Increased attendance in prolife parishes is related to prolife attitudes; (2) increased attendance in prochoice parishes is related to prochoice attitudes; (3) people who attend regularly are more likely to have prolife attitudes if they attend prolife churches; (4) among those people who attend infrequently, an inverse relationship exists between individual attitudes and the parish – individuals are more likely to have prochoice attitudes if they belong to prolife parishes.

The first three effects are directly interpretable, but the fourth effect requires more careful consideration. We may be witnessing a situation in which nonattendance serves as a shield against a parish context that the individual finds to be disagreeable. Thus, attendance serves to expose individuals to the climate of opinion in the parish, but parishioners control their own attendance patterns. And thus they may choose nonattendance as an articulated or unarticulated response to an environment that is at variance with their own viewpoint (cf. Finifter 1974).

In summary, parishes matter more than neighborhoods with respect to influencing abortion attitudes. The effect of parishes is, however, mediated by exposure. Regular attenders are more likely to be affected than infrequent attenders. Thus we see a pattern of effects in which the structure of social influence varies across attitudes and individuals in systematic ways.

THE SOURCE OF PARISH INFLUENCE

We may, of course, be witnessing the wagging tail rather than the barking dog. What is the source of the parish effect upon parishioners? Do they respond to commonly held beliefs among their coreligionists, or do their own opinions – and the opinions of other parishioners – respond to the theological positions of their churches? Four years after the original South Bend study, a team of interviewers conducted a follow-up study in which they interviewed the pastors of the parishes attended by the respondents. In some instances, of course, the interviewed parish pastor (or priest or rabbi) is not the same pastor who was in place four years earlier. For present purposes, however, this does not pose a significant problem.

Our goal is to assess the theological position of the respondent's church regarding abortion. Each pastor was asked to provide his or her own interpretation of the church's teaching on the abortion issue relative to the same set of circumstances regarding which the respondents had been asked to give their positions. Thus we have the judgment of a very well informed observer regarding the theological position of the church that the respondent reports attending – a judgment that is likely to be quite stable across time and across clergy within the same church.

Table 13.6 shows the distribution of Catholic and non-Catholic respon-

Table 13.6. *Distribution of respondents on the clergy-reported
position of church on abortion, by Catholics and non-Catholics*

	Catholics	Non-Catholics
Score on abortion scale		
0 (prolife)	67.1%	15.2
1	24.8	0.0
2	6.7	10.4
3	.5	40.0
4	0.0	0.0
5	0.0	0.0
6 (prochoice)	.8	34.4
N	371	125

dents across the clergy-provided measures of teaching regarding abortion. Not surprisingly, Catholics are skewed toward the prolife end of the scale. Indeed, the Catholics attending prochoice churches are not attending Catholic parishes. A very small number of Catholics report that they attend Protestant parishes, and these are the Catholics attending prochoice parishes. In contrast, non-Catholics attend churches represented by a broad range of theological positions regarding abortion. Nearly 50 percent lie at the midpoints on the scale, but another 50 percent lie at the two extremes.

An important question thus becomes: How well do the theological positions of the churches correspond to the attitudes of parishioners? As Table 13.7 shows, they correspond quite well for the sample as a whole, generating a correlation of .45. This correlation is a product of combining Catholics and non-Catholics, however. The correlation is dramatically reduced when Catholics and non-Catholics are considered separately. Indeed, the theological position of the church explains, at maximum, 2 percent of the variation in parishioner attitudes.

The weak correlation among Catholics is due at least in part to the very restricted range of variation in the interpreted positions of church teaching provided by Catholic clergy. A very different situation prevails among non-Catholics, however, where church teachings vary from consistently prochoice to consistently prolife. The prevailing attitudes of parishioners tend to be more moderate than the positions of their churches. Parishioners in prolife churches tend to be more prochoice than the clergy-interpreted position of their churches, and parishioners in prochoice churches tend to be more prolife. Thus, while the non-Catholic parishioners generally take the theological cue of the church, the slope of the relationship is fairly flat, and there are substantial aggregate deviations even from this modest relationship.

Finally, which factor does a better job of explaining individual attitudes

Table 13.7. *Correlation between clergy-reported position of church on abortion and the mean parish attitude*

	Pearson	N
All respondents	.45	496
Catholics	.04	371
Non-Catholics	.14	125

regarding abortion: the theological position of the individual's church or the positions held among other parishioners? In analyses not shown here, the models of Tables 13.4 and 13.5 were rerun with the clergy-supplied theological position substituted for the mean parish attitude, and the results were much less impressive. The climate of opinion measure provides much more statistical purchase than the clergy-reported theological position.

This does not mean, of course, that a church's theological position is unimportant to the beliefs of its members. Rather, the lesson would seem to be that, if a church wants to affect its members' positions regarding an issue of morality and church teaching, it must vigorously pursue the issue through education and persuasion. Merely adopting a theological stance that is divorced from member opinions is ineffective. Indeed, these results suggest that members learn more from one another than they do from formal pronouncements.

CONCLUSION

Social influence in politics is not idiosyncratic to the choices of individuals – citizens do not exercise lock-grip control over the political viewpoints and cues to which they are exposed. But neither is individual control without consequence for the location of citizens within social structure, and thus for the translation of social structure into a force on individual behavior.

People locate themselves in neighborhoods, churches, workplaces, clubs, and associations. They make these locational choices for good reasons on rational grounds, but in the process they also define – even if indirectly and unintentionally – the dimensions of their social experience. This social experience has relevance far beyond the basis of the original choice. In particular, it defines the composition of political preferences to which the individual is exposed.

As a matter of convenience and necessity, contextual studies of politics have typically summarized social experience in terms of geographical units – precincts, neighborhoods, counties, states. All too frequently these measurement procedures have obscured the multidimensional nature of social experience that is produced by the separate elements of social structure. Each structural element carries with it political implications that are potentially important. In some instances, multiple structural elements must be seen as being interdependent in the construction of a politically relevant social experience. In still other instances the importance of particular structural elements is best seen as the result of individual exposure, and individual exposure is best seen as a further manifestation of individual choice.

In summary, social influence in politics is structurally based, but it frequently depends upon multiple elements of social structure. It imposes itself upon individuals, but individual choice plays a major role in determining which individuals are exposed to which political cues and viewpoints. The emerging view is one in which social influence is structurally determined but in which the social influence process cannot be understood according to any simple deterministic logic (Boudon 1986). Rather, the end result of social influence in politics is created by the points of intersection between individual choice and the multiple bases of social experience.

14

Political consequences of interdependent citizens

The question arises quite naturally: What difference does it all make? We have argued that democratic citizenship involves something more than individually isolated and politically independent citizens making choices that are socially and politically divorced from their surroundings. Rather, citizens are fundamentally interdependent – they depend on one another for political information and guidance, and in the process of becoming informed they pass along distinctive interpretations and viewpoints. Moreover, the social communication of political information is itself subject to the political and social environment. Partisan dominance, party organization, and other organizational and institutional formations serve both to accelerate and impede the transmission and recognition of particular viewpoints. But if we are correct, does anything really change? Does the argument generate implications for political analysis in general and our understanding of democratic electoral politics in particular?

Perhaps the most important consequence lies in the ratification of something that Tip O'Neill knew all along: All politics *is* local politics. The Speaker may have had a different point of reference in mind when he made the observation, but our argument runs in a complementary direction. The point of reference for our own work is the construct of the national electorate. Journalists and pundits make reference to it, political scientists explain it, pollsters take its pulse. And while the concept of a national electorate is often quite useful, it remains an intellectual construct – a convenience for purposes of summarizing political behavior. The reality underlying this ubiquitous concept is that there is no single national electorate, but rather a multitude of subnational electorates. Some are organized geographically, while others are not. Some are organized around shared organizational affiliations, others around a common religious orientation, and others around shared values and symbols. Regardless of whether these electorates are organized geographically, or socially, or politically, the experience of the individual citizen is contingent on characteristics of the particular subelectorates within which the citizen is located.

It is not simply that being located within a particular subelectorate is an intrinsic characteristic of individuals that is correlated with preference and utility and hence choice. Rather, individual location is important primarily because it influences information flow and hence the political information and interpretations to which an individual is exposed. The key is communication – communication that is shaped and structured by individual surroundings.

Just as the national electorate is a construct, so is the concept of an average citizen. Citizens are distinctive, and this distinctiveness is not simply the result of individual characteristics, predispositions, and backgrounds – it also arises due to the particular microenvironments in which they live and work. In other words, citizens are distinctive in their responses to the social and political events and information that surround them on all sides. The distinctiveness of individual citizens and the viewpoints and opinions they hold is more profound than a simple summation of individually defined characteristics that translate unambiguously into corresponding interests. Instead, individual opinion and behavior is a product of social interaction, social communication, and the individual response to information obtained in this manner. Three sets of factors contribute to these responses: citizens' idiosyncratic social and political orientations, the information and viewpoints to which they are (socially) exposed, and the interplay between the two.

These elements constitute, in truncated form, our model of citizenship: the individual, the environment, and the complex relationship that exists between the individual and the environment. This final element – the individual–environmental nexus – is neither simple nor straightforward. Environments affect citizens by limiting and circumscribing individual choice, but citizens also exercise control over environments, and both processes occur imperfectly, incompletely, and simultaneously. Citizens do not exercise complete control, but neither are they wholly transformed by an external reality.

The relationships between individuals and environments are stochastic. People with multiple goals and imperfect information attempt to exercise control over the viewpoints to which they are exposed – they seek to impress their own views on the flow of incoming information. But even if they act efficiently and effectively, the stochastic nature of the environment makes itself felt. A citizen may select a lunch group composed of co-workers with whom she is comfortable and at ease, but she cannot be sure whether their political beliefs and opinions are fully congruent with the positions that are appropriate to someone with her own interests. Indeed, determining the appropriateness of alternative political positions is the primary purpose for obtaining political information, but information always and inevitably comes with a bias that probabilistically reflects its source. And thus, becoming informed is necessarily a political process that is only partially subject to the control of individual citizens.

STRUCTURES OF INFLUENCE

What elements of the external environment are particularly important in affecting the flow and supply of political information? First and foremost, other people play crucial roles, in various ways and at various environmental levels. The co-worker who complains about tax-and-spend liberals affects the flow of political information, as does the neighbor with the Democratic yard sign, and the wife who comes from a family of self-proclaimed political independents. Citizens encounter alternative viewpoints and information as they encounter one another, and these encounters – as well as their political content – neither are idiosyncratic to the citizen's own preferences nor do they lie wholly beyond the reach of individual control. Most of us avoid encounters with some people, just as we steer discussion away from politics with others. But our efforts are limited by availability and supply. When 85 percent of Mississippi whites voted for Ronald Reagan in 1984, a white Mississippi Mondale supporter may have had a difficult time avoiding the viewpoints of the surrounding population – a much more difficult time than Mondale supporters in Minnesota or Massachusetts or South Bend.

In short, the social and political composition of surrounding populations produces unavoidable and politically important consequences for the supply of information that is available to individual citizens. The incidence and magnitude of supportive and alternative viewpoints acquired through social communication are tied directly to the composition of particular populations. And this occurs in spite of individual efforts to control the incoming flow of information.

Political organization is also important. Many forms of social interaction with political content are induced by the systematic, institutionalized efforts of candidate and party organizations. Personal contact by a party worker, political yard signs, bumper stickers, and lapel pins are all important parts of partisan mobilization efforts, and they all further the social diffusion of political viewpoints. This means that the political consequence of social interaction is not simply a by-product of social structure. It is also a direct and systematic consequence of political structure and organization that are invoked by party strategy – strategic behavior imposed on a constraining, not wholly predictable, and complex social milieu.

It also means that political structure and organization are not simply the stuff of central committees and party chairmen – they are not divorced from the flesh and blood of citizens and their preferences. Indeed, to the extent that party organization is successful, such success is generally realized in terms of an underlying structure of mobilization and support within the electorate that typically depends on known social formations. That structure is not characterized by socially independent citizens who join partisan ranks in single-file lines, but rather by interacting information collectors who are affected by the viewpoints of fellow citizens. Above all, political mobilization is not an uncontrollable accident but rather the systematic consequence of party strategies traded in the currency of social communication and influence.

Third, the form and structure of social influence on politics are also an indirect result of political institutions and institutional design, primarily because various institutional devices inhibit or promote organized efforts to mobilize the electorate. Any institutional design that impedes partisan efforts to identify, locate, and mobilize supporters is also a device that impedes the social diffusion of political information, and hence the exercise of politically significant social influence. An intimate and complex relationship exists between the design of political institutions, the capacity of political parties to mobilize supporters, and the social diffusion of political information among citizens. And thus, any institutional design that inhibits party mobilization efforts also serves to undermine political discourse among citizens. A nonpartisan model of democratic politics is also, inevitably, an individualistic model that ignores the interdependence of citizens in the collective deliberations of democracy. Put a different way, parties are politically significant in part because party activity influences the political significance of social structure.

This is another way of reinforcing the argument of Powell (1986): The effect of individual level factors on turnout is weakest where party organizations and party mobilization efforts are strongest. Where parties are strong, individual-level predictors of turnout matter less. Where parties are weak, participation becomes more closely tied to individual-level processes and individually idiosyncratic characteristics. Politically significant social communication, social influence, and social interdependence are not accidental. If we want a democracy characterized by individually isolated citizens who are left to their own devices, there are some straightforward institutional devices available for producing such an outcome. In contrast, if we wish to produce a style of democratic politics in which citizens are highly interdependent and interconnected, organization becomes central, and no organization is more central than the political party.

Partisan organization is not the only form of social organization with important political consequences. A variety of other organizational forms serve intentionally or accidentally as vehicles of political mobilization, and thus they become important to the diffusion of political information. We have given deliberate attention to churches, but the list is certainly more extensive: bowling leagues, labor unions, bridge groups, neighborhood associations, and so on. Several features of organizations are particularly relevant. Not least important, individuals exercise a high degree of control over their exposure. They choose whether they will belong, and even though the choice is seldom predicated on an explicitly political basis, it may generate important political consequences. By choosing to belong and participate, people are often exposing themselves to one environment and shielding themselves from another. In this and many other ways, individual choice becomes crucially important to the flow of politically relevant information.

Just as institutional details become crucial for both the potential and the outcome of partisan organization, so also institutional peculiarities may have important implications for the political import of nonpartisan organizations. The post–World War II *embourgeoisement* of the American working class, to the extent that it occurred at all, might be understood in terms of the spatial dispersion of working-class populations into class-heterogeneous environments (Huckfeldt 1986; Stephens 1981). The relevant institutional effects would revolve around land use patterns, housing policies, and the other institutions that drove postwar suburbanization, thereby exposing affluent workers to non–working class environments.

As another example, the geographic basis of Catholic parish organization has important consequences for the political surroundings of Catholics, at the same time that it constrains the choices that Catholics are able to make in locating themselves in politically sympathetic surroundings. Whereas non-Catholics are typically able to attend parishes and congregations where they feel most at home, Catholics are encouraged, institutionally, to attend a nearby parish. As we have seen, this important institutional design feature has potentially important consequences for the construction of social and political environments, which in turn affect the flow of political information and the shape and form of social influence.

THE ORGANIZATION OF SOCIAL COMMUNICATION

A crucial ingredient in the transmission of political information within a population is not only the composition of the population with respect to social characteristics and political viewpoints, but also the patterns and organization of communication within the population. This is another way of saying that it is important to focus on the mechanisms of social influence – the means whereby a citizen's preferences are brought into correspondence with surrounding sentiment. But the focus on mechanisms too easily becomes a renewed focus on isolated individual characteristics: Do people reflect the surrounding political sentiment more completely if they are highly educated or modestly educated? Politically interested or disinterested? Politically knowledgeable or illiterate?

These are important questions because the characteristics of individual citizens are central to information exposure, to the control and manipulation of information sources, to the processing of incoming information, and to the ultimate political response. But these individual characteristics also become important when they are understood within the contexts and environments where information is transmitted. Social communication in politics becomes a more powerful concept when citizens are treated as both the recipients and the emitters of political information, and thus when social communication is understood in terms of social and political relationships.

None of this means that methodological individualism is sacrificed or that politics is understood as anything other than an individually experienced and constructed reality. Social and political life have meaning only as they are understood in terms of individual experience, but individual experience is realized through social interaction. How then is politics affected by the structure and pattern of social interaction? And how do individual differences affect social interaction? Two issues are particularly important, turning on the roles played by disagreement and intimacy.

First and foremost, citizens realize political disagreement through social interaction. Citizens do not only discuss politics with those who share their viewpoints, and neither are they wholly unable to recognize disagreement when it occurs. At one level this is not very surprising, and it corresponds with a number of arguments we have been making. But it is an important empirical issue, especially because expectations of disagreement are rendered problematic from several different theoretical vantage points. Some economists tell us that people quite reasonably obtain information from other people who share the same viewpoints, and some social psychologists tell us that people suppress and reinterpret information that conflicts with their own beliefs. And thus the one–two punch of political economy and social psychology has been to minimize the expectation of disagreement and, hence, the importance of social communication.

The economists and the social psychologists are certainly correct, but nuance is important here, and the extent to which they are correct should not be overestimated. Citizens search for information sources that correspond to their own political orientations, and they selectively misperceive and reinterpret information that diverges from their own viewpoints. Their control over information is compromised in several respects, however. Most important, they often do not know enough to disagree. That is, they are not sufficiently informed to hold an opinion regarding every issue. And thus they obtain information that proves to be influential, even when, in some objective sense, the information might be judged to be discrepant with their interests and orientations.

Moreover, citizens *do* experience disagreement, and they *do* recognize divergent opinions, and thus political discussion and social communication take on more meaning. Such disagreement is important because it creates the potential for politically influential social communication (McPhee 1963). Absent disagreement, influence is rendered meaningless, and social communication becomes wholly a reflection of idiosyncratic opinion without political consequence. In this context, disagreement takes on even more importance *because it need not be permanent or unalterable*. Citizens frequently encounter opinions that, while being different from their own, are not in opposition to their interests or beliefs in any fundamental sense.

Such disagreements are likely to carry high informational content, and hence to have a very high potential for influence. In these various ways, political discourse becomes more meaningful when people disagree, and we have shown that, indeed, they do disagree.

Second, social communication regarding politics does not only occur among intimates, and this fact is important for several reasons. As Granovetter has shown (1973), information that is conveyed only through intimate social ties does not travel well. The friends of my friends are quite frequently my friends too, and thus information conveyed through intimates tends to feed back on the source, thereby minimizing its spread. In contrast, information conveyed through casual social ties tends to keep traveling, and thus its spread is maximized. Not only have we seen that information is conveyed through casual contact, but casual acquaintances are no less influential than intimates.

A population in which the social transmission of political information is restricted to communication among intimates will, therefore, be characterized by political fragmentation and the creation of independent isolated cliques. Similar to an electorate organized around the independent individual citizen, the electorate would be organized around the independent and isolated small group. In such a population, the existence of a truly public opinion – an opinion that is created by, but independent from, individually held opinions – is rendered problematic (Stimson 1991).

Moreover, to the extent that information is transmitted through more casual social encounters, the political importance of the environment is accentuated. If citizens only receive political information from close friends and relatives, then the impact of the environments where they reside would be minimized. That is, if Joe obtains information only from his wife and best friend, then it does not much matter where he lives, works, goes to church, and so on. In contrast, if information obtained through more casual social relationships is important, then the citizen is directly connected to the locales that control the supply of such social contacts.

THE FOCUS ON INFORMATION

This book is motivated by a series of questions regarding the political consequences that arise due to social communication among interdependent citizens. To this end, we have been concerned with the ways that citizens obtain, control, and process political information. Such an undertaking places us within a major stream of research regarding citizens and elections, but with a different focus and orientation. Indeed, the ways in which citizens become informed, the content and effect of political information, and the effects of various information sources are among the most important topics being addressed in contemporary research on electoral politics. And their importance traces to fundamental issues of citizenship in democratic politics.

A dominant concern of electoral politics research during the past thirty years has been the effort to reconcile the citizenship requirements of democratic politics with the demonstrated capacity (or incapacity) of citizens to fulfill those requirements. The earliest empirical analyses of voters and elections, conducted during the 1940s and 1950s, startled contemporary readers with a picture of citizens who all-too-often seemed to be disinterested, inconsistent in their opinions, and poorly informed (Lazarsfeld et al. 1948; Berelson et al. 1954; Campbell et al. 1960). If the effective functioning of democracy required a knowledgeable and highly attentive citizenry, then the natural implication arose that democracy was in trouble. Viewed retrospectively, it is quite clear that these early empirical efforts defined a broadly based research agenda for the ensuing study of democratic politics.

Several different responses to this agenda subsequently emerged. Some wishfully thinking theorists simply rejected empirical research on voters, based on the premise that such research must be inevitably and fundamentally flawed. Other theorists began to reconsider the requirements of democracy (Schumpeter 1947). And still others (Dahl and Lindblom 1953; Dahl 1956, 1961; Riker 1982) initiated research programs aimed at alternative formulations and theoretical specifications of democratic politics. Many of these efforts were notable for the reduced role they ascribed to elections and individual voters. If traditionally defined democracy was in principle endangered by inadequately informed citizens at the same time that democratic politics seemed to be stable and thriving in a great many settings, perhaps it was because the role and importance of elections and voters had been overestimated in the first place.

An alternative body of research was aimed at resurrecting the democratic citizen, and its earliest exemplar came in the person of V. O. Key. Key recognized the challenge to democracy posed by the profile of the incompetent citizen, and responded with his now well known assertion that "voters are not fools" (1966: 7). Key's bold statement served to define a research program, and his effort to resurrect the role of the citizen in democratic politics is echoed in a long stream of subsequent research.

An important contribution to this stream of research was provided by the political economists who questioned whether it was reasonable to expect that anyone would willingly fulfill the requirements of traditionally defined citizenship. As Downs (1957) informed us, the costs of exercising citizenship cannot be ignored. Moreover, the impact of these costs is heightened by the individual realization that the political effect of an individual citizen, civics books to the contrary notwithstanding, is not likely to be great. In such a context, we should not be surprised when many citizens are poorly informed or less than fully engaged by their citizenship duties.

The contribution of cognitive psychology to political science has been to take such limitations seriously when thinking about the exercise of citizenship. Popkin (1991) reminds us of the ways in which citizens reduce the costs and burdens of acquiring and processing political information. Faced with an information overload as well as a variety of competing tasks and obligations, the citizen develops sensible coping strategies (Simon 1957, 1982). It is not that he or she does not care about the country and its future. Rather, the duties of citizenship are resource-consuming, and the likely return on any individual investment is not promising. Viewed in such a light, we should expect citizens to seek out shortcuts and economies in collecting and processing information (Lodge and Hamill 1986), and thus it is the relationship between the information source and the processing strategies of the recipient that determine political consequence. In the words we have been using, it is the nature of the relationship between the individual and the environment that determines political effect.

For example, Zaller (1992: 44–5) argues that "the likelihood of resisting persuasive communications that are inconsistent with one's political predispositions rises with a person's level of political attentiveness. Or, to put it the other way, politically inattentive persons will often be unaware of the implications of the persuasive communications they encounter, and so often end up 'mistakenly' accepting them." Zaller is concerned with information obtained from political elites, but his argument is not fundamentally different from our own. Namely, people exercise incomplete control over incoming information, and they may or may not reject information that, from an objective viewpoint, is in disagreement with their own interests and predispositions.

Some studies focus more intently on the ways in which citizens process information and reason about politics (Sniderman, Brody, and Tetlock 1991; Lodge and Hamill 1986). Others are more concerned with the temporal setting of information transmission (Bartels 1988). Still others focus on the particular features of alternative information sources, such as television (Iyengar and Kinder 1987; Iyengar 1991). But the unifying theme of all these studies, and our own, is the idea of citizens with limited resources attempting to understand politics on the basis of information obtained from distinctive sources. These studies are, in short, efforts to be more realistic regarding the capacities of citizens and the ways in which citizens become informed regarding politics. Moreover, they are fundamentally concerned to understand how characteristics of an external information source interact with information-processing strategies on the part of the recipient to produce distinctive political consequences.

In what ways do our own efforts diverge from these others? How is social communication different from other forms of information transmission? Most important, focusing on social communication helps to illuminate the relationship between electorates and citizens. If citizens are seen as individually disconnected information processors, we are unlikely to make significant progress toward relating the study of individual voters to the larger study of politics and electorates (Stimson 1991). Alternatively, to the extent that citizens are seen as being interdependent, then electorates become more than the simple summation of individual citizens. In order to understand electorates in this way, we must understand not only voters, but also the relationships that exist among citizens – the political organization of interdependence within the electorate.

CITIZENS AND SOCIAL COMMUNICATION

What is the view of the citizen that emerges from our analysis? First and foremost, citizens are not automata, and neither are they the inescapable products of their surroundings. We hold no determinate vision of the citizen as an environmental residue. Rather, citizens exercise control over their environments, they manipulate their surroundings, and they enforce their preferences and predispositions on the flow of incoming information.

Moreover, citizens act on the basis of their own goals and preferences. Certainly voters are *not* fools, and they engage in informational behaviors that are, on average, meaningful and comprehensible when viewed within the set of opportunities and constraints that confront a typical citizen (Boudon 1986; Weber 1966). Our effort falls squarely within the larger research tradition that seeks to redefine a meaningful model of citizen behavior in democratic politics. Rather than denigrating the capacities of individual citizens, our goal is to develop realistic expectations regarding citizen behavior.

At the same time, citizens are neither all powerful, all knowing, nor unlimited in their devotion to public affairs. Just as the environment is not determinate, neither is individual control over the flow of information. A Democrat might prefer to encounter a politically sympathetic environment, but such a preference may be difficult to realize if she marries into a Republican family, takes a job as a bank executive, and moves into an upper-class neighborhood in a Republican county. Citizens have preferences, but the preferences must be realized in particular places, at particular times, subject to particular constraints. The search for information is bounded and constrained by availability, and availability is environmentally imposed – the gentle coercion that arises inevitably in the context of the citizen.

Moreover, preferences must be informed, and information is socially transmitted. Preferences do not automatically and unambiguously arise from interests; citizens must rather define the nature of their interests and discover preferences that are coincidental. How do they carry out such complex tasks? Most important from our perspective, they get help from other citizens, but they do not know in advance whether the help they are getting is appropriate in some objective sense. Indeed, that is why they are acquiring information – to discover the nature of their interests and the means whereby those interests are realized. And thus their control over the flow of incoming information is further compromised.

Once again, the relationship between the citizen and the environment is doubly stochastic, both at the level of the environment and at the level of the individual. Everything else being equal, the typical Democrat will usually prefer to obtain information from a Democratic source. On average, people living in Republican counties are more likely to obtain information that coincides with a Republican viewpoint. There is slippage both at the level of individual choice and structure (Boudon 1986). This slippage reflects the less than determinate, inherently stochastic process of social communication – a process in which both choice and availability operate according to probabilistic rules.

In this way the environments surrounding the individual take on heightened importance for the individual exercise of citizenship. The same set of individually defined interests, characteristics, and preferences may lead to very different choices and behaviors as a function of individual surroundings. The citizen is an information processor, but information is environmentally supplied, and individual choices are imbedded within informational settings that systematically vary in time and space. Neither individual choice nor the environment is determinate in creating these informational settings, and hence the acquisition of political information is the end result of a complex interplay between individual choice and environmental supply. Just as the environment is composed of multiple dimensions of experience, so also is individual choice multidimensional, responding to disparate sets of preferences and goals. Not only are citizens understood in terms of environments, but environments take on political meaning in terms of interdependent citizens.

Bibliography

Abramowitz, Alan, John McGlennon, and Ronald Rapoport. 1981. "A Note on Strategic Voting in a Primary Election." *Journal of Politics* 43: 899–904.

Achen, Christopher H. 1986. *The Statistical Analysis of Quasi-Experiments*. Berkeley: University of California Press.

Adamany, David. 1976. "Cross-over Voting and the Democratic Party's Reform Rules." *American Political Science Review* 70: 536–41.

Alt, James. Forthcoming. "The Impact of the Voting Rights Act on Black and White Voter Registration in the South." In Chandler Davidson and Bernard Grofman, eds., *The Impact of the Voting Rights Act in the South*. Princeton: Princeton University Press.

Alwin, Duane F. 1976. "Assessing School Effects: Some Identities." *Sociology of Education* 49: 294–303.

Bartels, Larry M. 1988. *Presidential Primaries and the Dynamics of Public Choice*. Princeton: Princeton University Press.

Beck, Nathaniel. 1989. "Presidents, the Economy, and Elections: A Principal-Agent Perspective." In Paul Brace, Christine Harrington, and Gary King, eds., *The Presidency in American Politics,* pp. 121–49. New York: New York University Press.

Beck, Paul Allen. 1974. "Environment and Party: The Impact of Political and Demographic County Characteristics on Party Behavior." *American Political Science Review* 68: 1229–44.

Beck, Paul Allen. 1976. "A Socialization Theory of Partisan Realignment." In Richard G. Niemi and Herbert F. Weisberg, eds., *Controversies in American Voting Behavior,* pp. 396–411. San Francisco: Freeman.

Beck, Paul Allen. 1992. *Party Politics in America*. 7th ed. New York: Harper Collins.

Beck, Paul Allen, and M. Kent Jennings. 1975. "Parents as 'Middlepersons' in Political Socialization." *Journal of Politics* 37: 83–107.

Berelson, Bernard R., Paul F. Lazarsfeld, and William N. McPhee. 1954. *Voting: A Study of Opinion Formation in a Presidential Election*. Chicago: University of Chicago Press.

Berger, Bennett M. 1960. *Working-Class Suburb: A Study of Auto Workers in Suburbia*. Berkeley: University of California Press.

Bibby, John F., Cornelius P. Cotter, James L. Gibson, and Robert J. Huckshorn. 1983. "Parties in State Politics." In Virginia Gray, Herbert Jacob, and Kenneth N. Vines, eds., *Politics in the American States,* pp. 59–96. Boston: Little, Brown.

Blau, Peter M. 1956. "Social Mobility and Interpersonal Relations." *American Sociological Review* 21: 290–95.

Blau, Peter M. 1957. "Formal Organizations: Dimensions of Analysis." *American Journal of Sociology* 58: 58–69.
Blau, Peter M. 1960a. "Structural Effects." *American Sociological Review* 25: 178–93.
Blau, Peter M. 1960b. "A Theory of Social Integration." *American Journal of Sociology* 65: 545–56.
Bledsoe, Timothy, and Susan Welch. 1987. "Patterns of Political Party Activity among U.S. Cities." *Urban Affairs Quarterly* 23: 249–69.
Bobo, Lawrence. 1983. "Whites' Opposition to Busing: Symbolic Racism or Realistic Group Conflict?" *Journal of Personality and Social Psychology* 45: 1196–1210.
Bobo, Lawrence, 1988. "Attitudes toward the Black Political Movement: Trends, Meaning, and Effects on Racial Policy Preferences." *Social Psychology Quarterly* 51: 287–302.
Books, John W., and Charles L. Prysby. 1991. *Political Behavior and the Local Context.* New York: Praeger.
Boudon, Raymond. 1984. "The Individualistic Tradition in Sociology." Prepared for the Symposium on Micro and Macro Levels in Sociological Theories, Schloss Rauischolzhausen, June 21–23.
Boudon, Raymond. 1986. *Theories of Social Change.* Berkeley: University of California Press.
Bourque, Susan, and Jean Grossholtz. 1984. "Politics as Unnatural Practice: Political Science Looks at Female Participation." In J. Siltanen and M. Stanworth, eds., *Women and the Public Sphere,* pp. 103–21. New York: St. Martin's Press.
Boyd, Lawrence H., and Gudmund R. Iversen. 1979. *Contextual Analysis: Concepts and Statistical Techniques.* Belmont, Calif.: Wadsworth.
Brickell, Bettina, Robert Huckfeldt, and John Sprague. 1988. "Gender Effects on Political Discussion: The Political Networks of Men and Women." Presented at the annual meeting of the Midwest Political Science Association, Chicago.
Brown, Thad A. 1981. "On Contextual Change and Partisan Attitudes." *British Journal of Political Science* 11: 427–48.
Burt, Ronald S. 1987. "Social Contagion and Innovation: Cohesion versus Structural Equivalence." *American Journal of Sociology* 92: 1287–1335.
Bush, R. R., and F. Mosteller. 1955. *Stochastic Models for Learning.* New York: Wiley.
Butler, David, and Donald Stokes. 1974. *Political Change in Britain: The Evolution of Electoral Choice.* New York: St. Martin's.
Cadzow, James A. 1973. *Discrete Time Systems: An Introduction with Interdisciplinary Applications.* Englewood Cliffs, N.J.: Prentice-Hall.
Caldeira, Gregory A., Aage R. Clausen, and Samuel C. Patterson. 1990. "Partisan Mobilization and Electoral Participation." *Electoral Studies* 9: 191–204.
Caldeira, Gregory A., Samuel C. Patterson, and Gregory A. Markko 1985. "The Mobilization of Voters in Congressional Elections." *Journal of Politics* 47: 490–509.
Calvert, Randall L. 1985. "The Value of Biased Information: A Rational Choice Model of Political Advice." *Journal of Politics* 4: 530–55.
Campbell, Angus, Philip E. Converse, Warren E. Miller, and Donald E. Stokes. 1960. *The American Voter.* New York: Wiley.
Carmines, Edward G., and James H. Kuklinski. 1990. "Incentives, Opportunities, and the Logic of Public Opinion in American Political Representation." In John A. Ferejohn and James H. Kuklinski, eds., *Information and Democratic Processes,* pp. 240–68. Urbana: University of Illinois Press.
Carmines, Edward G., and James A. Stimson. 1989. *Issue Evolution: Race and the Transformation of American Politics.* Princeton: Princeton University Press.

Chaundy, T. W., and E. Phillips. 1936. "The Convergence of Sequences Defined by Quadratic Recurrence Formulae." *Quarterly Journal of Mathematics* 7: 74–80.

Coleman, James S. 1964. *Introduction to Mathematical Sociology.* New York: Free Press.

Coleman, James S., Elihu Katz, and Herbert Menzel. 1966. *Medical Innovation: A Diffusion Study.* Indianapolis: Bobbs-Merrill.

Converse, Philip E. 1962. "Information Flow and the Stability of Partisan Attitudes." *Public Opinion Quarterly* 26: 578–99.

Converse, Philip E. 1969. "Of Time and Partisan Stability." *Comparative Political Studies* 2: 139–71.

Cortes, Fernando, Adam Przeworski, and John Sprague. 1974. *Systems Analysis for Social Scientists.* New York: Wiley.

Cox, Kevin R. 1974. "The Spatial Structuring of Information Flow and Partisan Attitudes." In Mattei Dogan and Stein Rokkan, eds., *Social Ecology,* pp. 157–86. Cambridge, Mass.: MIT Press.

Crotty, William J. 1971. "Party Effort and Its Impact on the Vote." *American Political Science Review* 65: 439–50.

Cutright, Phillips. 1963. "Measuring the Impact of Local Party Activity on the General Election Vote." *Public Opinion Quarterly* 27: 372–86.

Cutright, Phillips, and Peter H. Rossi. 1958. "Grass Roots Politicians and the Vote." *American Sociological Review* 23: 171–9.

Dahl, Robert A. 1956. *A Preface to Democratic Theory.* Chicago: University of Chicago Press.

Dahl, Robert A. 1961. *Who Governs? Democracy and Power in an American City.* New Haven: Yale University Press.

Dahl, Robert A., and Charles E. Lindblom. 1953. *Politics, Economics, and Welfare.* New York: Harper.

Davis, James A. 1966. "The Campus as a Frog Pond: An Application of the Theory of Relative Deprivation to Career Decisions of College Men." *American Journal of Sociology* 72: 17–31.

Davis, James A., Joe L. Spaeth, and Carolyn Huson. 1961. "Analyzing Effects of Group Composition." *American Sociological Review* 26: 215–25.

Dawson, Richard E., Kenneth Prewitt, and Karen S. Dawson. 1977. *Political Socialization.* 2d ed. Boston: Little, Brown.

Deutsch, Karl W. 1953. *Nationalism and Social Communication: An Inquiry into the Foundations of Nationality.* Cambridge, Mass.: MIT Press.

Downs, Anthony. 1957. *An Economic Theory of Democracy.* New York: Harper and Row.

Durkheim, Emile. 1951. *Suicide.* Translated by John Spaulding. New York: Free Press. Originally published in 1897.

Engle, Robert F., David F. Hendry, and Jean-François Richard. 1983. "Exogeneity." *Econometrica* 51: 277–304.

Ennis, Philip H. 1962. "The Contextual Dimension in Voting." In William N. McPhee and William A. Glaser, eds., *Public Opinion and Congressional Elections,* pp. 180–211. New York: Free Press.

Erbring, Lutz, Edie N. Goldenberg, and Arthur H. Miller. 1980. "Front-Page News and Real-World Cues: A New Look at Agenda Setting by the Media." *American Journal of Political Science* 24: 16–49.

Erbring, Lutz, and Alice A. Young. 1979. "Individuals and Social Structure: Contextual Effects As Endogenous Feedback." *Sociological Methods and Research* 7: 396–430.

Erikson, Robert S., Gerald C. Wright, and John P. McIver. 1993. *Statehouse De-*

mocracy: Public Opinion and Policy in the American States. New York: Cambridge University Press.

Esser, Hartmut. 1982. "On the Explanation of Individual Behavior: The Case of Language Acquisition by Migrant Workers." In Werner Raub, ed., *Theoretical Models and Empirical Analyses: Contributions to the Explanation of Individual Actions and Collective Phenomena*, pp. 131–65. Utrecht: E. S. Publications.

Eulau, Heinz. 1986. *Politics, Self, and Society*. Cambridge, Mass.: Harvard University Press.

Eulau, Heinz, and Lawrence S. Rothenburg. 1986. "Life Space and Social Networks as Political Contexts." In Heinz Eulau, ed., *Politics, Self, and Society*, pp. 300–24. Cambridge, Mass.: Harvard University Press.

Farquharson, Robin. 1969. *Theory of Voting*. New Haven: Yale University Press.

Finifter, Ada. 1974. "The Friendship Group as a Protective Environment for Political Deviants." *American Political Science Review* 68: 607–25.

Finkel, Steven E., and Howard A. Scarrow. 1985. "Party Identification and Party Enrollment: The Difference and Consequence." *Journal of Politics* 47: 620–42.

Fiorina, Morris P. 1981. *Retrospective Voting in American National Elections*. New Haven: Yale University Press.

Franklin, Charles H., and John E. Jackson. 1983. "The Dynamics of Party Identification." *American Political Science Review* 77: 957–73.

Fuchs, Lawrence H. 1955. "American Jews and the Presidential Vote." *American Political Science Review* 49: 385–401.

Gans, Herbert J. 1967. *The Levittowners*. New York: Vintage.

Gibson, James L., Cornelius P. Cotter, John F. Bibby, and Robert J. Huckshorn. 1983. "Assessing Party Organizational Strength." *American Journal of Political Science* 27: 193–222.

Gibson, James L., Cornelius P. Cotter, John F. Bibby, and Robert J. Huckshorn. 1985. "Whither the Local Parties? A Cross-sectional and Longitudinal Analysis of the Strength of Party Organizations." *American Journal of Political Science* 29: 139–60.

Gilbert, Christopher P. 1993. *The Impact of Churches on Political Behavior: An Empirical Study*. Westport, Conn.: Greenwood Press.

Giles, Michael W., and Marilyn K. Dantico. 1982. "Political Participation and Neighborhood Social Context Revisited." *American Journal of Political Science* 26: 144–50.

Giles, Michael W., and Arthur S. Evans. 1985. "External Threat, Perceived Threat, and Group Identity." *Social Science Quarterly* 66: 50–66.

Goldberg, Samuel. 1958. *Introduction to Difference Equations: With Illustrative Examples from Economics, Psychology, and Sociology*. New York: Wiley.

Goodman, Leo A. 1953. "Ecological Regression and Behavior of Individuals." *American Sociological Review* 18: 663–4.

Goodman, Leo A. 1959. "Some Alternatives to Ecological Correlation." *American Journal of Sociology* 65: 610–25.

Goot, Murray, and Elizabeth Reid. 1984. "Women: If Not Apolitical, Then Conservative." In J. Siltanen and M. Stanworth, eds., *Women and the Public Sphere*, pp. 122–36. New York: St. Martin's Press.

Gosnell, Harold. 1927. *Getting Out the Vote: An Experiment in the Stimulation of Voting*. Chicago: University of Chicago Press.

Granovetter, Mark. 1973. "The Strength of Weak Ties." *American Journal of Sociology* 78: 1360–80.

Hannan, Michael T. 1971. *Aggregation and Disaggregation in Sociology*. Lexington, Mass.: D. C. Heath.

Hannan, Michael T., and Leigh Burstein. 1974. "Estimation from Grouped Observations." *American Sociological Review* 39: 374–92.

Hanushek, Eric A., and John E. Jackson. 1977. *Statistical Methods for Social Scientists*. New York: Academic Press.

Hanushek, Eric A., John E. Jackson, and John F. Kain. 1974. "Model Specification, Use of Aggregate Data, and the Ecological Correlation Fallacy." *Political Methodology* 1: 89–107.

Harder, Theodor, and Franz Urban Pappi. 1969. "Multiple Regression Analysis of Survey and Ecological Data." *Social Science Information* 8: 43–67.

Harvey, Andrew C. 1989. *Forecasting, Structural Time Series Models and the Kalman Filter*. Cambridge: Cambridge University Press.

Hauser, Robert M. 1974. "Contextual Analysis Revisited." *Sociological Methods and Research* 2: 365–75.

Hawley, Willis D. 1973. *Nonpartisan Elections and the Case for Party Politics*. New York: Wiley.

Heard, Alexander. 1952. *A Two-Party South*. Chapel Hill: University of North Carolina Press.

Hedlund, Ronald D., and Meredith W. Watts. 1986. "The Wisconsin Open Primary: 1968–1984." *American Politics Quarterly* 14: 55–74.

Hofstetter, Richard C. 1973. "Interparty Competition and Electoral Turnout: The Case of Indiana." *American Journal of Political Science* 17: 351–66.

Huckfeldt, Robert. 1979. "Political Participation and the Neighborhood Social Context." *American Journal of Political Science* 23: 579–92.

Huckfeldt, Robert. 1983a. "The Social Context of Political Change: Durability, Volatility, and Social Influence." *American Political Science Review* 77: 929–44.

Huckfeldt, Robert. 1983b. "Social Contexts, Social Networks, and Urban Neighborhoods: Environmental Constraints on Friendship Choice." *American Journal of Sociology* 89: 651–69.

Huckfeldt, Robert. 1984. "Political Loyalties and Social Class Ties: The Mechanisms of Contextual Influence." *American Journal of Political Science* 28: 399–417.

Huckfeldt, Robert. 1986. *Politics in Context: Assimilation and Conflict in Urban Neighborhoods*. New York: Agathon.

Huckfeldt, Robert, and Carol W. Kohfeld. 1989. *Race and the Decline of Class in American Politics*. Urbana: University of Illinois Press.

Huckfeldt, Robert, Carol W. Kohfeld, and Thomas W. Likens. 1982. *Dynamic Modeling: An Introduction*. Beverly Hills, Calif.: Sage.

Huckfeldt, Robert, Eric Plutzer, and John Sprague. 1993. "Alternative Contexts of Political Behavior: Churches, Neighborhoods, and Individuals." *Journal of Politics* 55: 365–81.

Huckfeldt, Robert, and John Sprague. 1987. "Networks in Context: The Social Flow of Political Information." *American Political Science Review* 81: 1197–1216.

Huckfeldt, Robert, and John Sprague. 1988. "Choice, Social Structure, and Political Information: The Informational Coercion of Minorities." *American Journal of Political Science* 32: 467–82.

Huckfeldt, Robert, and John Sprague. 1990. "Social Order and Political Chaos: The Structural Setting of Political Information." In John A. Ferejohn and James H. Kuklinski, eds., *Information and Democratic Processes*, pp. 23–58. Urbana: University of Illinois Press.

Huckfeldt, Robert, and John Sprague. 1991. "Discussant Effects on Vote Choice: Intimacy, Structure, and Interdependence." *Journal of Politics* 53: 122–58.

Huckfeldt, Robert, and John Sprague. 1992. "Political Parties and Electoral Mobilization: Political Structure, Social Structure, and the Party Canvass." *American Political Science Review* 86: 70–86.

Huckfeldt, Robert, and John Sprague. 1993. "Citizens, Contexts, and Politics." In Ada Finifter, ed., *Political Science: The State of the Discipline II,* pp. 281–303. Washington, D.C.: American Political Science Association.

Iversen, Gudmund R. 1991. *Contextual Analysis.* Newbury Park, Calif.: Sage.

Iyengar, Shanto. 1990. "Shortcuts to Political Knowledge: The Role of Selective Attention and Accessibility." In John A. Ferejohn and James H. Kuklinski, eds., *Information and Democratic Processes,* pp. 160–85. Urbana: University of Illinois Press.

Iyengar, Shanto. 1991. *Is Anyone Responsible? How Television Frames Political Issues.* Chicago: University of Chicago Press.

Iyengar, Shanto, and Donald R. Kinder. 1987. *News That Matters: Television and American Opinion.* Chicago: University of Chicago Press.

Jennings, M. Kent. 1983. "Gender Roles and Inequalities in Political Participation: Results from an Eight-Nation Study." *Western Political Quarterly* 36: 364–85.

Jennings, M. Kent, and Richard G. Niemi. 1968. "The Transmission of Political Values from Parent to Child." *American Political Science Review* 62: 169–84.

Jennings, M. Kent, and Richard G. Niemi. 1974. *The Political Character of Adolescence.* Princeton: Princeton University Press.

Jennings, M. Kent, and Richard G. Niemi. 1981. *Generations and Politics: A Panel Study of Young Adults and Their Parents.* Princeton: Princeton University Press.

Jewell, Malcolm. 1984. *Parties and Primaries: Nominating State Governors.* New York: Praeger.

Jewell, Malcolm, and David Olson. 1982. *Political Parties and Elections in American States.* Homewood, Ill.: Dorsey Press.

Jones, Edward E. 1986. "Interpreting Interpersonal Behavior: The Effects of Expectancies." *Science* 234: 41–6.

Katosh, John P., and Michael W. Traugott. 1981. "The Consequences of Validated and Self-Reported Voting Measures." *Public Opinion Quarterly* 45: 519–35.

Katz, Daniel, and Samuel J. Eldersveld. 1961. "The Impact of Local Party Activities upon the Electorate." *Public Opinion Quarterly* 25: 1–24.

Katz, Elihu. 1957. "The Two-Step Flow of Communication: An Up-to-Date Report on a Hypothesis." *Public Opinion Quarterly* 21: 61–78.

Katz, Elihu, and Paul F. Lazarsfeld. 1955. *Personal Influence: The Part Played by People in the Flow of Mass Communications.* Glencoe, Ill.: Free Press.

Keller, Suzanne. 1968. *The Urban Neighborhood: A Sociological Perspective.* New York: Random House.

Kelley, Jonathon, and Ian McAllister. 1985. "Social Context and Electoral Behavior in Britain." *American Journal of Political Science* 29: 564–86.

Key, V. O., Jr., with Alexander Heard. 1949. *Southern Politics: In State and Nation.* New York: Alfred A. Knopf.

Key, V. O., Jr., with Milton C. Cummings, Jr. 1966. *The Responsible Electorate: Rationality in Presidential Voting, 1936–1960.* Cambridge, Mass.: Belknap Press of Harvard University Press.

Key, V. O., Jr., and Frank Munger. 1959. "Social Determinism and Electoral Decision: The Case of Indiana." In Eugene Burdick and Arthur J. Brodbeck, eds., *American Voting Behavior,* pp. 281–99. Glencoe, Ill.: Free Press.

Kornhauser, William. 1959. *The Politics of Mass Society.* New York: Free Press.

Kramer, Gerald. 1970–1. "The Effects of Precinct-Level Canvassing on Voter Behavior." *Public Opinion Quarterly* 34: 560–72.

Kramer, Gerald. 1975. "Short-term Fluctuations in U.S. Voting Behavior: 1896–1964." *American Political Science Review* 65: 131–43.

Krassa, Michael A. 1985. "Contextually Conditioned Political Interactions: Party

Activity and Mass Behavior Response." Ph.D. dissertation, Washington University, St. Louis.

Krassa, Michael A. 1988. "Context and the Canvass: The Mechanisms of Interaction." *Political Behavior* 10: 233–46.

Krassa, Michael A. 1989. "Getting Out the Black Vote: The Party Canvass and the Black Response." In Lucius Barker, ed., *New Perspectives in American Politics.* Vol. 1 of *National Political Science Review,* pp. 58–75. New Brunswick, N.J.: Transaction Publishers.

Langton, Kenneth P., and Ronald Rapoport. 1975. "Social Structure, Social Context, and Partisan Mobilization: Urban Workers in Chile." *Comparative Political Studies* 8: 318–44.

Lasswell, Harold D. 1948. "The Structure and Function of Communication in Society." In Lyman Bryson, ed., *The Communication of Ideas,* pp. 37–51. New York: Harper and Row.

Latane, Bibb. 1981. "The Psychology of Social Impact." *American Psychologist* 36: 343–56.

Laumann, Edward O. 1973. *Bonds of Pluralism: The Form and Substance of Urban Social Networks.* New York: Wiley.

Lazarsfeld, Paul, Bernard Berelson, and Hazel Gaudet. 1948. *The People's Choice: How the Voter Makes Up His Mind in a Presidential Campaign.* New York: Columbia University Press.

Leege, David C., and Michael R. Welch. 1989. "Religious Roots of Political Orientations." *Journal of Politics* 52: 137–62.

Lewis-Beck, Michael. 1986. "Comparative Economic Voting: Britain, France, Germany, Italy." *American Journal of Political Science* 30: 315–46.

Lipset, Seymour Martin. 1981. *Political Man.* Expanded edition. Baltimore: Johns Hopkins University Press.

Lodge, Milton, and Ruth Hamill. 1986. "A Partisan Schema for Political Information Processing." *American Political Science Review* 80: 505–19.

Lodge, Milton, Kathleen M. McGraw, and Patrick Stroh. 1989. "An Impression-Driven Model of Candidate Evaluation." *American Political Science Review* 83: 399–419.

MacKuen, Michael B. 1990. "Speaking of Politics: Individual Conversational Choice, Public Opinion, and the Prospects for Deliberative Democracy." In John A. Ferejohn and James H. Kuklinski, eds., *Information and Democratic Politics,* pp. 59–99. Urbana: University of Illinois Press.

MacKuen, Michael B., and Courtney Brown. 1987. "Political Context and Attitude Change." *American Political Science Review* 81: 471–90.

MacKuen, Michael B., and Steven Lane Combs. 1981. *More Than News: Media Power in Public Affairs.* Beverly Hills, Calif.: Sage.

Macoby, Eleanor E., Richard E. Matthews, and Alton S. Morton. 1954. "Youth and Political Change." In Heinz Eulau, Samuel J. Eldersveld, and Morris Janowitz, eds., *Political Behavior: A Reader in Theory and Research,* pp. 299–307. Glencoe, Ill.: Free Press.

Maddala, G. S. 1977. *Econometrics.* New York: McGraw-Hill.

Maddala, G. S. 1983. *Limited-Dependent and Qualitative Variables in Econometrics.* Cambridge: Cambridge University Press.

Marsden, Peter V. 1987. "Core Discussion Networks of Americans." *American Sociological Review* 52: 122–31.

Matthews, Donald R., and James W. Prothro. 1963. "Social and Economic Factors and Negro Voter Registration in the South." *American Political Science Review* 57: 24–44.

May, Robert M. 1974. *Stability and Complexity in Model Ecosystems.* 2d ed. Princeton: Princeton University Press.

Mayhew, David R. 1986. *Placing Parties in American Politics: Organization, Electoral Settings, and Government Activity in the Twentieth Century.* Princeton: Princeton University Press.

McClosky, Herbert, and Harold E. Dahlgren. 1959. "Primary Group Influence on Party Loyalty." *American Political Science Review* 53: 757–76.

McPhee, William N. 1963. "Note on a Campaign Simulator." In William N. McPhee, *Formal Theories of Mass Behavior,* pp. 169–83. New York: Free Press.

McPhee, William N., with Robert B. Smith and Jack Ferguson. 1963. "A Theory of Informal Social Influence." In William N. McPhee, *Formal Theories of Mass Behavior,* pp. 74–203. New York: Free Press.

McPhee, William N., and Jack Ferguson. 1962. "Political Immunization." In William N. McPhee and William A. Glaser, eds., *Public Opinion and Congressional Elections,* pp. 155–79. New York: Macmillan.

McPhee, William N., and Robert B. Smith. 1962. "A Model For Analyzing Voting Systems." In William N. McPhee and William A. Glaser, eds., *Public Opinion and Congressional Elections,* pp. 123–54. New York: Macmillan.

Mill, James Stuart. 1956. *On Liberty.* Edited with an introduction by C. V. Shields. Indianapolis: Bobbs-Merrill. Originally published in 1859.

Miller, Warren E. 1956. "One-Party Politics and the Voter." *American Political Science Review* 50: 707–25.

Mondak, Jeffery J. 1990. "Determinants of Coattail Voting." *Political Behavior* 12: 265–88.

Noelle-Neumann, Elizabeth. 1984. *The Spiral of Silence: Public Opinion – Our Social Skin.* Chicago: University of Chicago Press.

Orbell, John M. 1970. "An Information Flow Theory of Community Influence." *Journal of Politics* 32: 322–38.

Ostrom, Elinor. 1972. "Metropolitan Reform: Propositions Derived from Two Traditions." *Social Science Quarterly* 53: 474–93.

Ottati, Victor C., and Robert S. Wyer, Jr. 1990. "The Cognitive Mediators of Political Choice: Toward a Comprehensive Model of Political Information Processing." In John A. Ferejohn and James H. Kuklinski, eds., *Information and Democratic Processes,* pp. 186–218. Urbana: University of Illinois Press.

Patterson, Samuel C., and Gregory A. Caldeira. 1953. "Getting Out the Vote: Participation in Gubernatorial Elections." *American Political Science Review* 77: 675–89.

Pimlott, Ben. 1972. "Does Local Party Organization Matter?" *British Journal of Political Science* 2: 381–3.

Pimlott, Ben. 1973. "Local Party Organization, Turnout and Marginality." *British Journal of Political Science* 3: 252–5.

Popkin, Samuel L. 1991. *The Reasoning Voter: Communication and Persuasion in Presidential Campaigns.* Chicago: University of Chicago Press.

Powell, G. Bingham Jr. 1986. "American Voter Turnout in Comparative Perspective." *American Political Science Review* 80: 17–44.

Przeworski, Adam. 1974. "Contextual Models of Political Behavior." *Political Methodology* 1: 27–61.

Przeworski, Adam, and Henry Teune. 1970. *The Logic of Comparative Social Inquiry.* New York: Wiley-Interscience.

Putnam, Linda L. 1982. "In Search of Gender: A Critique of Communication and Sex-Rules Research." *Women's Studies in Communications* 5: 1–9.

Putnam, Robert D. 1966. "Political Attitudes and the Local Community." *American Political Science Review* 60: 640–54.

Rakow, Lana F. 1986. "Rethinking Gender Research in Communication." *Journal of Communication* 36: 11–26.

Ranney, Austin. 1972. "Turnout and Representation in Presidential Primary Elections." *American Political Science Review* 66: 21–37.

Richardson, Lewis F. 1960. *Arms and Insecurity.* Pittsburgh: Boxwood.

Riker, William H. 1982. *Liberalism against Populism: A Confrontation between the Theory of Democracy and Theory of Social Choice.* San Francisco: Freeman.

Robinson, W. S. 1950. "Ecological Correlations and the Behavior of Individuals." *American Sociological Review* 15: 351–7.

Ross, Lee, Gunter Bierbrauer, and Susan Hoffman. 1976. "The Role of Attribution Processes in Conformity and Dissent." *American Psychologist* 31: 148–57.

Sapiro, Virginia. 1983. *The Political Integration of Women.* Urbana: University of Illinois Press.

Schattschneider, E. E. 1960. *The Semi-Sovereign People.* New York: Holt, Rinehart and Winston.

Schelling, Thomas C. 1978. *Micromotives and Macrobehavior.* New York: Norton.

Schumpeter, Joseph A. 1947. *Capitalism, Socialism, and Democracy.* New York: Harper.

Segal, David R., and Marshall W. Meyer. 1974. "The Social Context of Political Partisanship." In Mattei Dogan and Stein Rokkan, eds., *Social Ecology,* pp. 217–32. Cambridge, Mass.: MIT Press.

Shafer, Byron E. 1983. *Quiet Revolution: The Struggle for the Democratic Party and the Shaping of Post-Reform Politics.* New York: Russell Sage Foundation.

Shafer, Byron E. 1988. *Bifurcated Politics: Evolution and Reform in the National Party Convention.* Cambridge, Mass.: Harvard University Press.

Shaffer, William R. 1972. *Computer Simulations of Voting Behavior.* New York: Oxford University Press.

Shepsle, Kenneth A. 1972. "The Strategy of Ambiguity: Uncertainty and Electoral Competition." *American Political Science Review* 66: 555–68.

Shively, W. Phillips. 1987. "Cross-Level Inference as an Identification Problem." University of Minnesota, Minneapolis. Photocopy.

Siltanen, Janet, and Michelle Stanworth. 1984. "The Politics of Private Woman and Public Man." In J. Siltanen and M. Stanworth, eds., *Women and the Public Sphere,* pp. 185–208. New York: St. Martin's Press.

Simon, Herbert A. 1957. *Models of Man.* New York: Wiley.

Simon, Herbert A. 1982. *Models of Bounded Rationality.* Cambridge, Mass.: MIT Press.

Skinner, B. F. 1938. *The Behavior of Organisms.* New York: Appleton-Century.

Sniderman, Paul M., Richard A. Brody, and Philip E. Tetlock. 1991. *Reasoning and Choice: Explorations in Political Psychology.* Cambridge: Cambridge University Press.

Sprague, John. 1969. "A Nonlinear Difference Equation." Washington University, St. Louis. Working paper.

Sprague, John. 1976. "Estimating a Boudon Type Contextual Model: Some Practical and Theoretical Problems of Measurement." *Political Methodology* 3: 333–53.

Sprague, John. 1980. "Two Variants of Aggregation Processes and Problems in Elementary Dynamic and Contextual Causal Formulations." Presented at the Department of Political Science, University of Iowa under the auspices of the Shambaugh Fund, April 7–11.

Sprague, John. 1982. "Is There a Micro Theory Consistent with Contextual Analysis?" In Elinor Ostrom, eds., *Strategies of Political Inquiry,* pp. 99–121. Beverly Hills, Calif.: Sage.

Sprague, John, and Lewis P. Westefield. 1979. "An Interpretive Reconstruction of Some Aggregate Models of Contextual Effects." Presented at the annual meeting of the Southern Political Science Association, Gatlinburg, November 1–3.

Stabrowski, Donald. 1984. "A Political Machine, an Ethnic Community, and South Bend's West Side: 1900–1980." Ph.D. dissertation, University of Notre Dame, South Bend.

Stephens, John D. 1981. "The Changing Swedish Electorate: Class Voting, Contextual Effects, and Voter Volatility." *Comparative Political Studies* 14: 163–204.

Stimson, James A. 1991. *Public Opinion in America: Moods, Cycles, and Swings.* Boulder, Colo.: Westview Press.

Stokes, Donald E. 1966. "Some Dynamic Elements of Contests for the Presidency." *American Political Science Review* 60: 19–28.

Straits, Bruce C. 1990. "The Social Context of Voter Turnout." *Public Opinion Quarterly* 54: 64–73.

Suttles, Gerald D. 1972. *The Social Construction of Communities.* Chicago: University of Chicago Press.

Tedin, Kent L. 1974. "The Influence of Parents on the Political Attitudes of Adolescents." *American Political Science Review* 68: 1579–92.

Tingsten, Herbert. 1963. *Political Behavior: Studies in Election Statistics.* Translated by V. Hammarling. Totowa, N.J.: Bedminster. Originally published in 1937.

Traugott, Michael W., and John P. Katosh. 1979. "Response Validity in Surveys of Voting Behavior." *Public Opinion Quarterly* 43: 359–77.

Tufte, Edward R. 1975. "Determinants of the Outcomes of Midterm Congressional Elections." *American Political Science Review* 69: 812–26.

Wald, Kenneth D., Dennis E. Owen, and Samuel S. Hill, Jr. 1988. "Churches as Political Communities." *American Political Science Review* 82: 531–48.

Wald, Kenneth D., Dennis E. Owen, and Samuel S. Hill, Jr. 1990. "Political Cohesion in Churches." *Journal of Politics* 52: 195–215.

Weatherford, M. Stephen. 1980. "The Politics of School Busing: Contextual Effects and Community Polarization." *Journal of Politics* 42: 747–65.

Weatherford, M. Stephen. 1982. "Interpersonal Networks and Political Behavior." *American Journal of Political Science* 26: 117–43.

Weber, Max. 1966. "On the Concept of Sociology and the Meaning of Social Conduct." In *Basic Concepts in Sociology,* translated by H. P. Secher, pp. 29–58. New York: Citadel Press. Originally published posthumously in 1925 as Chapter 1 of *Wirtschaft und Gessellschaft.*

Weimann, Gabriel. 1982. "On the Importance of Marginality: One More Step into the Two-Step Flow of Communication." *American Sociological Review* 47: 764–73.

Welch, Susan. 1977. "Women as Political Animals? A Test of Some Explanations for Male-Female Political Participation Differences." *American Journal of Political Science* 4: 711–30.

Wolfinger, Raymond. 1963. "The Influence of Precinct Work on Voting Behavior." *Public Opinion Quarterly* 27: 387–98.

Wonnacott, Ronald J., and Thomas H. Wonnacott. 1979. *Econometrics.* 2d ed. New York: Wiley.

Wright, Gerald C., Jr. 1976. "Community Structure and Voting in the South." *Public Opinion Quarterly* 40: 200–15.

Wright, Gerald C., Jr. 1977. "Contextual Models of Electoral Behavior: The Southern Wallace Vote." *American Political Science Review* 71: 497–508.

Zaller, John R. 1992. *The Nature and Origins of Mass Opinion.* Cambridge: Cambridge University Press.

Index